高雄右京

ToHeart ①

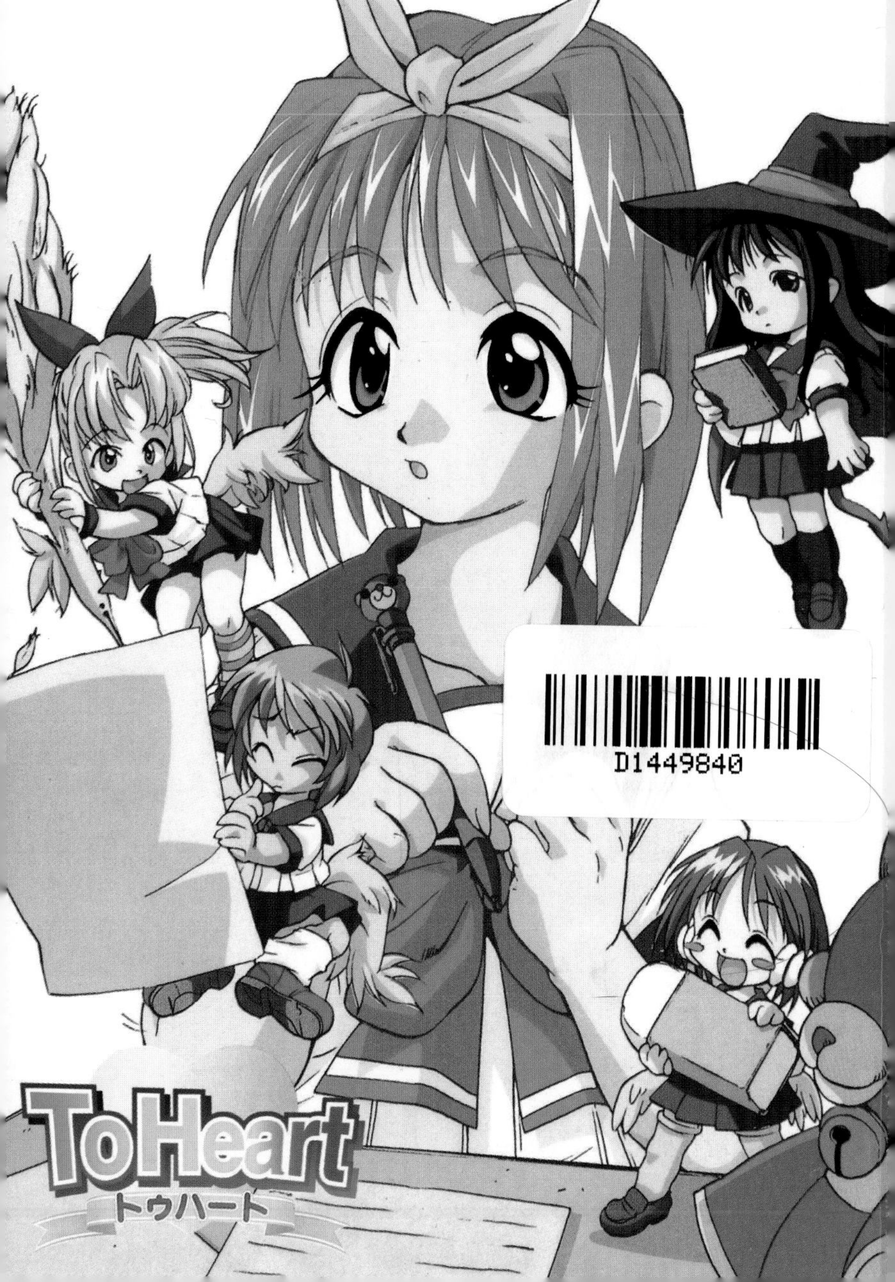
ToHeart
トゥハート

Episode 1
『Cherry Blossom Time』
~Akari Kamigishi I~

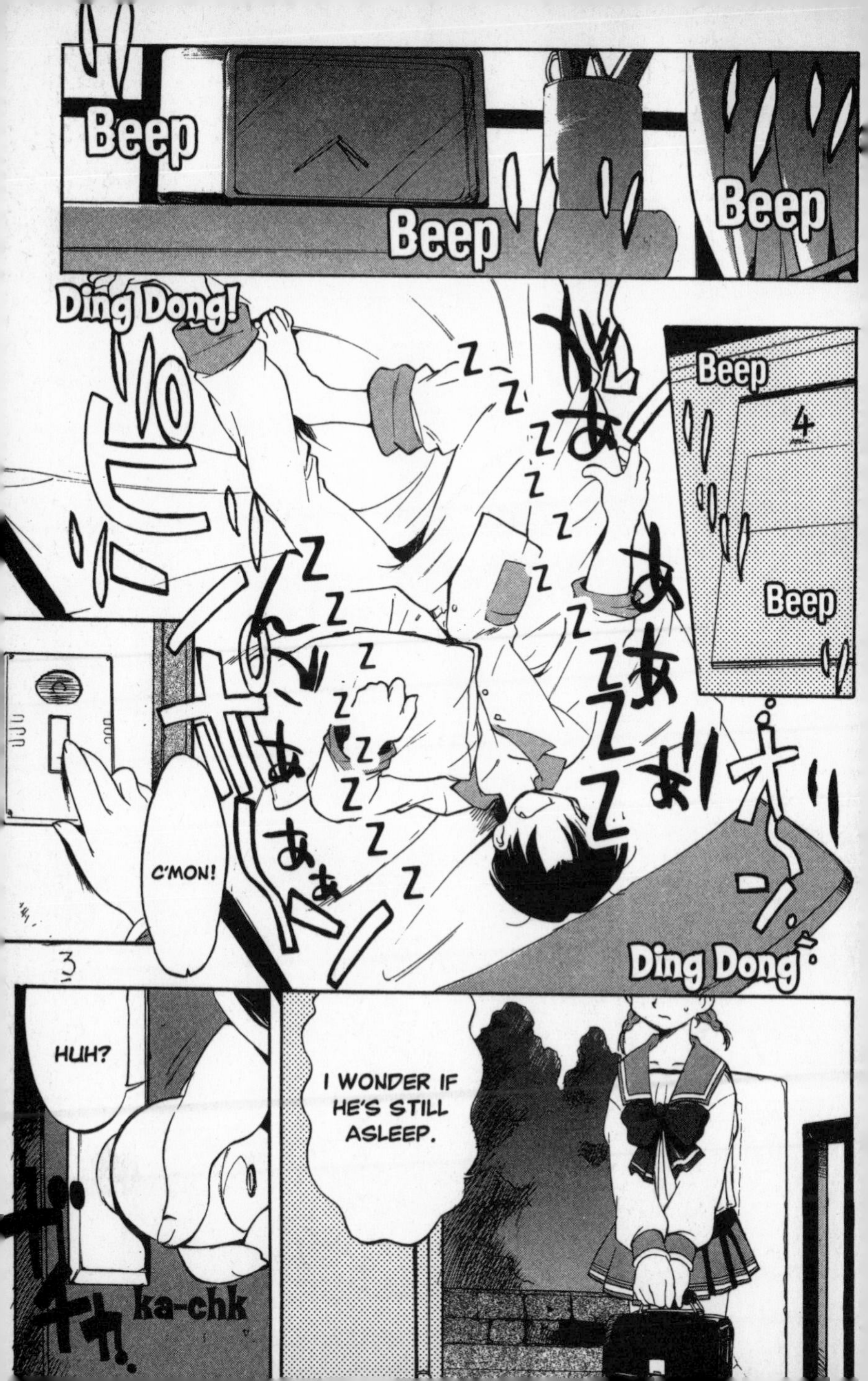
Beep
Beep
Beep
Ding Dong!
Beep
Beep
Ding Dong
C'MON!
I WONDER IF HE'S STILL ASLEEP.
HUH?
ka-chk

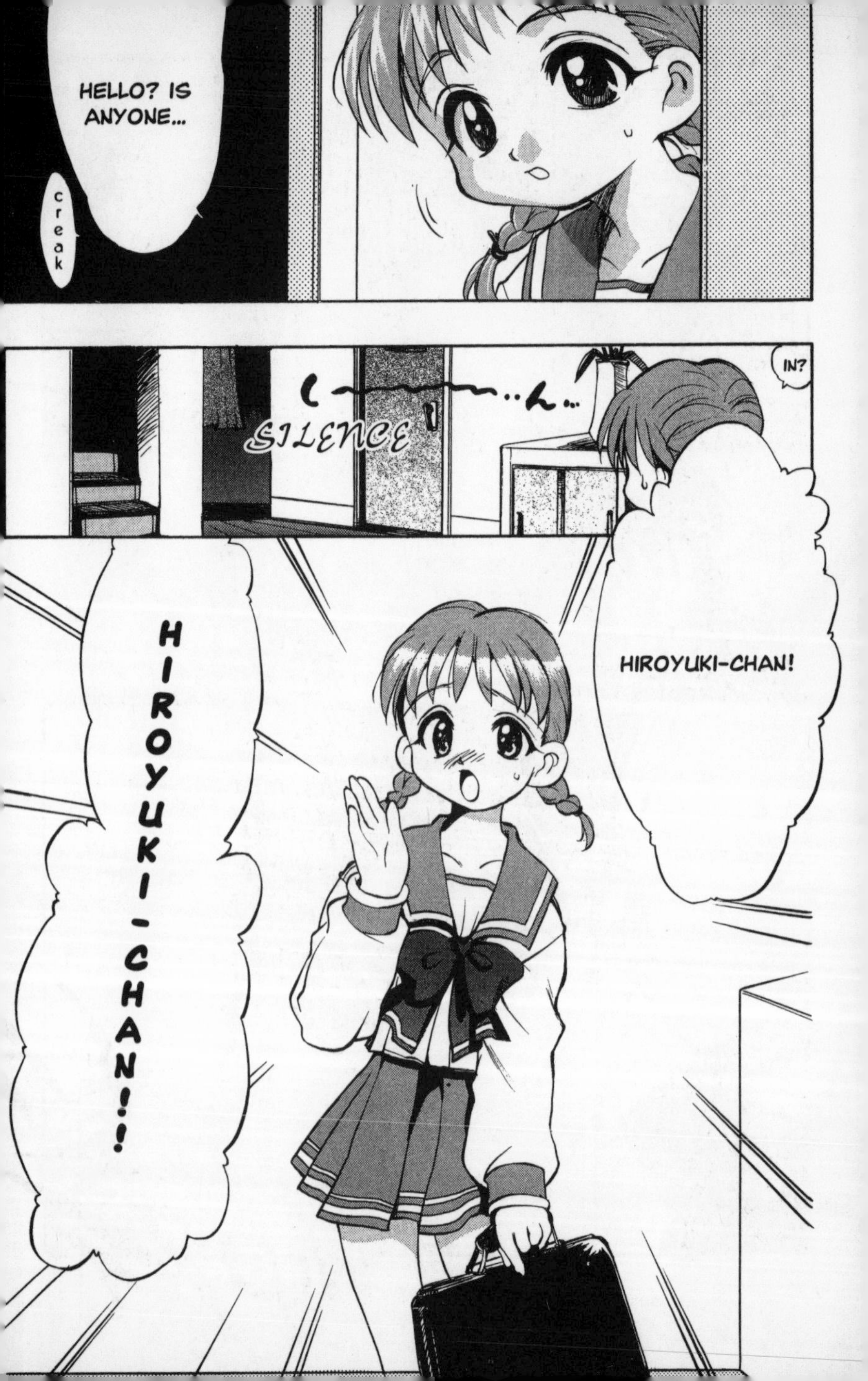
HELLO? IS ANYONE...
creak
IN?
SILENCE
HIROYUKI-CHAN!
HIROYUKI-CHAN!!

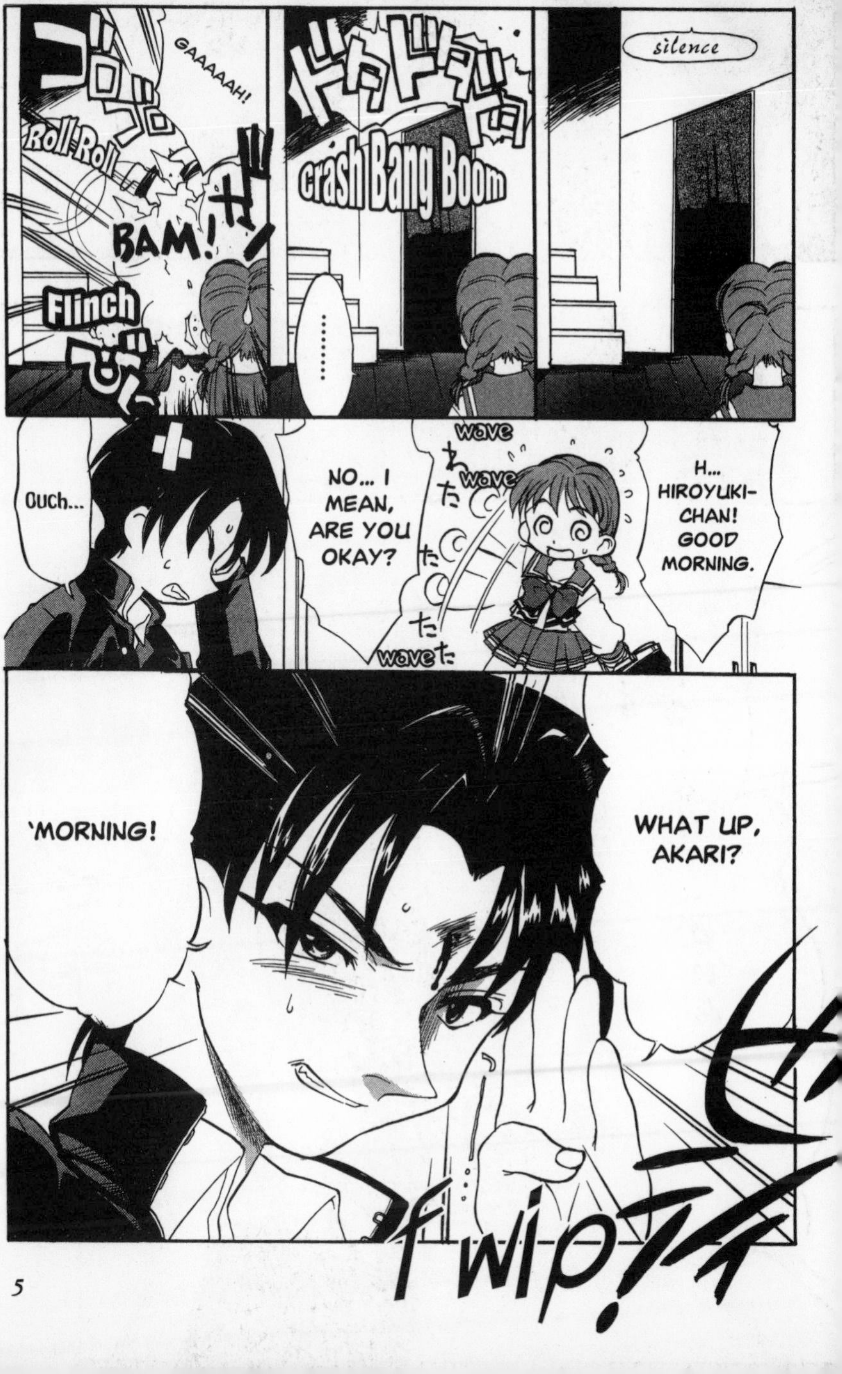
silence
crash Bang Boom
GAAAAAH!
Roll Roll
BAM!
Flinch
H... HIROYUKI-CHAN! GOOD MORNING.
wave wave wave
NO... I MEAN, ARE YOU OKAY?
Ouch...
WHAT UP, AKARI?
'MORNING!
fwip!

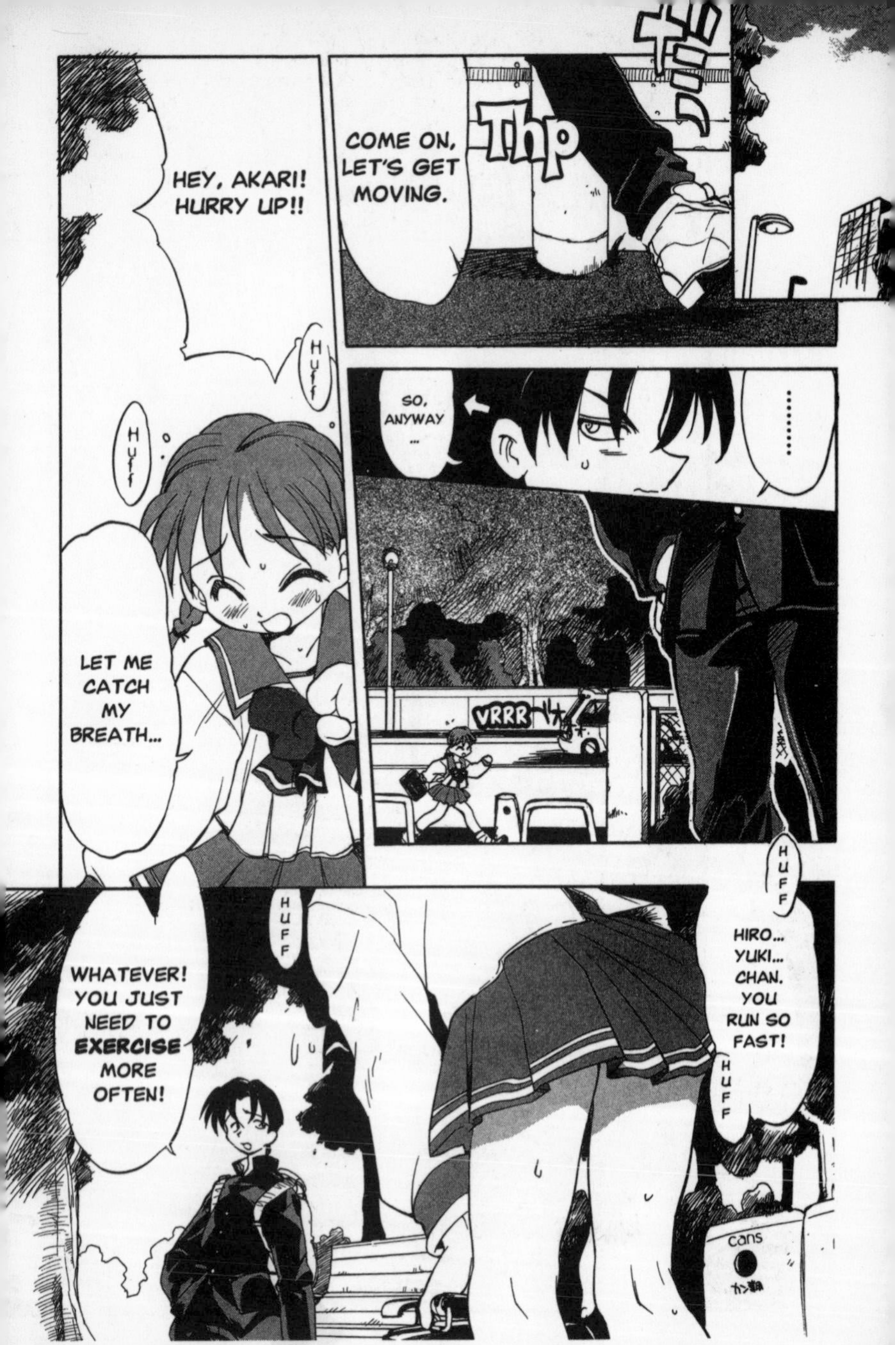
Thp
COME ON, LET'S GET MOVING.
HEY, AKARI! HURRY UP!!
Huff
Huff
LET ME CATCH MY BREATH...
SO, ANYWAY ...
....
VRRR
HUFF
HIRO... YUKI... CHAN. YOU RUN SO FAST!
HUFF
HUFF
WHATEVER! YOU JUST NEED TO EXERCISE MORE OFTEN!
cans

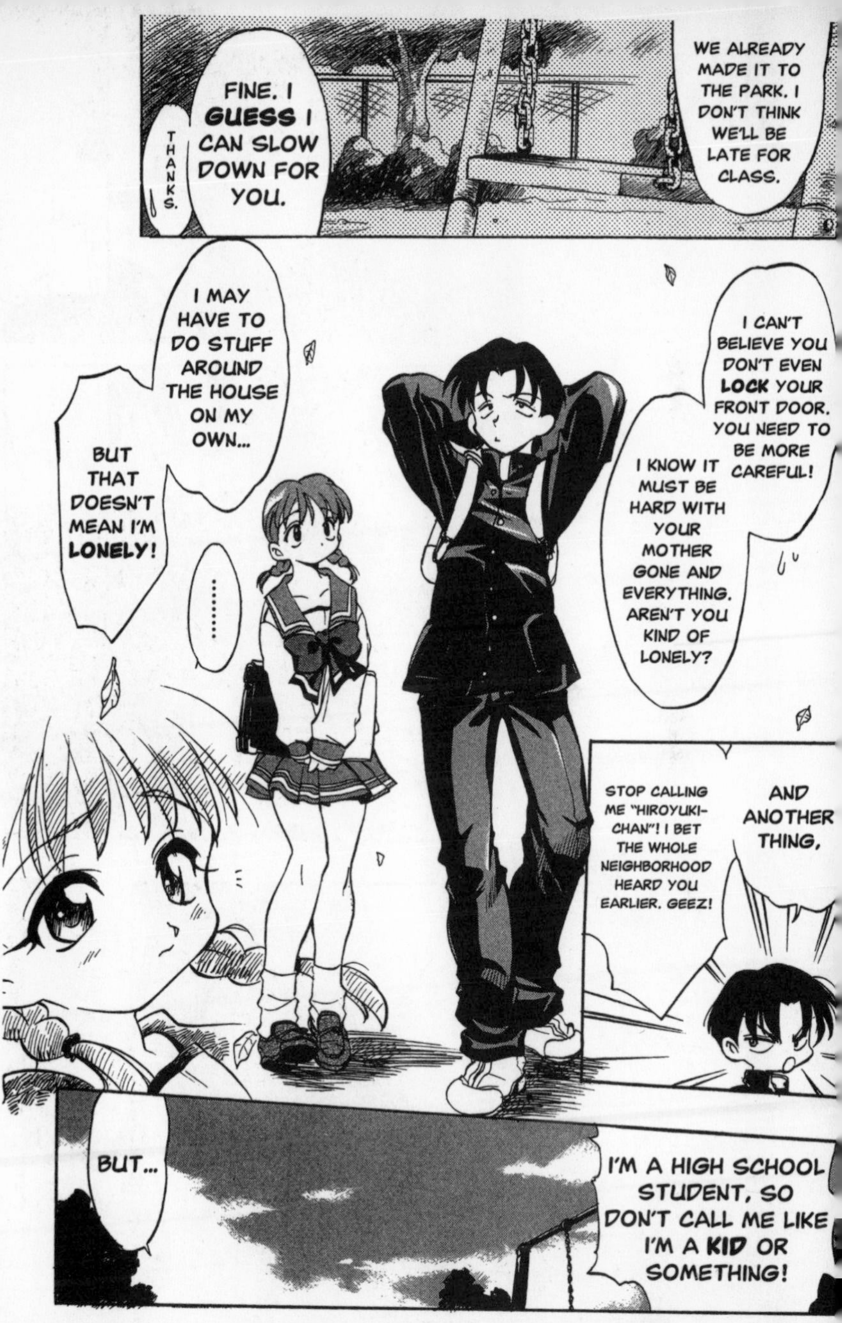
WE ALREADY MADE IT TO THE PARK. I DON'T THINK WE'LL BE LATE FOR CLASS.
FINE. I GUESS I CAN SLOW DOWN FOR YOU.
THANKS.
I CAN'T BELIEVE YOU DON'T EVEN LOCK YOUR FRONT DOOR. YOU NEED TO BE MORE CAREFUL!
I KNOW IT MUST BE HARD WITH YOUR MOTHER GONE AND EVERYTHING. AREN'T YOU KIND OF LONELY?
I MAY HAVE TO DO STUFF AROUND THE HOUSE ON MY OWN...
BUT THAT DOESN'T MEAN I'M LONELY!
....
AND ANOTHER THING,
STOP CALLING ME "HIROYUKI-CHAN"! I BET THE WHOLE NEIGHBORHOOD HEARD YOU EARLIER. GEEZ!
I'M A HIGH SCHOOL STUDENT, SO DON'T CALL ME LIKE I'M A KID OR SOMETHING!
BUT...

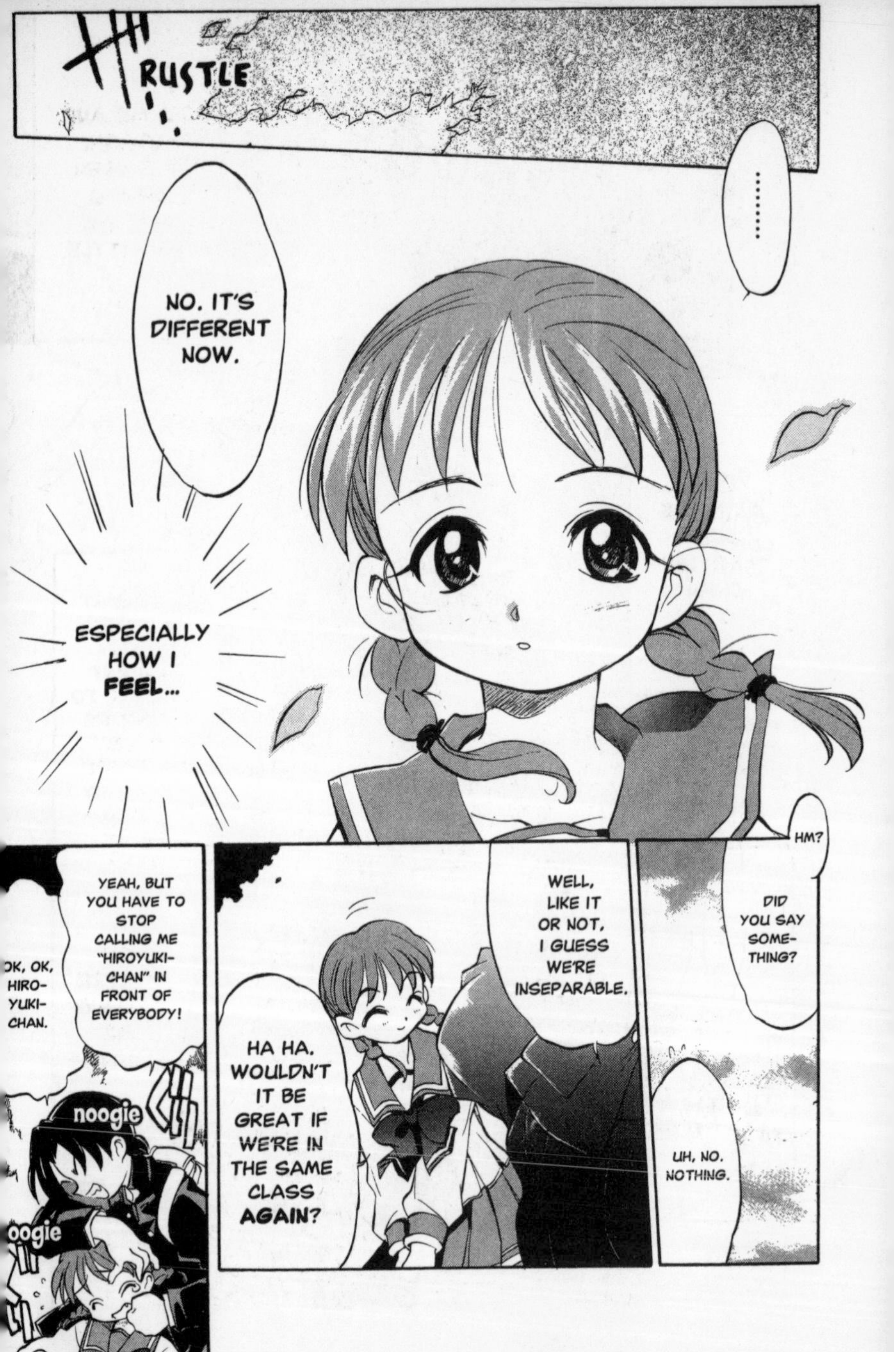
RUSTLE
......
NO. IT'S DIFFERENT NOW.
ESPECIALLY HOW I FEEL...
HM?
DID YOU SAY SOME-THING?
UH, NO. NOTHING.
WELL, LIKE IT OR NOT, I GUESS WE'RE INSEPARABLE.
HA HA. WOULDN'T IT BE GREAT IF WE'RE IN THE SAME CLASS AGAIN?
YEAH, BUT YOU HAVE TO STOP CALLING ME "HIROYUKI-CHAN" IN FRONT OF EVERYBODY!
OK, OK, HIRO-YUKI-CHAN.
noogie
oogie

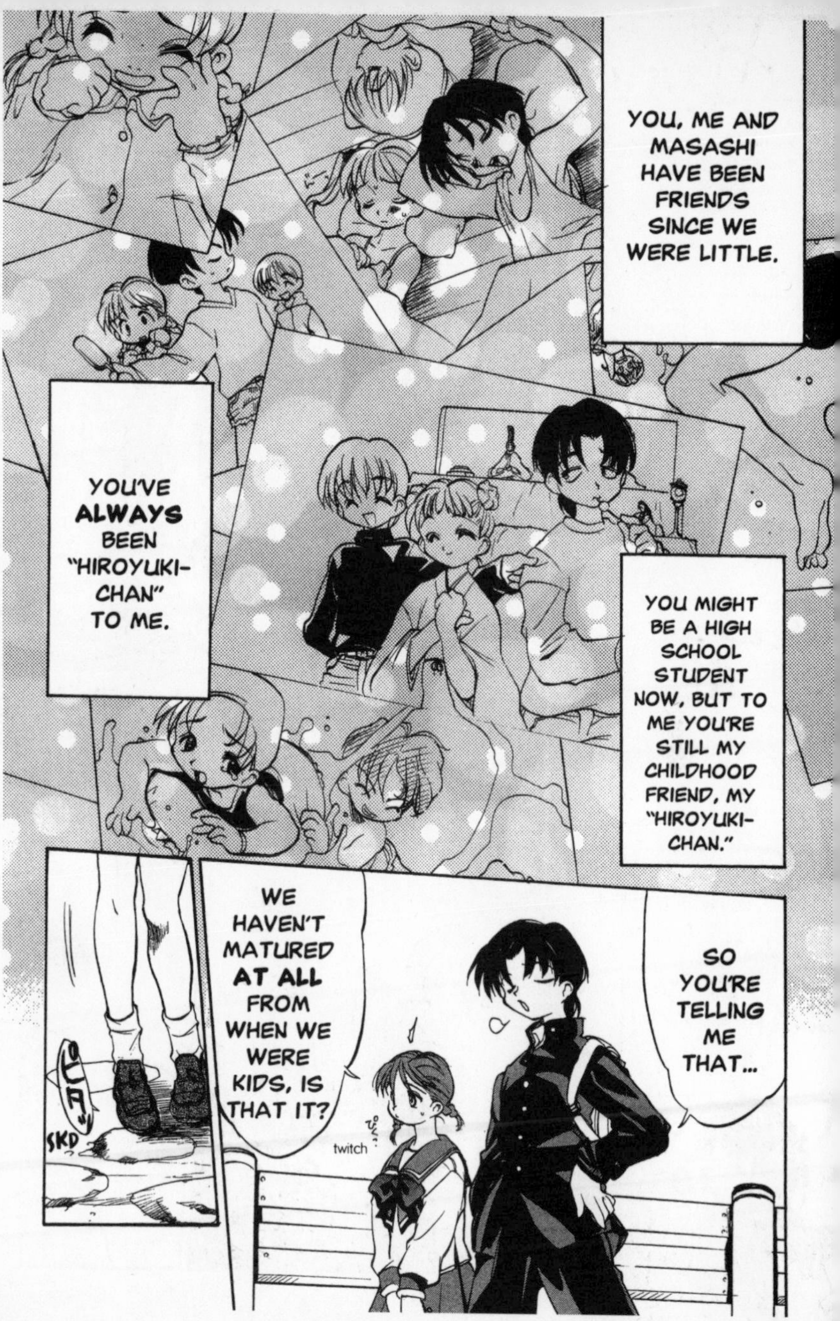
YOU, ME AND MASASHI HAVE BEEN FRIENDS SINCE WE WERE LITTLE.
YOU'VE **ALWAYS** BEEN "HIROYUKI-CHAN" TO ME.
YOU MIGHT BE A HIGH SCHOOL STUDENT NOW, BUT TO ME YOU'RE STILL MY CHILDHOOD FRIEND, MY "HIROYUKI-CHAN."
SO YOU'RE TELLING ME THAT...
WE HAVEN'T MATURED **AT ALL** FROM WHEN WE WERE KIDS, IS THAT IT?
twitch
SKD

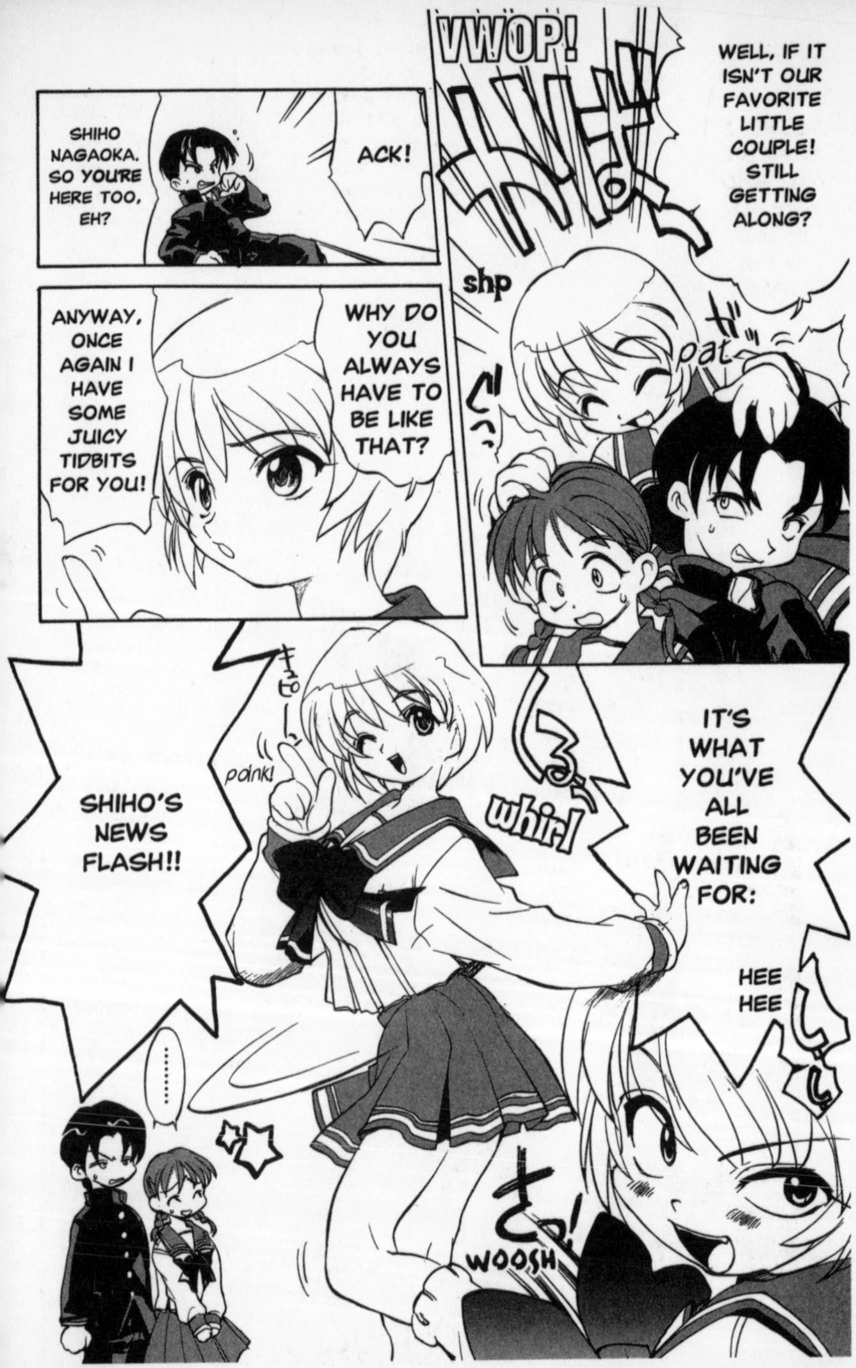
VWOP!
WELL, IF IT ISN'T OUR FAVORITE LITTLE COUPLE! STILL GETTING ALONG?
shp
pat
ACK!
SHIHO NAGAOKA. SO YOU'RE HERE TOO, EH?
WHY DO YOU ALWAYS HAVE TO BE LIKE THAT?
ANYWAY, ONCE AGAIN I HAVE SOME JUICY TIDBITS FOR YOU!
whirl
IT'S WHAT YOU'VE ALL BEEN WAITING FOR:
poink!
SHIHO'S NEWS FLASH!!
HEE HEE
WOOSH
......

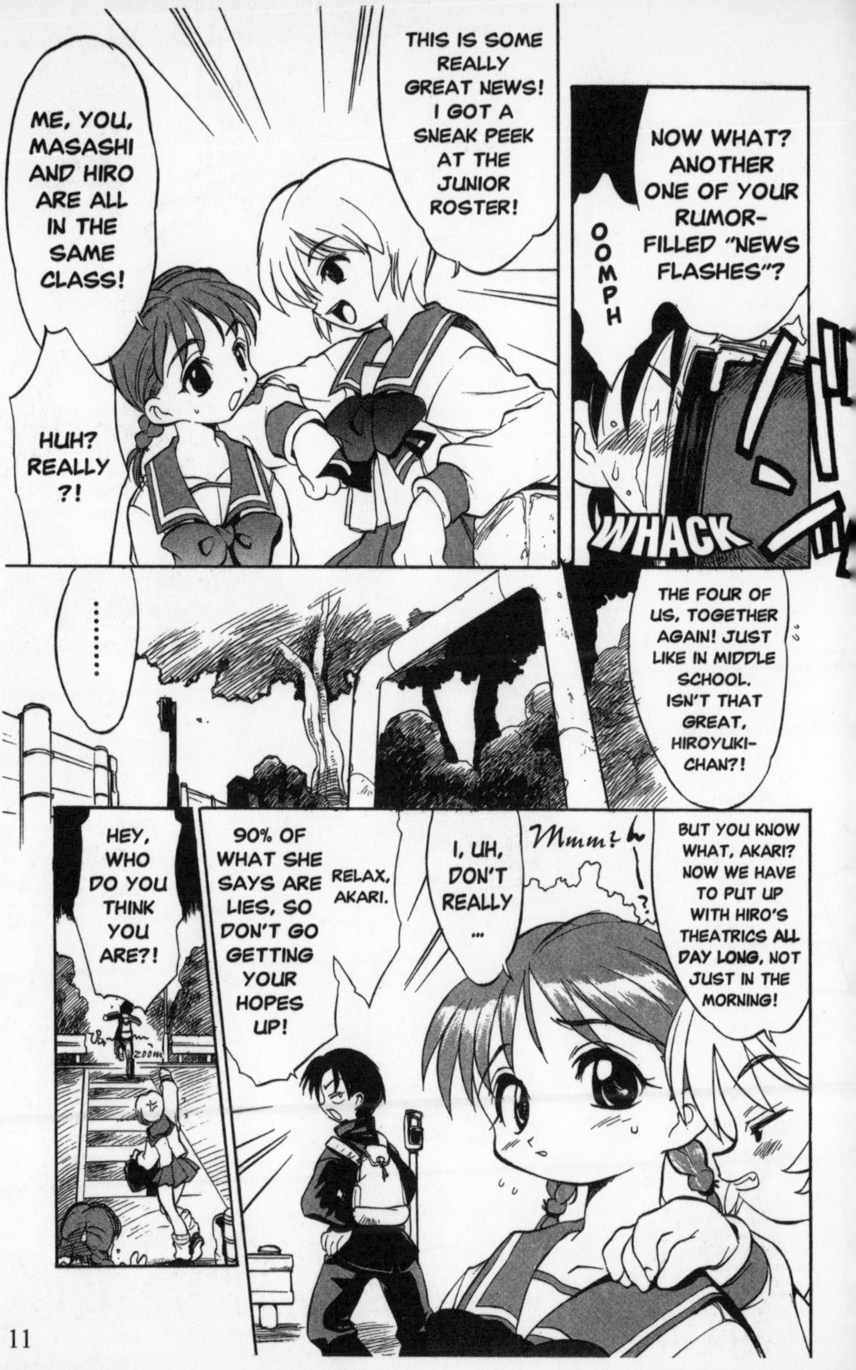
OOMPH
WHACK
NOW WHAT? ANOTHER ONE OF YOUR RUMOR-FILLED "NEWS FLASHES"?
THIS IS SOME REALLY GREAT NEWS! I GOT A SNEAK PEEK AT THE JUNIOR ROSTER!
ME, YOU, MASASHI AND HIRO ARE ALL IN THE SAME CLASS!
HUH? REALLY?!
THE FOUR OF US, TOGETHER AGAIN! JUST LIKE IN MIDDLE SCHOOL. ISN'T THAT GREAT, HIROYUKI-CHAN?!
....
BUT YOU KNOW WHAT, AKARI? NOW WE HAVE TO PUT UP WITH HIRO'S THEATRICS ALL DAY LONG, NOT JUST IN THE MORNING!
Mmm?
I, UH, DON'T REALLY...
RELAX, AKARI.
90% OF WHAT SHE SAYS ARE LIES, SO DON'T GO GETTING YOUR HOPES UP!
HEY, WHO DO YOU THINK YOU ARE?!

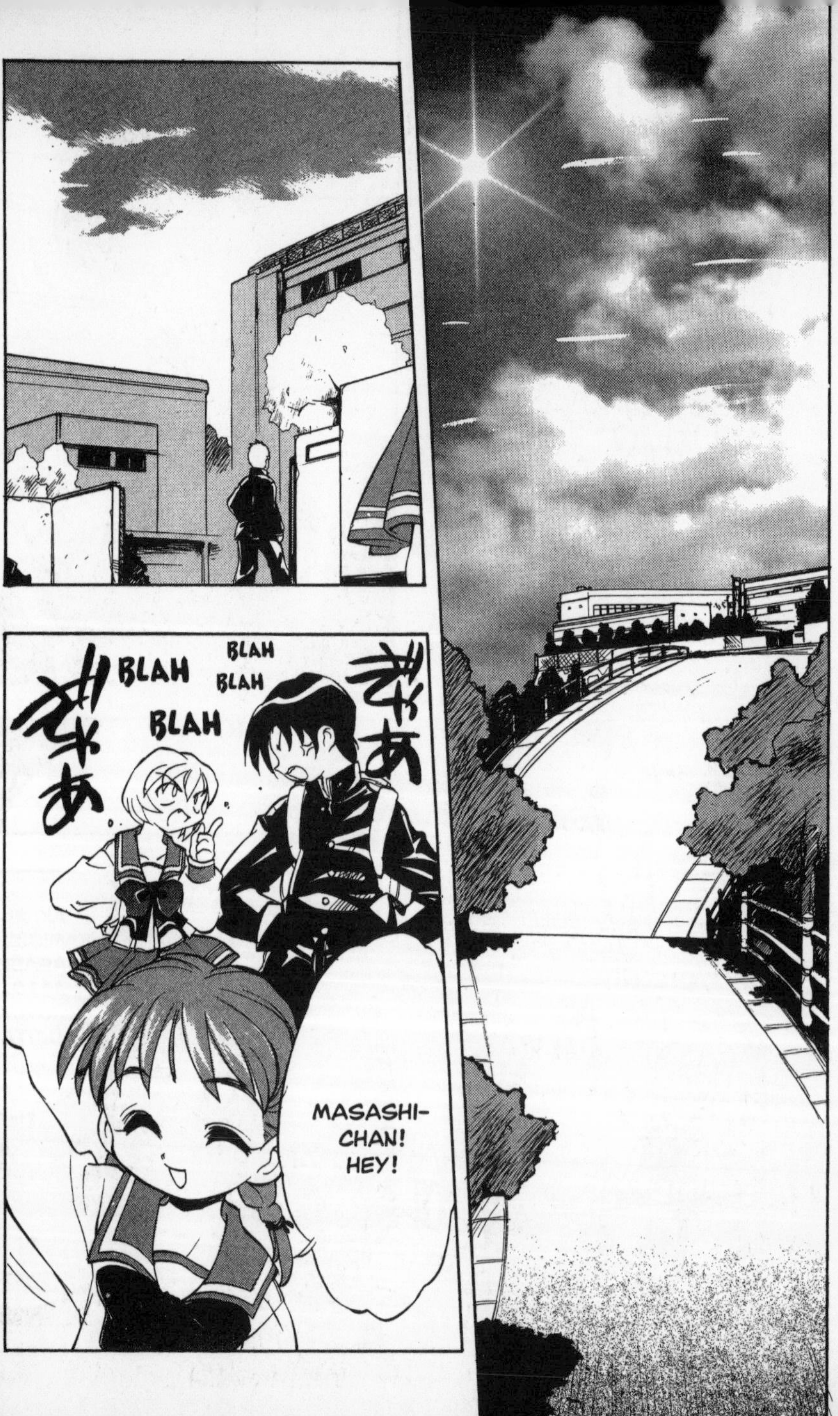
ぎゃあ
BLAH
BLAH
BLAH
BLAH
ぎゃあ
MASASHI-CHAN! HEY!

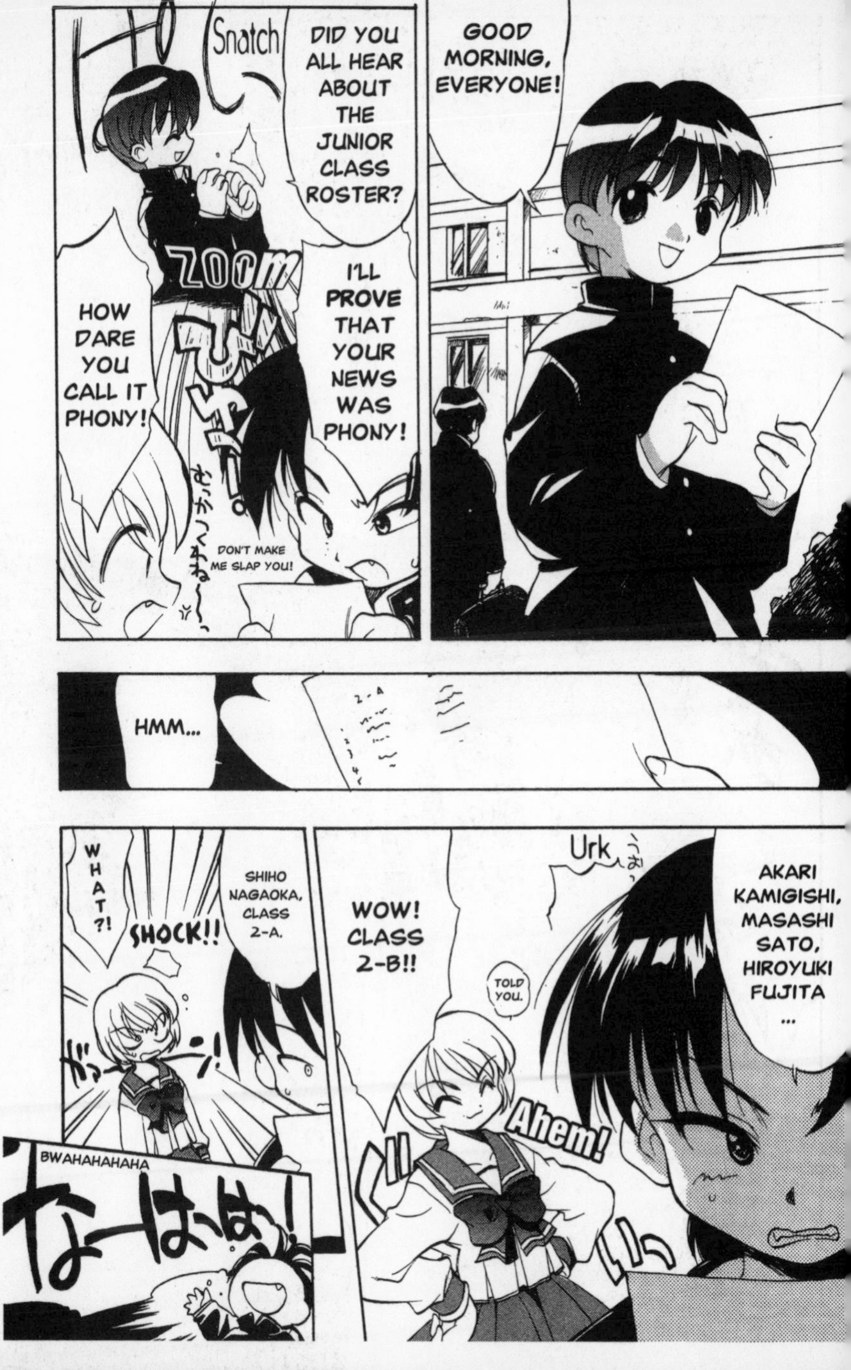

GOOD MORNING, EVERYONE!
DID YOU ALL HEAR ABOUT THE JUNIOR CLASS ROSTER?
Snatch
I'LL PROVE THAT YOUR NEWS WAS PHONY!
ZOOM
HOW DARE YOU CALL IT PHONY!
DON'T MAKE ME SLAP YOU!
HMM...
AKARI KAMIGISHI, MASASHI SATO, HIROYUKI FUJITA ...
Urk
WOW! CLASS 2-B!!
TOLD YOU.
Ahem!
SHIHO NAGAOKA, CLASS 2-A.
WHAT?!
SHOCK!!
BWAHAHAHAHA

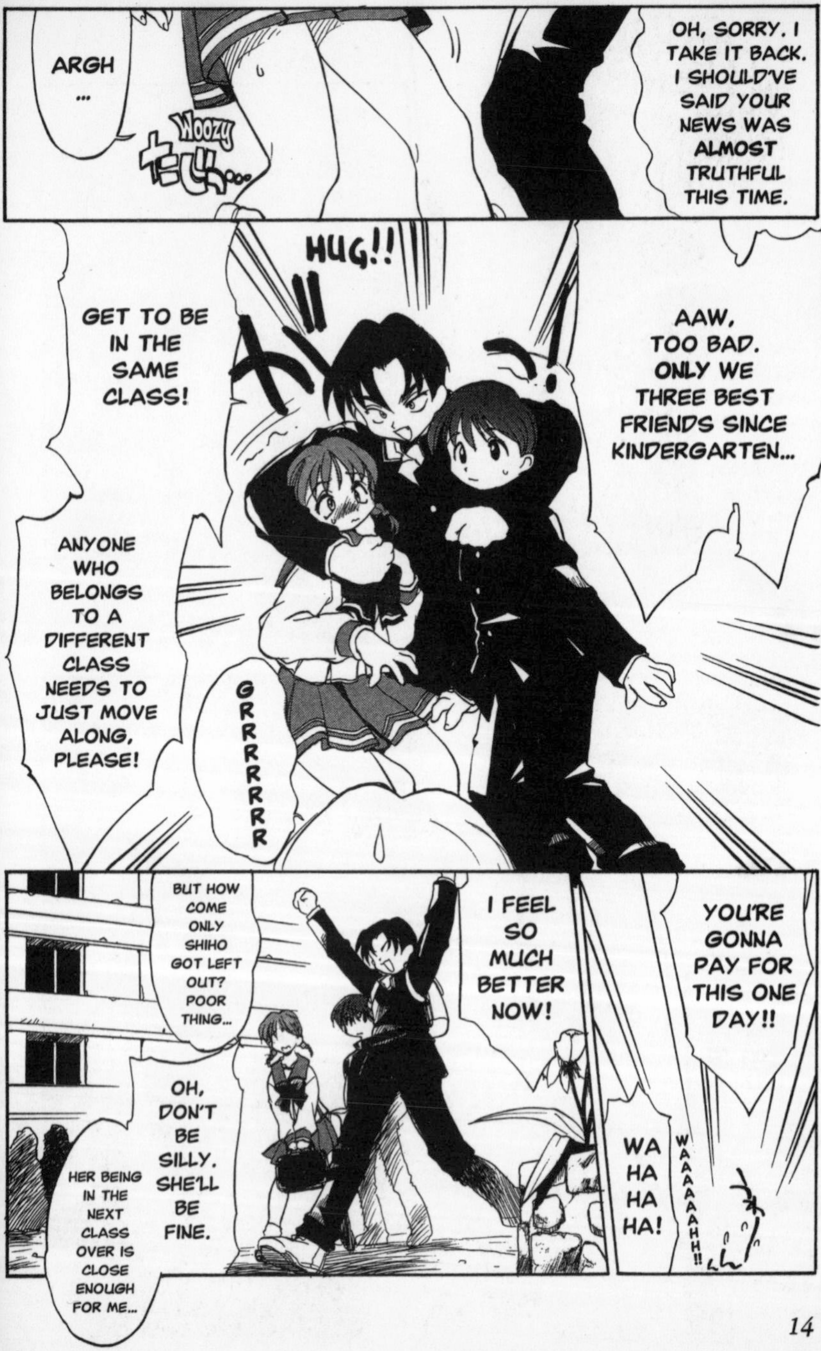
OH, SORRY. I TAKE IT BACK. I SHOULD'VE SAID YOUR NEWS WAS ALMOST TRUTHFUL THIS TIME.
ARGH ...
Woozy
AAW, TOO BAD. ONLY WE THREE BEST FRIENDS SINCE KINDERGARTEN...
HUG!!
GET TO BE IN THE SAME CLASS!
ANYONE WHO BELONGS TO A DIFFERENT CLASS NEEDS TO JUST MOVE ALONG, PLEASE!
GRRRRRRR
YOU'RE GONNA PAY FOR THIS ONE DAY!!
WA HA HA HA!
WAAAAAAAHH!!
I FEEL SO MUCH BETTER NOW!
BUT HOW COME ONLY SHIHO GOT LEFT OUT? POOR THING...
OH, DON'T BE SILLY. SHE'LL BE FINE.
HER BEING IN THE NEXT CLASS OVER IS CLOSE ENOUGH FOR ME...

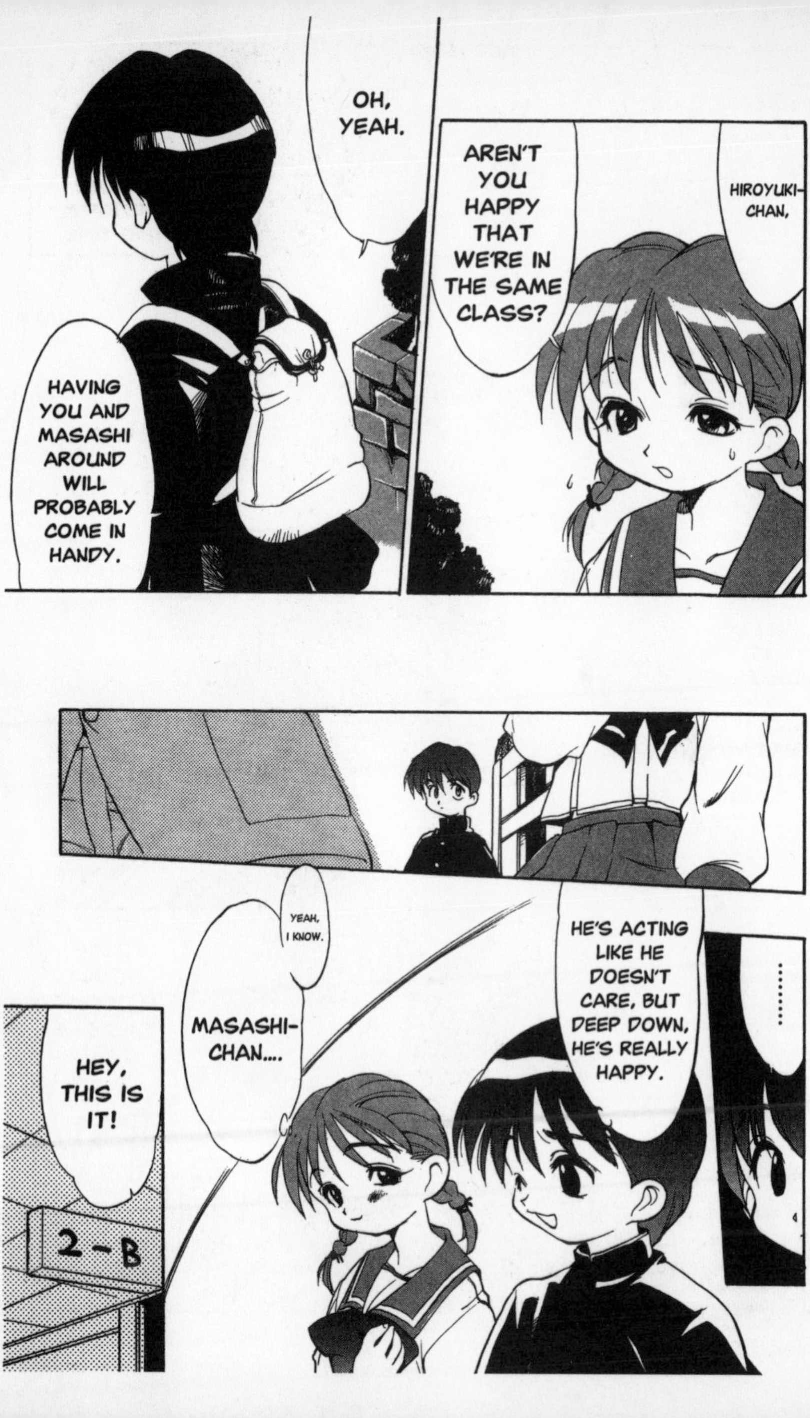
HIROYUKI-CHAN,
AREN'T YOU HAPPY THAT WE'RE IN THE SAME CLASS?
OH, YEAH.
HAVING YOU AND MASASHI AROUND WILL PROBABLY COME IN HANDY.
......
HE'S ACTING LIKE HE DOESN'T CARE, BUT DEEP DOWN, HE'S REALLY HAPPY.
MASASHI-CHAN....
YEAH, I KNOW.
HEY, THIS IS IT!
2-B

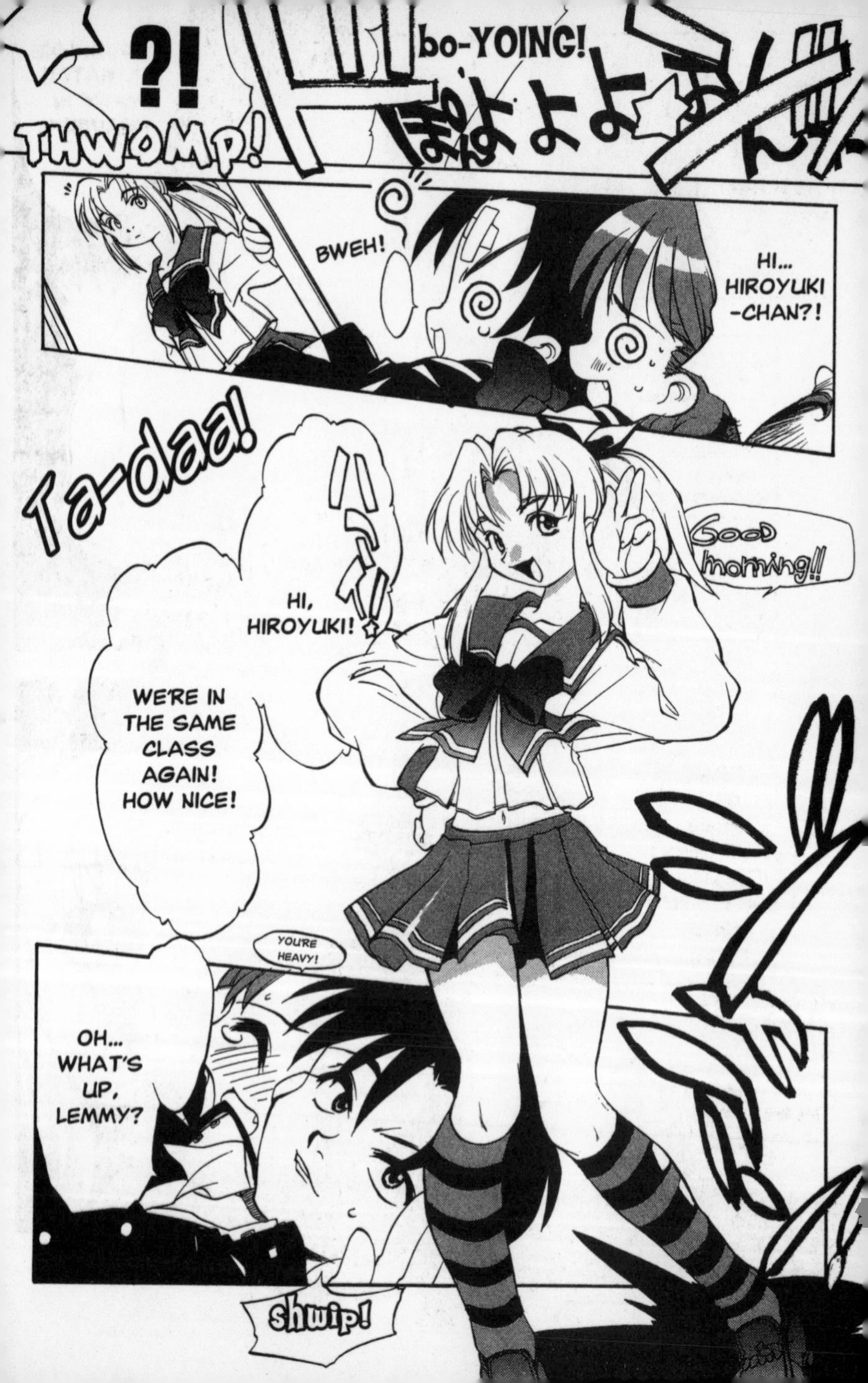
?!
bo-YOING!
ぽよよよ☆よん!!
THWOMP!
BWEH!
HI... HIROYUKI -CHAN?!
Ta-daa!
Good morning!!
HI, HIROYUKI!
WE'RE IN THE SAME CLASS AGAIN! HOW NICE!
YOU'RE HEAVY!
OH... WHAT'S UP, LEMMY?
shwip!

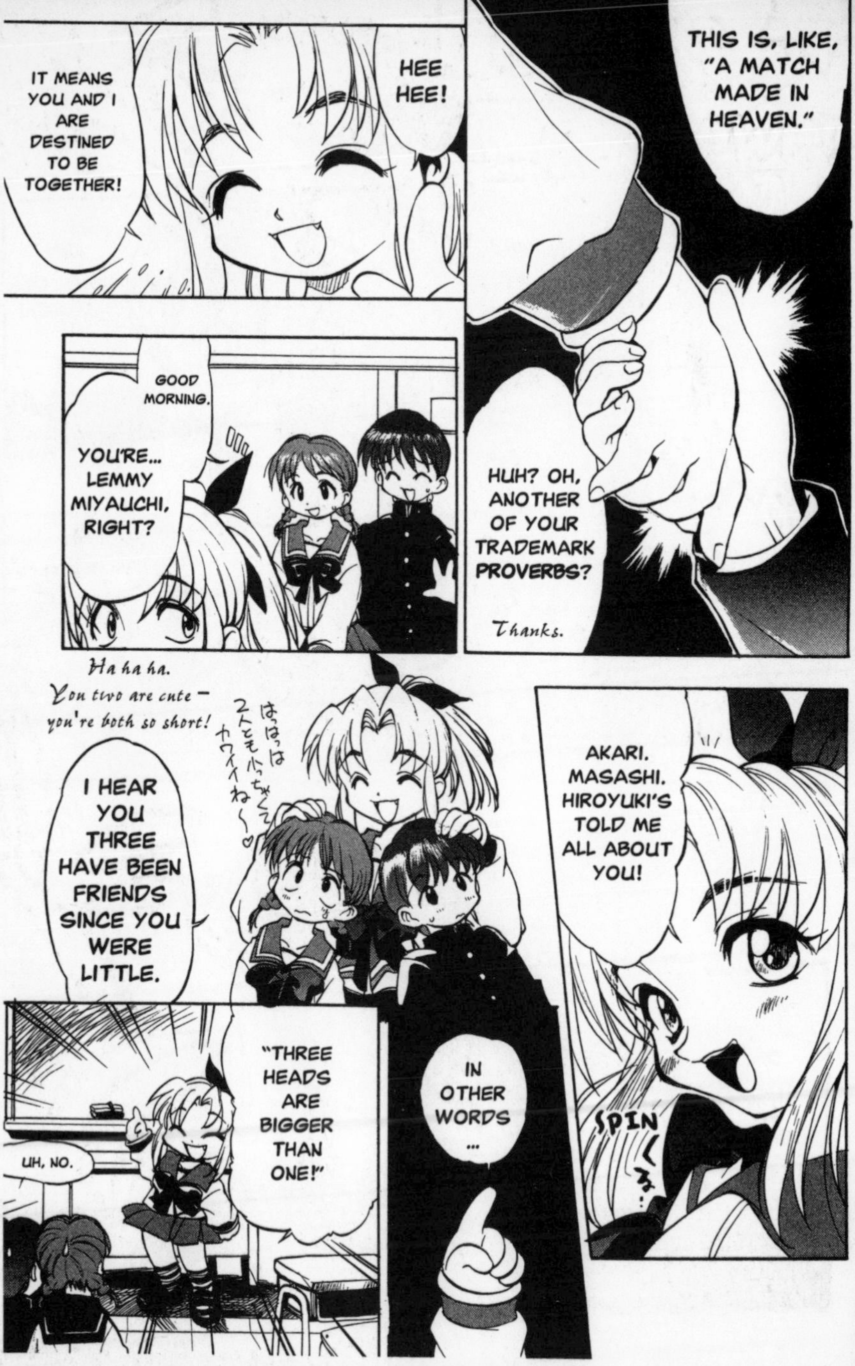
THIS IS, LIKE, "A MATCH MADE IN HEAVEN."
HEE HEE!
IT MEANS YOU AND I ARE DESTINED TO BE TOGETHER!
HUH? OH, ANOTHER OF YOUR TRADEMARK PROVERBS?
Thanks.
GOOD MORNING.
YOU'RE... LEMMY MIYAUCHI, RIGHT?
AKARI. MASASHI. HIROYUKI'S TOLD ME ALL ABOUT YOU!
SPIN くる…
I HEAR YOU THREE HAVE BEEN FRIENDS SINCE YOU WERE LITTLE.
Ha ha ha. You two are cute — you're both so short!
はっはっは 2人とも小っちゃくてカワイイね～♡
IN OTHER WORDS...
"THREE HEADS ARE BIGGER THAN ONE!"
UH, NO.

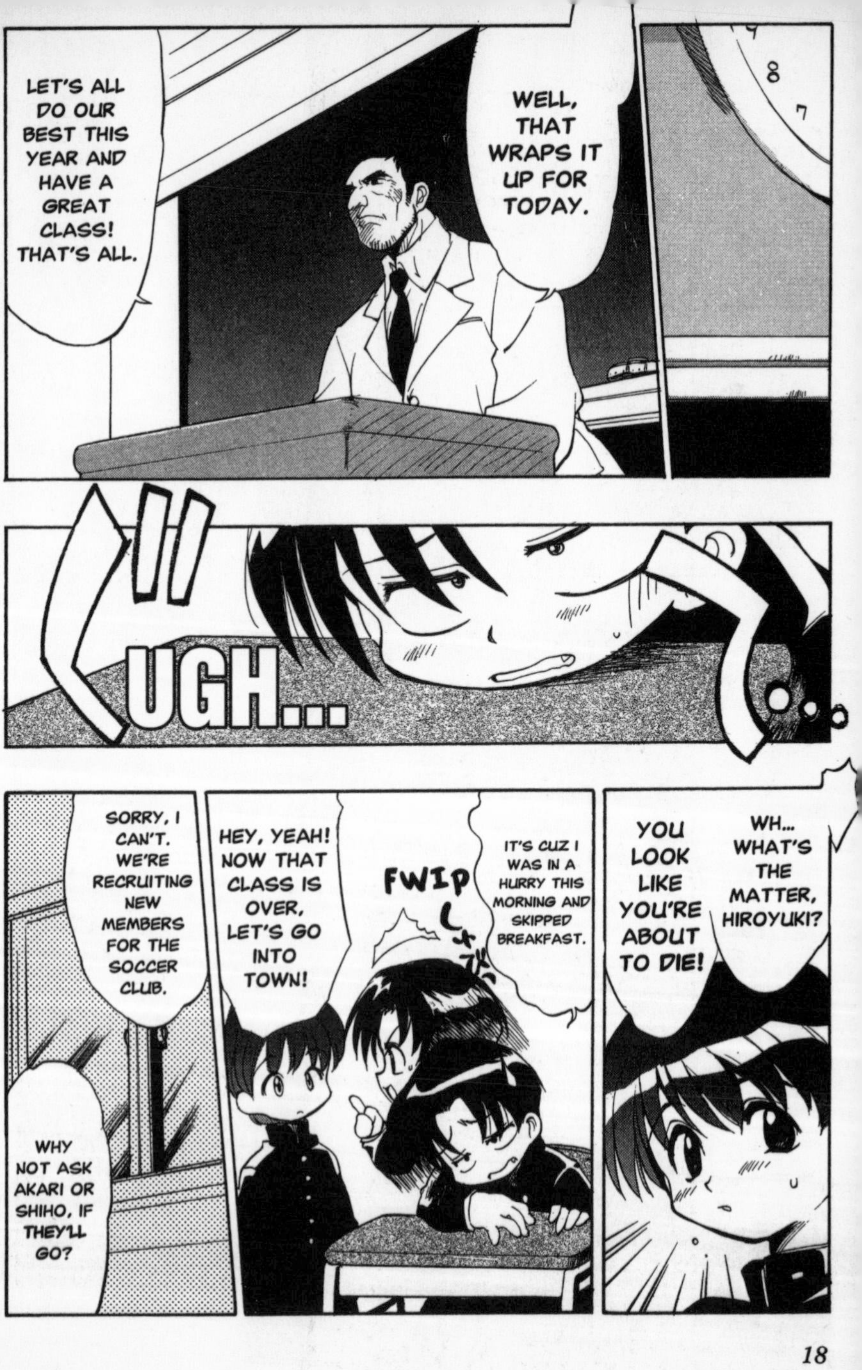
WELL, THAT WRAPS IT UP FOR TODAY.
LET'S ALL DO OUR BEST THIS YEAR AND HAVE A GREAT CLASS! THAT'S ALL.
UGH...
WH... WHAT'S THE MATTER, HIROYUKI?
YOU LOOK LIKE YOU'RE ABOUT TO DIE!
IT'S CUZ I WAS IN A HURRY THIS MORNING AND SKIPPED BREAKFAST.
FWIP
HEY, YEAH! NOW THAT CLASS IS OVER, LET'S GO INTO TOWN!
SORRY, I CAN'T. WE'RE RECRUITING NEW MEMBERS FOR THE SOCCER CLUB.
WHY NOT ASK AKARI OR SHIHO, IF THEY'LL GO?

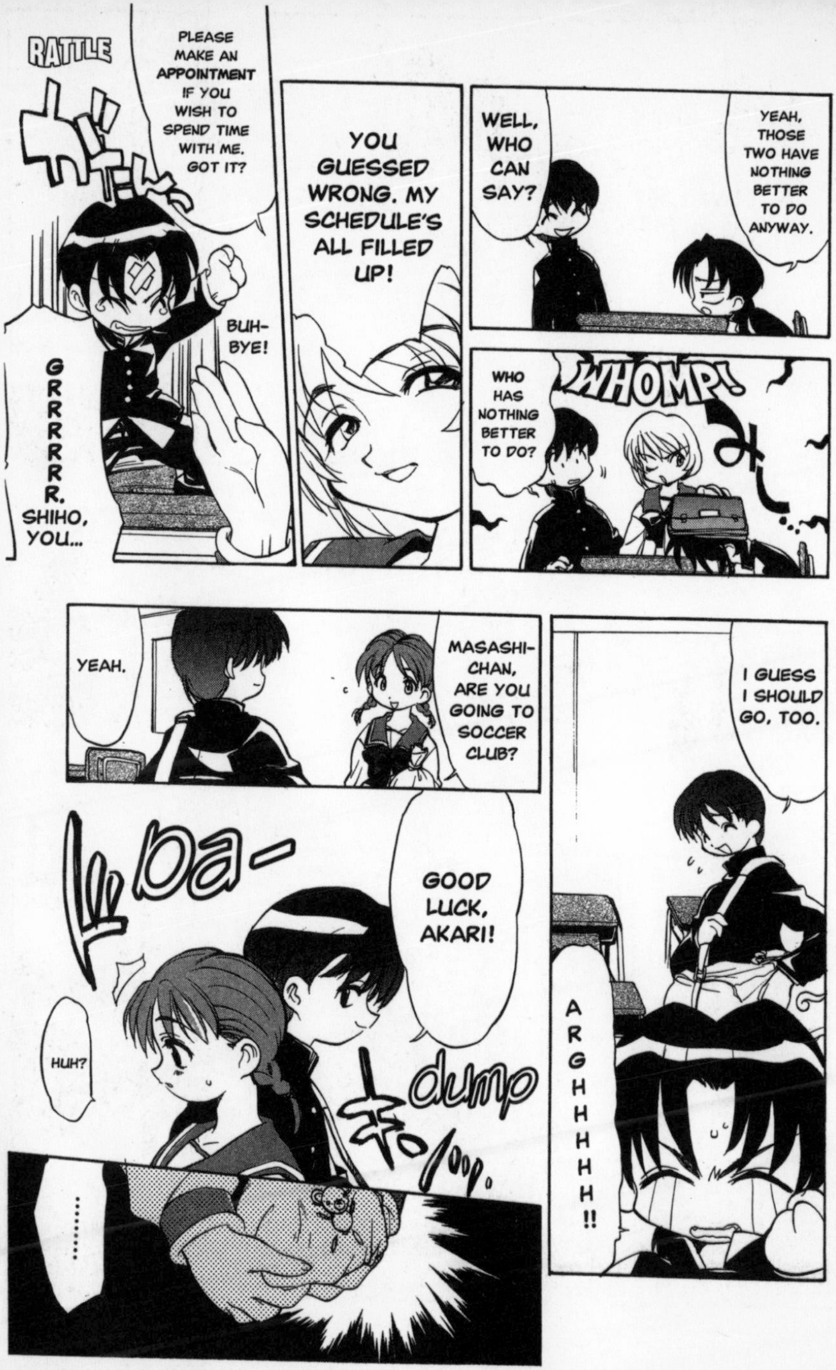

YEAH, THOSE TWO HAVE NOTHING BETTER TO DO ANYWAY.
WELL, WHO CAN SAY?
WHOMP!
WHO HAS NOTHING BETTER TO DO?
YOU GUESSED WRONG. MY SCHEDULE'S ALL FILLED UP!
BUH-BYE!
RATTLE
PLEASE MAKE AN APPOINTMENT IF YOU WISH TO SPEND TIME WITH ME. GOT IT?
GRRRRRR. SHIHO, YOU...
I GUESS I SHOULD GO, TOO.
ARGHHHHH!!
MASASHI-CHAN, ARE YOU GOING TO SOCCER CLUB?
YEAH.
ba-
GOOD LUCK, AKARI!
dump
HUH?
....

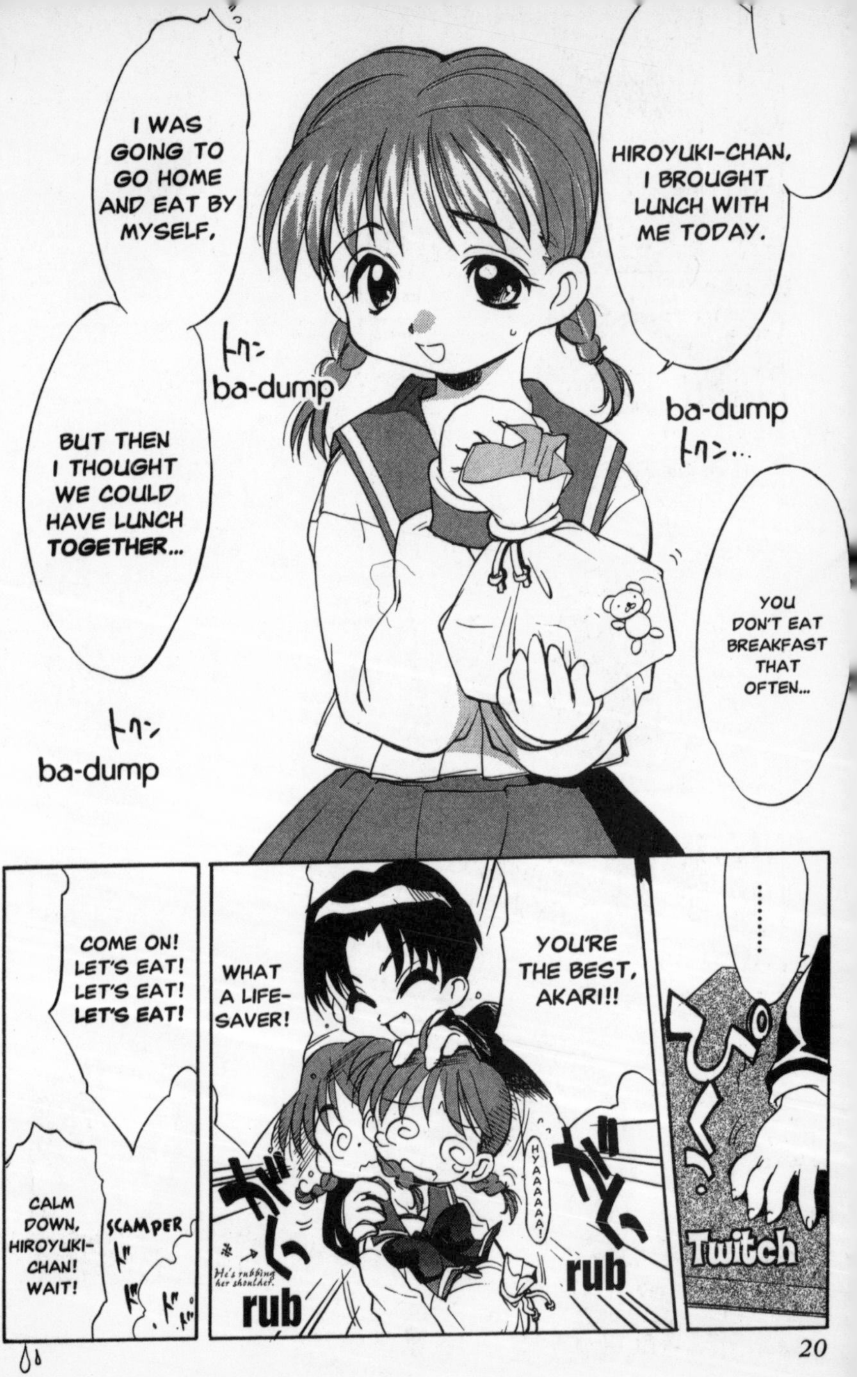
HIROYUKI-CHAN, I BROUGHT LUNCH WITH ME TODAY.
I WAS GOING TO GO HOME AND EAT BY MYSELF,
トクン
ba-dump
ba-dump
トクン…
YOU DON'T EAT BREAKFAST THAT OFTEN...
BUT THEN I THOUGHT WE COULD HAVE LUNCH TOGETHER...
トクン
ba-dump
......
Twitch
YOU'RE THE BEST, AKARI!!
WHAT A LIFE-SAVER!
HYAAAAAA!
rub
rub
He's rubbing her shoulder.
COME ON! LET'S EAT! LET'S EAT! LET'S EAT!
SCAMPER
CALM DOWN, HIROYUKI-CHAN! WAIT!

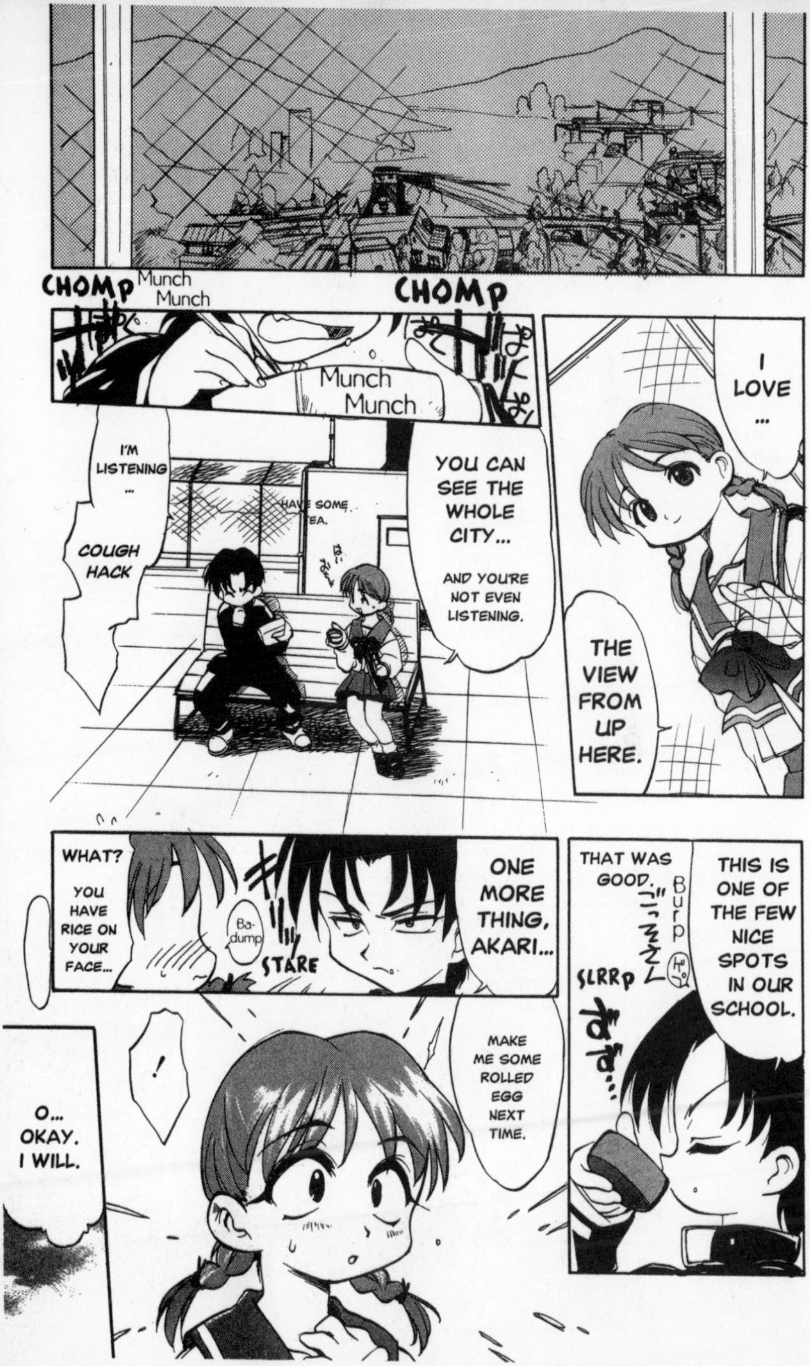

CHOMP
Munch Munch
CHOMP
Munch Munch
I LOVE ...
THE VIEW FROM UP HERE.
YOU CAN SEE THE WHOLE CITY...
AND YOU'RE NOT EVEN LISTENING.
HAVE SOME TEA.
I'M LISTENING ...
COUGH HACK
THIS IS ONE OF THE FEW NICE SPOTS IN OUR SCHOOL.
THAT WAS GOOD.
Burp
SLRRp
ONE MORE THING, AKARI...
STARE
Ba-dump
WHAT?
YOU HAVE RICE ON YOUR FACE...
MAKE ME SOME ROLLED EGG NEXT TIME.
!
O... OKAY. I WILL.

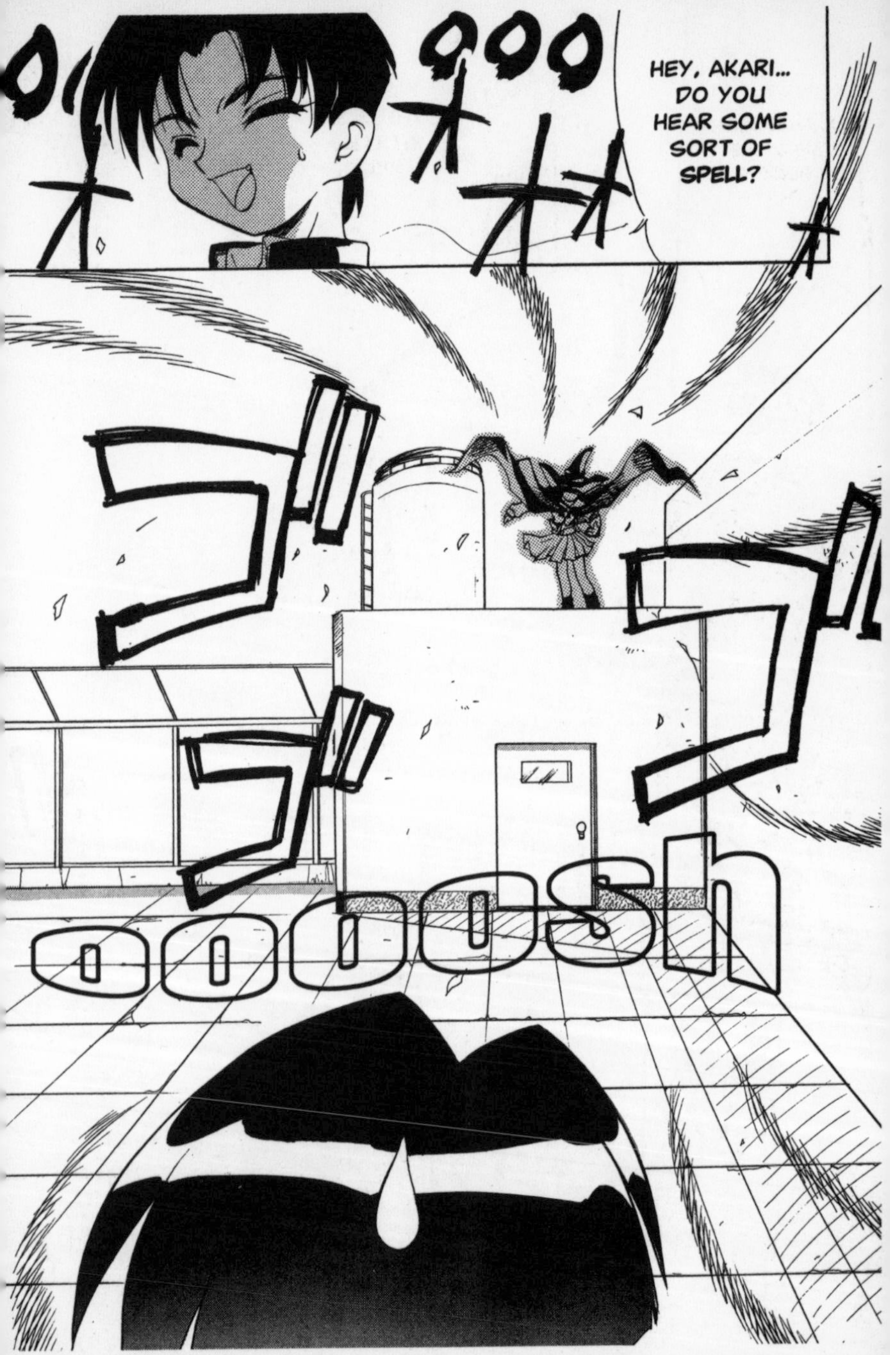

HEY, AKARI... DO YOU HEAR SOME SORT OF SPELL?
ooooosh

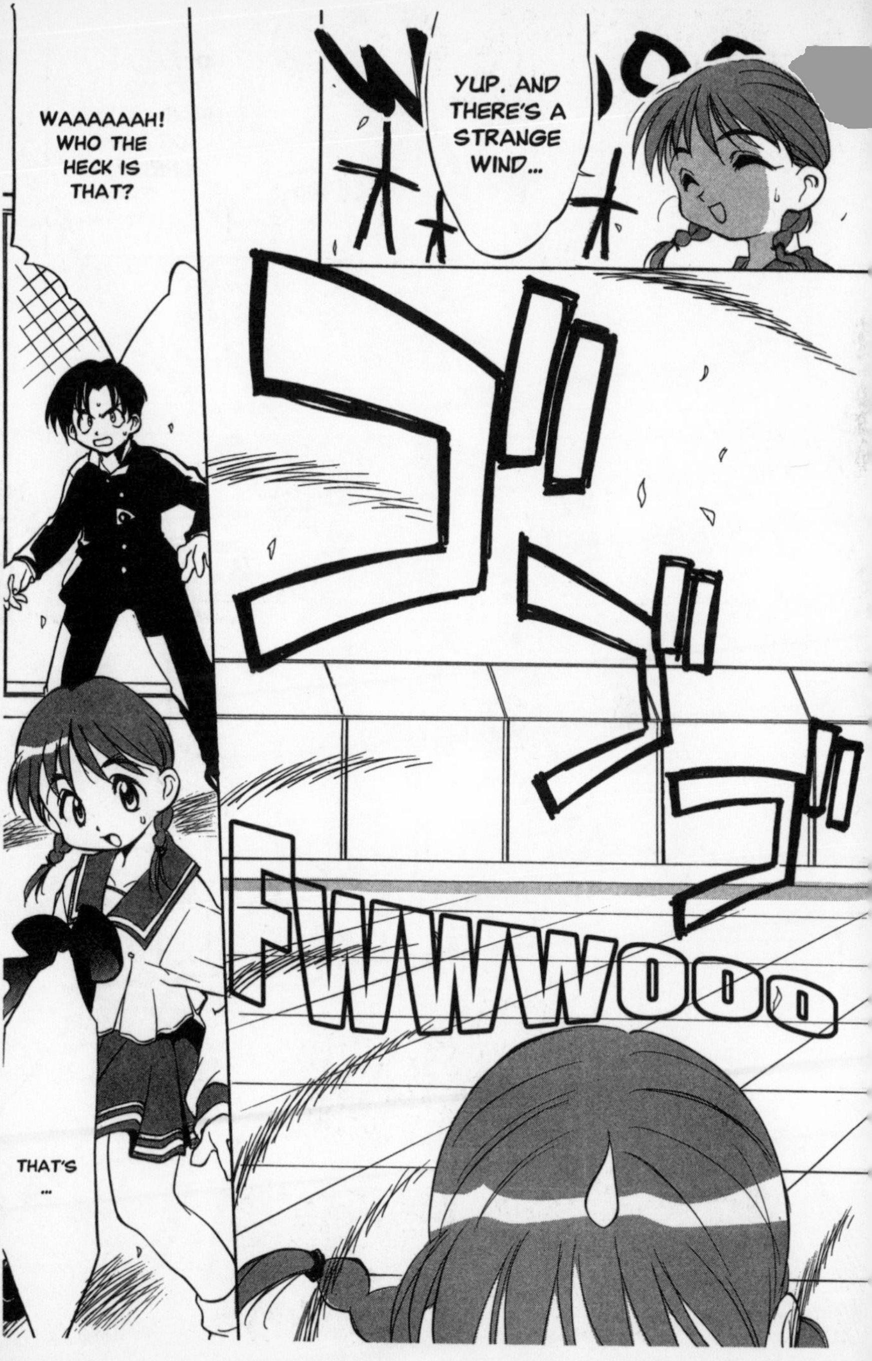

YUP. AND THERE'S A STRANGE WIND...
WAAAAAAH! WHO THE HECK IS THAT?
FWWWOOO
THAT'S ...

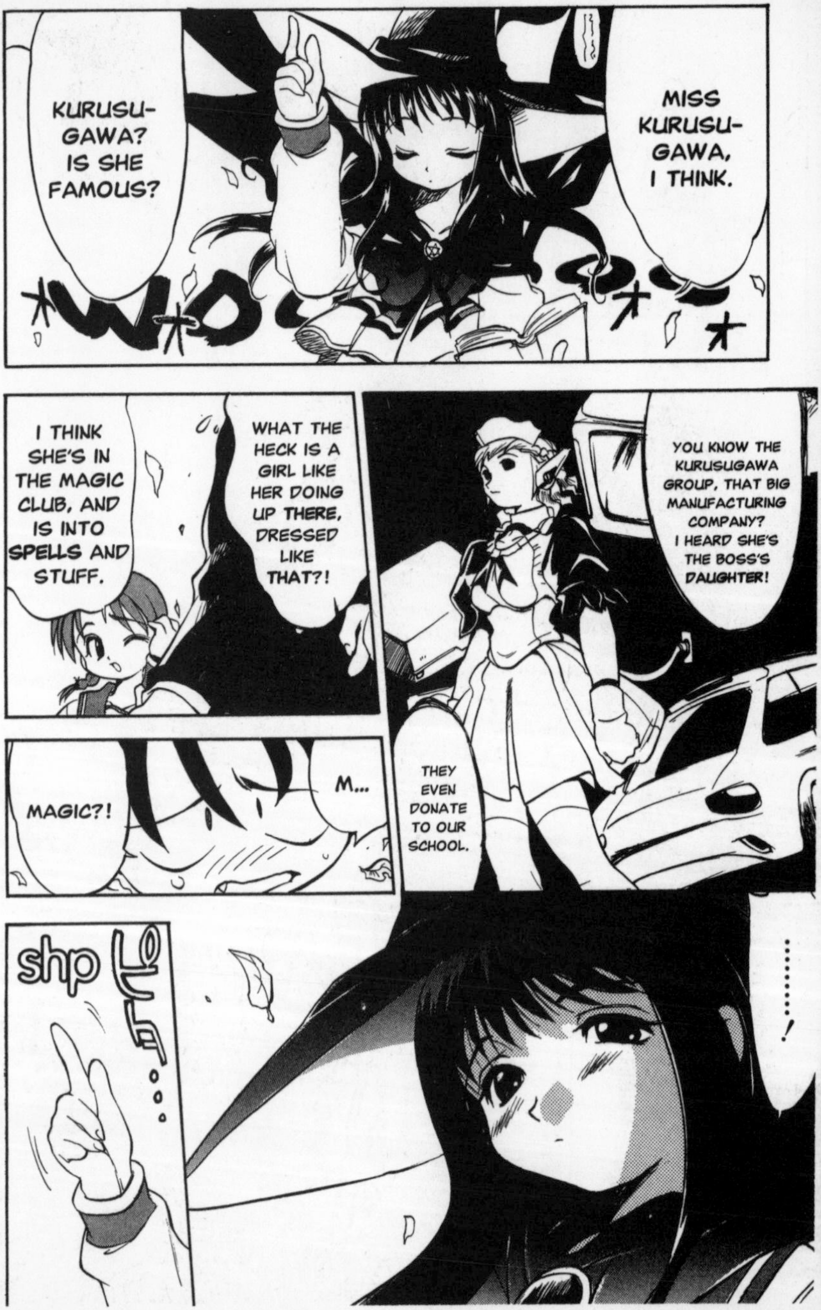
MISS KURUSU-GAWA, I THINK.
KURUSU-GAWA? IS SHE FAMOUS?
YOU KNOW THE KURUSUGAWA GROUP, THAT BIG MANUFACTURING COMPANY? I HEARD SHE'S THE BOSS'S DAUGHTER!
WHAT THE HECK IS A GIRL LIKE HER DOING UP THERE, DRESSED LIKE THAT?!
I THINK SHE'S IN THE MAGIC CLUB, AND IS INTO SPELLS AND STUFF.
THEY EVEN DONATE TO OUR SCHOOL.
M...
MAGIC?!
......!
shp

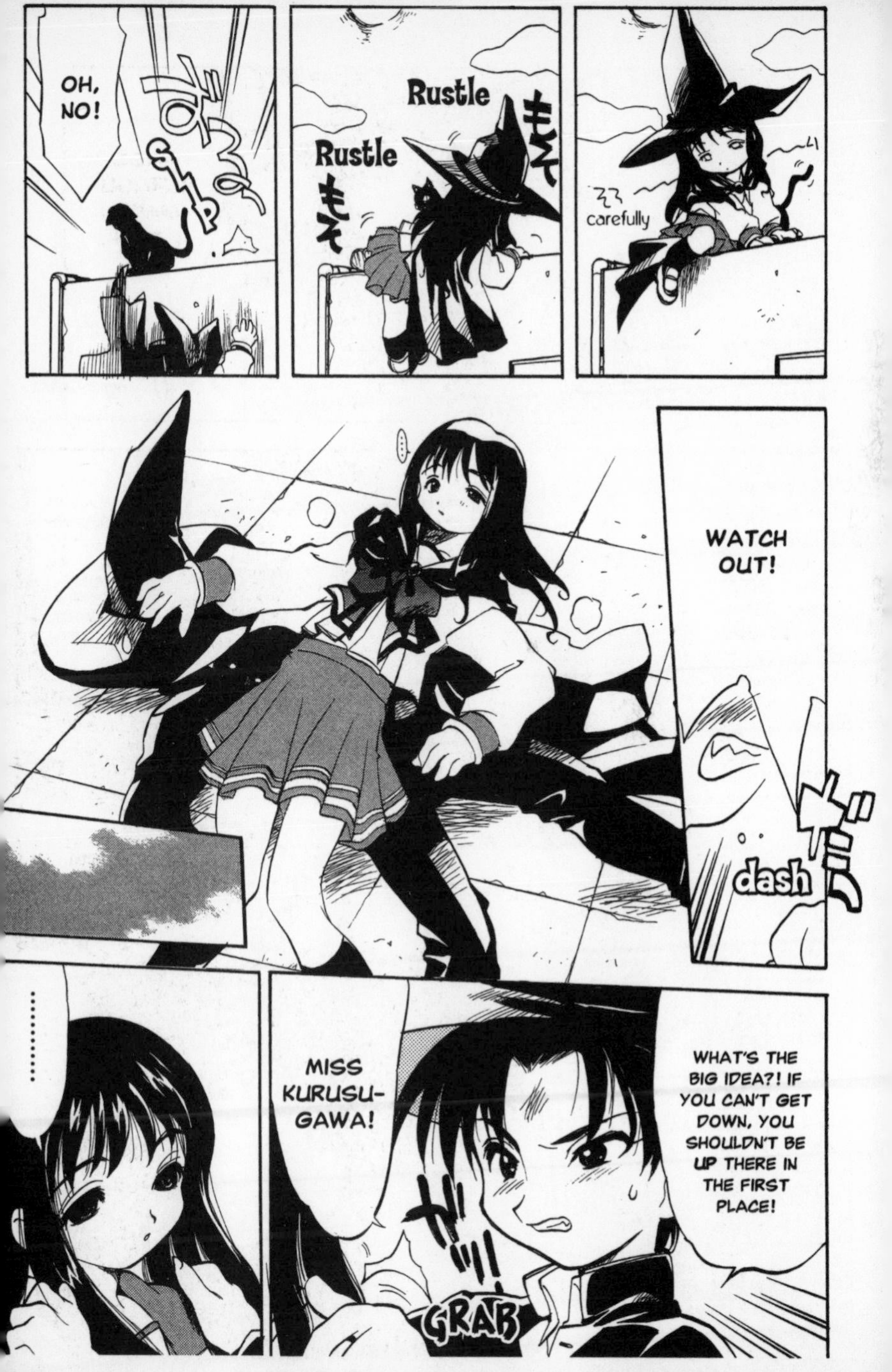

carefully
Rustle
Rustle
OH, NO!
WATCH OUT!
dash
WHAT'S THE BIG IDEA?! IF YOU CAN'T GET DOWN, YOU SHOULDN'T BE UP THERE IN THE FIRST PLACE!
GRAB
MISS KURUSU-GAWA!
....

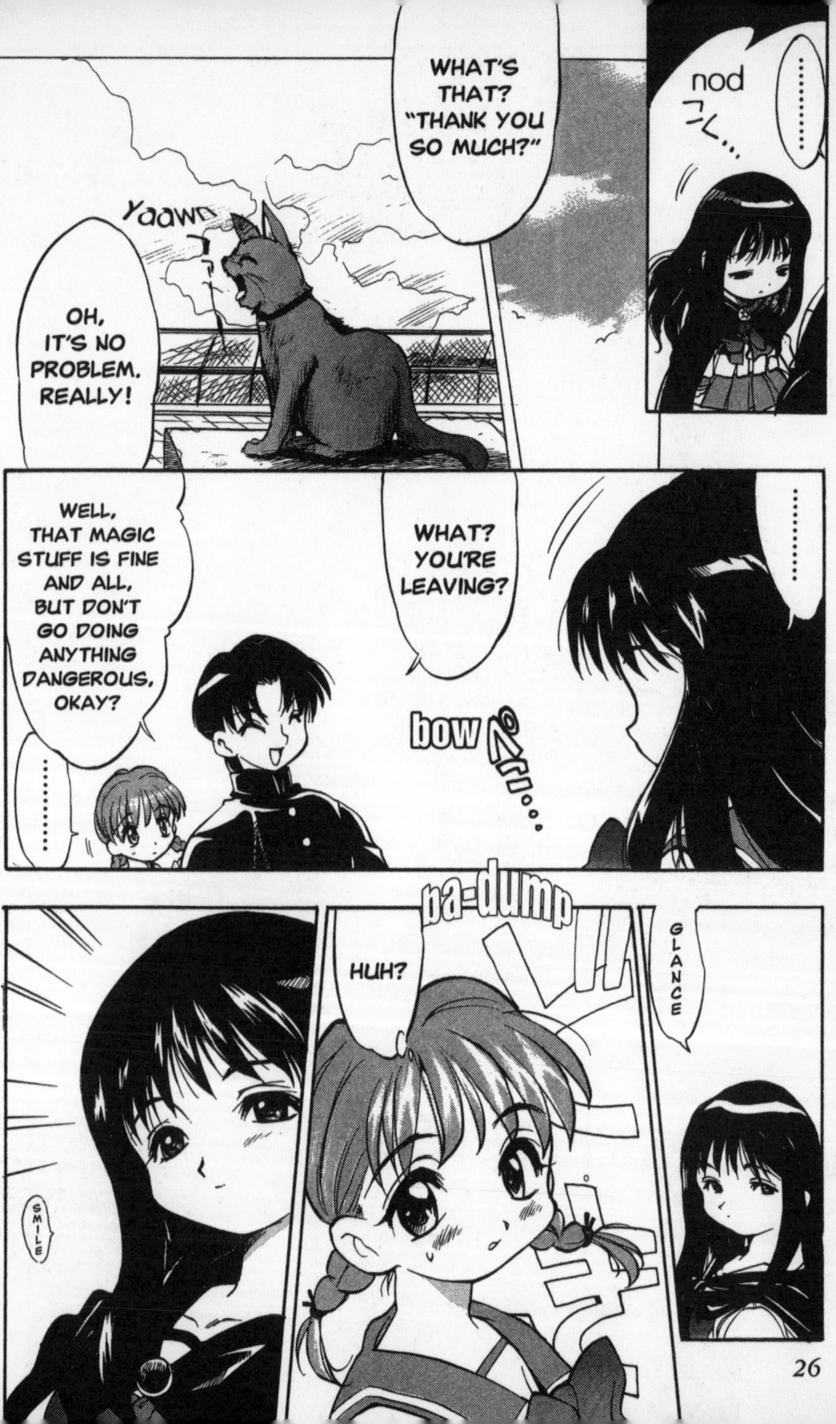
nod
......
WHAT'S THAT? "THANK YOU SO MUCH?"
Yaawn
OH, IT'S NO PROBLEM. REALLY!
......
bow
WHAT? YOU'RE LEAVING?
WELL, THAT MAGIC STUFF IS FINE AND ALL, BUT DON'T GO DOING ANYTHING DANGEROUS, OKAY?
......
GLANCE
ba-dump
HUH?
SMILE

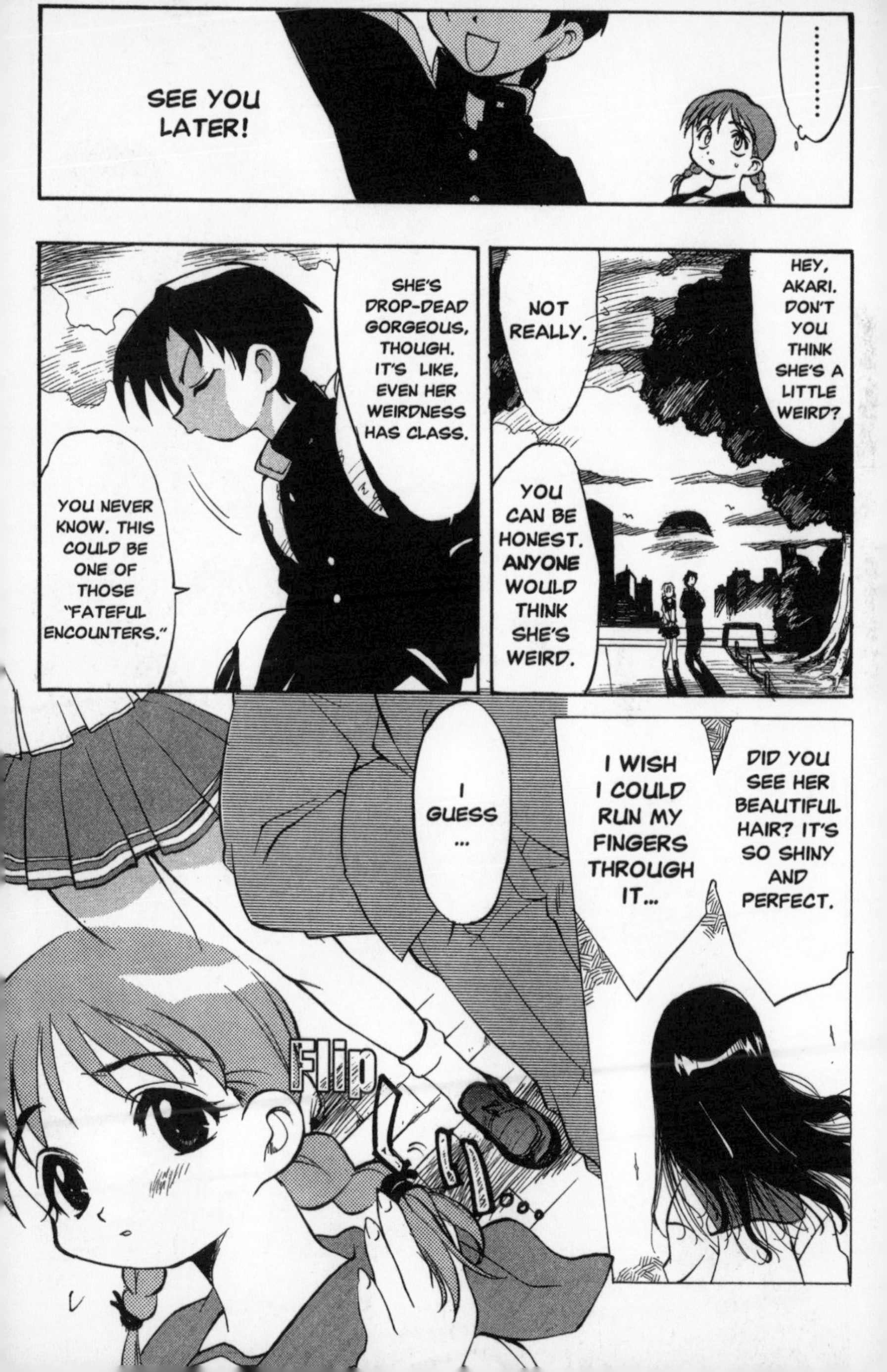
......
SEE YOU LATER!
HEY, AKARI. DON'T YOU THINK SHE'S A LITTLE WEIRD?
NOT REALLY.
YOU CAN BE HONEST. ANYONE WOULD THINK SHE'S WEIRD.
SHE'S DROP-DEAD GORGEOUS, THOUGH. IT'S LIKE, EVEN HER WEIRDNESS HAS CLASS.
YOU NEVER KNOW. THIS COULD BE ONE OF THOSE "FATEFUL ENCOUNTERS."
DID YOU SEE HER BEAUTIFUL HAIR? IT'S SO SHINY AND PERFECT.
I WISH I COULD RUN MY FINGERS THROUGH IT...
I GUESS ...
Flip

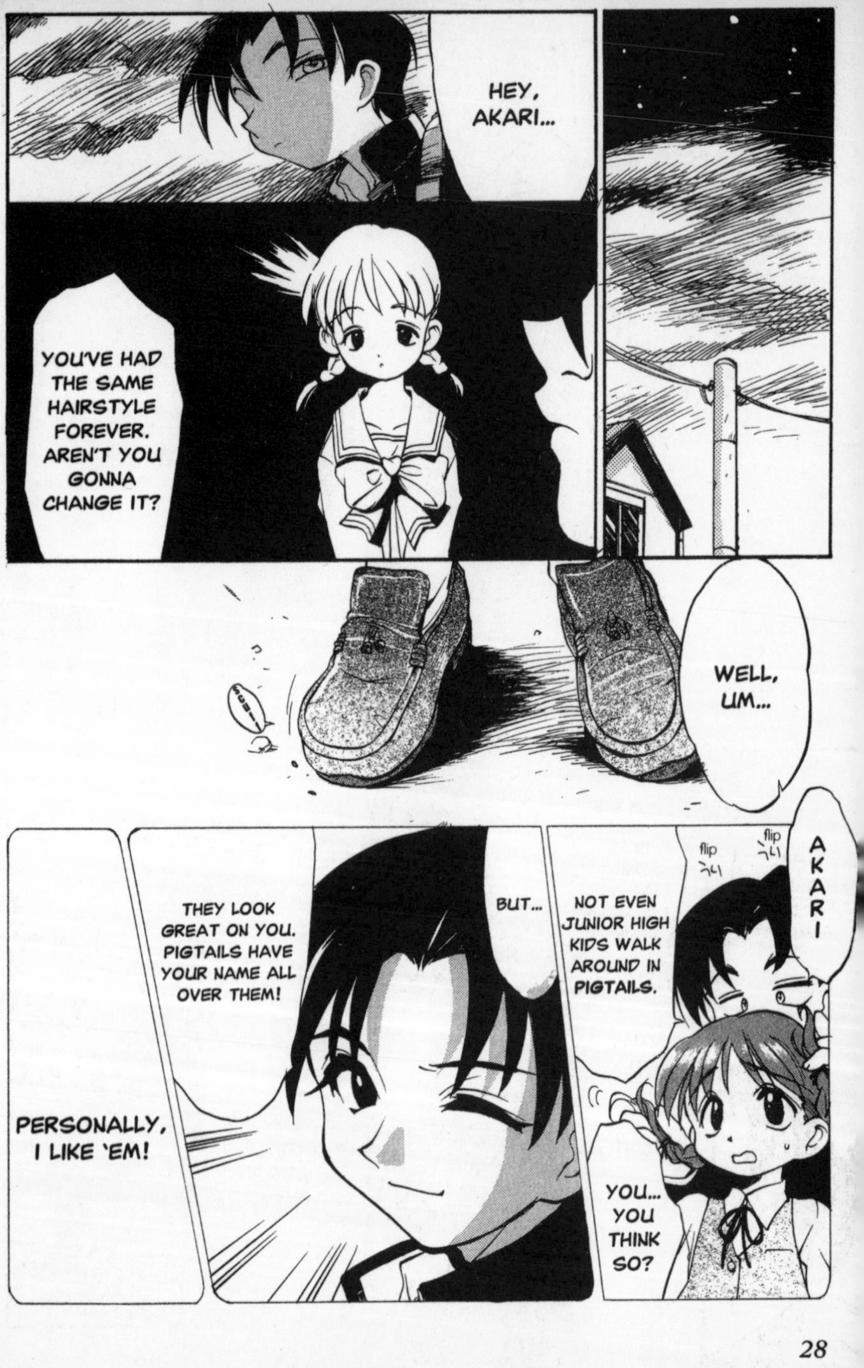
HEY, AKARI...
YOU'VE HAD THE SAME HAIRSTYLE FOREVER. AREN'T YOU GONNA CHANGE IT?
WELL, UM...
AKARI
flip
flip
NOT EVEN JUNIOR HIGH KIDS WALK AROUND IN PIGTAILS.
YOU... YOU THINK SO?
BUT...
THEY LOOK GREAT ON YOU. PIGTAILS HAVE YOUR NAME ALL OVER THEM!
PERSONALLY, I LIKE 'EM!

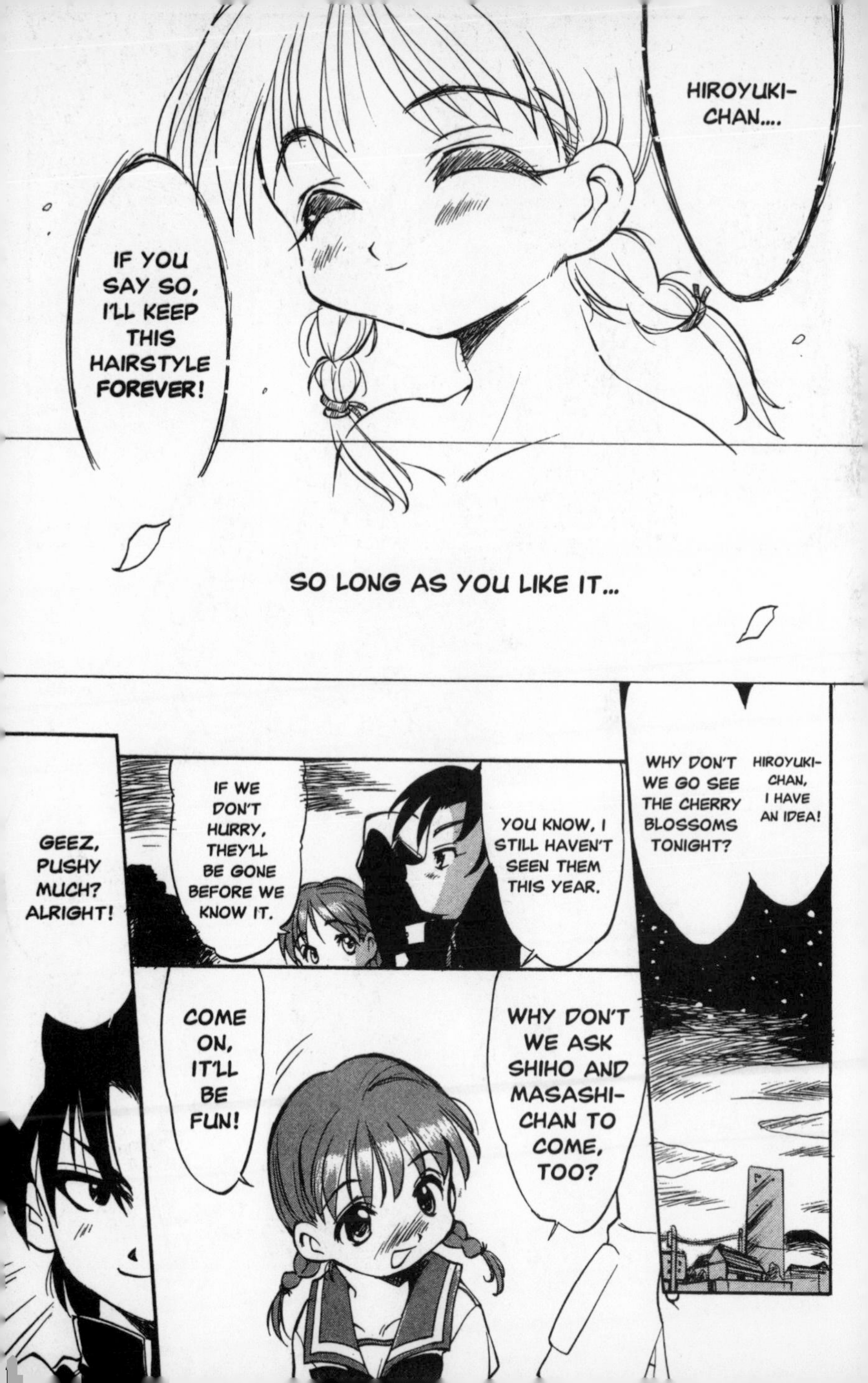
HIROYUKI-CHAN....
IF YOU SAY SO, I'LL KEEP THIS HAIRSTYLE FOREVER!
SO LONG AS YOU LIKE IT...
HIROYUKI-CHAN, I HAVE AN IDEA!
WHY DON'T WE GO SEE THE CHERRY BLOSSOMS TONIGHT?
YOU KNOW, I STILL HAVEN'T SEEN THEM THIS YEAR.
IF WE DON'T HURRY, THEY'LL BE GONE BEFORE WE KNOW IT.
WHY DON'T WE ASK SHIHO AND MASASHI-CHAN TO COME, TOO?
COME ON, IT'LL BE FUN!
GEEZ, PUSHY MUCH? ALRIGHT!

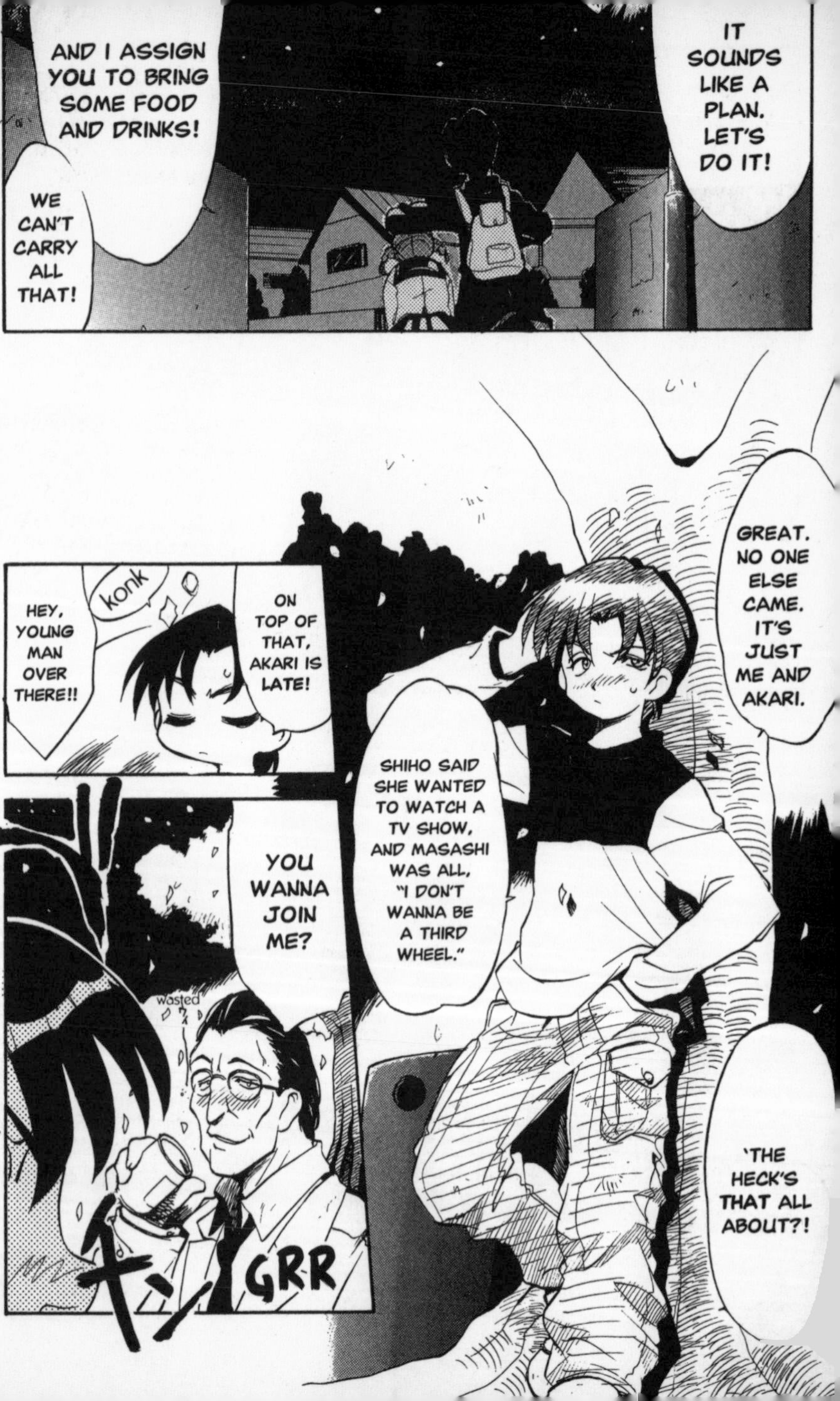
IT SOUNDS LIKE A PLAN. LET'S DO IT!
AND I ASSIGN YOU TO BRING SOME FOOD AND DRINKS!
WE CAN'T CARRY ALL THAT!
GREAT. NO ONE ELSE CAME. IT'S JUST ME AND AKARI.
SHIHO SAID SHE WANTED TO WATCH A TV SHOW, AND MASASHI WAS ALL, "I DON'T WANNA BE A THIRD WHEEL."
'THE HECK'S THAT ALL ABOUT?!
ON TOP OF THAT, AKARI IS LATE!
konk
HEY, YOUNG MAN OVER THERE!!
YOU WANNA JOIN ME?
wasted
GRR

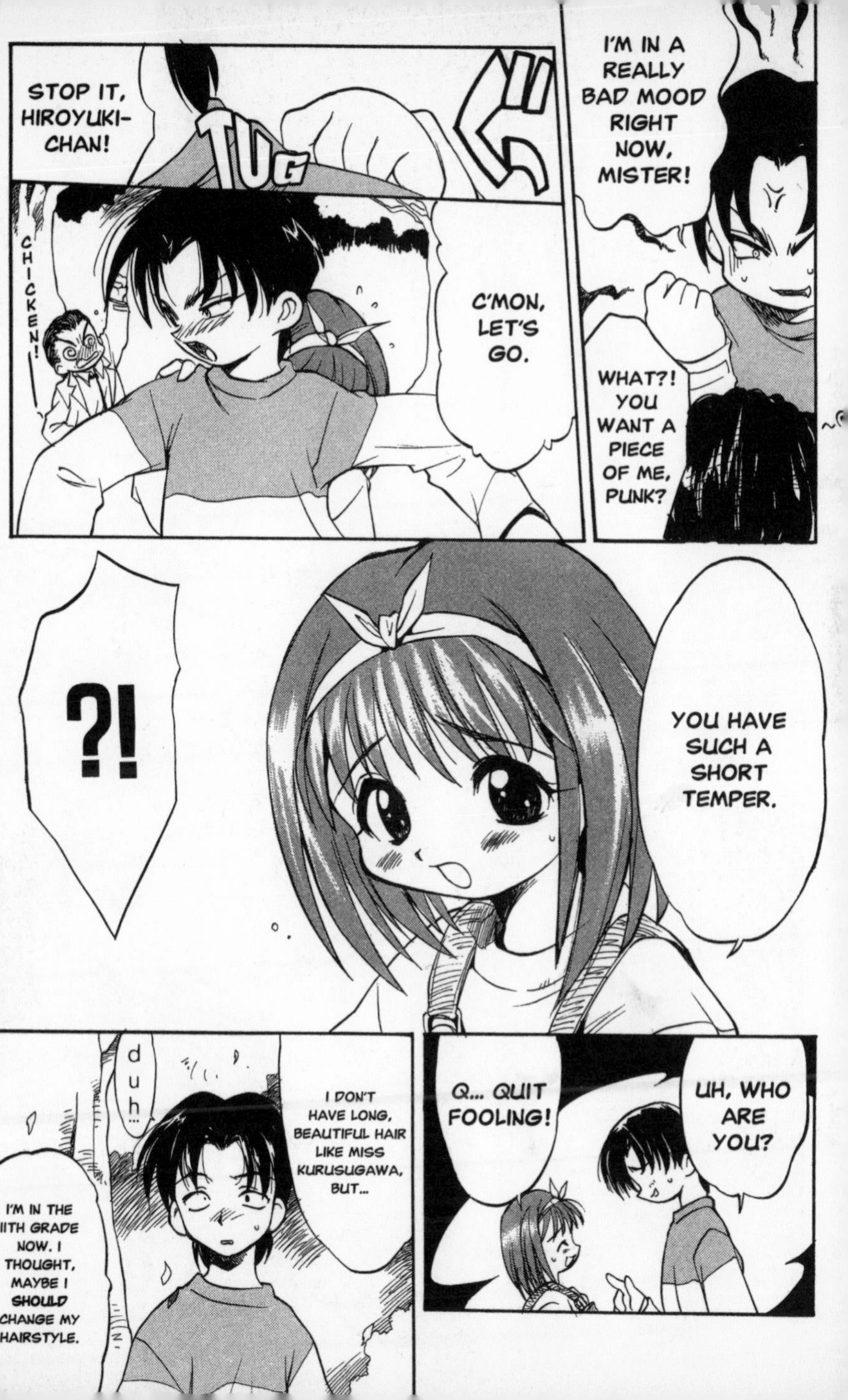
I'M IN A REALLY BAD MOOD RIGHT NOW, MISTER!
WHAT?! YOU WANT A PIECE OF ME, PUNK?
STOP IT, HIROYUKI-CHAN!
TUG
C'MON, LET'S GO.
CHICKEN!
YOU HAVE SUCH A SHORT TEMPER.
?!
UH, WHO ARE YOU?
Q... QUIT FOOLING!
I DON'T HAVE LONG, BEAUTIFUL HAIR LIKE MISS KURUSUGAWA, BUT...
I'M IN THE 11TH GRADE NOW. I THOUGHT, MAYBE I SHOULD CHANGE MY HAIRSTYLE.
duh...

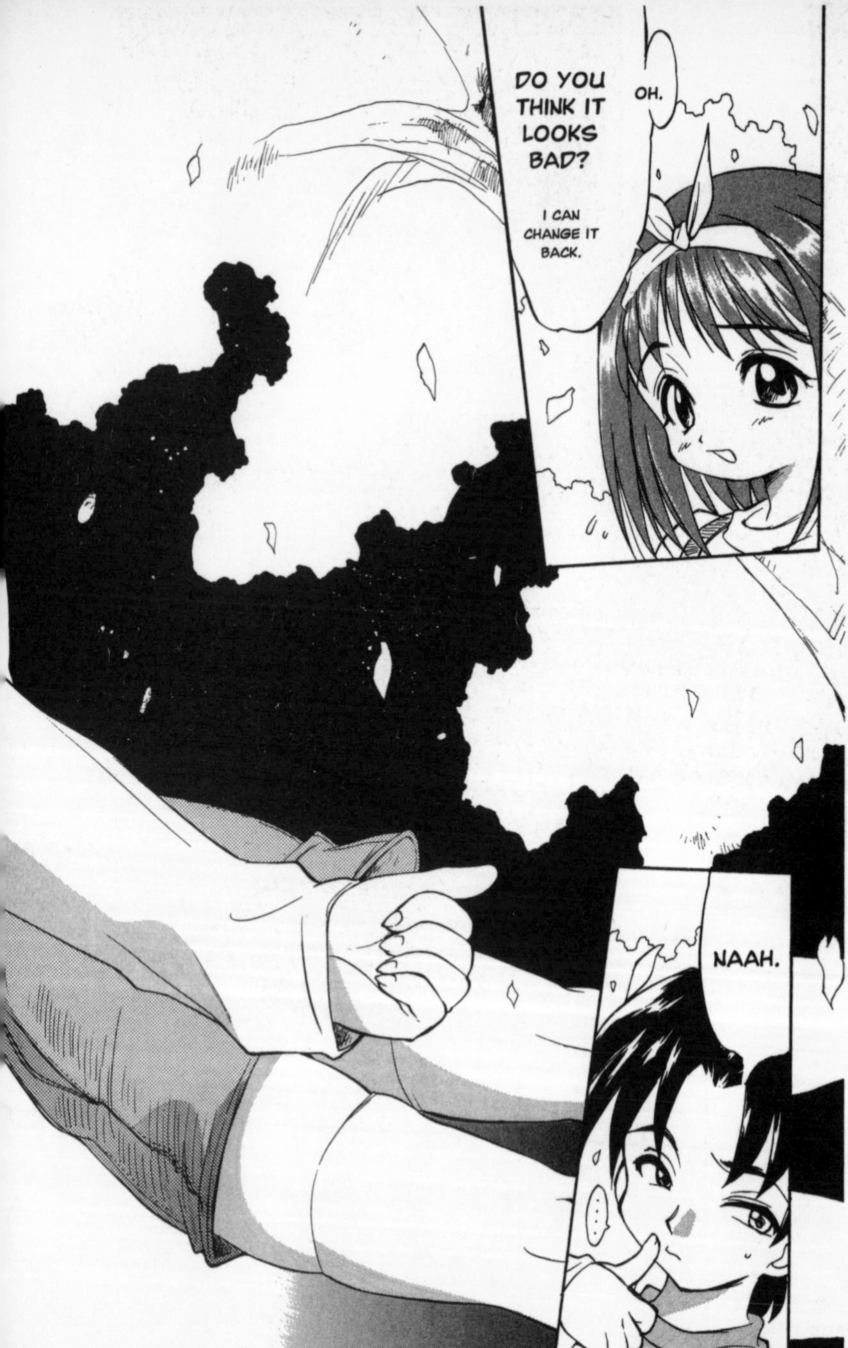
OH.
DO YOU THINK IT LOOKS BAD?
I CAN CHANGE IT BACK.
NAAH.

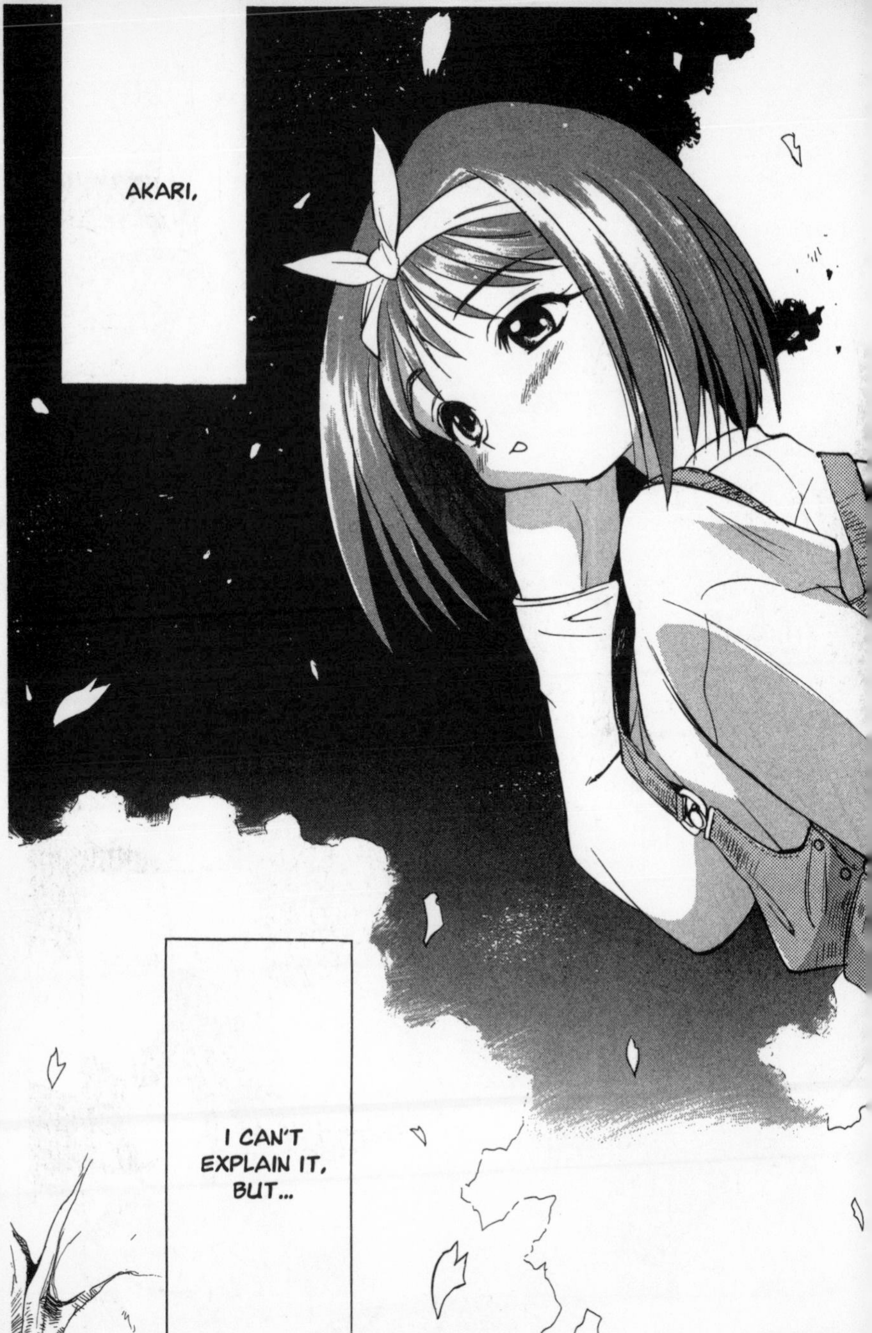
AKARI,
I CAN'T EXPLAIN IT, BUT...

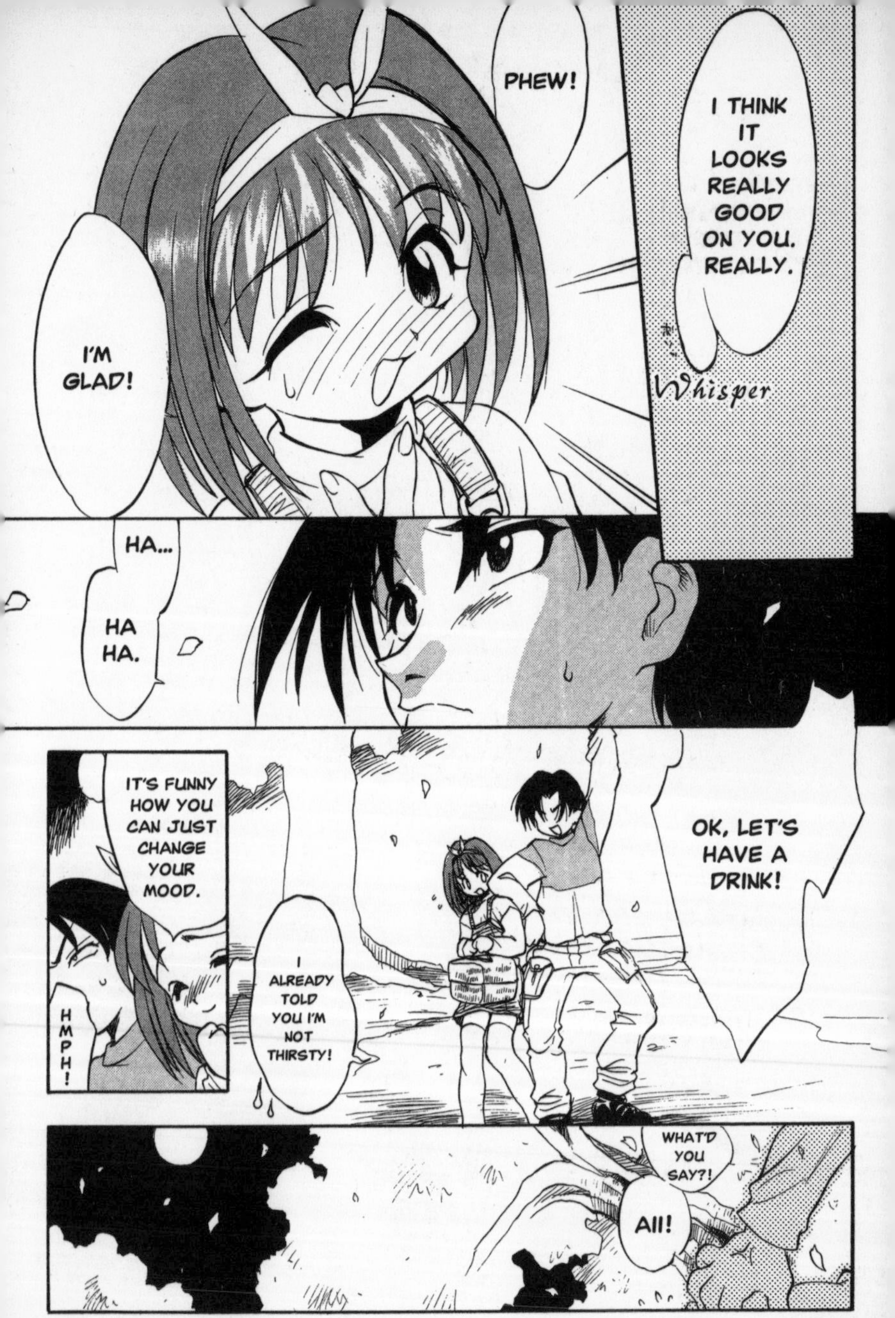
I THINK IT LOOKS REALLY GOOD ON YOU. REALLY.
Whisper
PHEW!
I'M GLAD!
HA... HA HA.
OK, LET'S HAVE A DRINK!
I ALREADY TOLD YOU I'M NOT THIRSTY!
IT'S FUNNY HOW YOU CAN JUST CHANGE YOUR MOOD.
HMPH!
WHAT'D YOU SAY?!
AII!

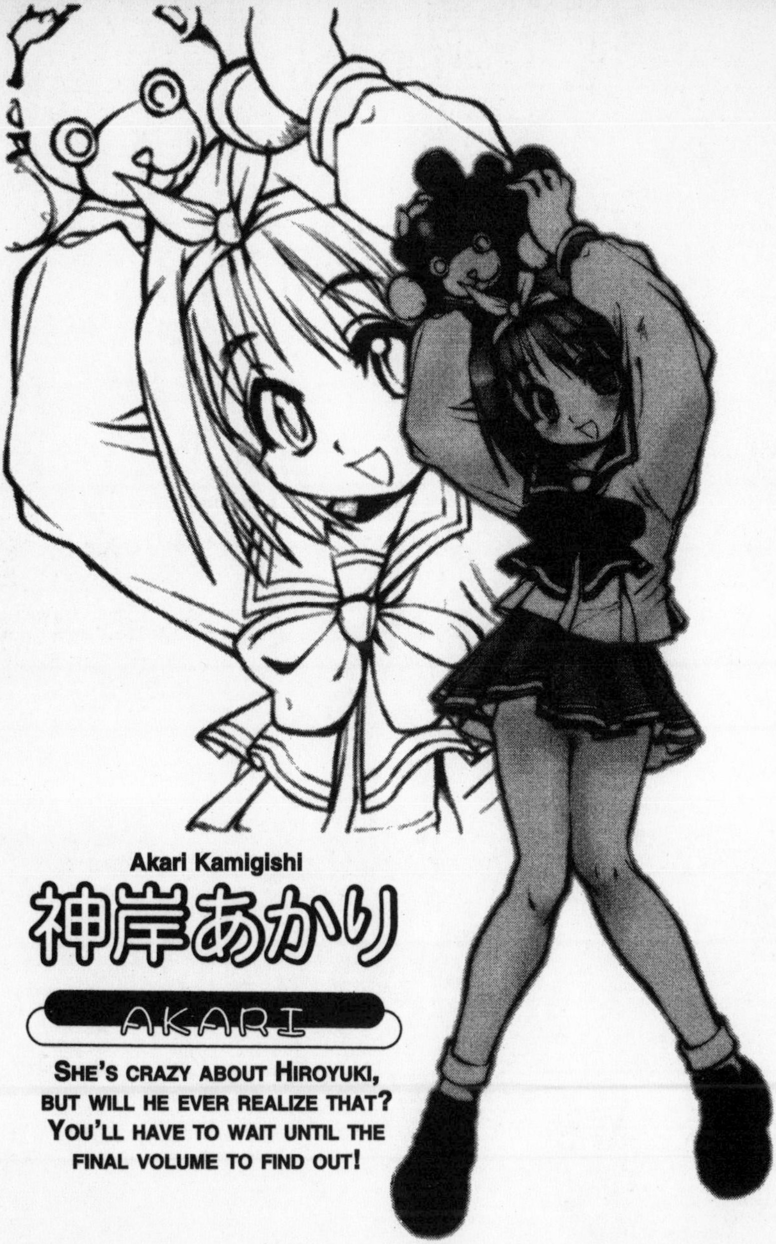

Akari Kamigishi

神岸あかり

AKARI

SHE'S CRAZY ABOUT HIROYUKI, BUT WILL HE EVER REALIZE THAT? YOU'LL HAVE TO WAIT UNTIL THE FINAL VOLUME TO FIND OUT!

Episode 2
『Pure』
～HMX-12 Multi～

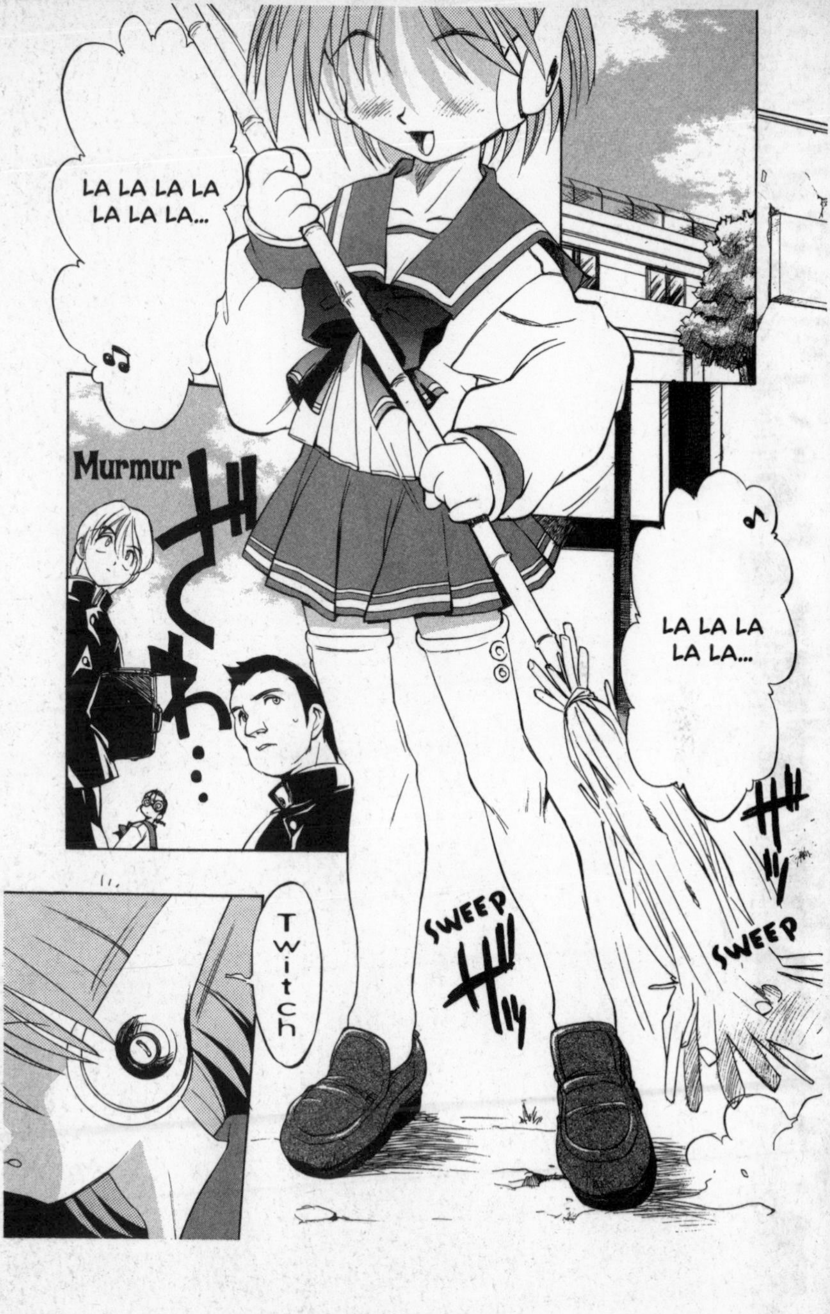
LA LA LA LA
LA LA LA...
LA LA LA
LA LA...
SWEEP
SWEEP
Murmur
ざわ...
Twitch

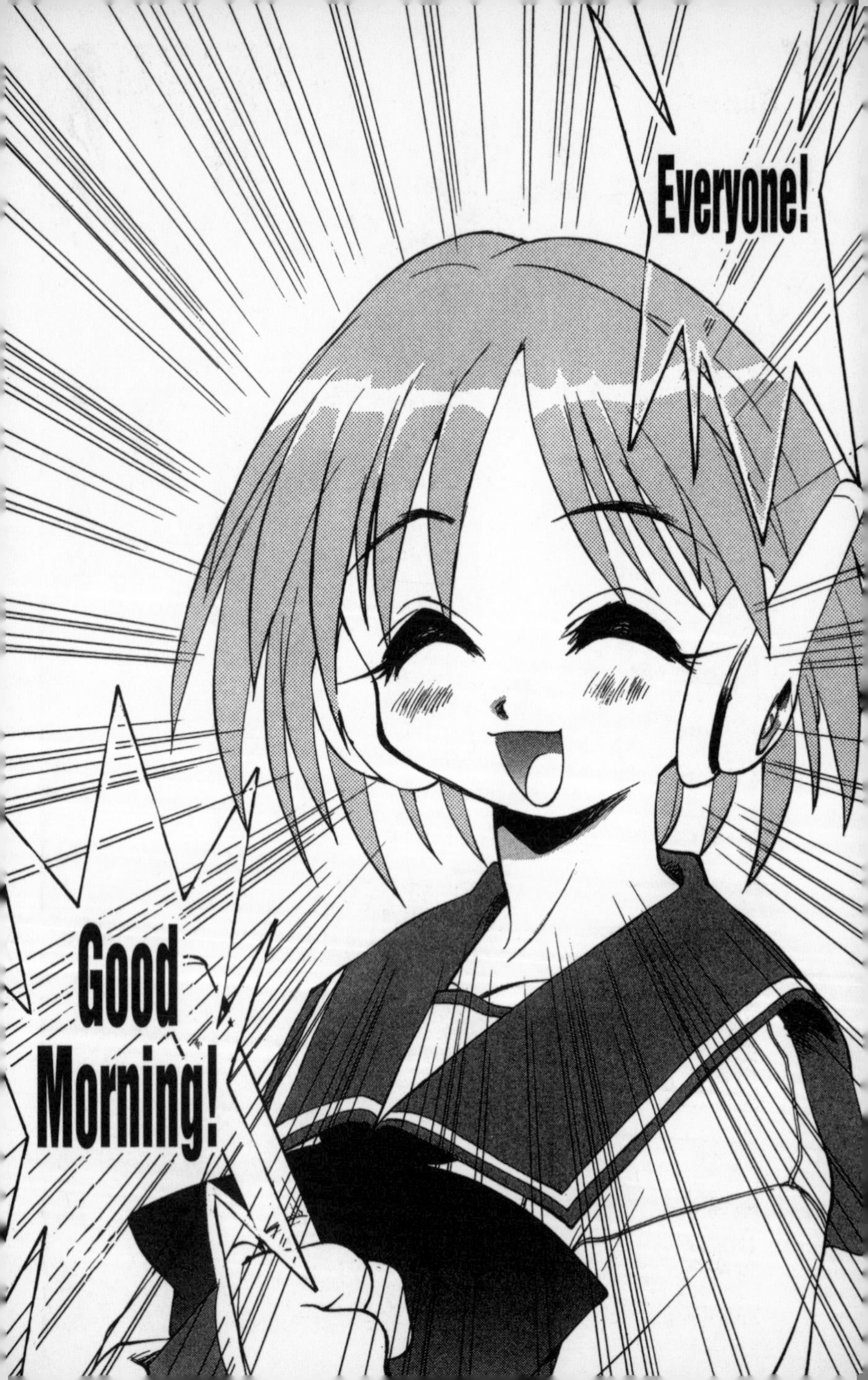
Everyone!
Good Morning!

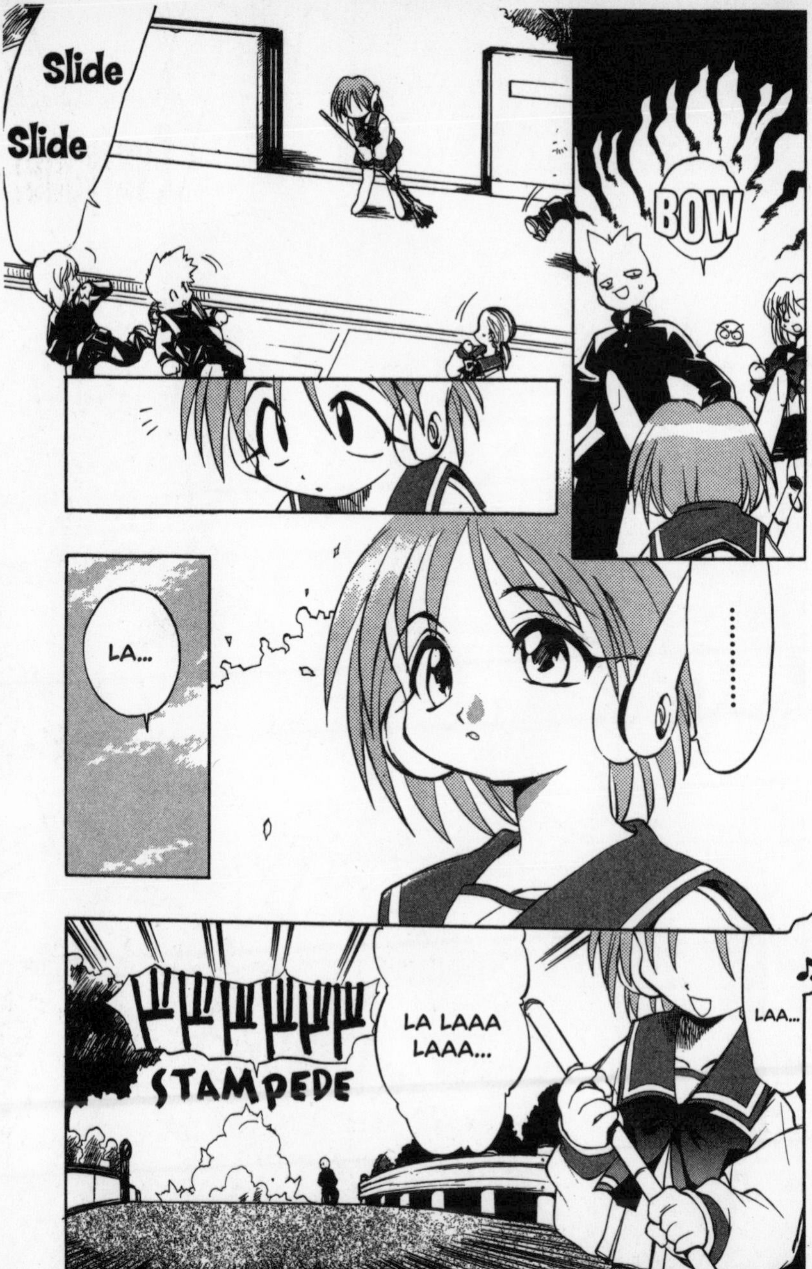
BOW
Slide
Slide
LA...
....
STAMPEDE
LAA...
LA LAAA LAAA...

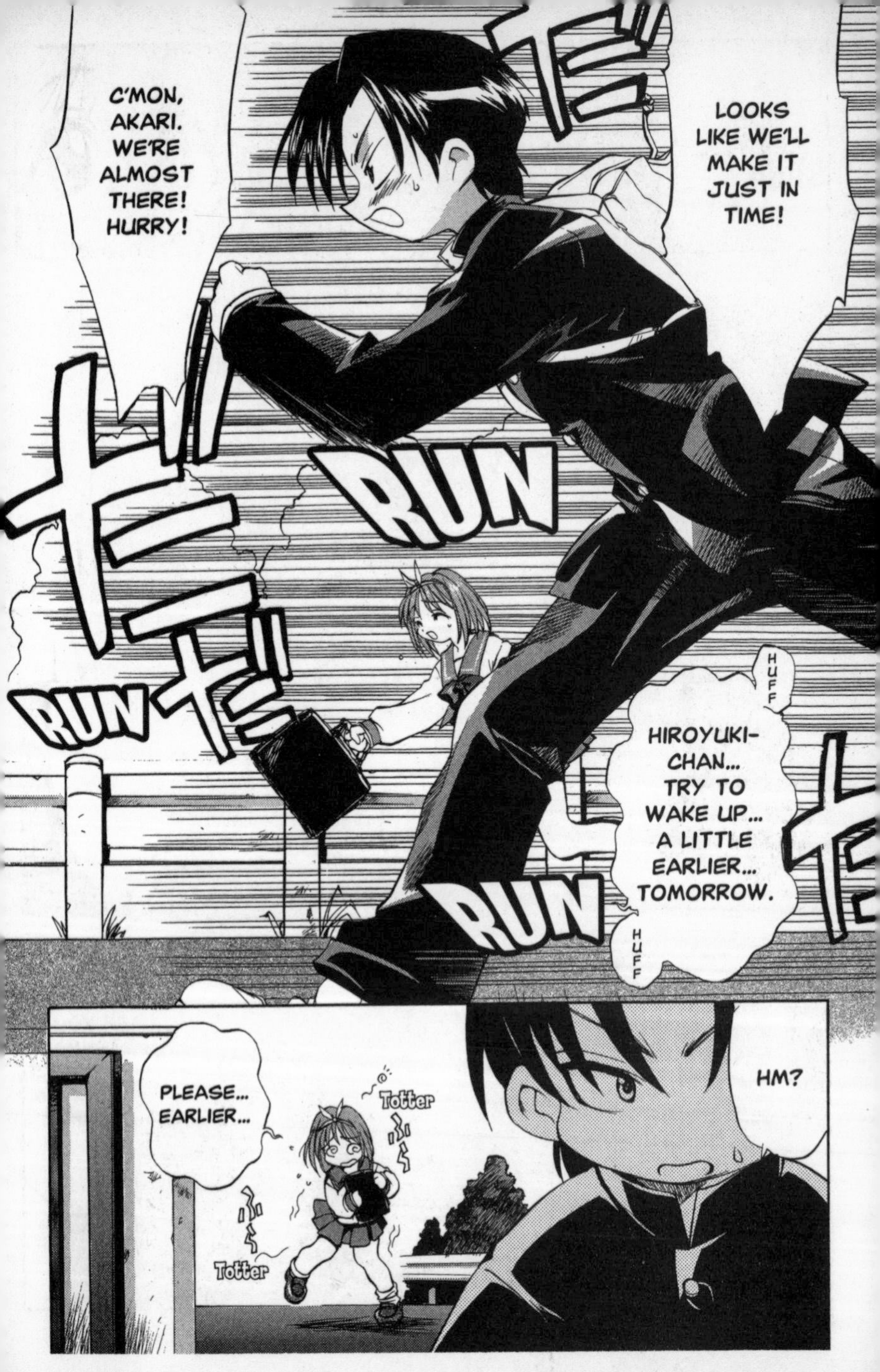
LOOKS LIKE WE'LL MAKE IT JUST IN TIME!
C'MON, AKARI. WE'RE ALMOST THERE! HURRY!
RUN
RUN
RUN
HUFF
HIROYUKI-CHAN... TRY TO WAKE UP... A LITTLE EARLIER... TOMORROW.
HUFF
HM?
Totter
PLEASE... EARLIER...
Totter

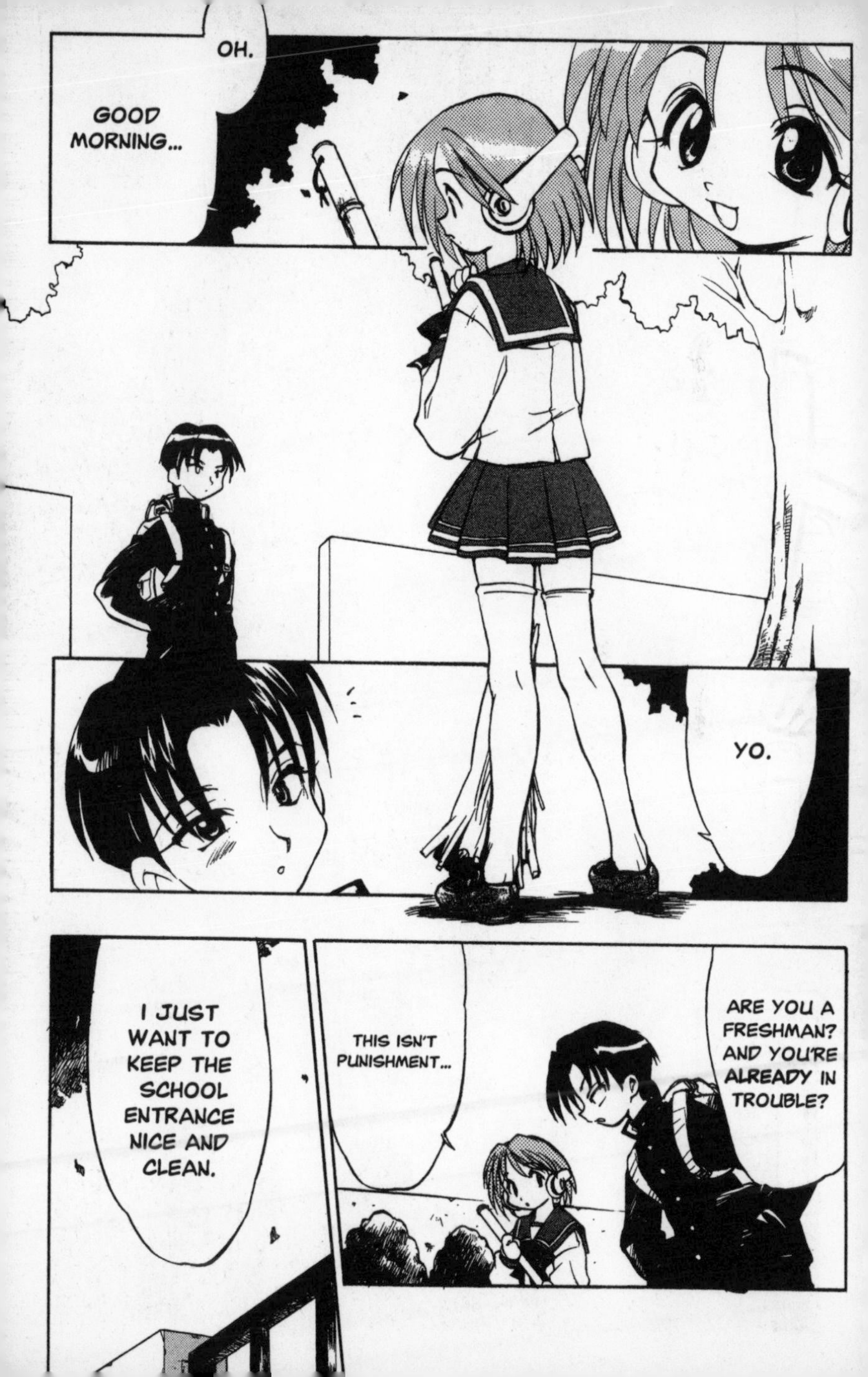
OH.
GOOD MORNING...
YO.
ARE YOU A FRESHMAN? AND YOU'RE ALREADY IN TROUBLE?
THIS ISN'T PUNISHMENT...
I JUST WANT TO KEEP THE SCHOOL ENTRANCE NICE AND CLEAN.

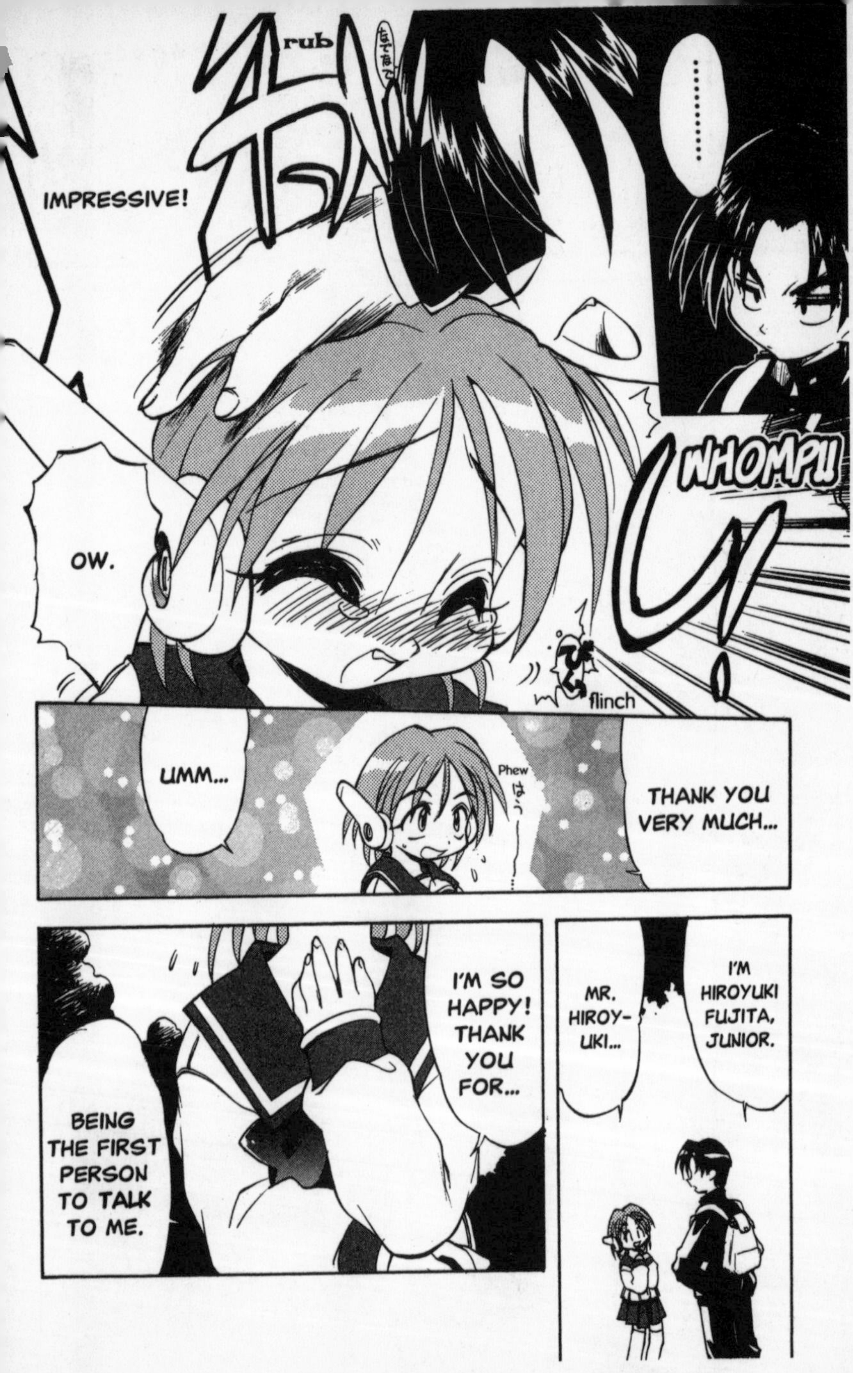
rub
なでなで
......
IMPRESSIVE!
WHOMP!!
flinch
OW.
THANK YOU VERY MUCH...
Phew
UMM...
I'M HIROYUKI FUJITA, JUNIOR.
MR. HIROY-UKI...
I'M SO HAPPY! THANK YOU FOR...
BEING THE FIRST PERSON TO TALK TO ME.

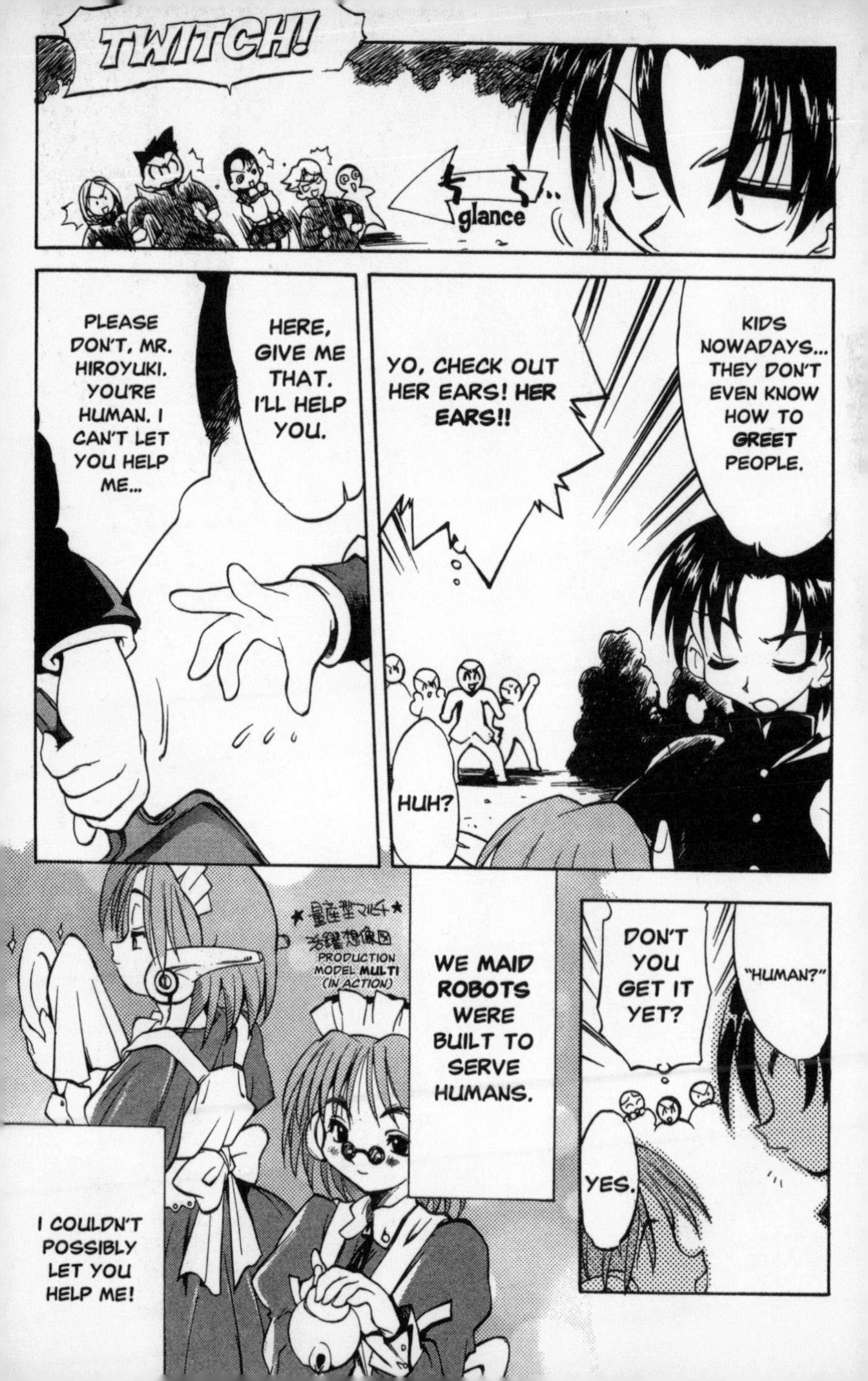
TWITCH!
glance
KIDS NOWADAYS... THEY DON'T EVEN KNOW HOW TO GREET PEOPLE.
YO, CHECK OUT HER EARS! HER EARS!!
HUH?
HERE, GIVE ME THAT. I'LL HELP YOU.
PLEASE DON'T, MR. HIROYUKI. YOU'RE HUMAN. I CAN'T LET YOU HELP ME...
"HUMAN?"
DON'T YOU GET IT YET?
YES.
WE MAID ROBOTS WERE BUILT TO SERVE HUMANS.
I COULDN'T POSSIBLY LET YOU HELP ME!
★量産型マルチ★
活躍想像図
PRODUCTION MODEL MULTI (IN ACTION)

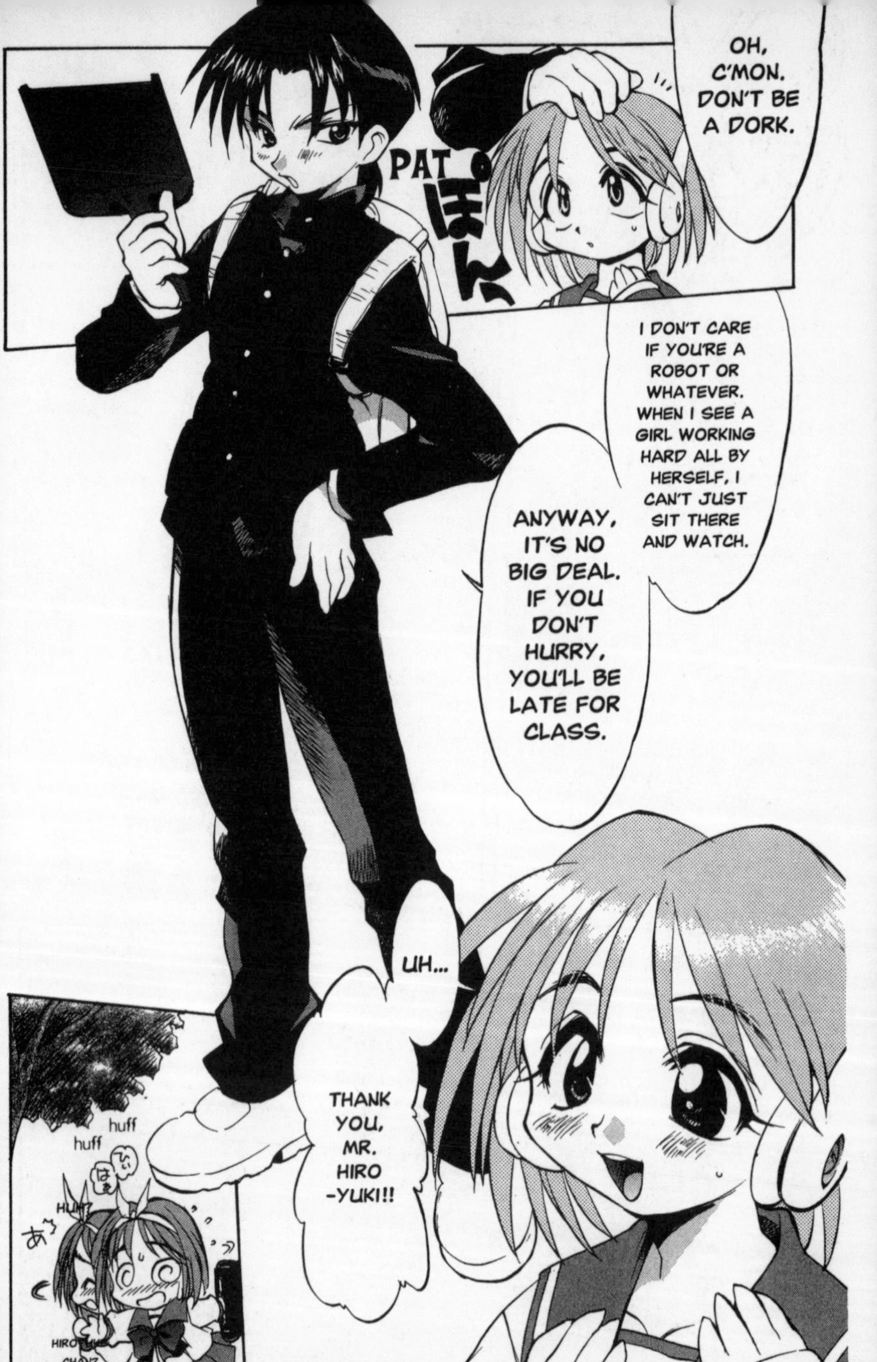
OH, C'MON. DON'T BE A DORK.
PAT
ぽん
I DON'T CARE IF YOU'RE A ROBOT OR WHATEVER. WHEN I SEE A GIRL WORKING HARD ALL BY HERSELF, I CAN'T JUST SIT THERE AND WATCH.
ANYWAY, IT'S NO BIG DEAL. IF YOU DON'T HURRY, YOU'LL BE LATE FOR CLASS.
UH...
THANK YOU, MR. HIRO-YUKI!!
huff
huff
ひぃ
はぁ
CHAN?

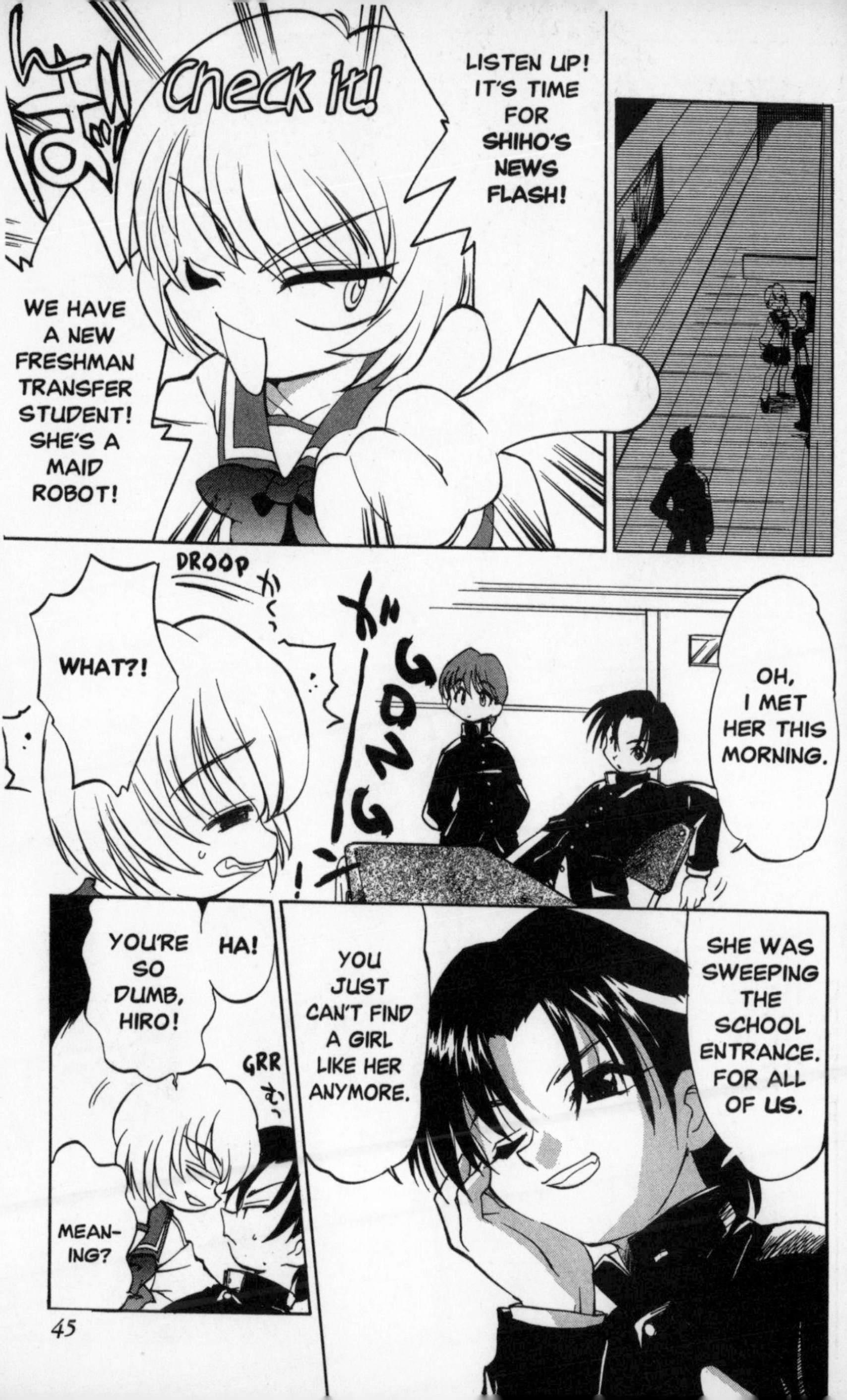
Check it!
LISTEN UP! IT'S TIME FOR SHIHO'S NEWS FLASH!
WE HAVE A NEW FRESHMAN TRANSFER STUDENT! SHE'S A MAID ROBOT!
OH, I MET HER THIS MORNING.
GONG
DROOP
WHAT?!
SHE WAS SWEEPING THE SCHOOL ENTRANCE. FOR ALL OF US.
YOU JUST CAN'T FIND A GIRL LIKE HER ANYMORE.
HA!
YOU'RE SO DUMB, HIRO!
GRR
MEAN-ING?

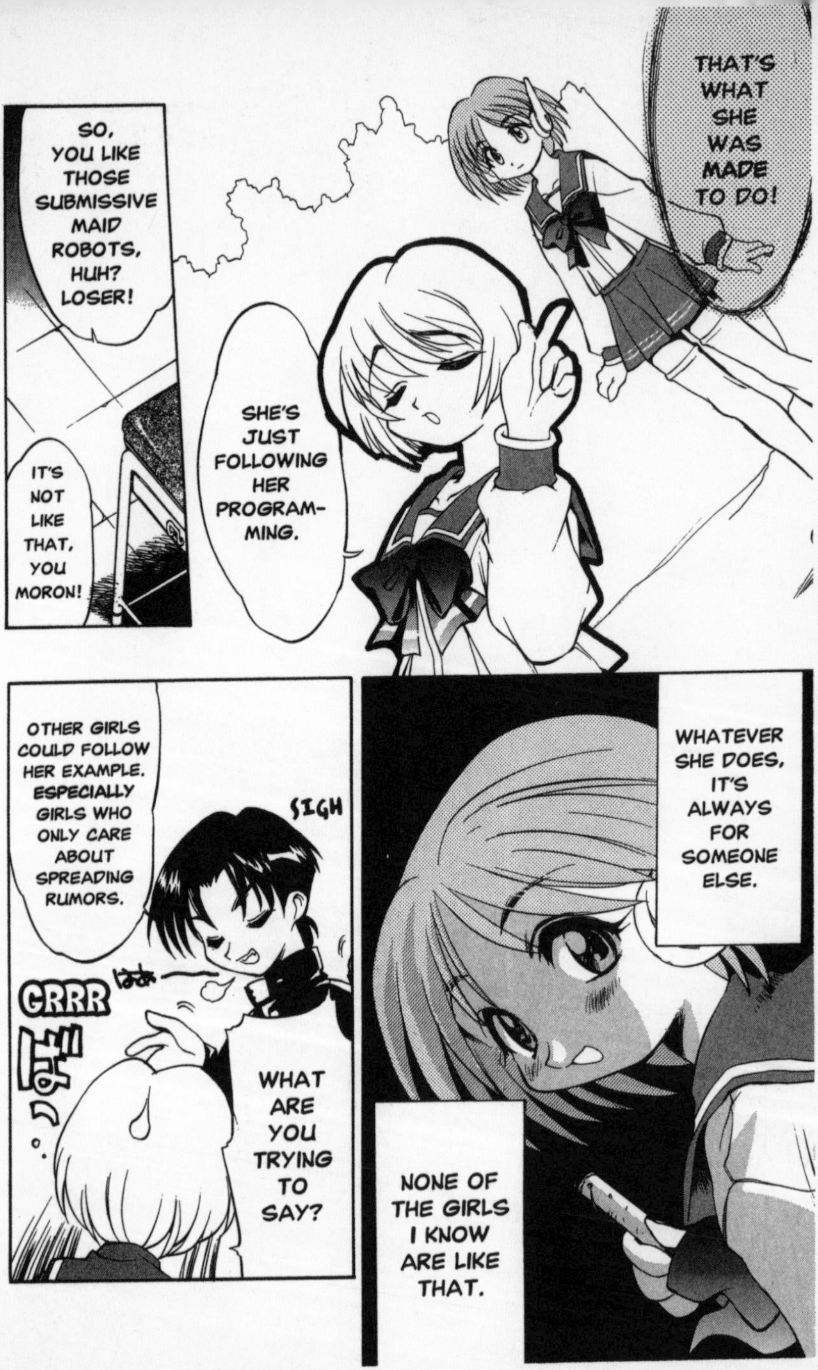

THAT'S WHAT SHE WAS MADE TO DO!
SHE'S JUST FOLLOWING HER PROGRAM-MING.
SO, YOU LIKE THOSE SUBMISSIVE MAID ROBOTS, HUH? LOSER!
IT'S NOT LIKE THAT, YOU MORON!
WHATEVER SHE DOES, IT'S ALWAYS FOR SOMEONE ELSE.
NONE OF THE GIRLS I KNOW ARE LIKE THAT.
OTHER GIRLS COULD FOLLOW HER EXAMPLE. ESPECIALLY GIRLS WHO ONLY CARE ABOUT SPREADING RUMORS.
SIGH
GRRR
WHAT ARE YOU TRYING TO SAY?

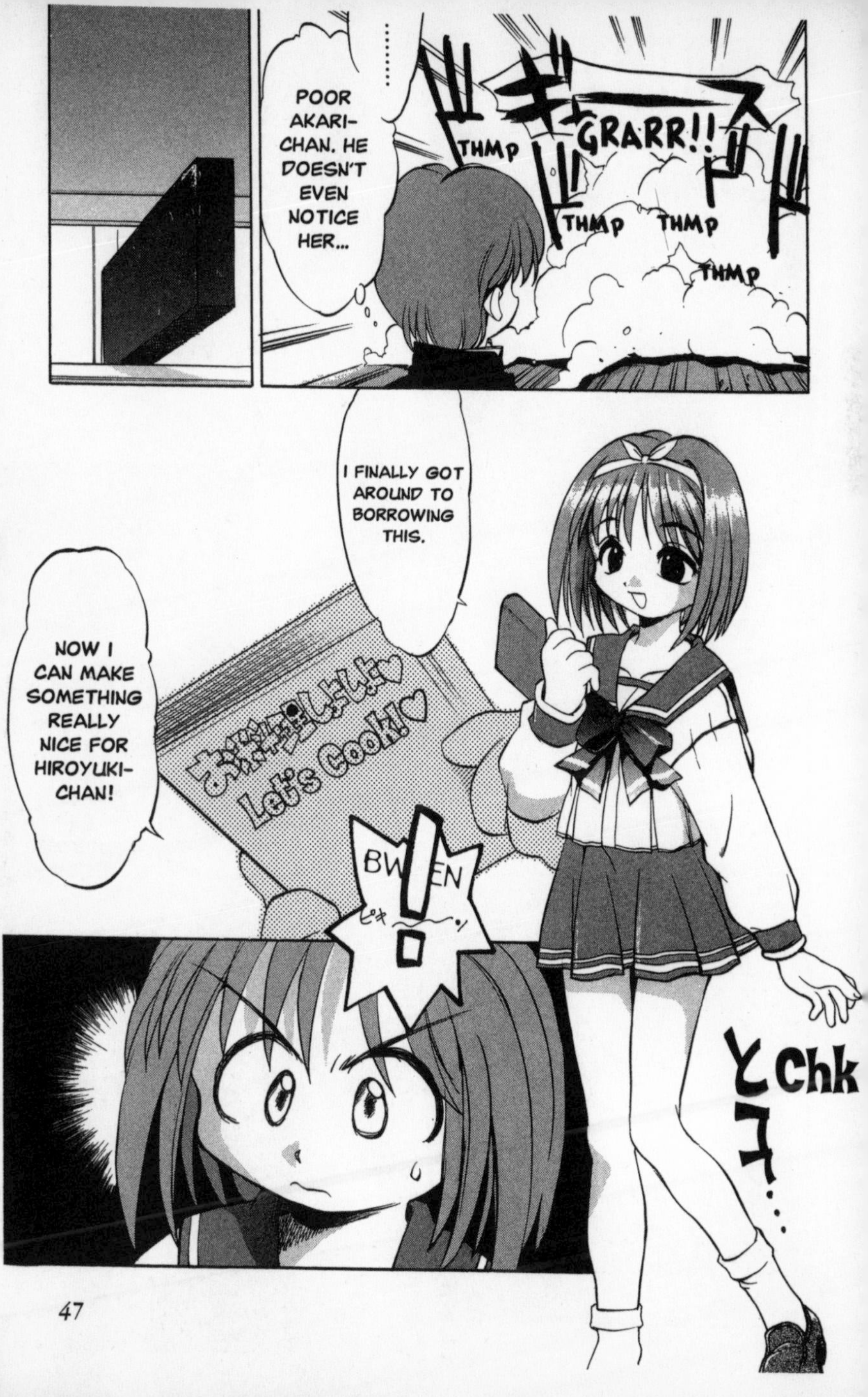

GRARR!!
THMP
THMP
THMP
THMP
......
POOR AKARI-CHAN. HE DOESN'T EVEN NOTICE HER...
I FINALLY GOT AROUND TO BORROWING THIS.
NOW I CAN MAKE SOMETHING REALLY NICE FOR HIROYUKI-CHAN!
Let's Cook!
BW EN
!
Chk

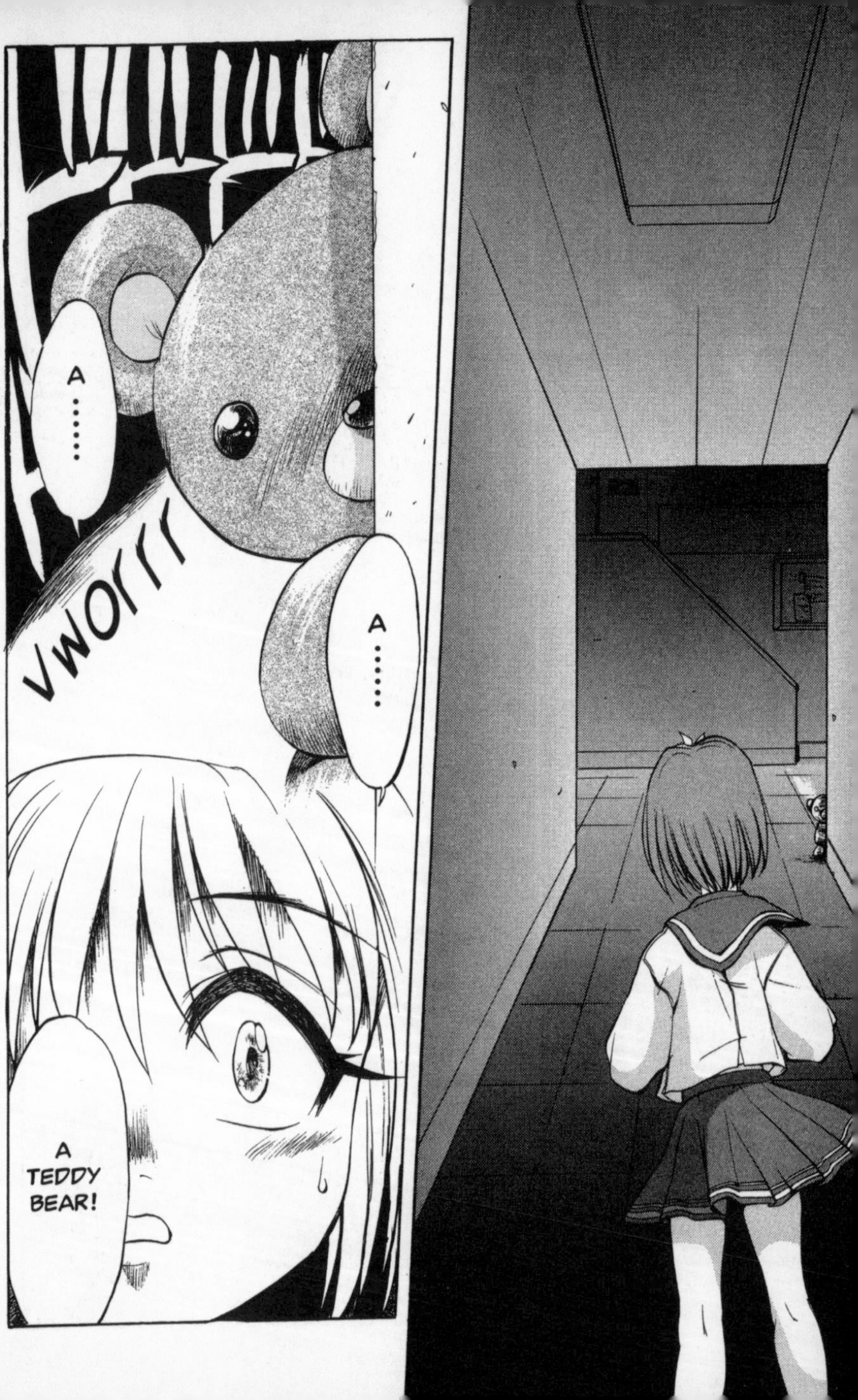

A......
VWORRR
A......
A TEDDY BEAR!

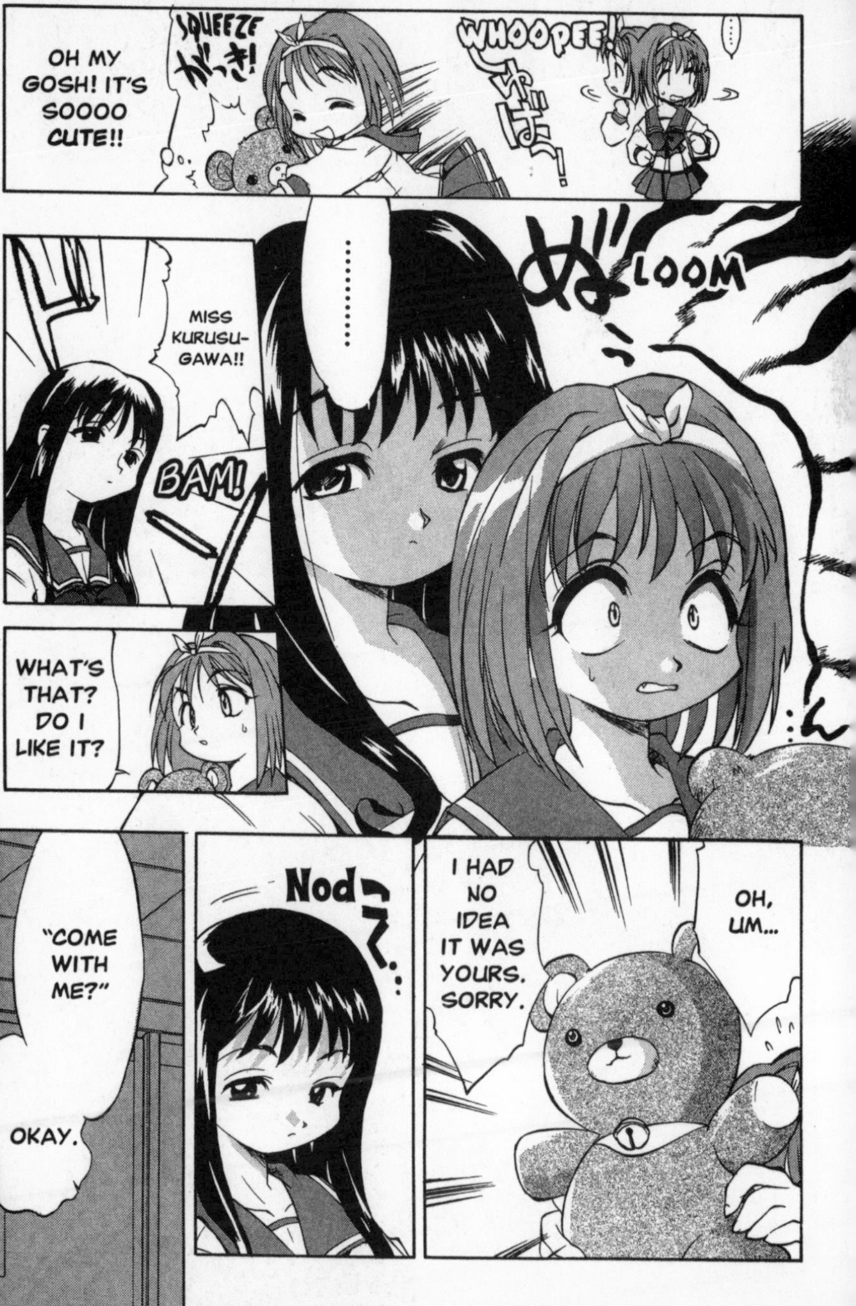

…!
WHOOPEE!!
ひゃっほ〜!
SQUEEZE
がっきー!
OH MY GOSH! IT'S SOOOO CUTE!!
ぬ
LOOM
……ん
……
MISS KURUSU-GAWA!!
BAM!
WHAT'S THAT? DO I LIKE IT?
OH, UM...
I HAD NO IDEA IT WAS YOURS. SORRY.
Nod
こく
"COME WITH ME?"
OKAY.

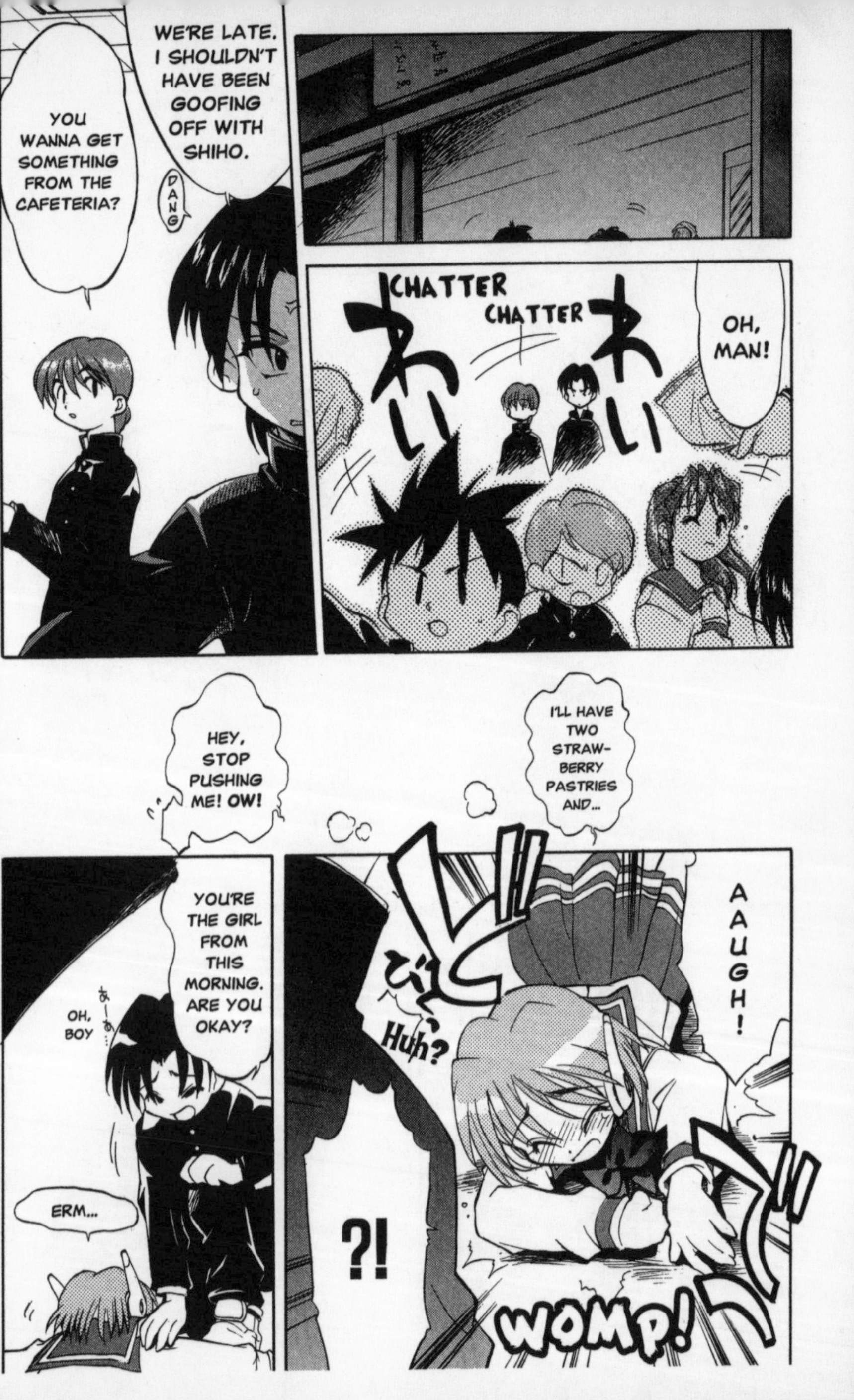

OH, MAN!
CHATTER
CHATTER
WE'RE LATE. I SHOULDN'T HAVE BEEN GOOFING OFF WITH SHIHO.
DANG
YOU WANNA GET SOMETHING FROM THE CAFETERIA?
I'LL HAVE TWO STRAW-BERRY PASTRIES AND...
HEY, STOP PUSHING ME! OW!
AAUGH!
Huh?
?!
WOMP!
YOU'RE THE GIRL FROM THIS MORNING. ARE YOU OKAY?
OH, BOY
ERM...

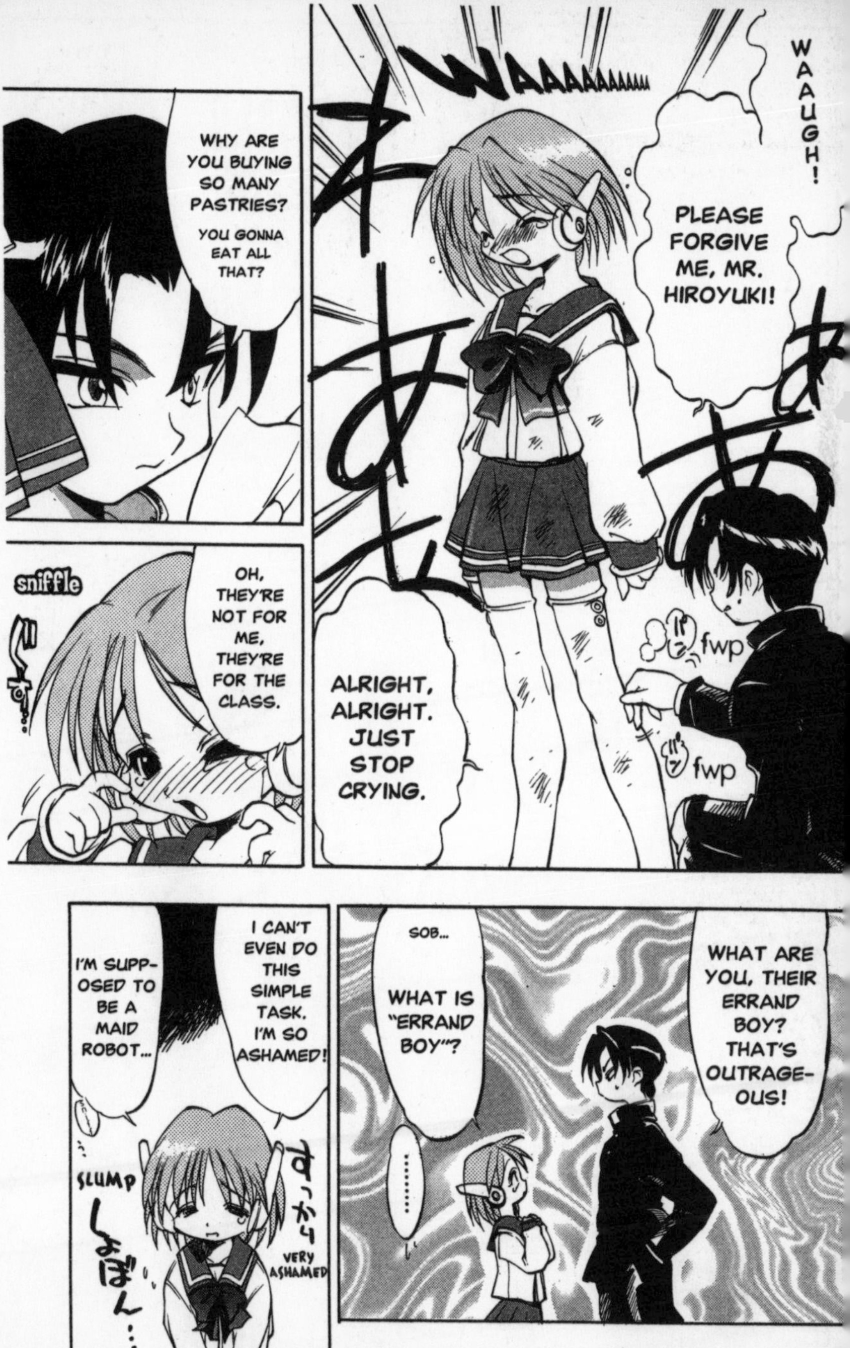
WAAAAAAAAAAA
WAAUGH!
PLEASE FORGIVE ME, MR. HIROYUKI!
WHY ARE YOU BUYING SO MANY PASTRIES?
YOU GONNA EAT ALL THAT?
fwp
fwp
ALRIGHT, ALRIGHT. JUST STOP CRYING.
sniffle
OH, THEY'RE NOT FOR ME, THEY'RE FOR THE CLASS.
WHAT ARE YOU, THEIR ERRAND BOY? THAT'S OUTRAGE-OUS!
SOB...
WHAT IS "ERRAND BOY"?
....
I CAN'T EVEN DO THIS SIMPLE TASK. I'M SO ASHAMED!
I'M SUPP-OSED TO BE A MAID ROBOT...
VERY ASHAMED
SLUMP

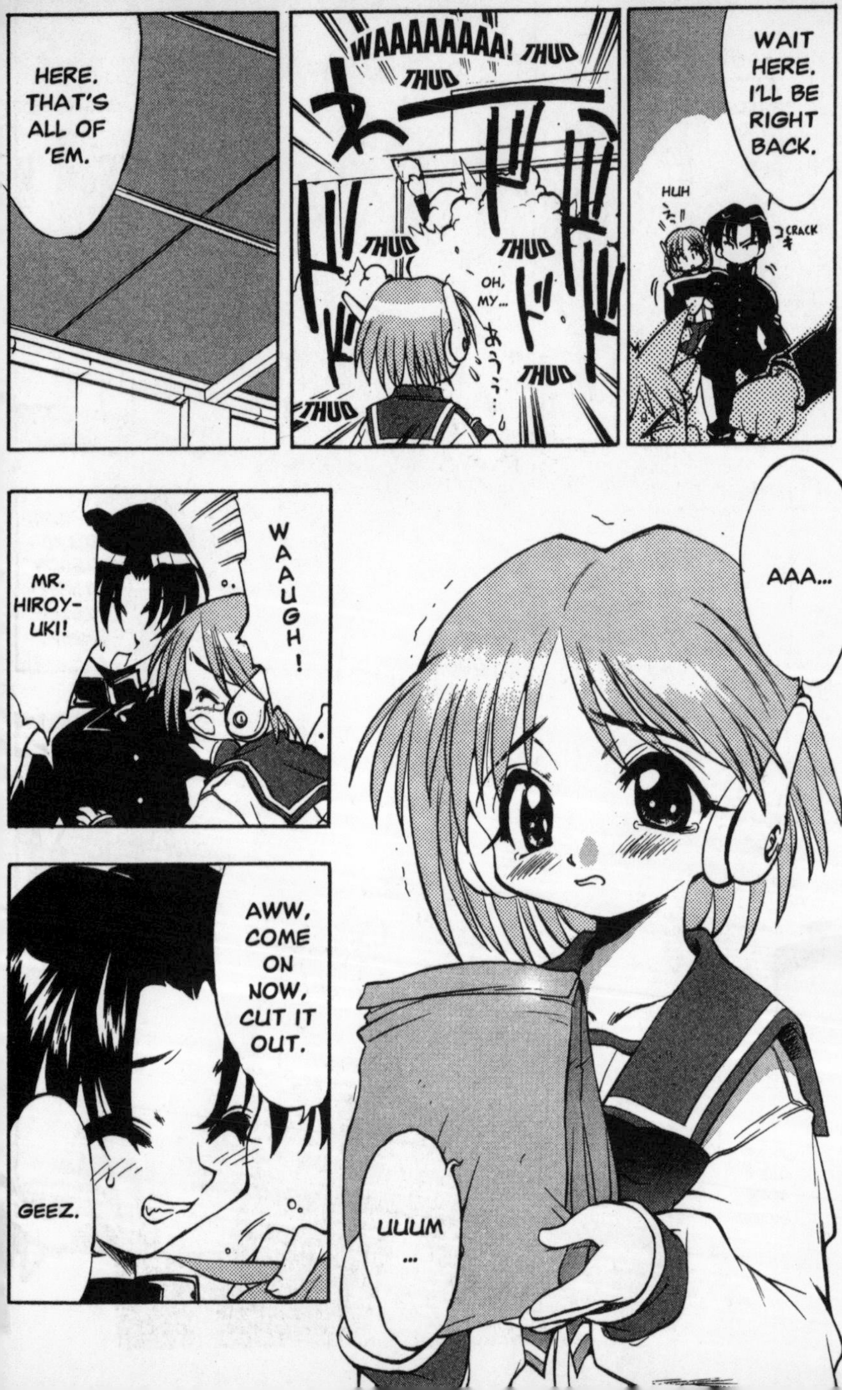
WAIT HERE. I'LL BE RIGHT BACK.
HUH
CRACK
WAAAAAAAA! THUD
THUD
THUD
THUD
OH, MY...
THUD
THUD
HERE. THAT'S ALL OF 'EM.
AAA...
WAAUGH!
MR. HIROY-UKI!
AWW, COME ON NOW, CUT IT OUT.
UUUM ...
GEEZ.

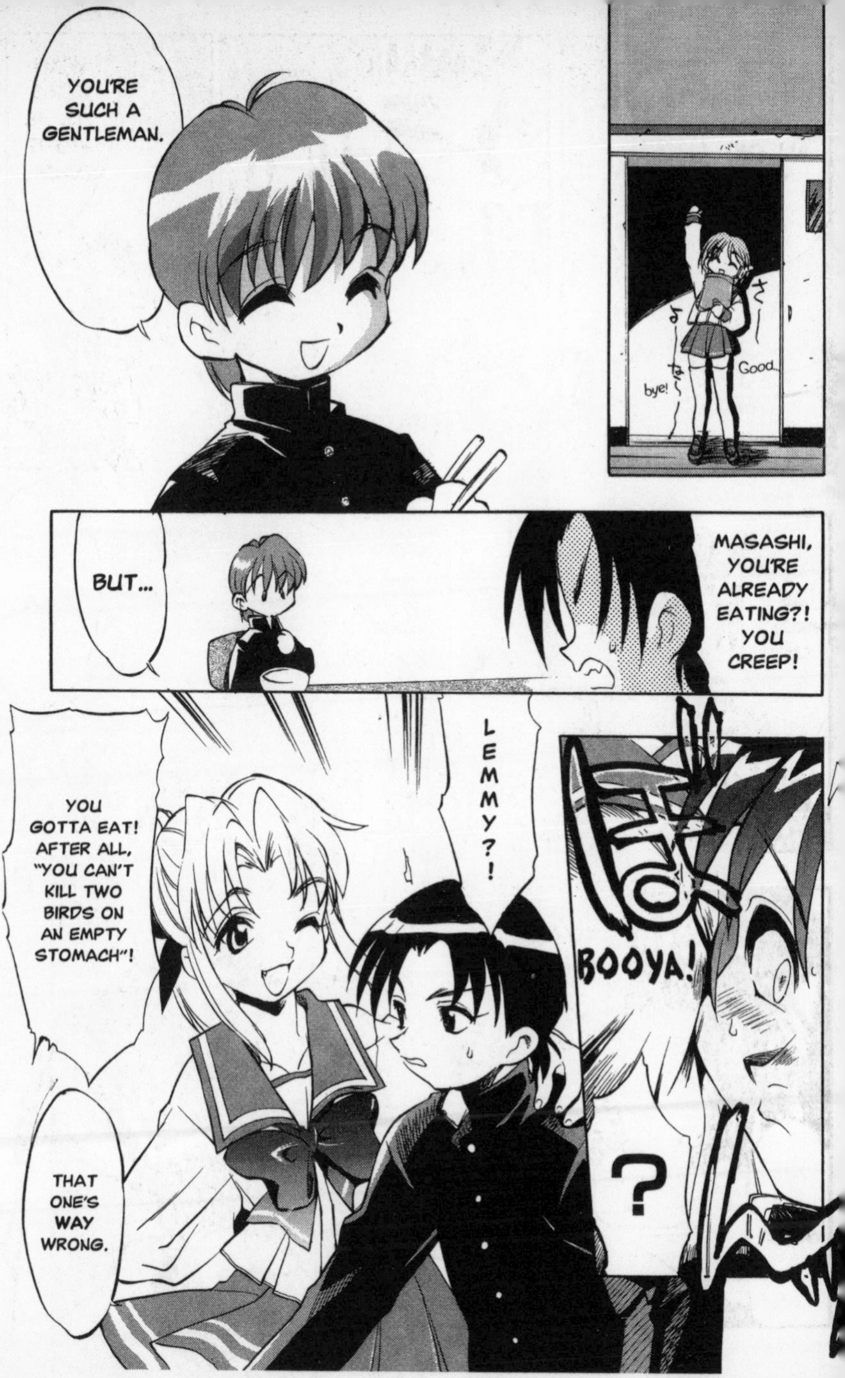
Good...
bye!
YOU'RE SUCH A GENTLEMAN.
MASASHI, YOU'RE ALREADY EATING?! YOU CREEP!
BUT...
BOOYA!
?
LEMMY?!
YOU GOTTA EAT! AFTER ALL, "YOU CAN'T KILL TWO BIRDS ON AN EMPTY STOMACH"!
THAT ONE'S WAY WRONG.

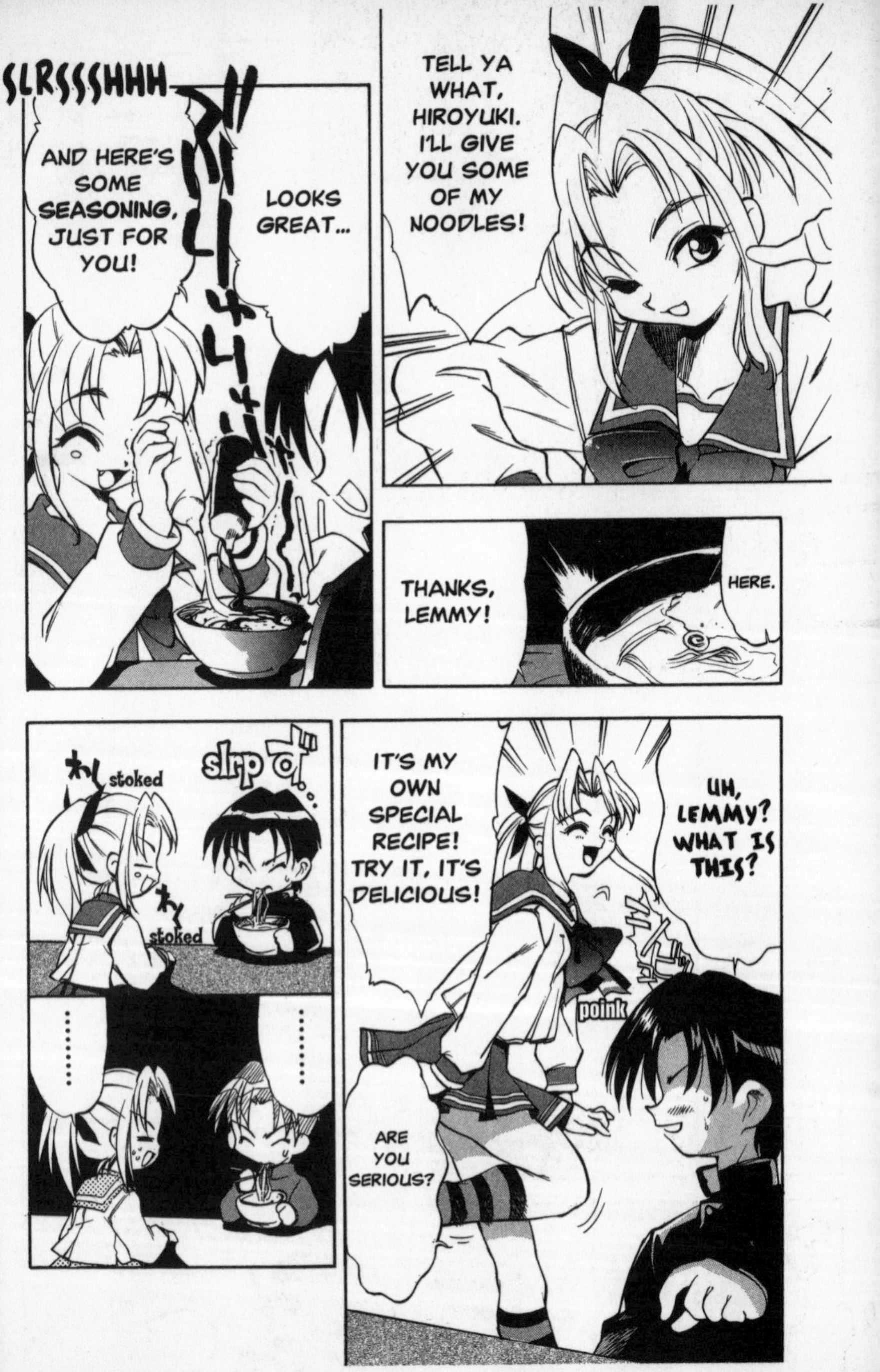

TELL YA WHAT, HIROYUKI. I'LL GIVE YOU SOME OF MY NOODLES!
LOOKS GREAT...
AND HERE'S SOME SEASONING, JUST FOR YOU!
SLRSSSSHHH
HERE.
THANKS, LEMMY!
UH, LEMMY? WHAT IS THIS?
IT'S MY OWN SPECIAL RECIPE! TRY IT, IT'S DELICIOUS!
poink
ARE YOU SERIOUS?
slrp
stoked
stoked
......
......

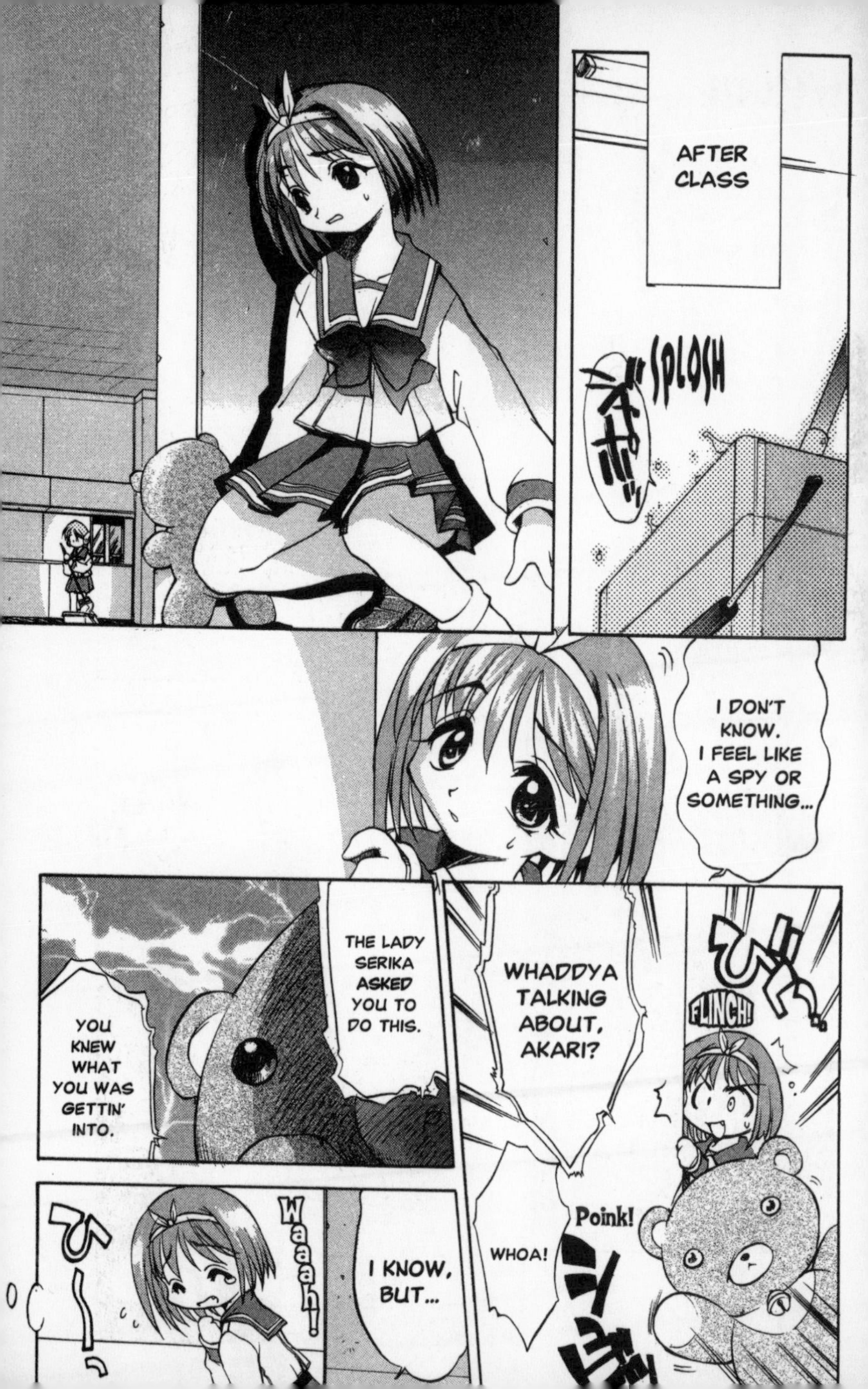
AFTER CLASS
SPLOSH
I DON'T KNOW. I FEEL LIKE A SPY OR SOMETHING...
FLINCH!
WHADDYA TALKING ABOUT, AKARI?
THE LADY SERIKA ASKED YOU TO DO THIS.
YOU KNEW WHAT YOU WAS GETTIN' INTO.
Poink!
WHOA!
I KNOW, BUT...
Waaah!

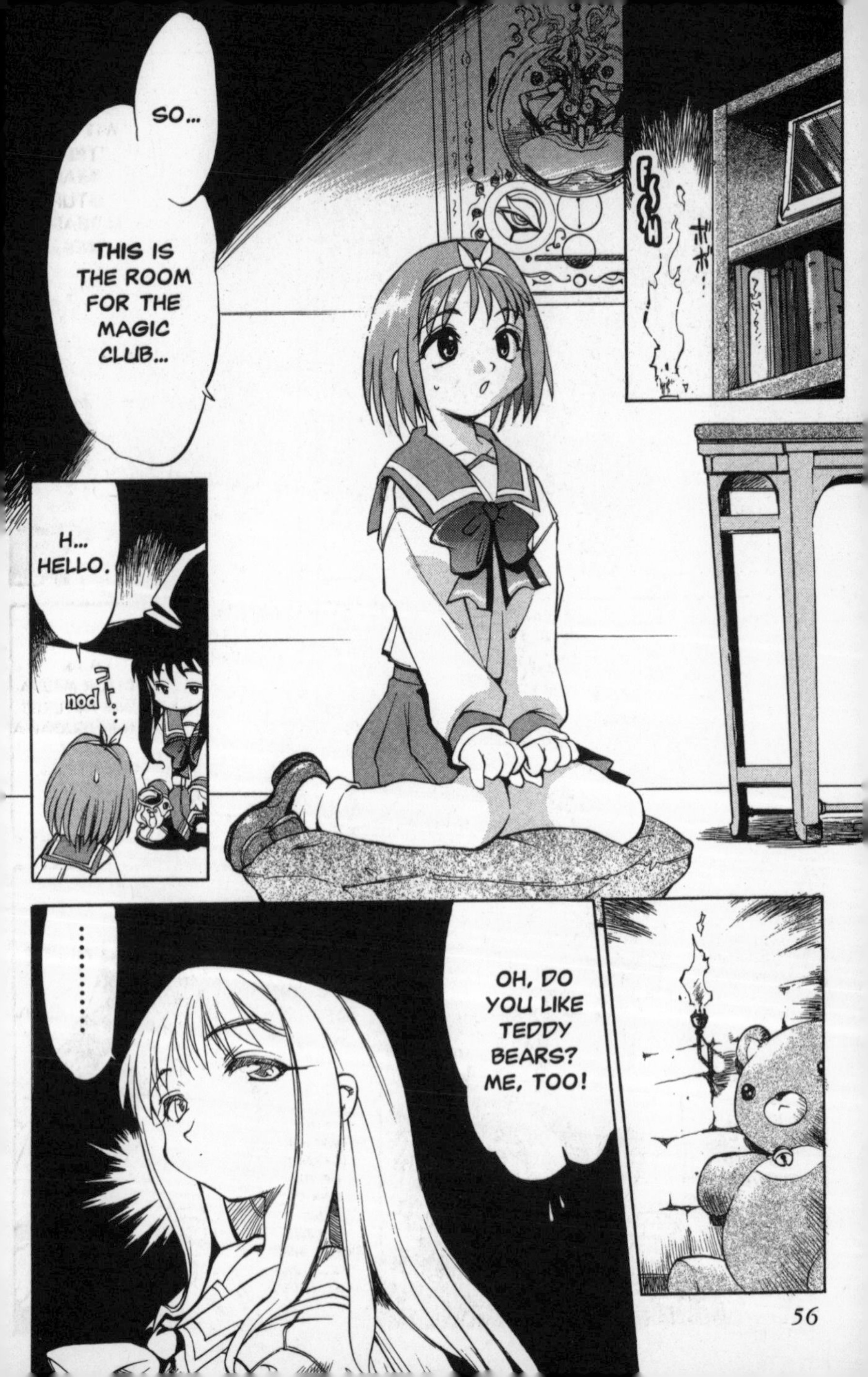
FSSH
ボボ…
SO...
THIS IS THE ROOM FOR THE MAGIC CLUB...
H... HELLO.
nod
OH, DO YOU LIKE TEDDY BEARS? ME, TOO!
....

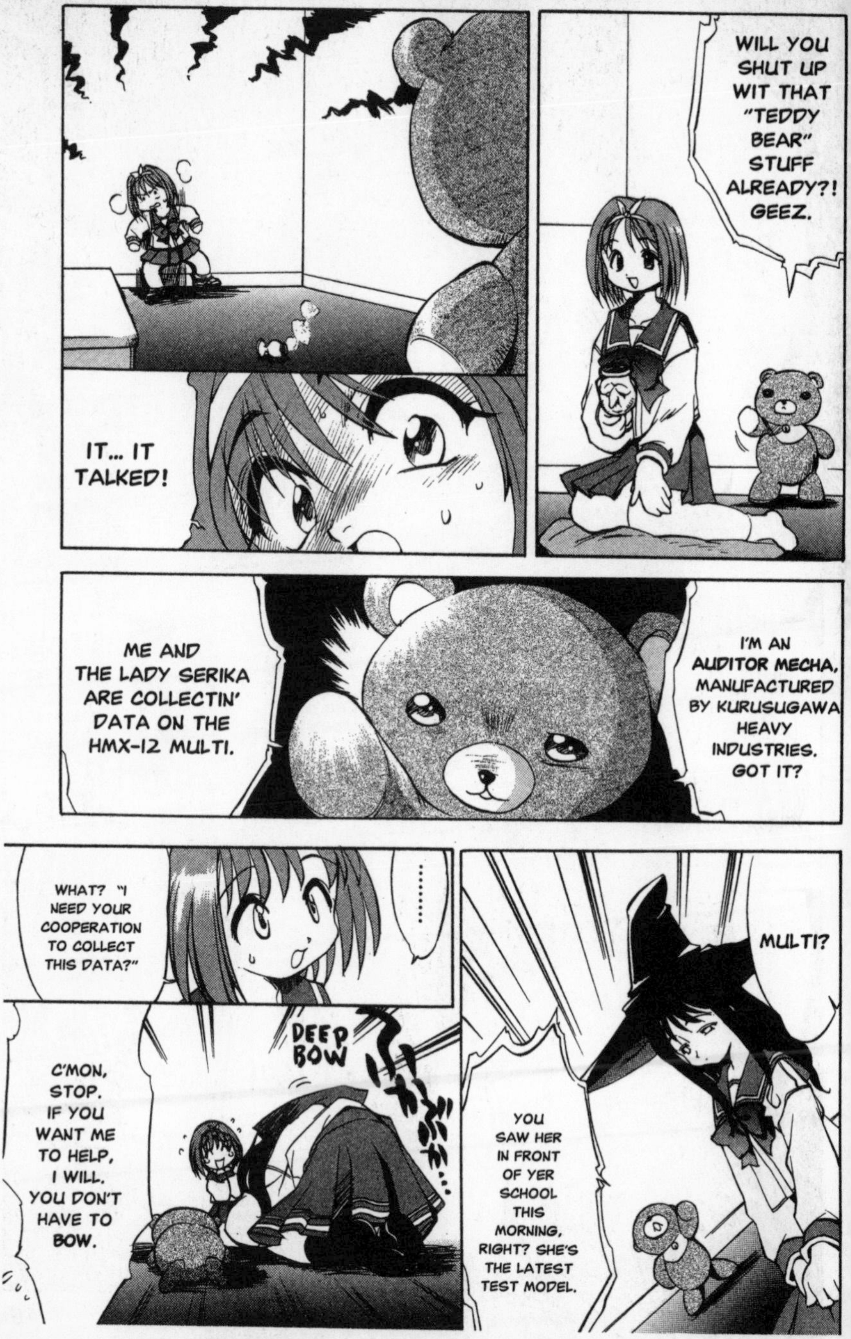
WILL YOU SHUT UP WIT THAT "TEDDY BEAR" STUFF ALREADY?! GEEZ.
IT... IT TALKED!
I'M AN AUDITOR MECHA, MANUFACTURED BY KURUSUGAWA HEAVY INDUSTRIES. GOT IT?
ME AND THE LADY SERIKA ARE COLLECTIN' DATA ON THE HMX-12 MULTI.
MULTI?
YOU SAW HER IN FRONT OF YER SCHOOL THIS MORNING, RIGHT? SHE'S THE LATEST TEST MODEL.
......
WHAT? "I NEED YOUR COOPERATION TO COLLECT THIS DATA?"
DEEP BOW
C'MON, STOP. IF YOU WANT ME TO HELP, I WILL. YOU DON'T HAVE TO BOW.

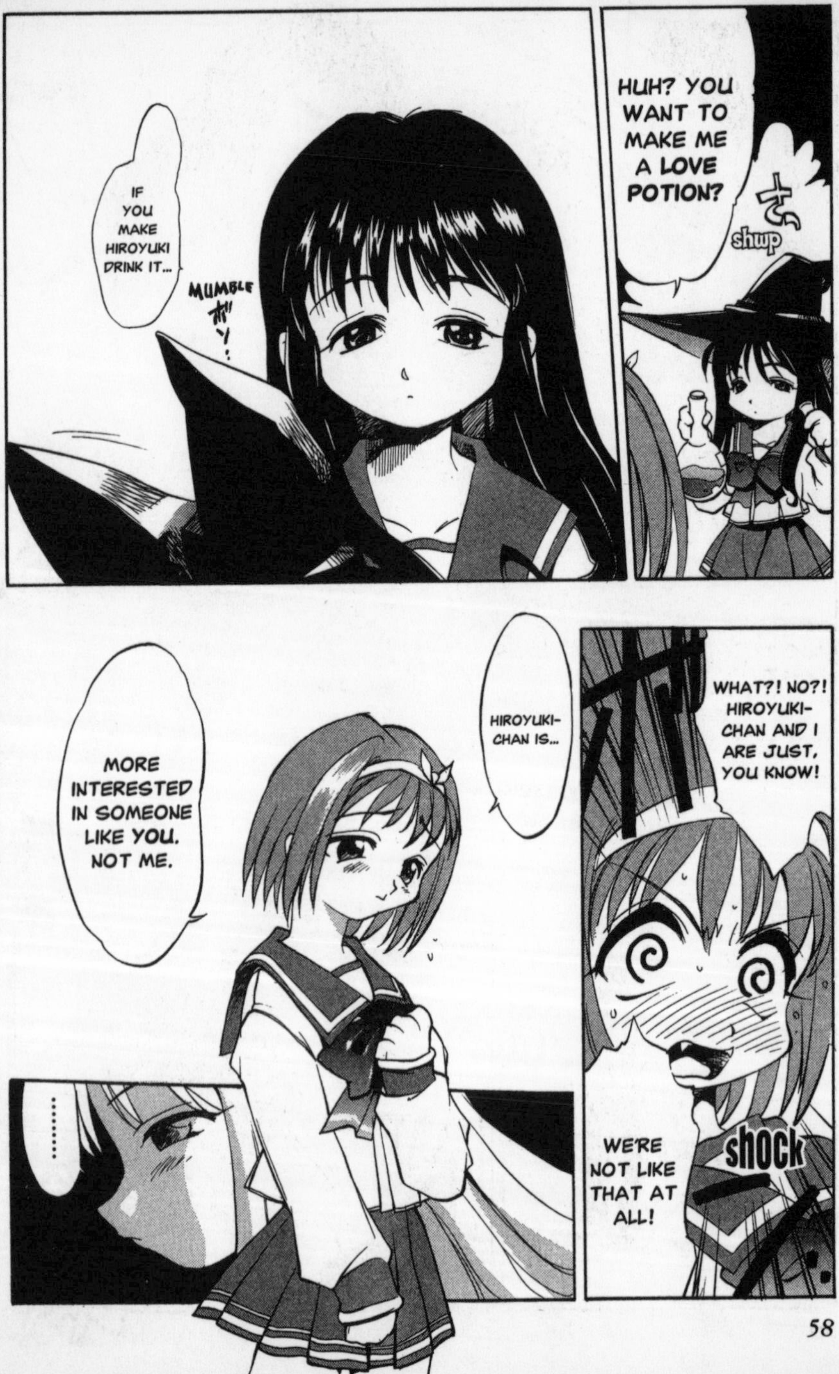
HUH? YOU WANT TO MAKE ME A LOVE POTION?
shwp
IF YOU MAKE HIROYUKI DRINK IT...
MUMBLE
WHAT?! NO?! HIROYUKI-CHAN AND I ARE JUST, YOU KNOW!
shock
WE'RE NOT LIKE THAT AT ALL!
HIROYUKI-CHAN IS...
MORE INTERESTED IN SOMEONE LIKE YOU. NOT ME.
....

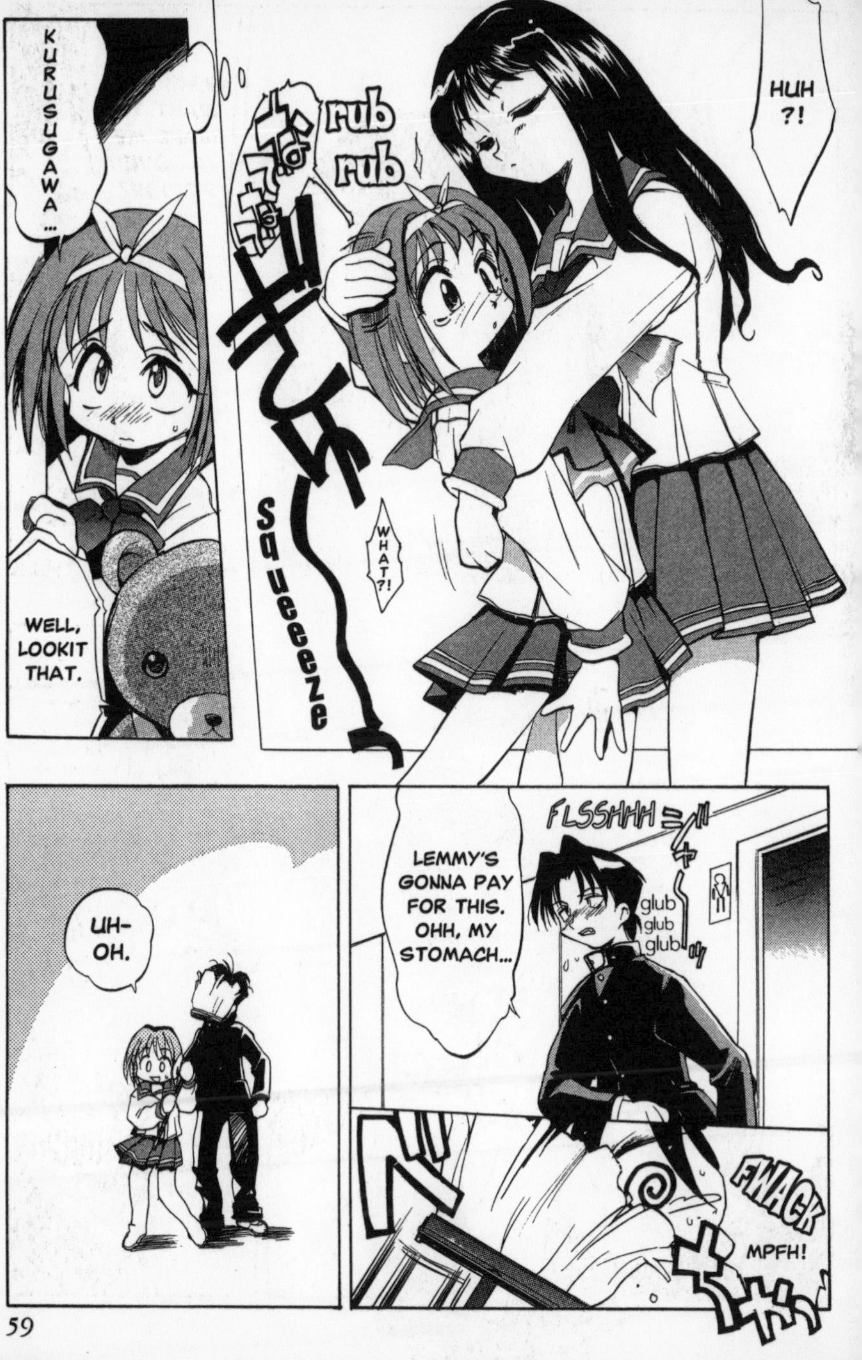

HUH ?!
KURUSUGAWA ...
rub rub
WELL, LOOKIT THAT.
squeeeze
WHAT?!
FLSSHHH
glub glub glub
LEMMY'S GONNA PAY FOR THIS. OHH, MY STOMACH...
FWACK
MPFH!
UH-OH.

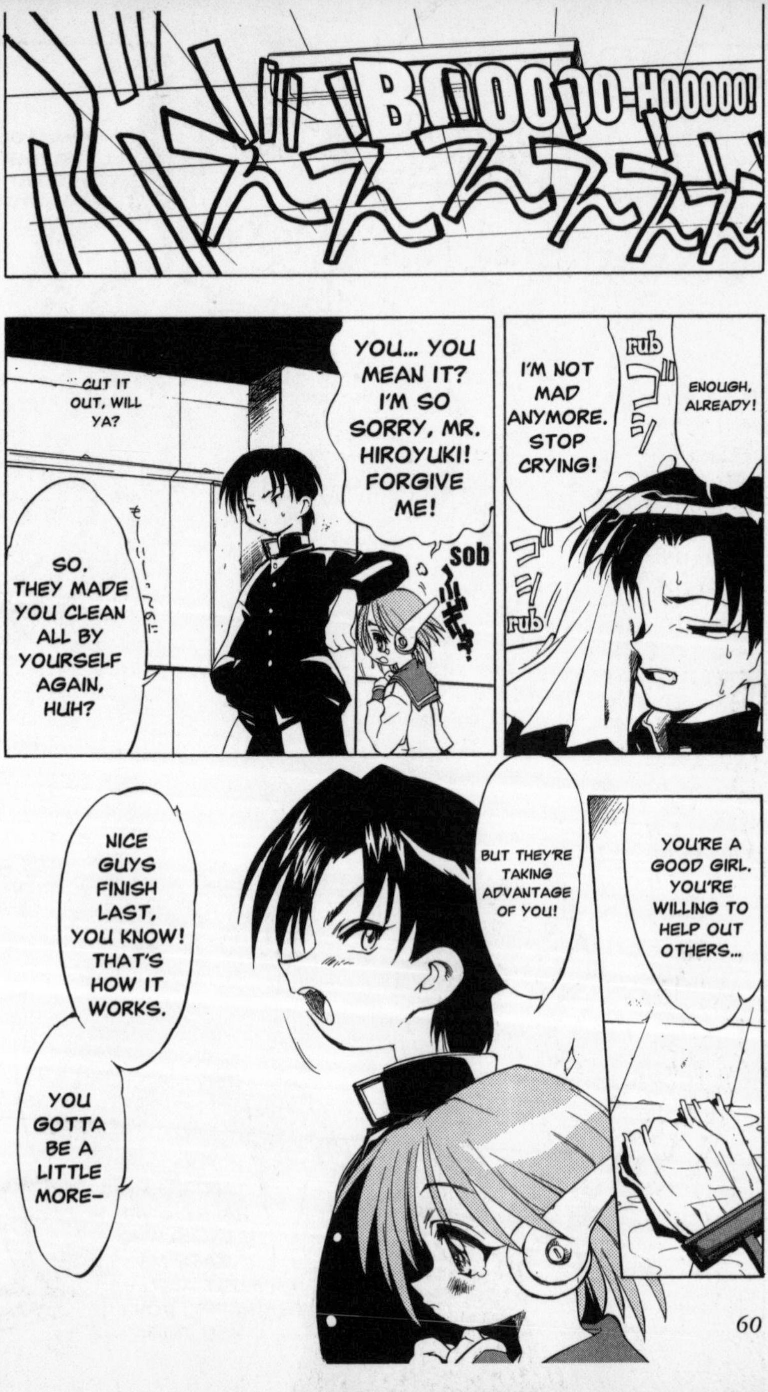
BOOOOO-HOOOOO!
ENOUGH, ALREADY!
rub
I'M NOT MAD ANYMORE. STOP CRYING!
rub
YOU... YOU MEAN IT? I'M SO SORRY, MR. HIROYUKI! FORGIVE ME!
sob
CUT IT OUT, WILL YA?
SO. THEY MADE YOU CLEAN ALL BY YOURSELF AGAIN, HUH?
YOU'RE A GOOD GIRL. YOU'RE WILLING TO HELP OUT OTHERS...
BUT THEY'RE TAKING ADVANTAGE OF YOU!
NICE GUYS FINISH LAST, YOU KNOW! THAT'S HOW IT WORKS.
YOU GOTTA BE A LITTLE MORE-

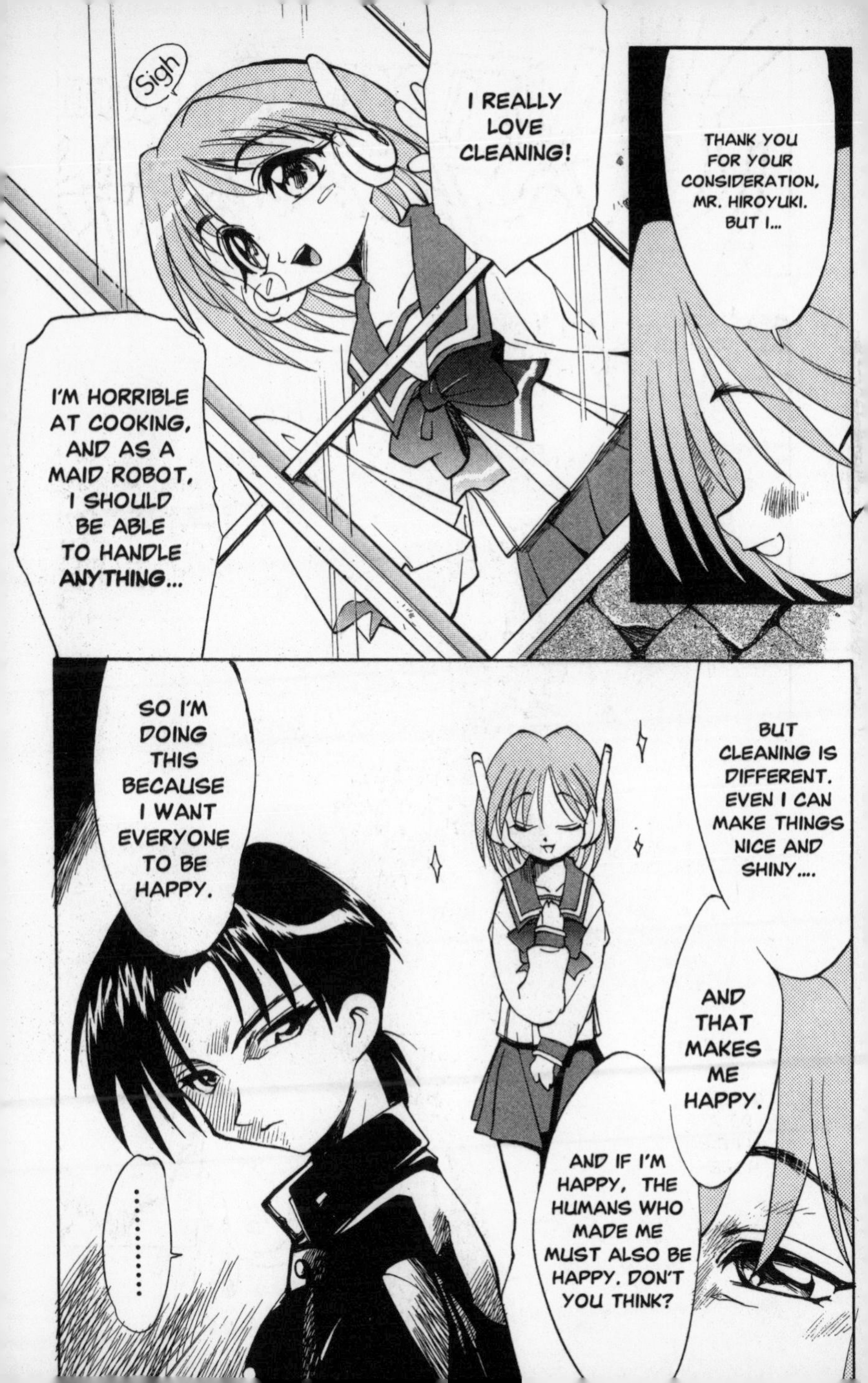
THANK YOU FOR YOUR CONSIDERATION, MR. HIROYUKI. BUT I...
I REALLY LOVE CLEANING!
Sigh
I'M HORRIBLE AT COOKING, AND AS A MAID ROBOT, I SHOULD BE ABLE TO HANDLE ANYTHING...
BUT CLEANING IS DIFFERENT. EVEN I CAN MAKE THINGS NICE AND SHINY....
AND THAT MAKES ME HAPPY.
AND IF I'M HAPPY, THE HUMANS WHO MADE ME MUST ALSO BE HAPPY. DON'T YOU THINK?
SO I'M DOING THIS BECAUSE I WANT EVERYONE TO BE HAPPY.
....

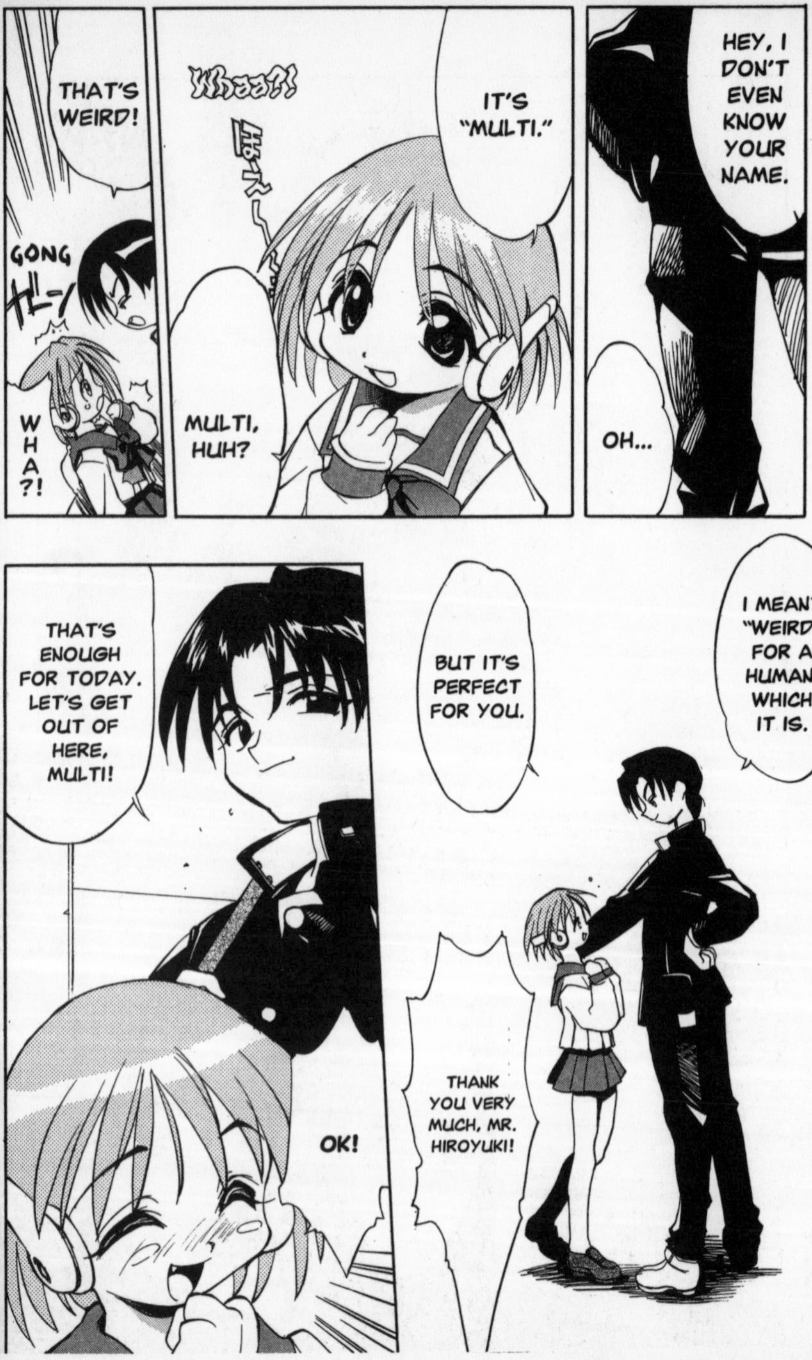
HEY, I DON'T EVEN KNOW YOUR NAME.
OH...
IT'S "MULTI."
Whaa?!
MULTI, HUH?
THAT'S WEIRD!
GONG
WHA?!
I MEANT "WEIRD" FOR A HUMAN. WHICH IT IS.
BUT IT'S PERFECT FOR YOU.
THANK YOU VERY MUCH, MR. HIROYUKI!
THAT'S ENOUGH FOR TODAY. LET'S GET OUT OF HERE, MULTI!
OK!

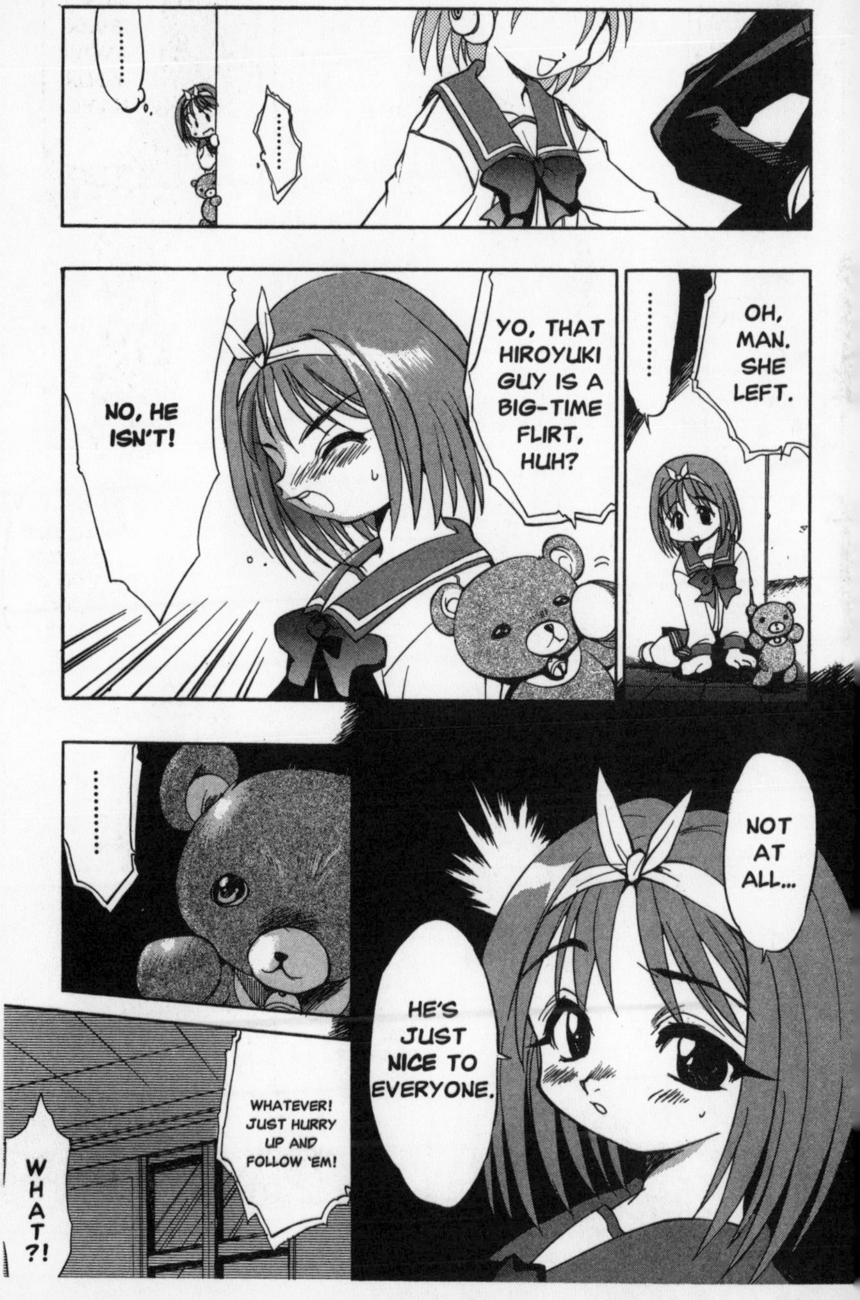
......
......
OH, MAN. SHE LEFT.
......
YO, THAT HIROYUKI GUY IS A BIG-TIME FLIRT, HUH?
NO, HE ISN'T!
NOT AT ALL...
HE'S JUST NICE TO EVERYONE.
......
WHATEVER! JUST HURRY UP AND FOLLOW 'EM!
WHAT?!

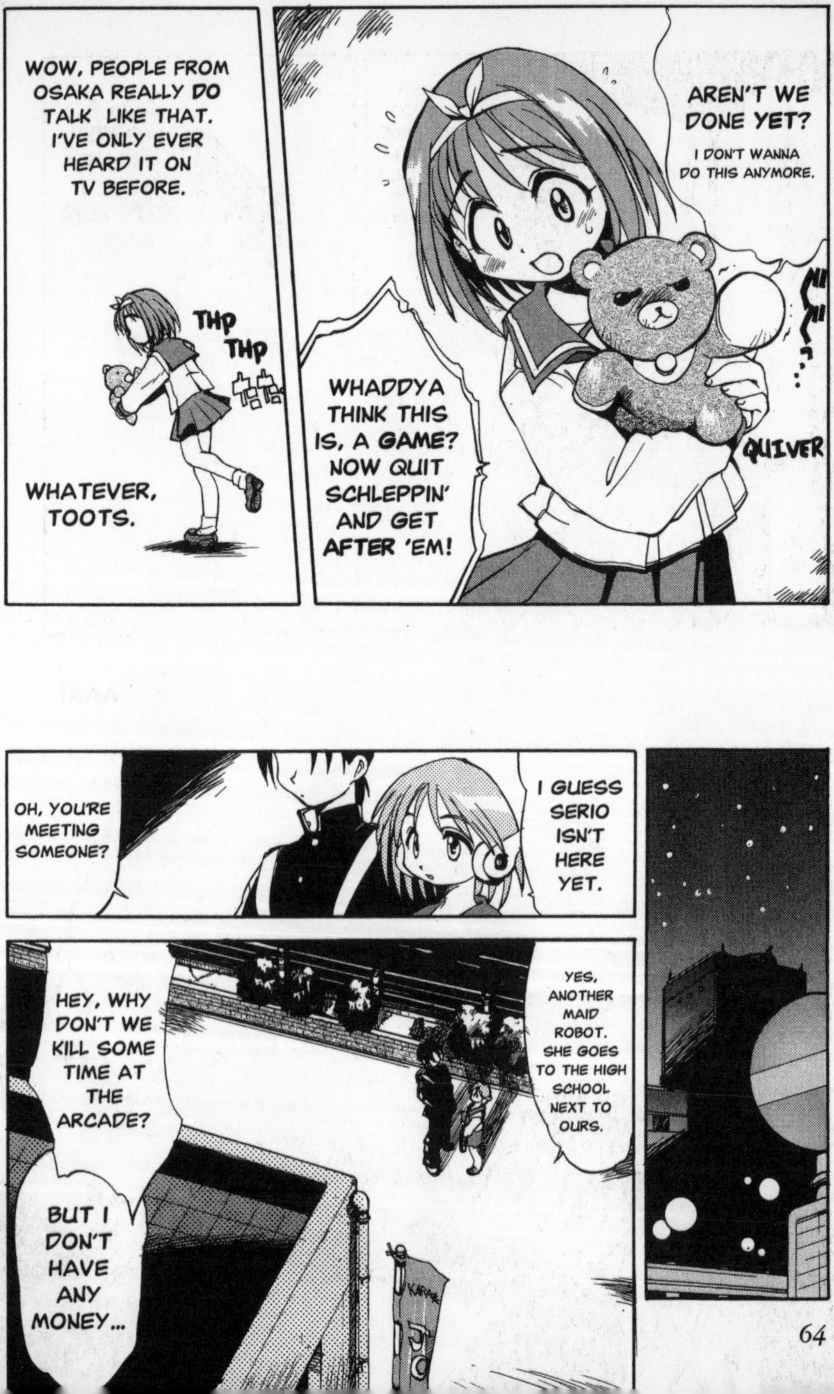
AREN'T WE DONE YET?
I DON'T WANNA DO THIS ANYMORE.
QUIVER
WHADDYA THINK THIS IS, A GAME? NOW QUIT SCHLEPPIN' AND GET AFTER 'EM!
WOW, PEOPLE FROM OSAKA REALLY DO TALK LIKE THAT. I'VE ONLY EVER HEARD IT ON TV BEFORE.
THP
THP
WHATEVER, TOOTS.
I GUESS SERIO ISN'T HERE YET.
OH, YOU'RE MEETING SOMEONE?
YES, ANOTHER MAID ROBOT. SHE GOES TO THE HIGH SCHOOL NEXT TO OURS.
HEY, WHY DON'T WE KILL SOME TIME AT THE ARCADE?
BUT I DON'T HAVE ANY MONEY...

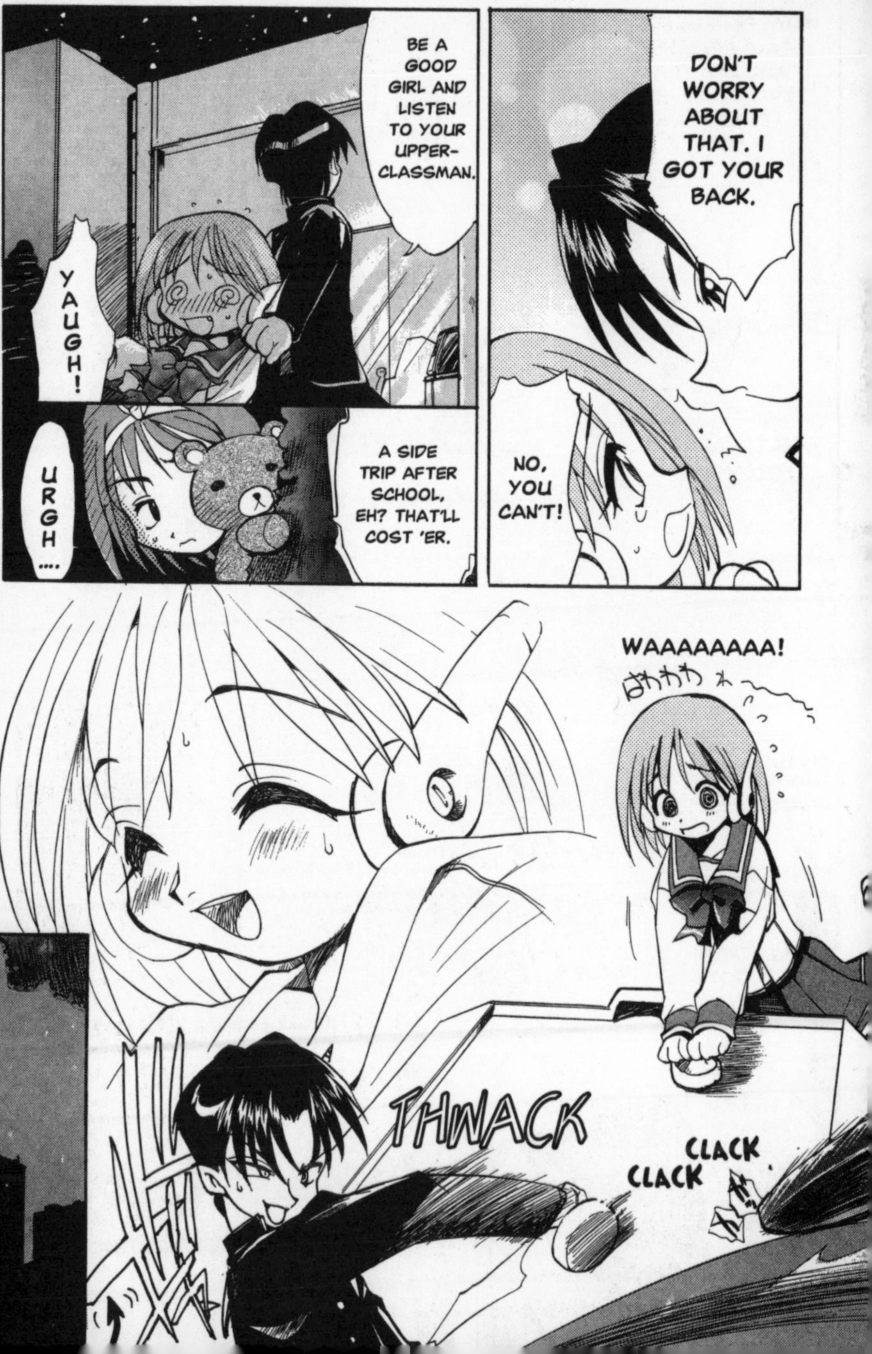
BE A GOOD GIRL AND LISTEN TO YOUR UPPER-CLASSMAN.
YAUGH!
DON'T WORRY ABOUT THAT. I GOT YOUR BACK.
A SIDE TRIP AFTER SCHOOL, EH? THAT'LL COST 'ER.
URGH....
NO, YOU CAN'T!
WAAAAAAAA!
THWACK
CLACK
CLACK

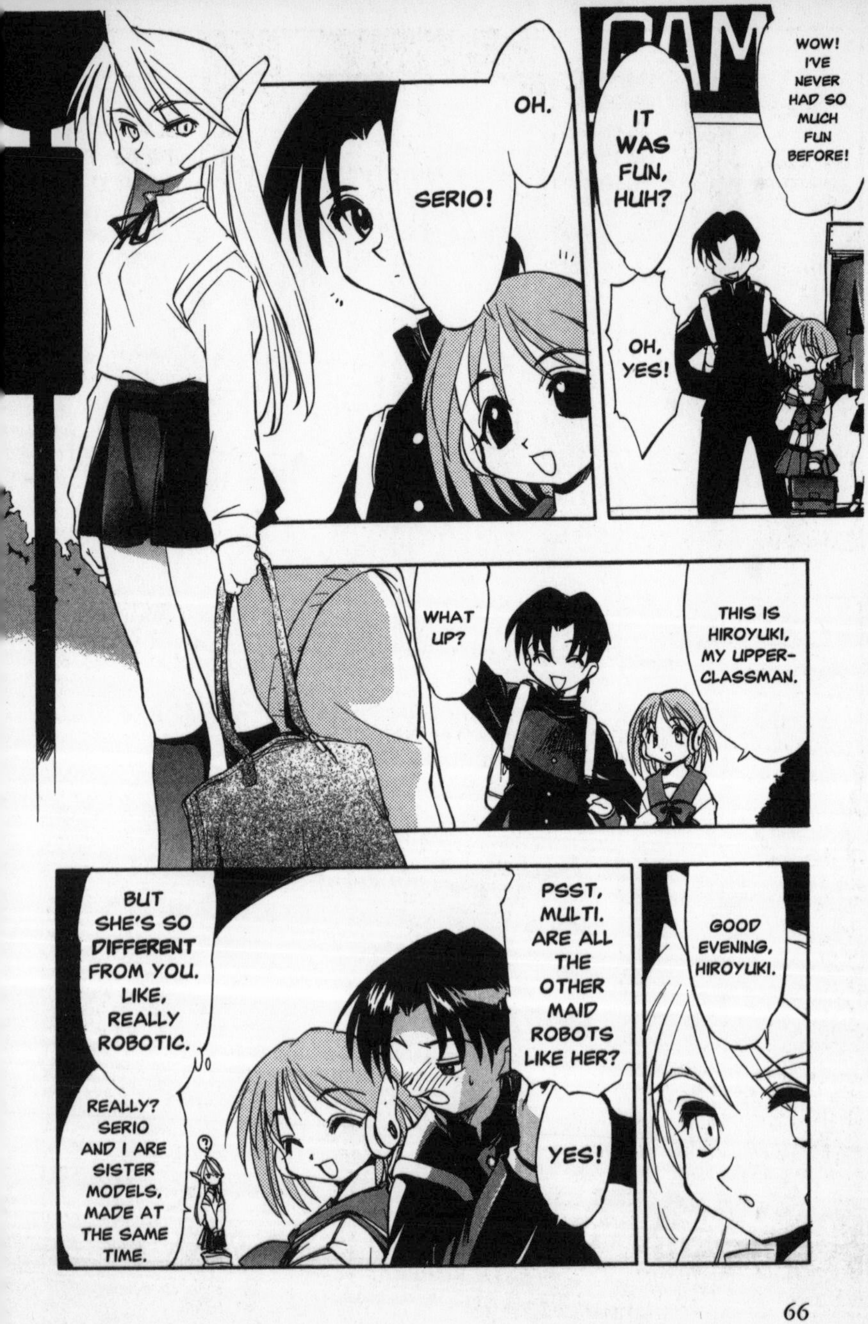
WOW! I'VE NEVER HAD SO MUCH FUN BEFORE!
IT WAS FUN, HUH?
OH, YES!
OH.
SERIO!
THIS IS HIROYUKI, MY UPPER-CLASSMAN.
WHAT UP?
GOOD EVENING, HIROYUKI.
PSST, MULTI. ARE ALL THE OTHER MAID ROBOTS LIKE HER?
YES!
BUT SHE'S SO DIFFERENT FROM YOU. LIKE, REALLY ROBOTIC.
REALLY? SERIO AND I ARE SISTER MODELS, MADE AT THE SAME TIME.

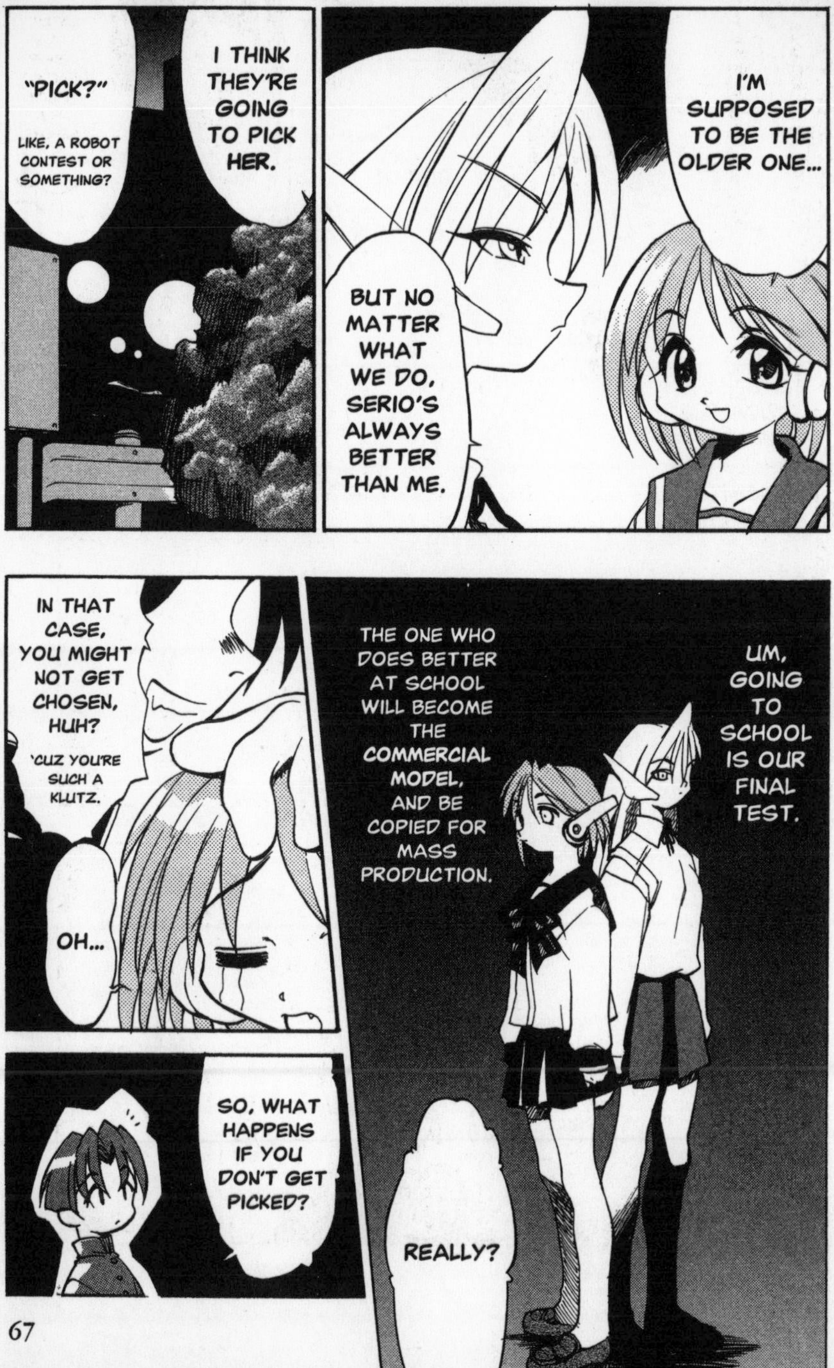
I'M SUPPOSED TO BE THE OLDER ONE...
BUT NO MATTER WHAT WE DO, SERIO'S ALWAYS BETTER THAN ME.
I THINK THEY'RE GOING TO PICK HER.
"PICK?"
LIKE, A ROBOT CONTEST OR SOMETHING?
UM, GOING TO SCHOOL IS OUR FINAL TEST.
THE ONE WHO DOES BETTER AT SCHOOL WILL BECOME THE COMMERCIAL MODEL, AND BE COPIED FOR MASS PRODUCTION.
REALLY?
IN THAT CASE, YOU MIGHT NOT GET CHOSEN, HUH?
'CUZ YOU'RE SUCH A KLUTZ.
OH...
SO, WHAT HAPPENS IF YOU DON'T GET PICKED?

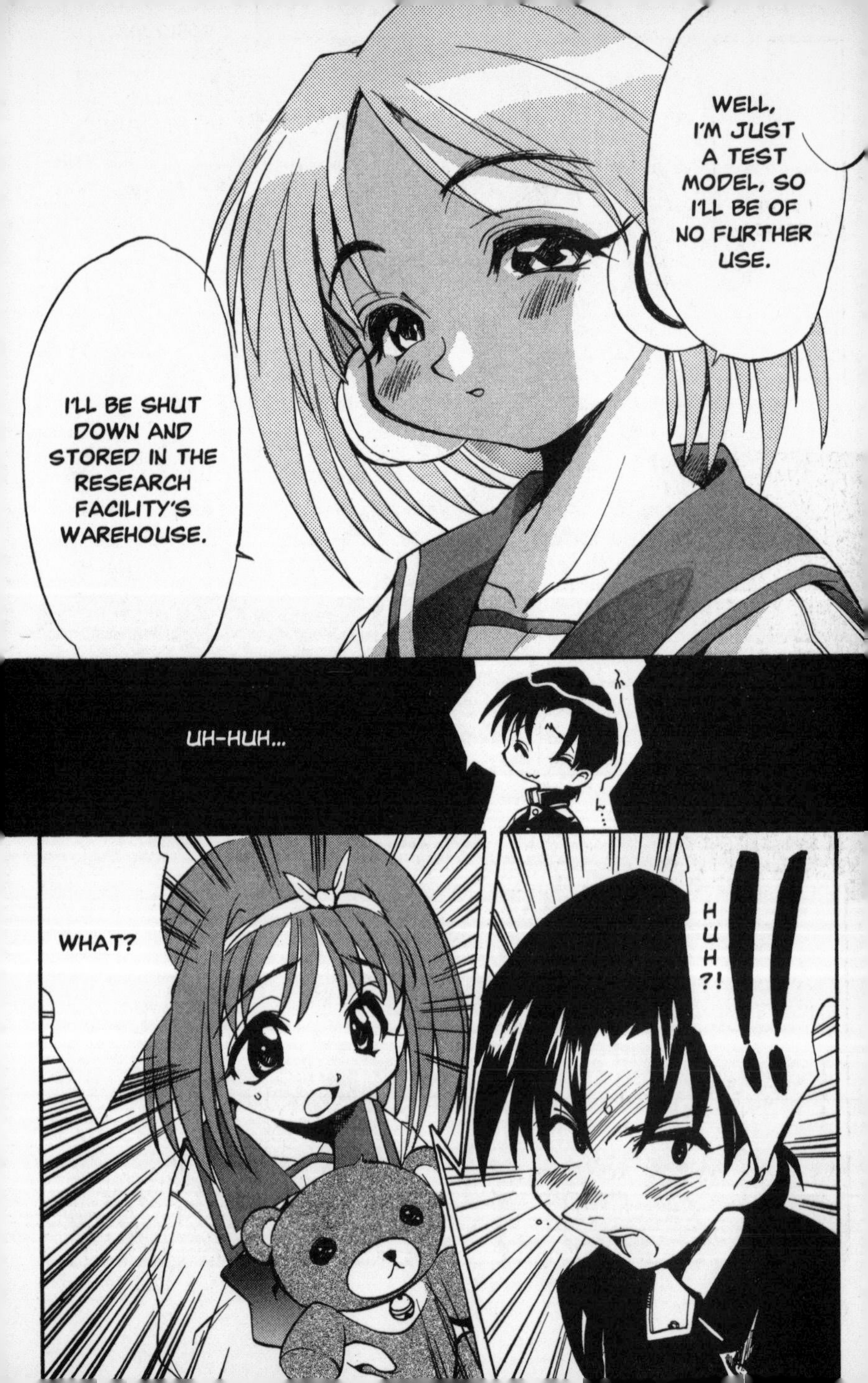
WELL, I'M JUST A TEST MODEL, SO I'LL BE OF NO FURTHER USE.
I'LL BE SHUT DOWN AND STORED IN THE RESEARCH FACILITY'S WAREHOUSE.
UH-HUH...
HUH?!
WHAT?

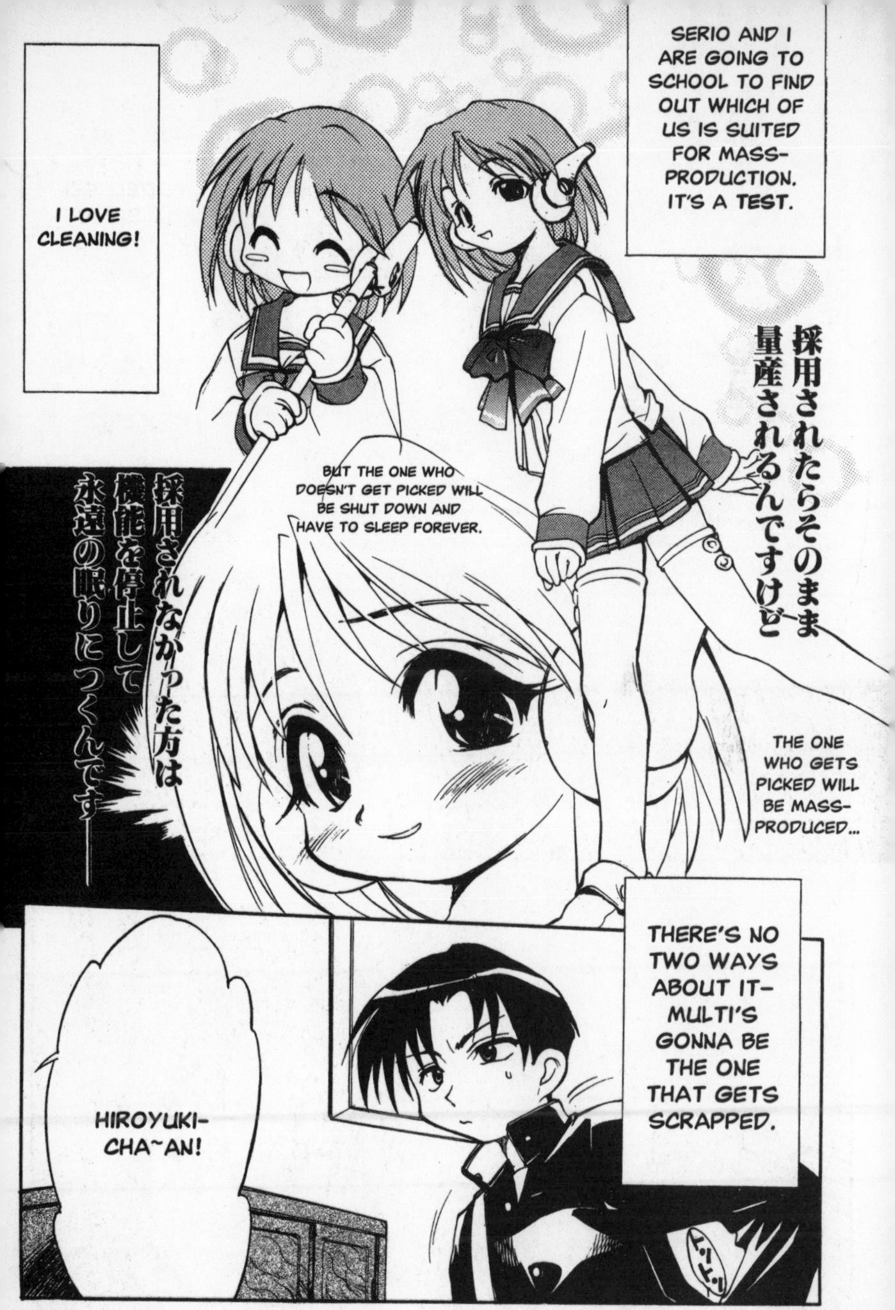
SERIO AND I ARE GOING TO SCHOOL TO FIND OUT WHICH OF US IS SUITED FOR MASS-PRODUCTION. IT'S A TEST.
I LOVE CLEANING!
採用されたらそのまま量産されるんですけど
THE ONE WHO GETS PICKED WILL BE MASS-PRODUCED...
採用されなかった方は機能を停止して永遠の眠りにつくんです——
BUT THE ONE WHO DOESN'T GET PICKED WILL BE SHUT DOWN AND HAVE TO SLEEP FOREVER.
THERE'S NO TWO WAYS ABOUT IT- MULTI'S GONNA BE THE ONE THAT GETS SCRAPPED.
HIROYUKI-CHA~AN!

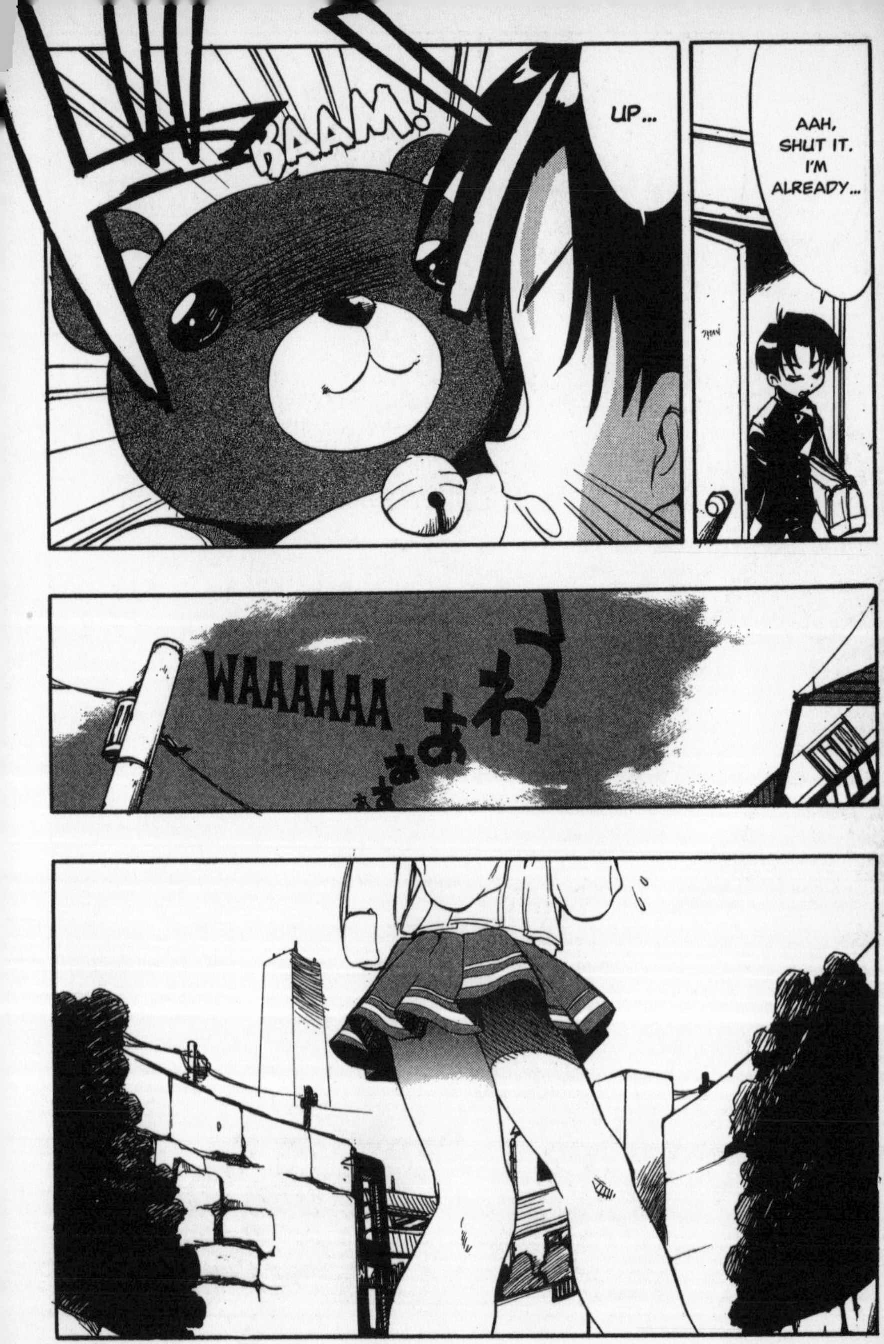
AAH, SHUT IT. I'M ALREADY...
UP...
BAAM!
WAAAAAA

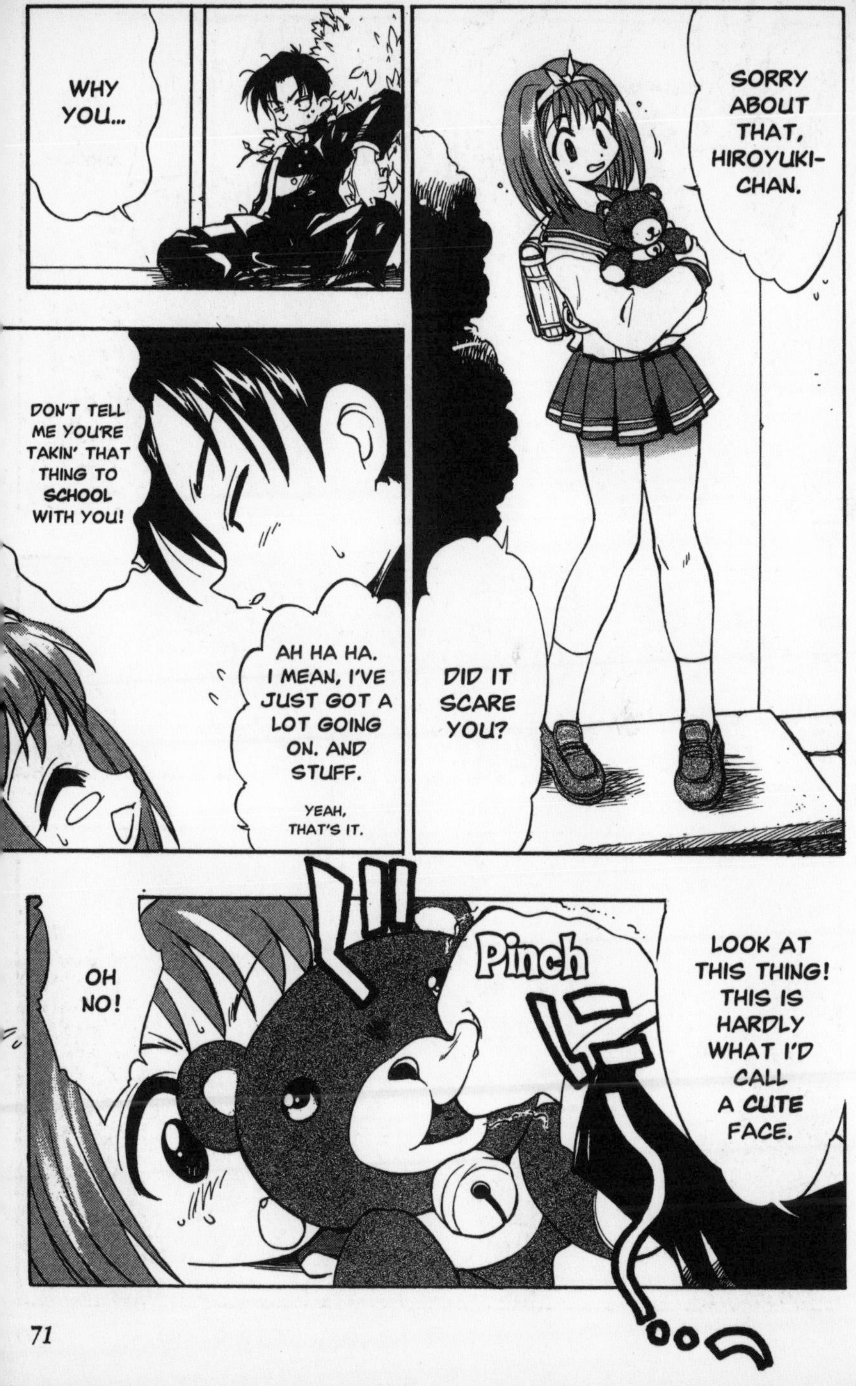
SORRY ABOUT THAT, HIROYUKI-CHAN.
WHY YOU...
DID IT SCARE YOU?
DON'T TELL ME YOU'RE TAKIN' THAT THING TO SCHOOL WITH YOU!
AH HA HA. I MEAN, I'VE JUST GOT A LOT GOING ON. AND STUFF.
YEAH, THAT'S IT.
LOOK AT THIS THING! THIS IS HARDLY WHAT I'D CALL A CUTE FACE.
Pinch
OH NO!

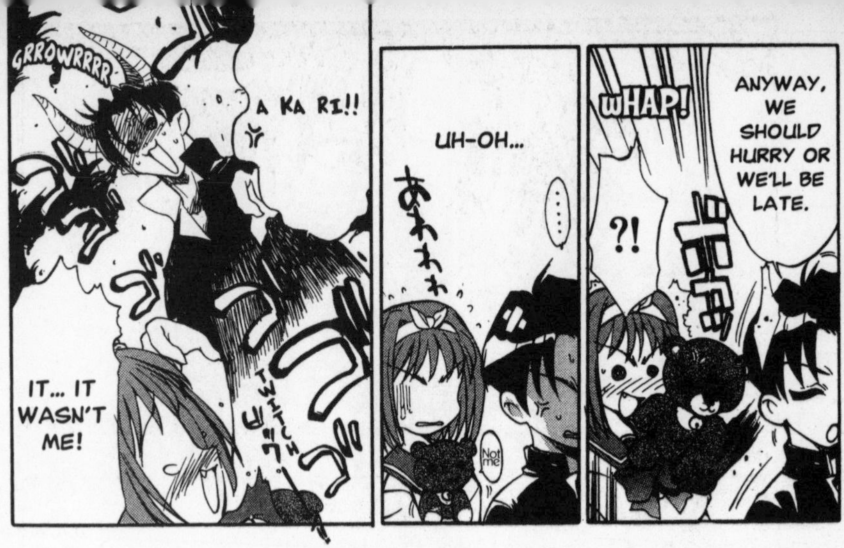
WHAP!
ANYWAY, WE SHOULD HURRY OR WE'LL BE LATE.
?!
UH-OH...
あわわわ
...
Not me
GRROWRRRR
A KA RI!!
TWITCH
IT... IT WASN'T ME!

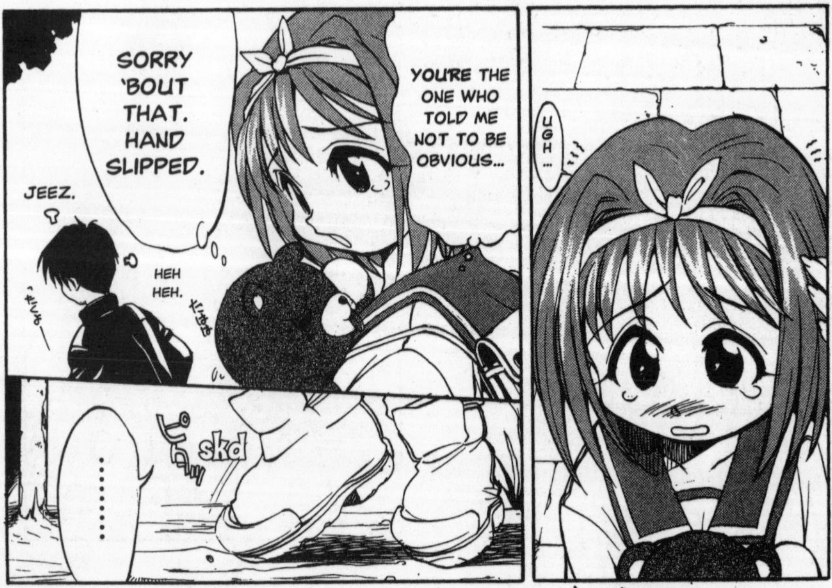
UGH...
YOU'RE THE ONE WHO TOLD ME NOT TO BE OBVIOUS...
SORRY 'BOUT THAT. HAND SLIPPED.
JEEZ.
HEH HEH.
skd
......

↑ グリグリされた
POST-NOOGIE

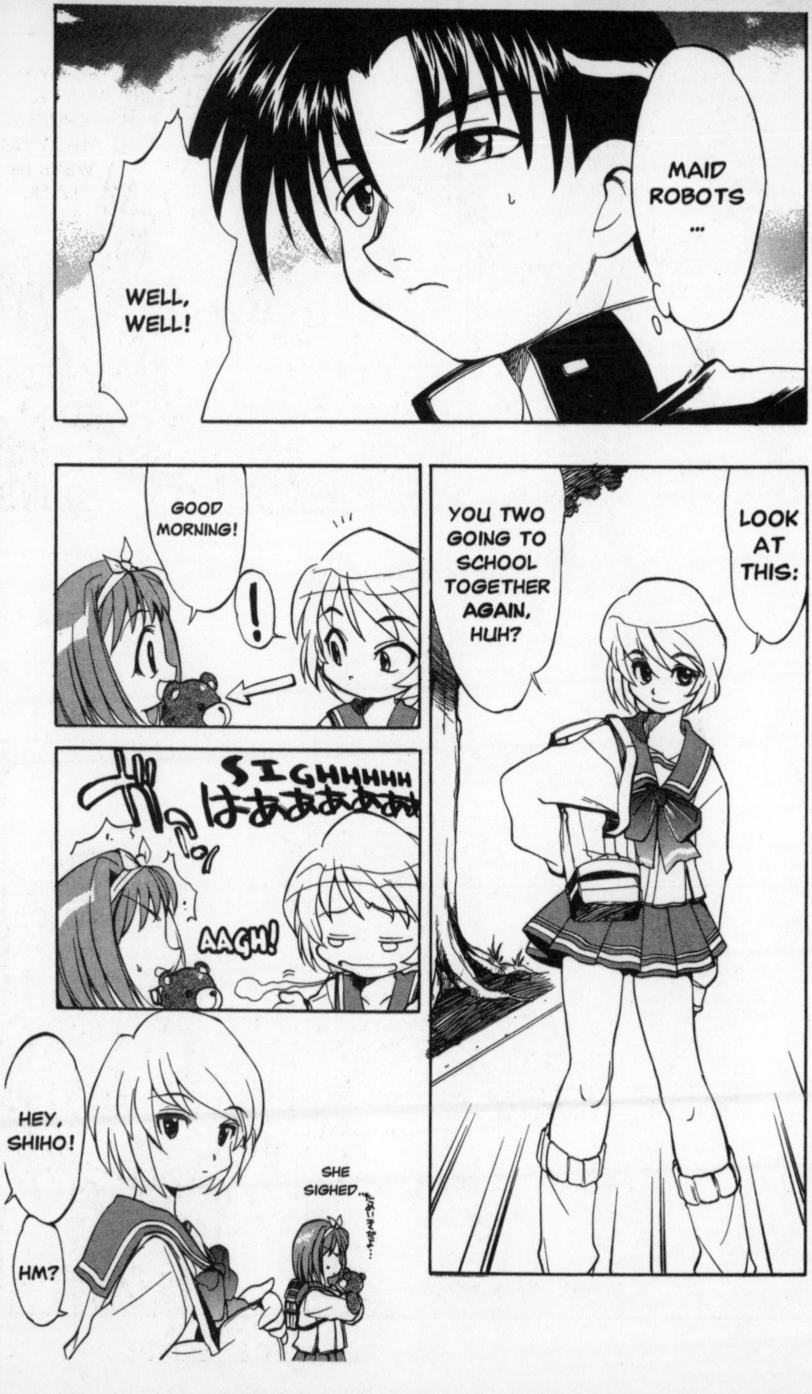
MAID ROBOTS ...
WELL, WELL!
LOOK AT THIS:
YOU TWO GOING TO SCHOOL TOGETHER AGAIN, HUH?
GOOD MORNING!
!
SIGHHHHH
AAGH!
HEY, SHIHO!
HM?
SHE SIGHED...

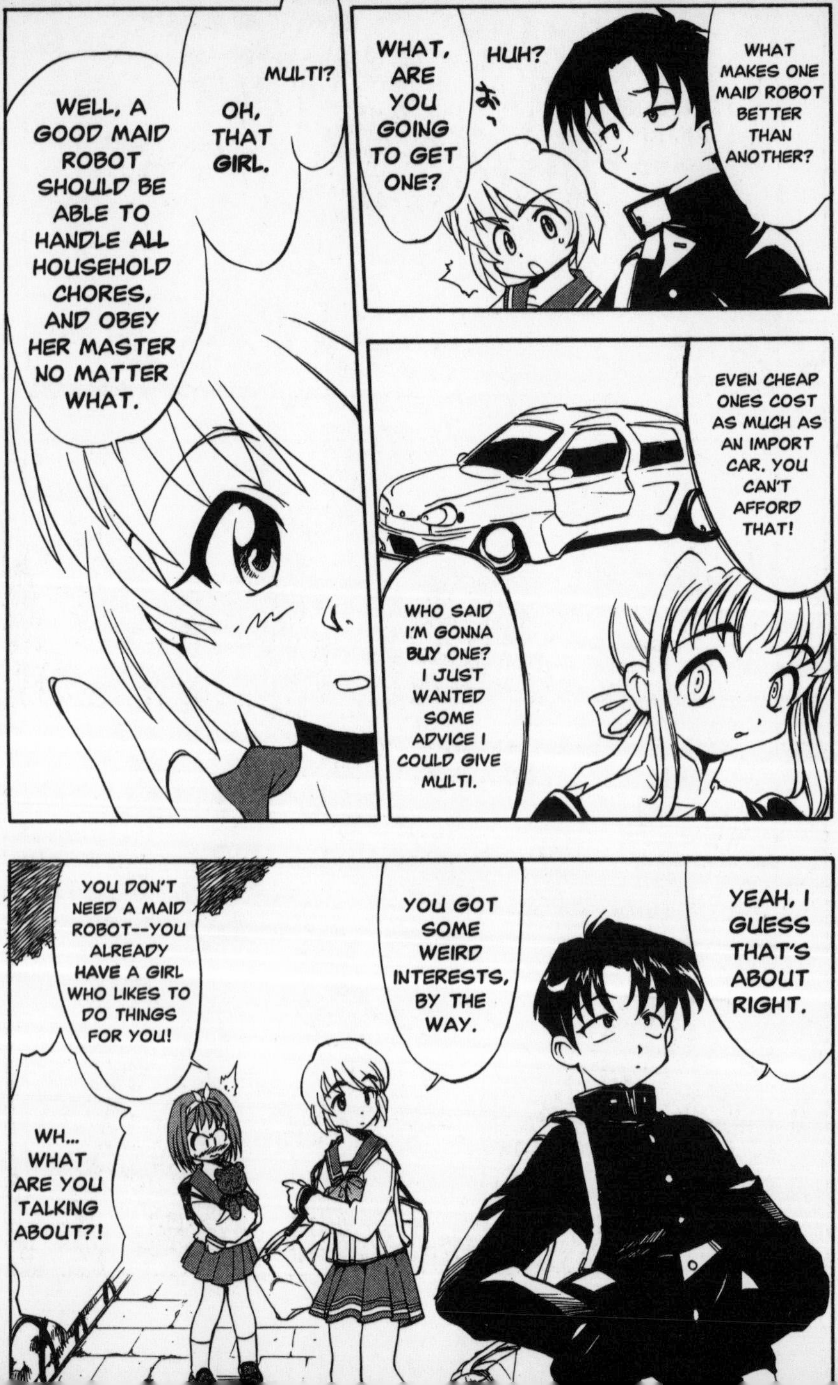
WHAT MAKES ONE MAID ROBOT BETTER THAN ANOTHER?
HUH?
お、
WHAT, ARE YOU GOING TO GET ONE?
EVEN CHEAP ONES COST AS MUCH AS AN IMPORT CAR. YOU CAN'T AFFORD THAT!
WHO SAID I'M GONNA BUY ONE? I JUST WANTED SOME ADVICE I COULD GIVE MULTI.
MULTI?
OH, THAT GIRL.
WELL, A GOOD MAID ROBOT SHOULD BE ABLE TO HANDLE ALL HOUSEHOLD CHORES, AND OBEY HER MASTER NO MATTER WHAT.
YEAH, I GUESS THAT'S ABOUT RIGHT.
YOU GOT SOME WEIRD INTERESTS, BY THE WAY.
YOU DON'T NEED A MAID ROBOT--YOU ALREADY HAVE A GIRL WHO LIKES TO DO THINGS FOR YOU!
WH... WHAT ARE YOU TALKING ABOUT?!

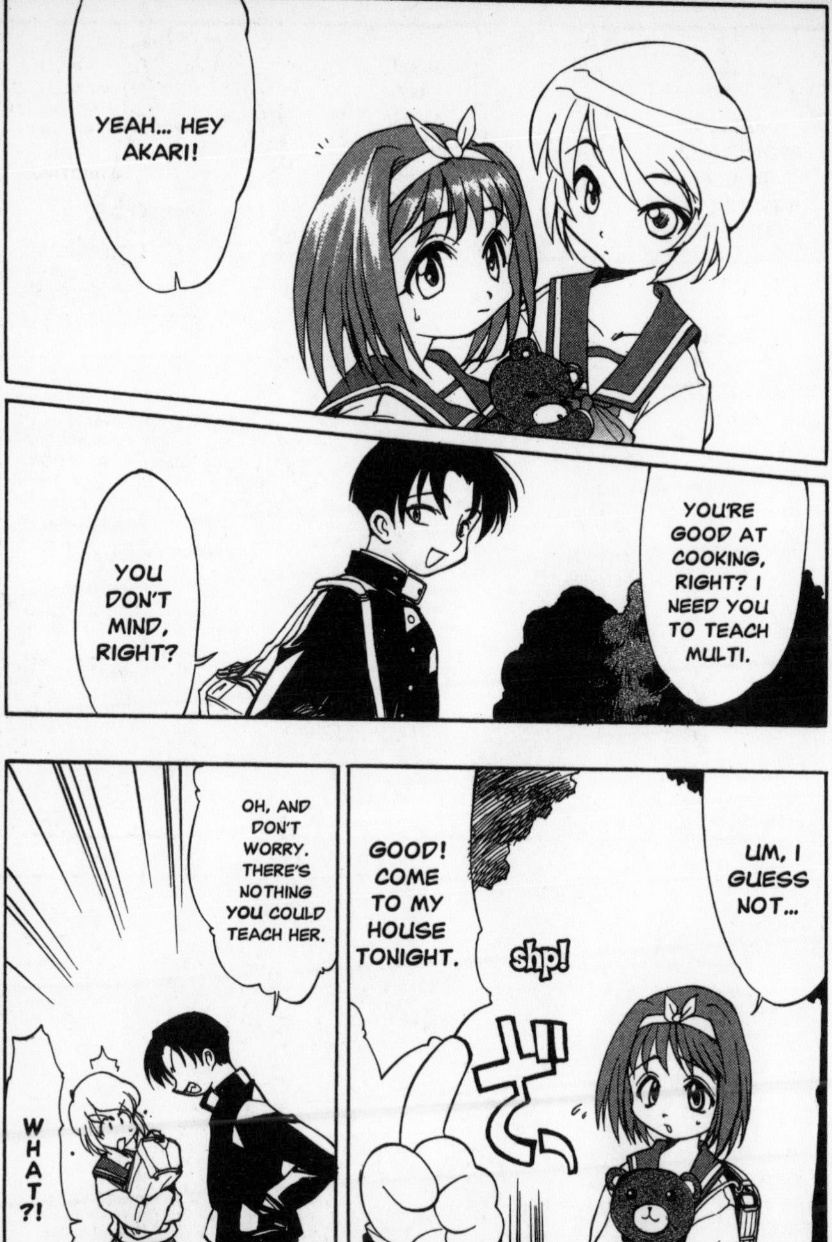
YEAH... HEY AKARI!
YOU'RE GOOD AT COOKING, RIGHT? I NEED YOU TO TEACH MULTI.
YOU DON'T MIND, RIGHT?
UM, I GUESS NOT...
GOOD! COME TO MY HOUSE TONIGHT.
shp!
OH, AND DON'T WORRY. THERE'S NOTHING YOU COULD TEACH HER.
WHAT?!

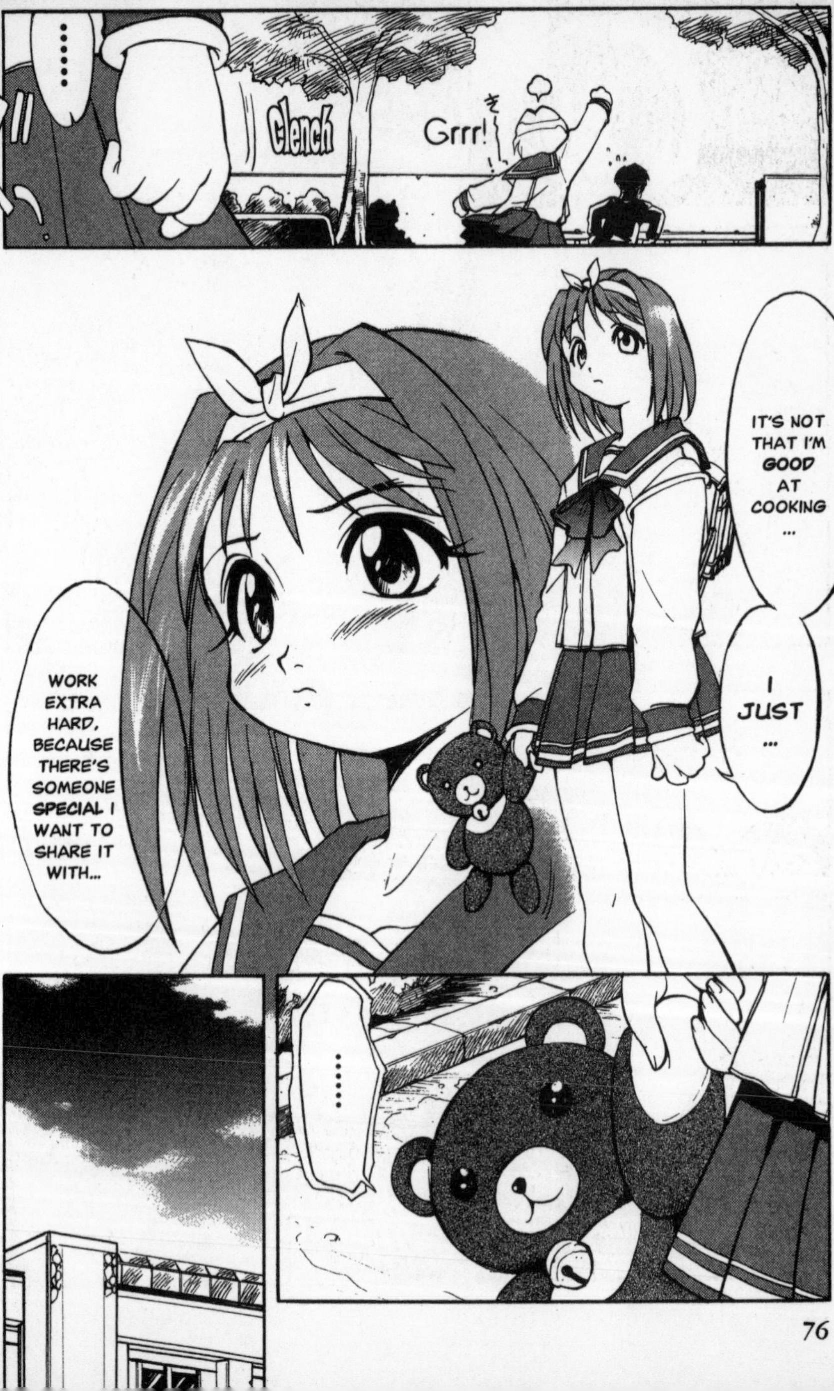
......
Clench
Grrr!
IT'S NOT THAT I'M GOOD AT COOKING ...
I JUST ...
WORK EXTRA HARD, BECAUSE THERE'S SOMEONE SPECIAL I WANT TO SHARE IT WITH...
......

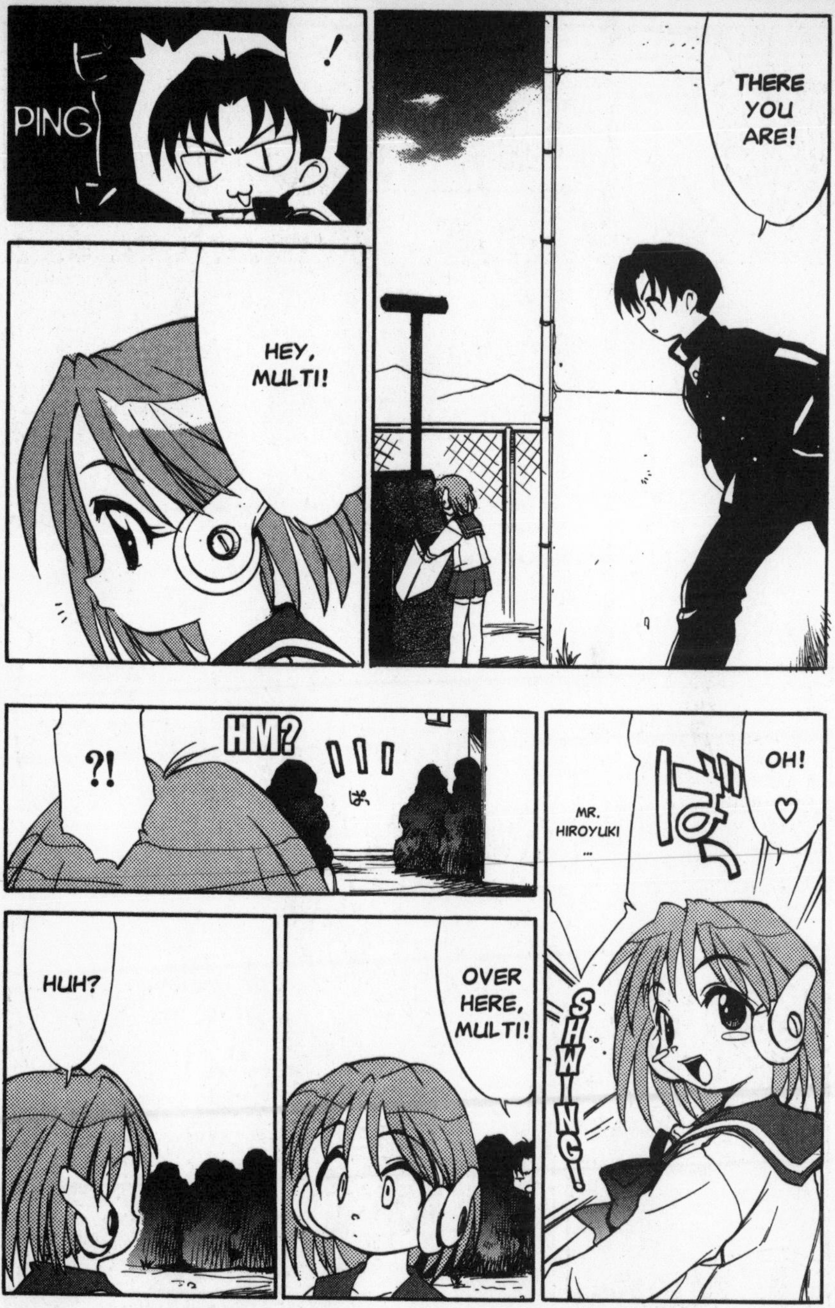
THERE YOU ARE!
!
PING
HEY, MULTI!
OH! ♥
MR. HIROYUKI ...
HM?
?!
SHWING!
OVER HERE, MULTI!
HUH?

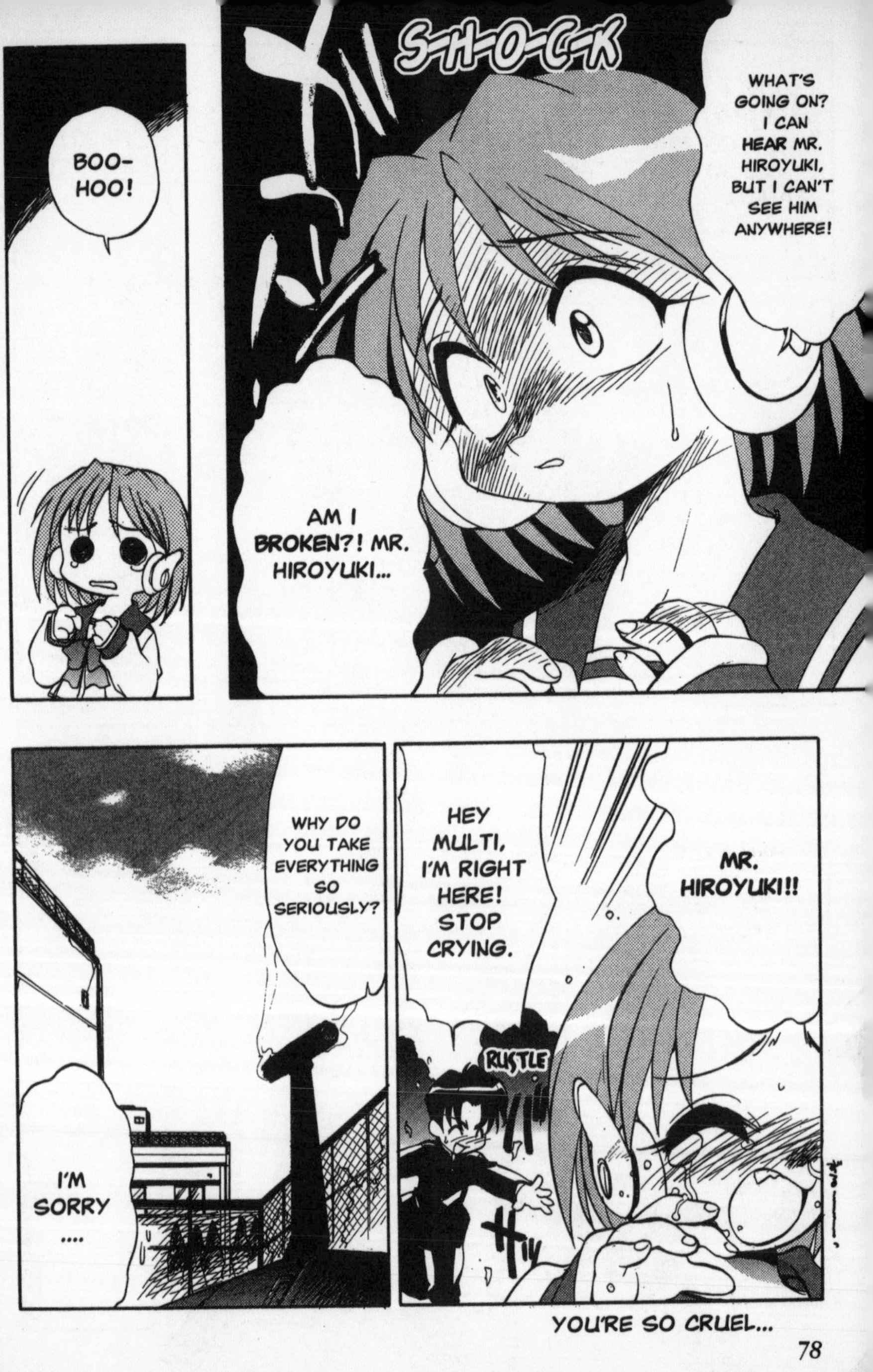
S-H-O-C-K
WHAT'S GOING ON? I CAN HEAR MR. HIROYUKI, BUT I CAN'T SEE HIM ANYWHERE!
AM I BROKEN?! MR. HIROYUKI...
BOO-HOO!
MR. HIROYUKI!!
HEY MULTI, I'M RIGHT HERE! STOP CRYING.
RUSTLE
WHY DO YOU TAKE EVERYTHING SO SERIOUSLY?
I'M SORRY ....
YOU'RE SO CRUEL...

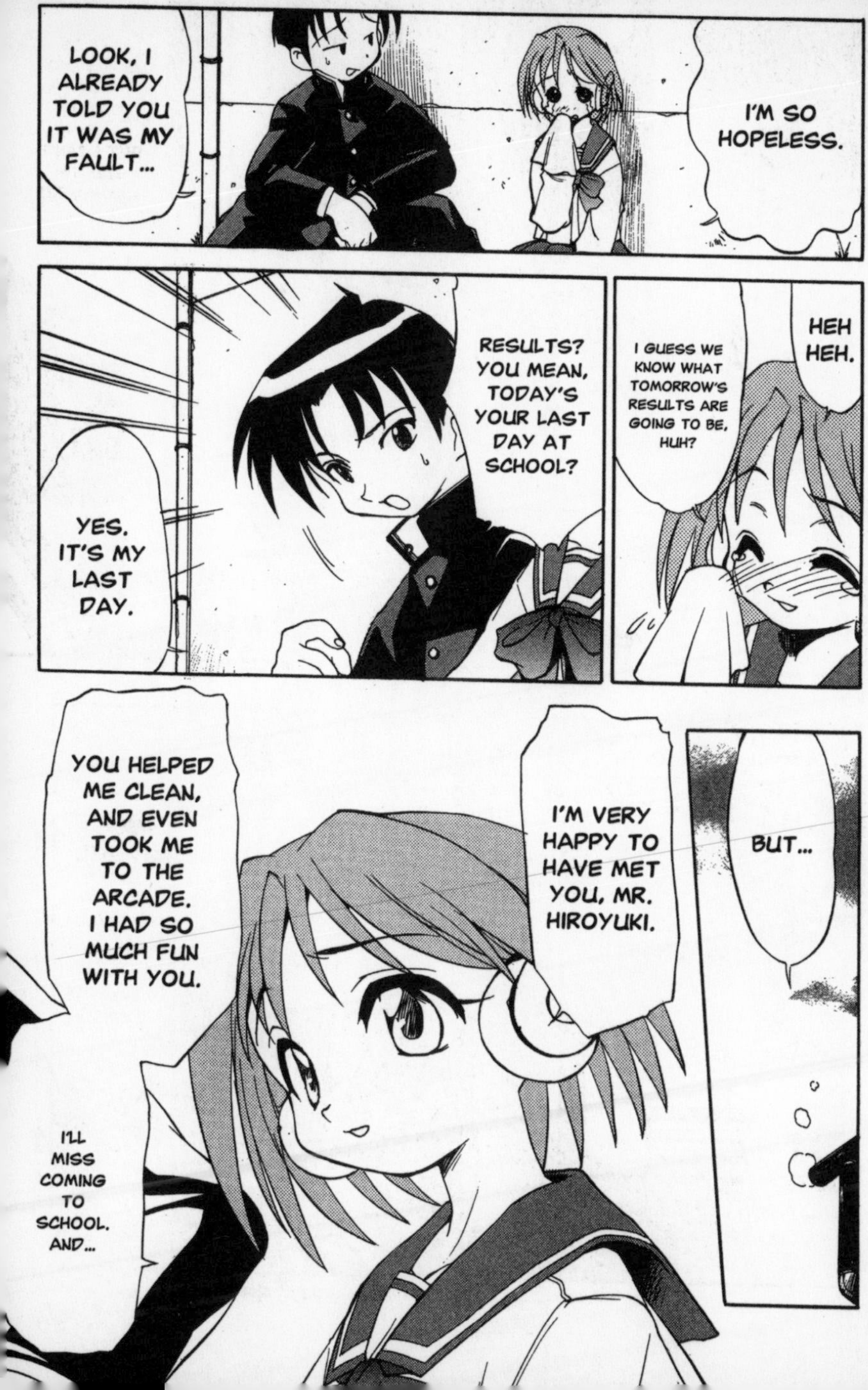
I'M SO HOPELESS.
LOOK, I ALREADY TOLD YOU IT WAS MY FAULT...
HEH HEH.
I GUESS WE KNOW WHAT TOMORROW'S RESULTS ARE GOING TO BE, HUH?
RESULTS? YOU MEAN, TODAY'S YOUR LAST DAY AT SCHOOL?
YES. IT'S MY LAST DAY.
BUT...
I'M VERY HAPPY TO HAVE MET YOU, MR. HIROYUKI.
YOU HELPED ME CLEAN, AND EVEN TOOK ME TO THE ARCADE. I HAD SO MUCH FUN WITH YOU.
I'LL MISS COMING TO SCHOOL. AND...

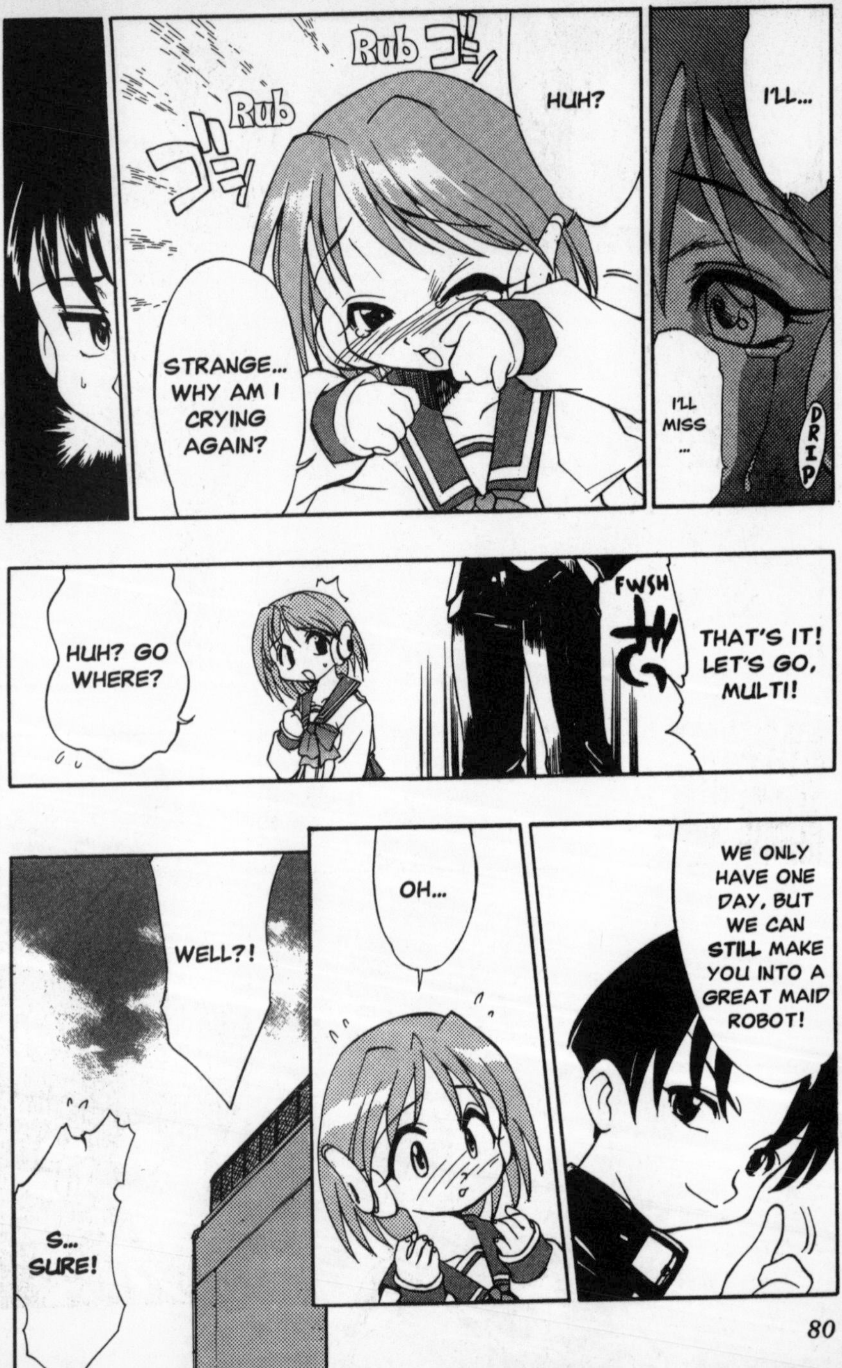
I'LL...
I'LL MISS ...
DRIP
Rub
Rub
HUH?
STRANGE... WHY AM I CRYING AGAIN?
THAT'S IT! LET'S GO, MULTI!
FWSH
HUH? GO WHERE?
WE ONLY HAVE ONE DAY, BUT WE CAN STILL MAKE YOU INTO A GREAT MAID ROBOT!
OH...
WELL?!
S... SURE!

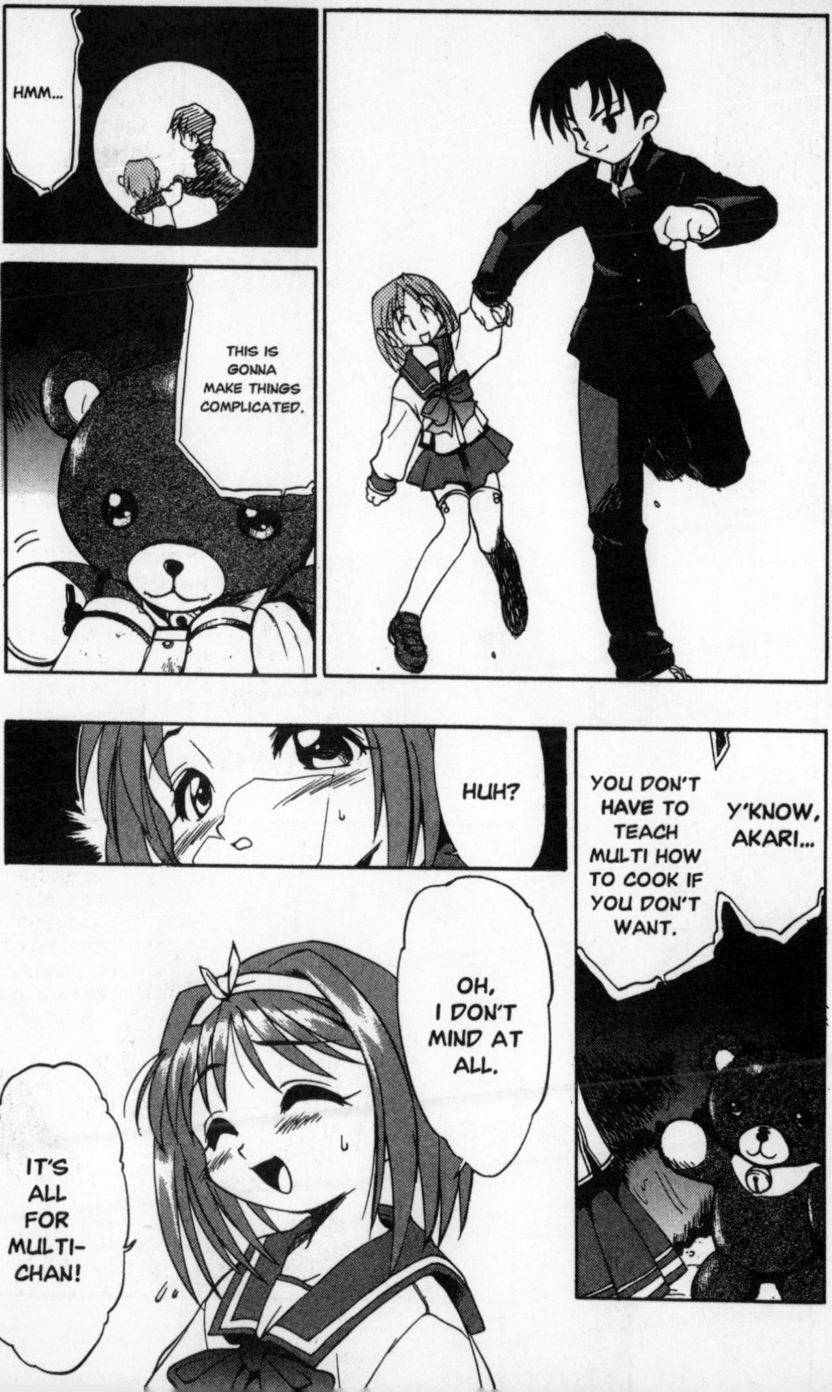
HMM...
THIS IS GONNA MAKE THINGS COMPLICATED.
Y'KNOW, AKARI...
YOU DON'T HAVE TO TEACH MULTI HOW TO COOK IF YOU DON'T WANT.
HUH?
OH, I DON'T MIND AT ALL.
IT'S ALL FOR MULTI-CHAN!

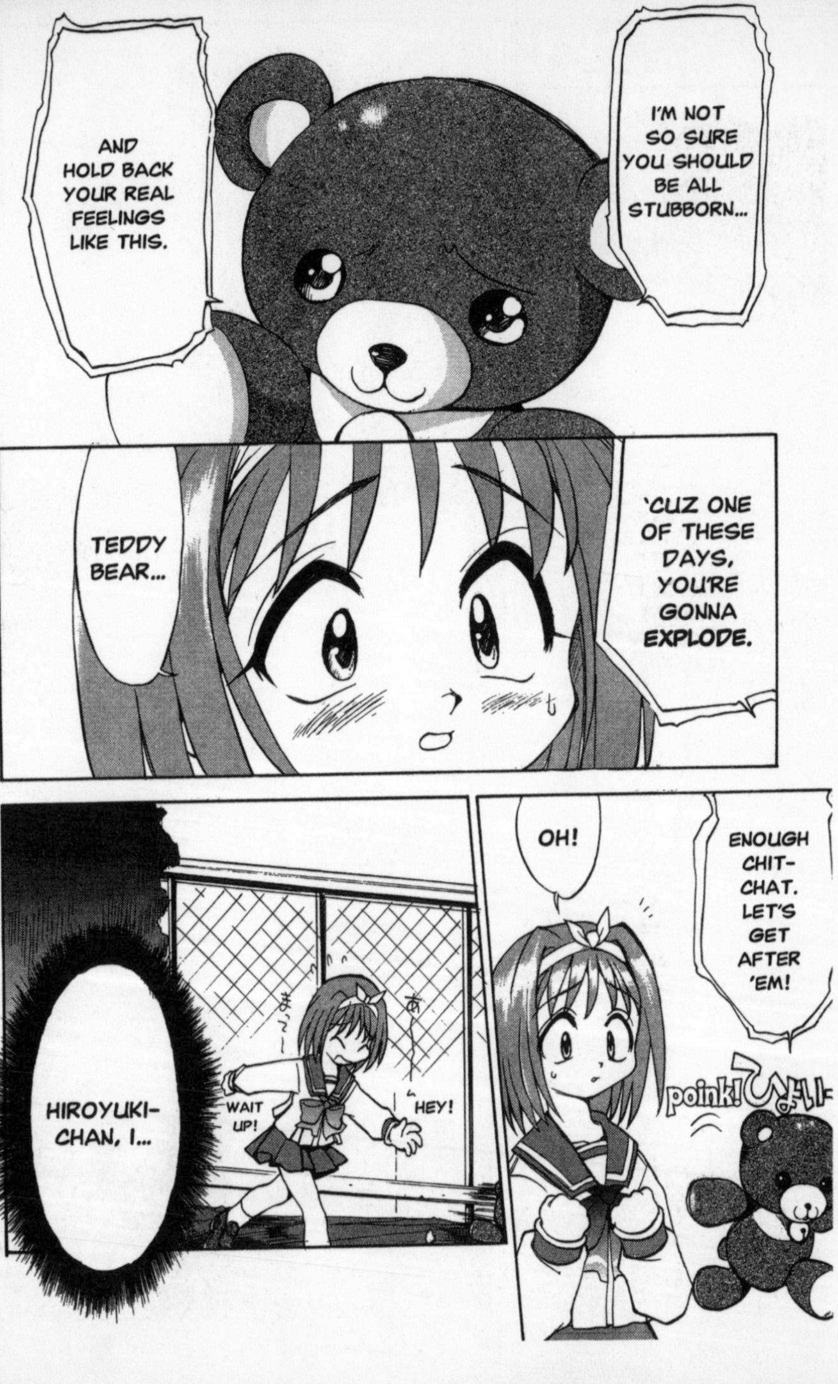
I'M NOT SO SURE YOU SHOULD BE ALL STUBBORN...
AND HOLD BACK YOUR REAL FEELINGS LIKE THIS.
'CUZ ONE OF THESE DAYS, YOU'RE GONNA EXPLODE.
TEDDY BEAR...
ENOUGH CHIT-CHAT. LET'S GET AFTER 'EM!
OH!
poink!
HEY!
WAIT UP!
HIROYUKI-CHAN, I...

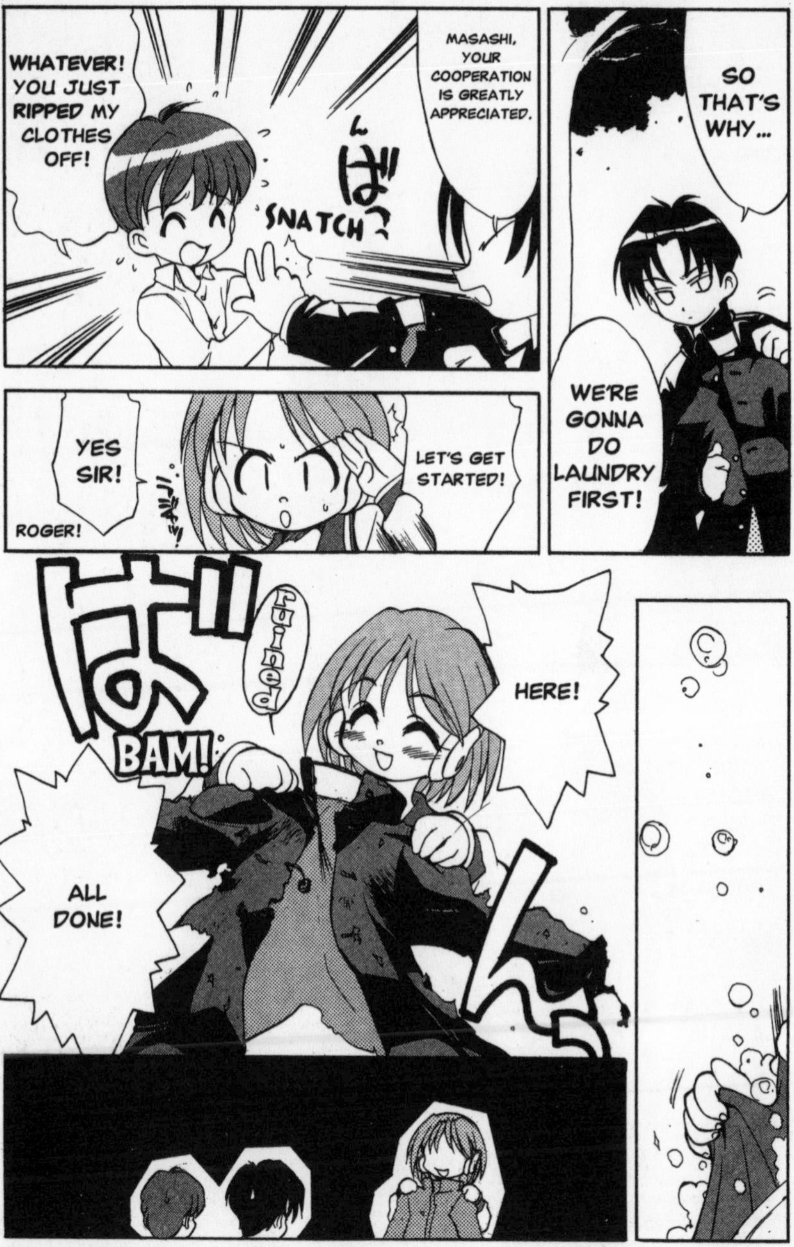
SO THAT'S WHY...
WE'RE GONNA DO LAUNDRY FIRST!
MASASHI, YOUR COOPERATION IS GREATLY APPRECIATED.
SNATCH
WHATEVER! YOU JUST RIPPED MY CLOTHES OFF!
LET'S GET STARTED!
YES SIR!
ROGER!
HERE!
ruined
BAM!
ALL DONE!

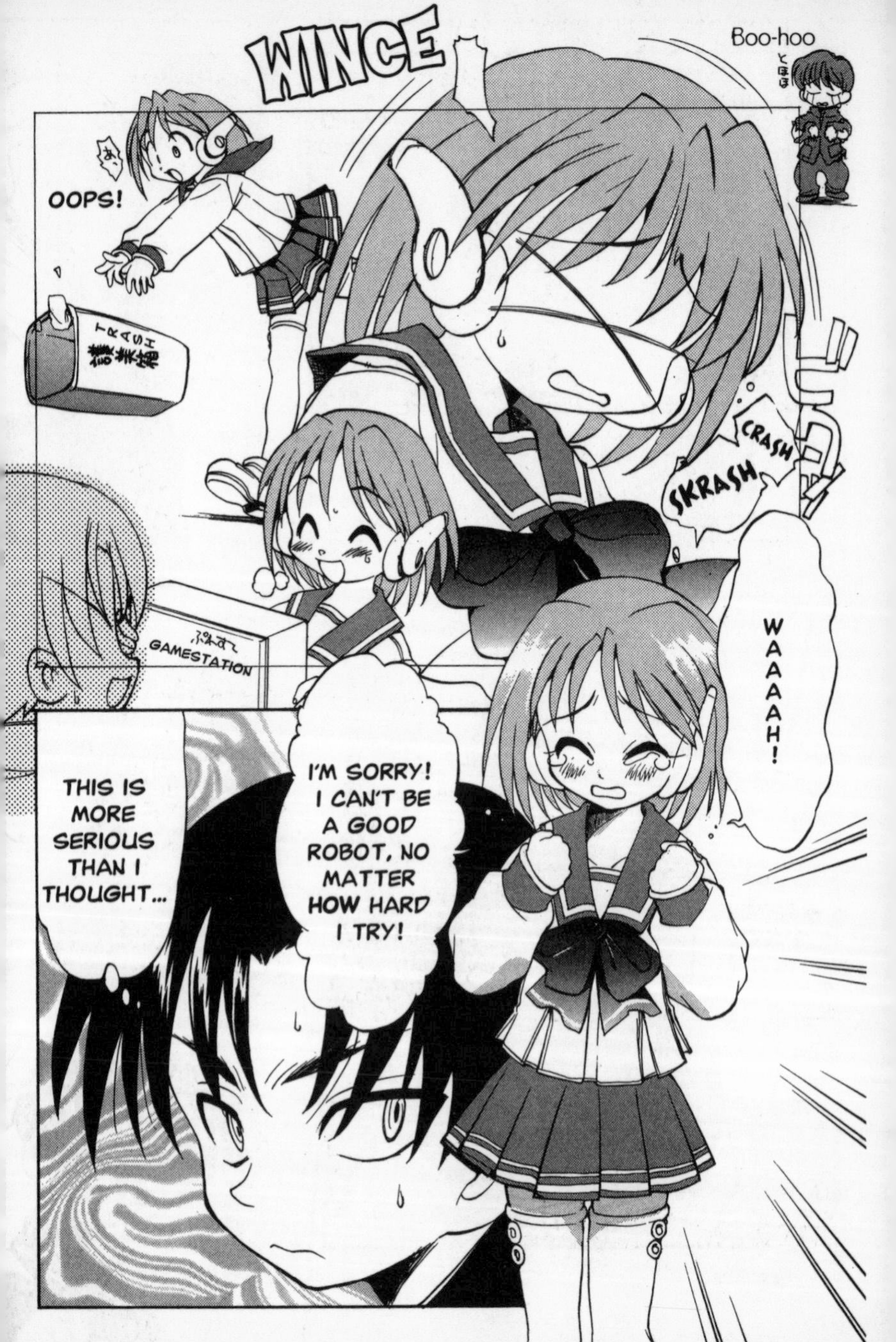
Boo-hoo
とほほ
WINCE
OOPS!
あっ
TRASH
CRASH
SKRASH
GAMESTATION
WAAAAAH!
I'M SORRY! I CAN'T BE A GOOD ROBOT, NO MATTER HOW HARD I TRY!
THIS IS MORE SERIOUS THAN I THOUGHT...

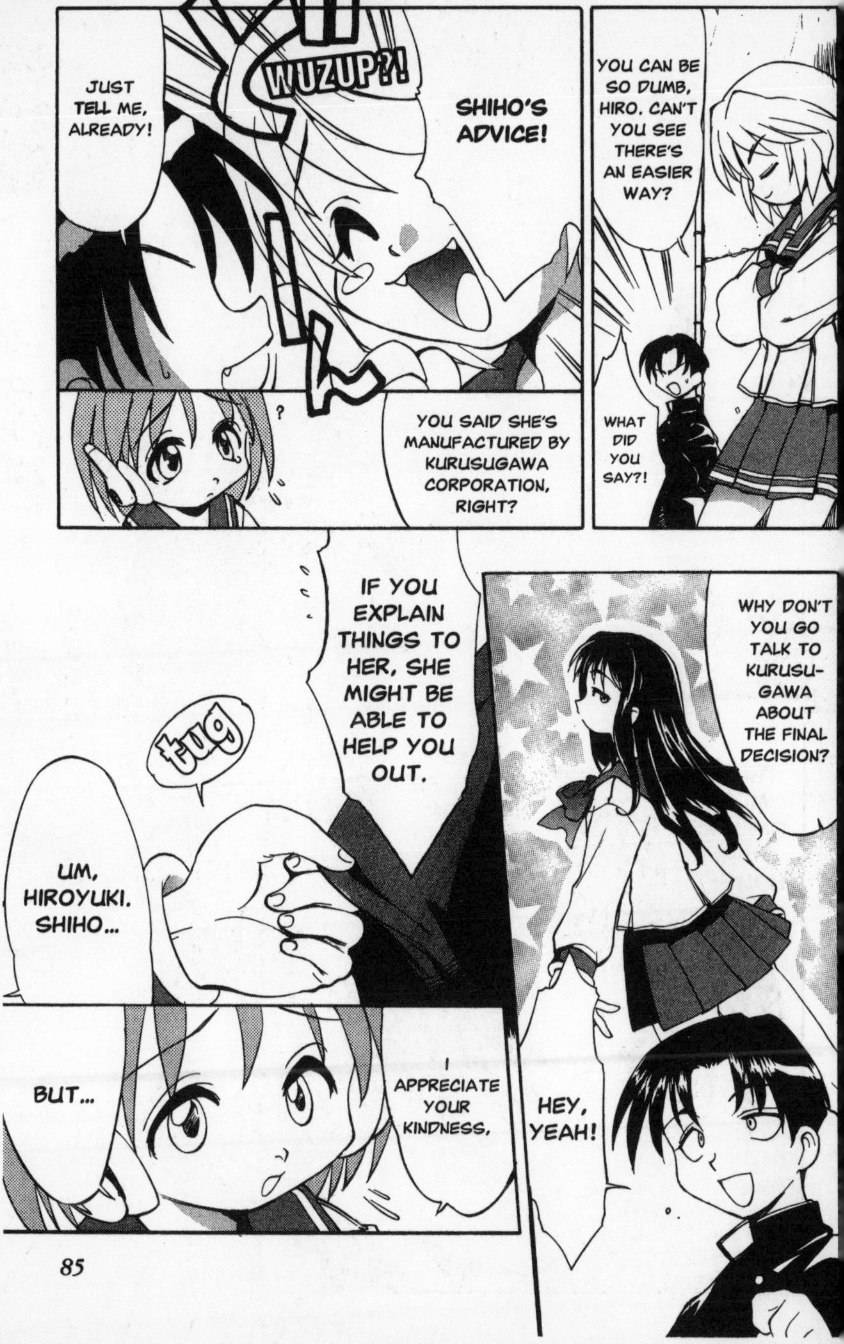

YOU CAN BE SO DUMB, HIRO. CAN'T YOU SEE THERE'S AN EASIER WAY?
WHAT DID YOU SAY?!
JUST TELL ME, ALREADY!
WUZUP?!
SHIHO'S ADVICE!
?
YOU SAID SHE'S MANUFACTURED BY KURUSUGAWA CORPORATION, RIGHT?
IF YOU EXPLAIN THINGS TO HER, SHE MIGHT BE ABLE TO HELP YOU OUT.
WHY DON'T YOU GO TALK TO KURUSU-GAWA ABOUT THE FINAL DECISION?
HEY, YEAH!
tug
UM, HIROYUKI. SHIHO...
I APPRECIATE YOUR KINDNESS,
BUT...

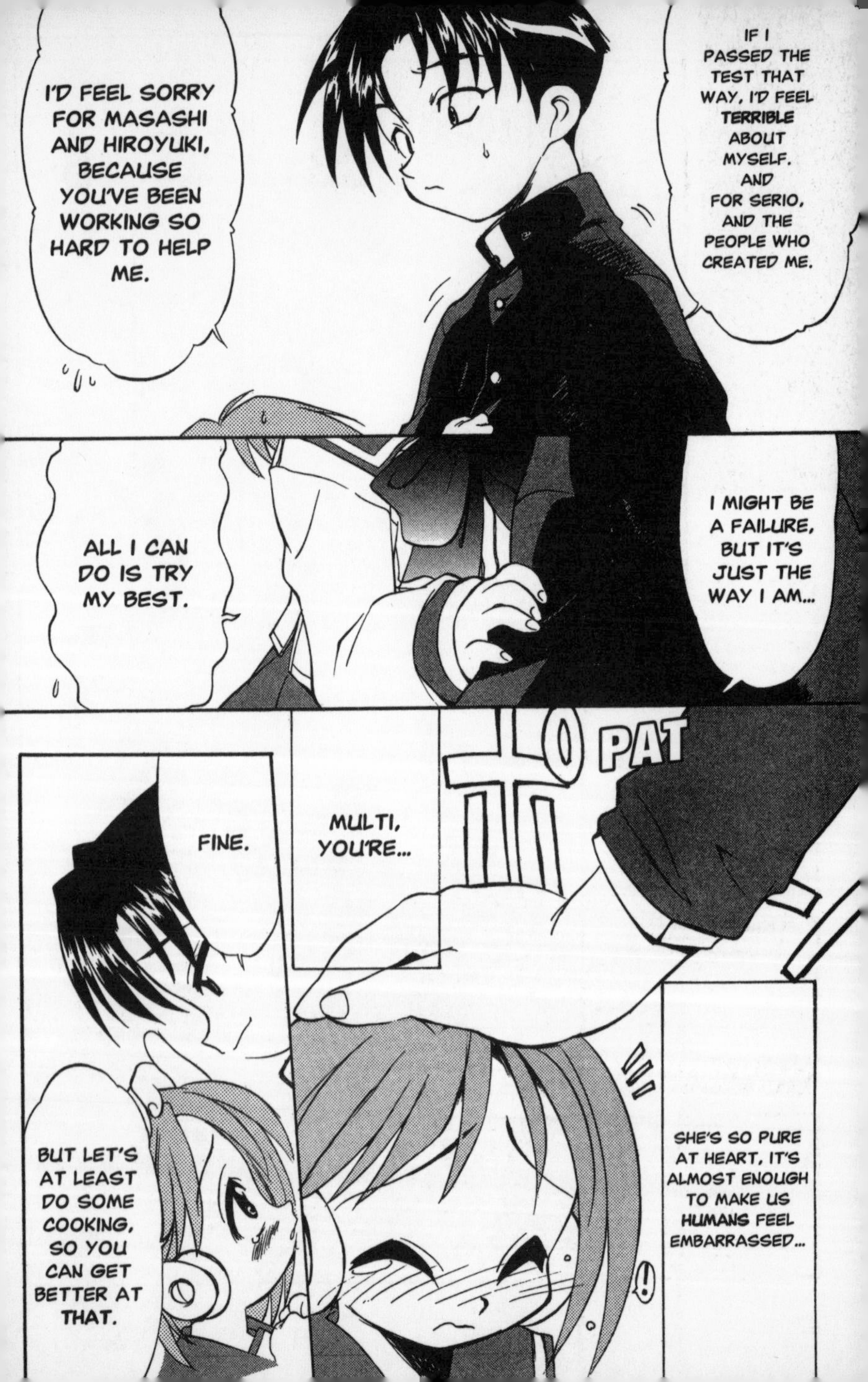
IF I PASSED THE TEST THAT WAY, I'D FEEL TERRIBLE ABOUT MYSELF. AND FOR SERIO, AND THE PEOPLE WHO CREATED ME.
I'D FEEL SORRY FOR MASASHI AND HIROYUKI, BECAUSE YOU'VE BEEN WORKING SO HARD TO HELP ME.
I MIGHT BE A FAILURE, BUT IT'S JUST THE WAY I AM...
ALL I CAN DO IS TRY MY BEST.
PAT
MULTI, YOU'RE...
FINE.
!
SHE'S SO PURE AT HEART, IT'S ALMOST ENOUGH TO MAKE US HUMANS FEEL EMBARRASSED...
BUT LET'S AT LEAST DO SOME COOKING, SO YOU CAN GET BETTER AT THAT.

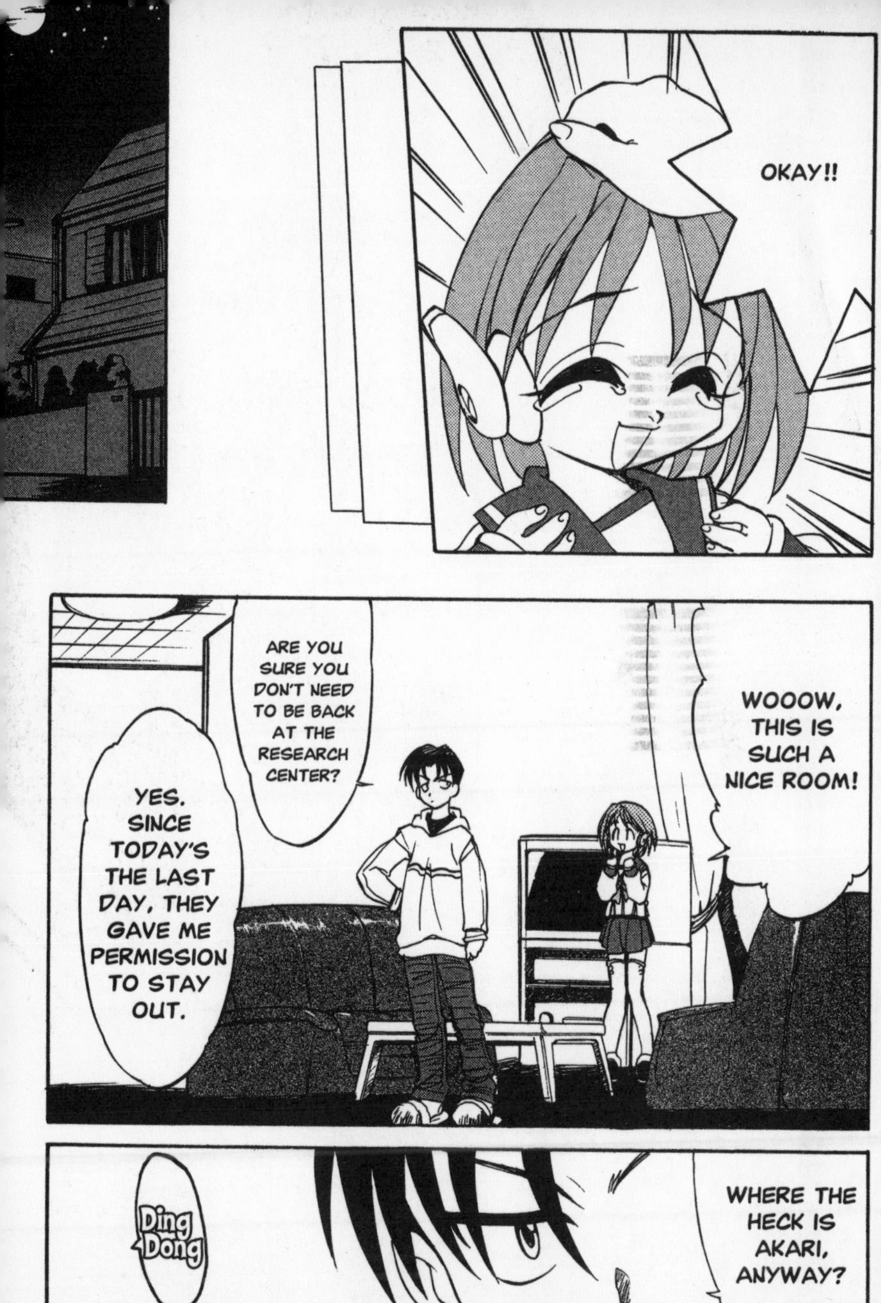
OKAY!!
WOOOW, THIS IS SUCH A NICE ROOM!
ARE YOU SURE YOU DON'T NEED TO BE BACK AT THE RESEARCH CENTER?
YES. SINCE TODAY'S THE LAST DAY, THEY GAVE ME PERMISSION TO STAY OUT.
WHERE THE HECK IS AKARI, ANYWAY?
Ding Dong

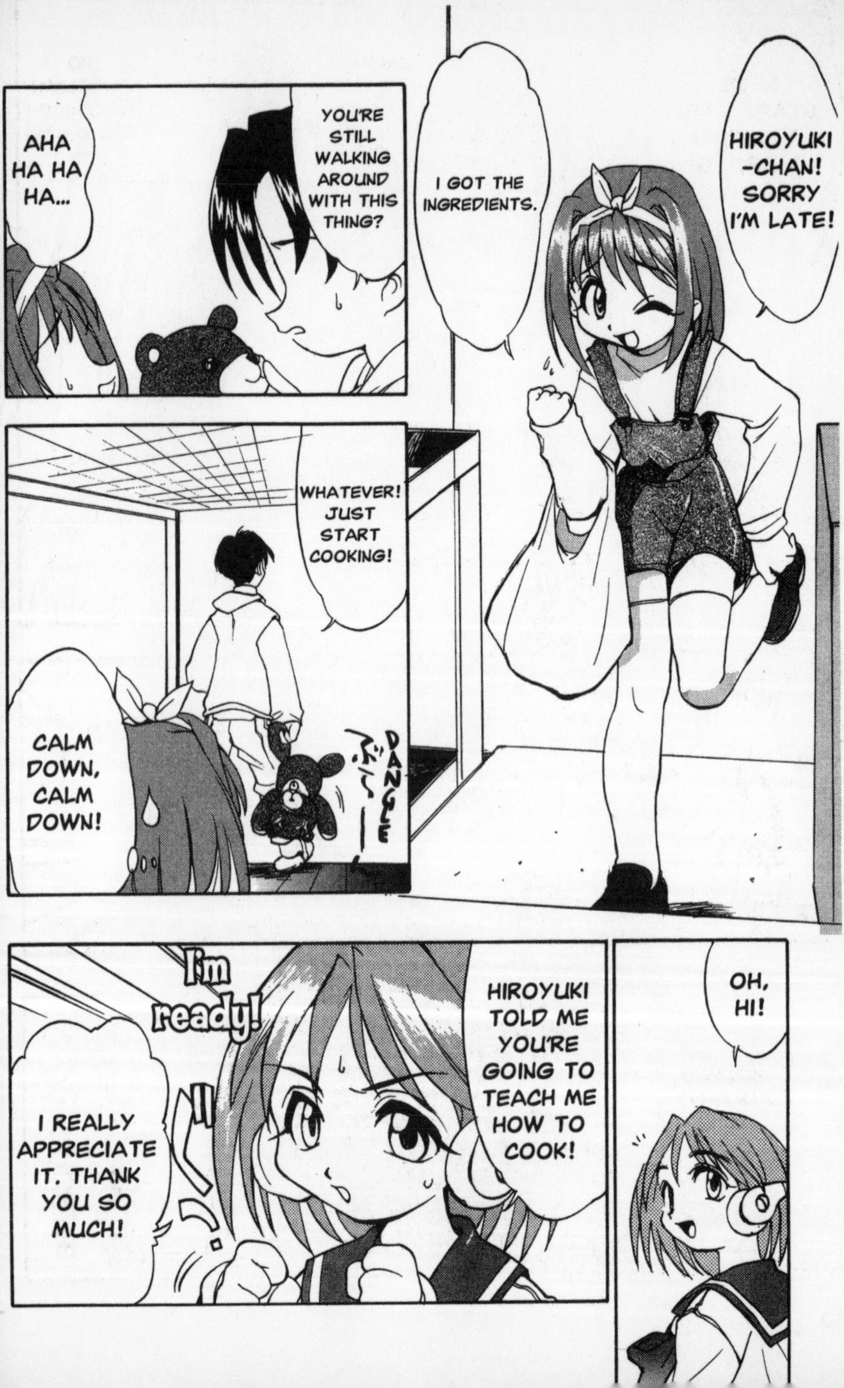
HIROYUKI -CHAN! SORRY I'M LATE!
I GOT THE INGREDIENTS.
YOU'RE STILL WALKING AROUND WITH THIS THING?
AHA HA HA HA...
WHATEVER! JUST START COOKING!
DANGLE
CALM DOWN, CALM DOWN!
OH, HI!
HIROYUKI TOLD ME YOU'RE GOING TO TEACH ME HOW TO COOK!
I'm ready!
I REALLY APPRECIATE IT. THANK YOU SO MUCH!

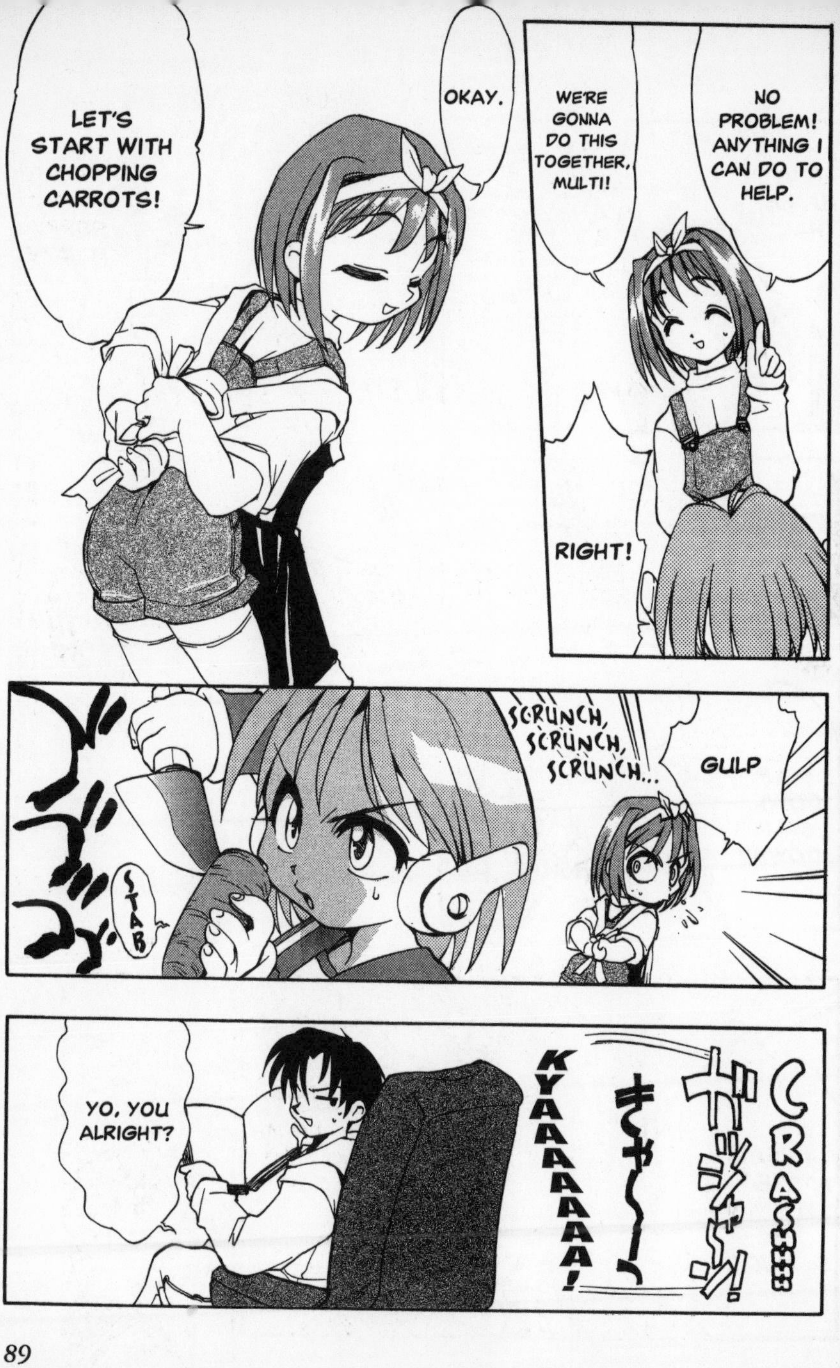
NO PROBLEM! ANYTHING I CAN DO TO HELP.
WE'RE GONNA DO THIS TOGETHER, MULTI!
RIGHT!
OKAY.
LET'S START WITH CHOPPING CARROTS!
GULP
SCRUNCH, SCRUNCH, SCRUNCH...
STAB
CRASH!!!
KYAAAAAAAA!
YO, YOU ALRIGHT?

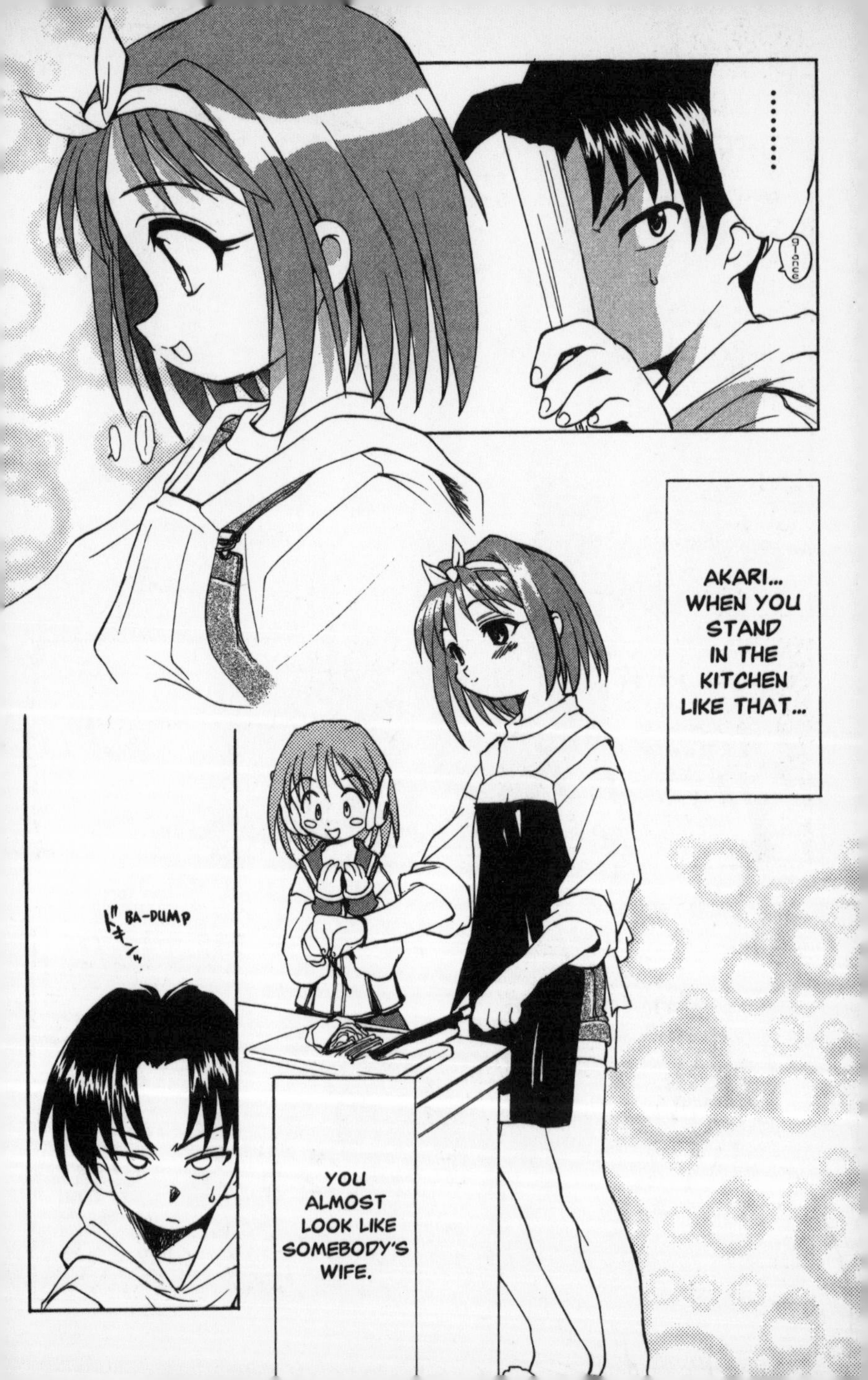

......
glance
AKARI... WHEN YOU STAND IN THE KITCHEN LIKE THAT...
BA-DUMP
YOU ALMOST LOOK LIKE SOMEBODY'S WIFE.

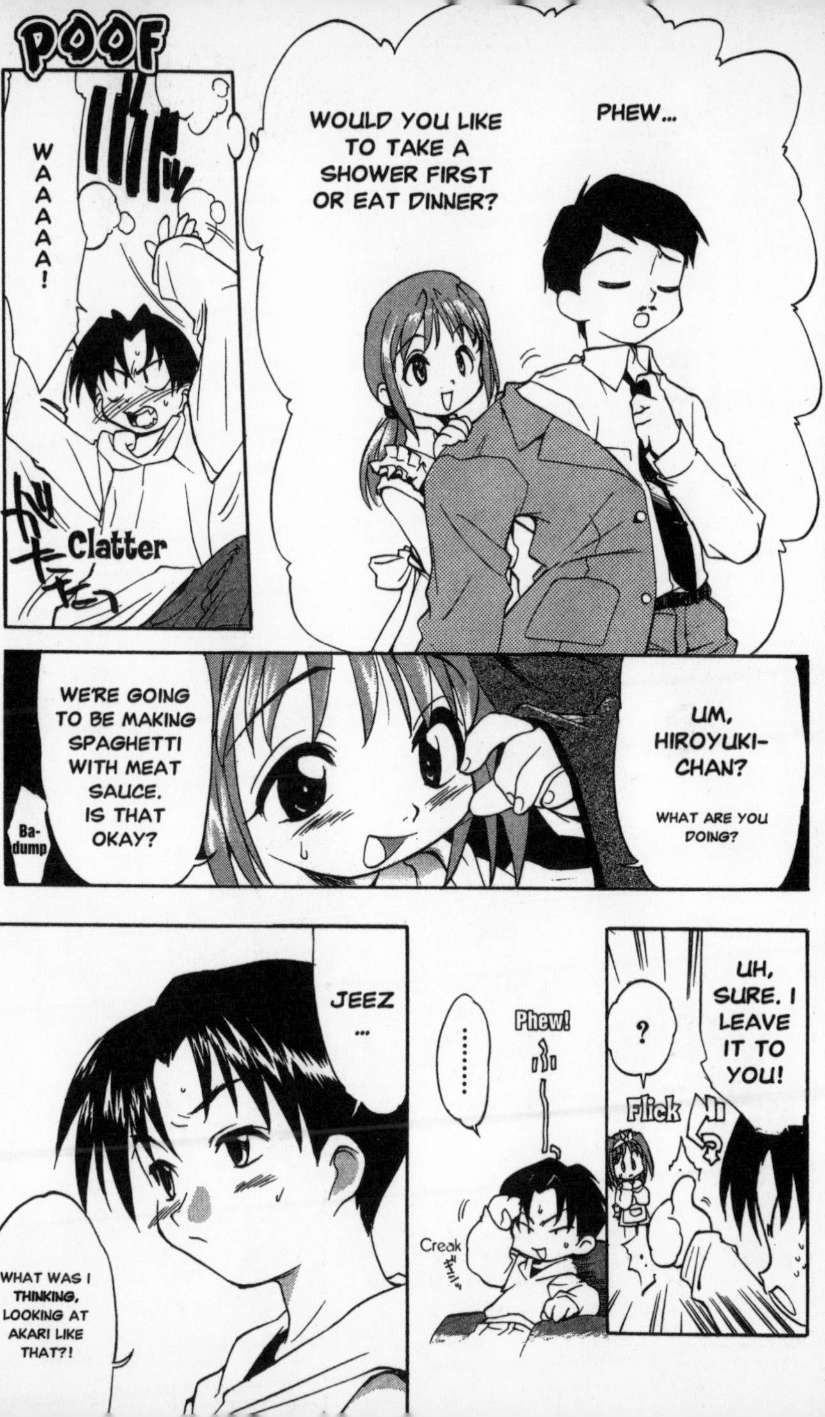
PHEW...
WOULD YOU LIKE TO TAKE A SHOWER FIRST OR EAT DINNER?
POOF
WAAAAAA!
Clatter
UM, HIROYUKI-CHAN?
WHAT ARE YOU DOING?
WE'RE GOING TO BE MAKING SPAGHETTI WITH MEAT SAUCE. IS THAT OKAY?
Ba-dump
UH, SURE. I LEAVE IT TO YOU!
?
Flick
Phew!
Creak
....
JEEZ...
WHAT WAS I THINKING, LOOKING AT AKARI LIKE THAT?!

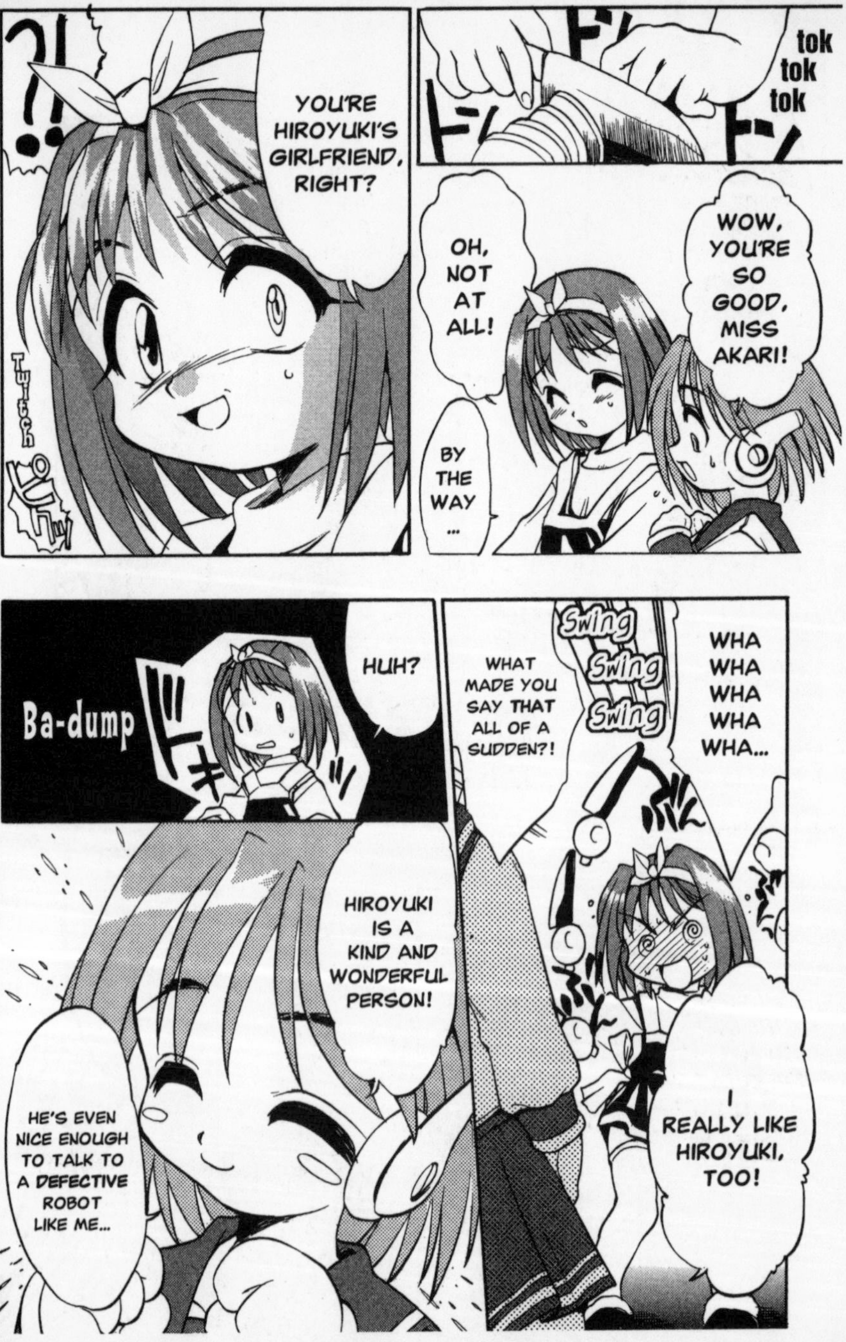
tok
tok
tok
ドン
ドン
WOW, YOU'RE SO GOOD, MISS AKARI!
OH, NOT AT ALL!
BY THE WAY ...
YOU'RE HIROYUKI'S GIRLFRIEND, RIGHT?
?!
Twitch
Ba-dump
HUH?
WHA WHA WHA WHA WHA...
Swing
Swing
Swing
WHAT MADE YOU SAY THAT ALL OF A SUDDEN?!
HIROYUKI IS A KIND AND WONDERFUL PERSON!
HE'S EVEN NICE ENOUGH TO TALK TO A DEFECTIVE ROBOT LIKE ME...
I REALLY LIKE HIROYUKI, TOO!

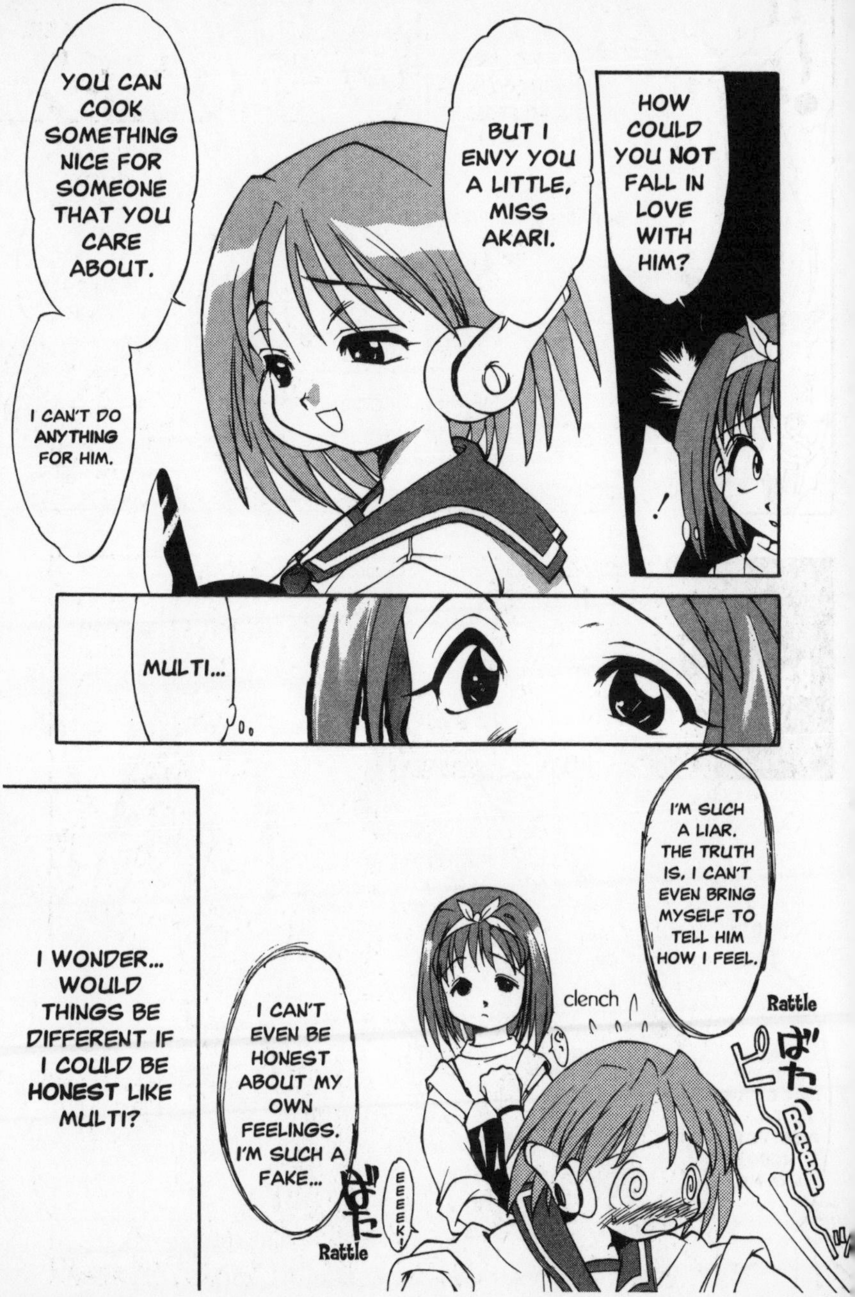
HOW COULD YOU NOT FALL IN LOVE WITH HIM?
!
BUT I ENVY YOU A LITTLE, MISS AKARI.
YOU CAN COOK SOMETHING NICE FOR SOMEONE THAT YOU CARE ABOUT.
I CAN'T DO ANYTHING FOR HIM.
MULTI...
I'M SUCH A LIAR. THE TRUTH IS, I CAN'T EVEN BRING MYSELF TO TELL HIM HOW I FEEL.
clench
Rattle
Beeep
I CAN'T EVEN BE HONEST ABOUT MY OWN FEELINGS. I'M SUCH A FAKE...
EEEEK!
Rattle
I WONDER... WOULD THINGS BE DIFFERENT IF I COULD BE HONEST LIKE MULTI?

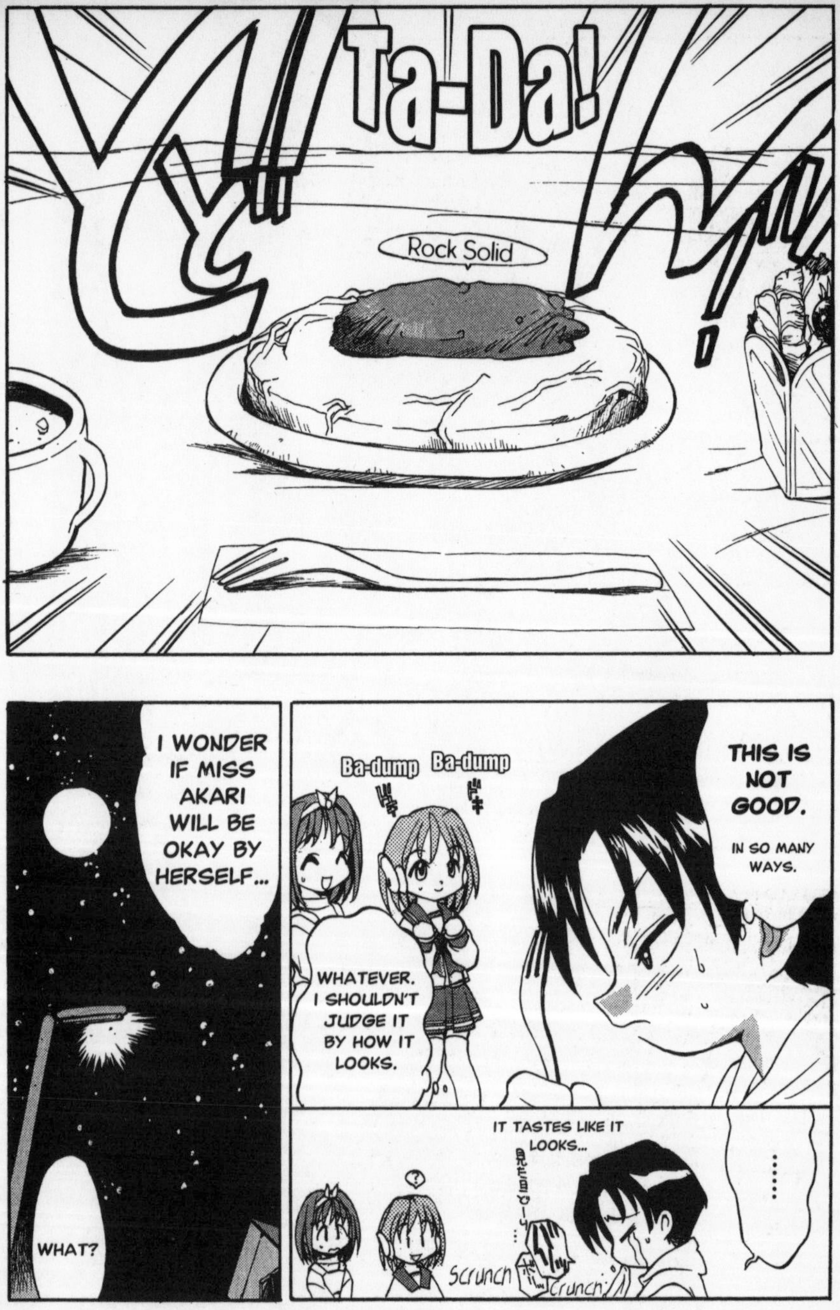
Ta-Da!
Rock Solid
THIS IS NOT GOOD.
IN SO MANY WAYS.
Ba-dump
Ba-dump
WHATEVER. I SHOULDN'T JUDGE IT BY HOW IT LOOKS.
I WONDER IF MISS AKARI WILL BE OKAY BY HERSELF...
......
IT TASTES LIKE IT LOOKS...
?
Scrunch
Crunch
WHAT?

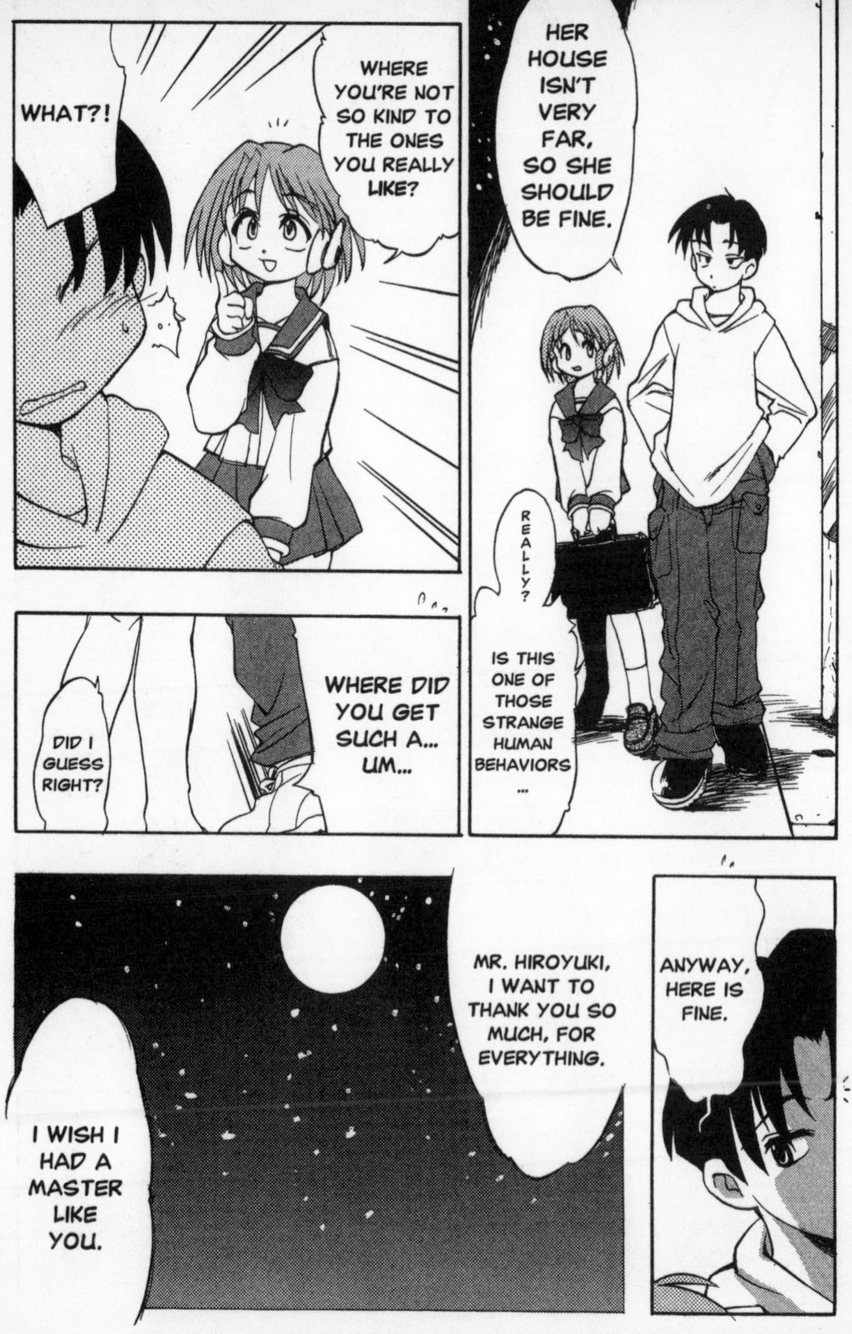
HER HOUSE ISN'T VERY FAR, SO SHE SHOULD BE FINE.
REALLY?
IS THIS ONE OF THOSE STRANGE HUMAN BEHAVIORS...
WHERE YOU'RE NOT SO KIND TO THE ONES YOU REALLY LIKE?
WHAT?!
WHERE DID YOU GET SUCH A... UM...
DID I GUESS RIGHT?
ANYWAY, HERE IS FINE.
MR. HIROYUKI, I WANT TO THANK YOU SO MUCH, FOR EVERYTHING.
I WISH I HAD A MASTER LIKE YOU.

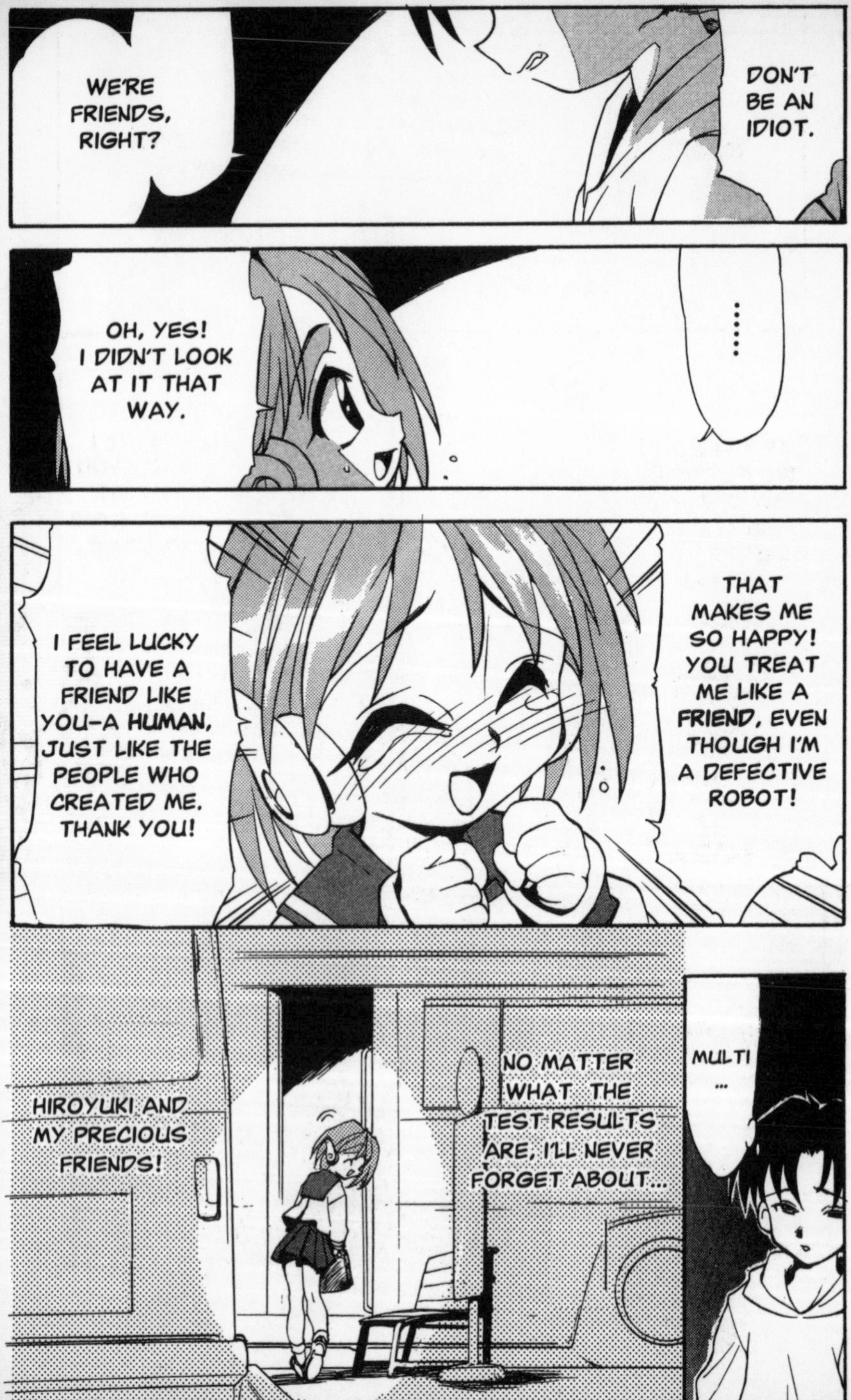
WE'RE FRIENDS, RIGHT?
DON'T BE AN IDIOT.
OH, YES! I DIDN'T LOOK AT IT THAT WAY.
......
I FEEL LUCKY TO HAVE A FRIEND LIKE YOU–A HUMAN, JUST LIKE THE PEOPLE WHO CREATED ME. THANK YOU!
THAT MAKES ME SO HAPPY! YOU TREAT ME LIKE A FRIEND, EVEN THOUGH I'M A DEFECTIVE ROBOT!
NO MATTER WHAT THE TEST RESULTS ARE, I'LL NEVER FORGET ABOUT...
HIROYUKI AND MY PRECIOUS FRIENDS!
MULTI ...

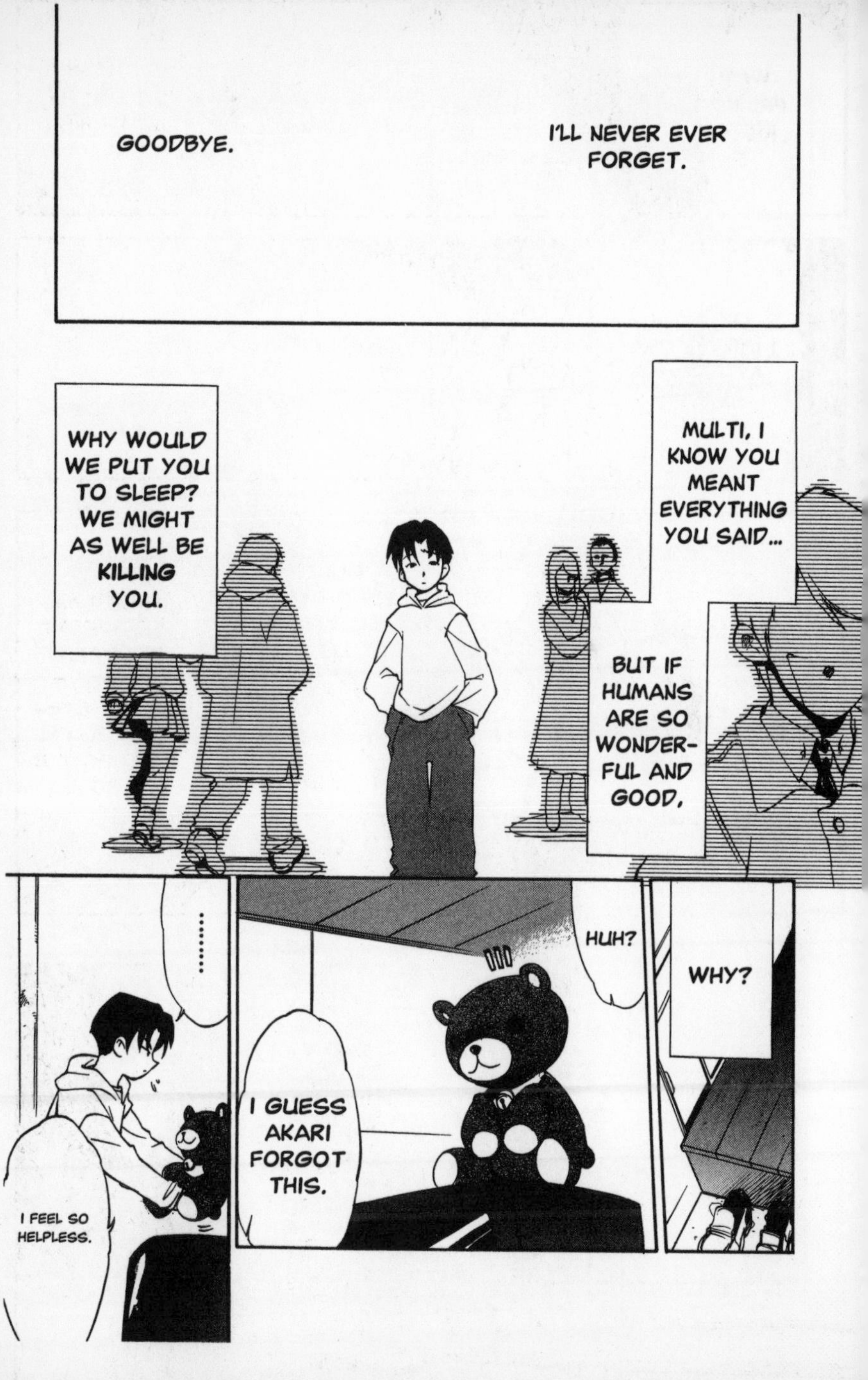
I'LL NEVER EVER FORGET.
GOODBYE.
MULTI, I KNOW YOU MEANT EVERYTHING YOU SAID...
BUT IF HUMANS ARE SO WONDER-FUL AND GOOD,
WHY WOULD WE PUT YOU TO SLEEP? WE MIGHT AS WELL BE KILLING YOU.
WHY?
HUH?
I GUESS AKARI FORGOT THIS.
....
I FEEL SO HELPLESS.

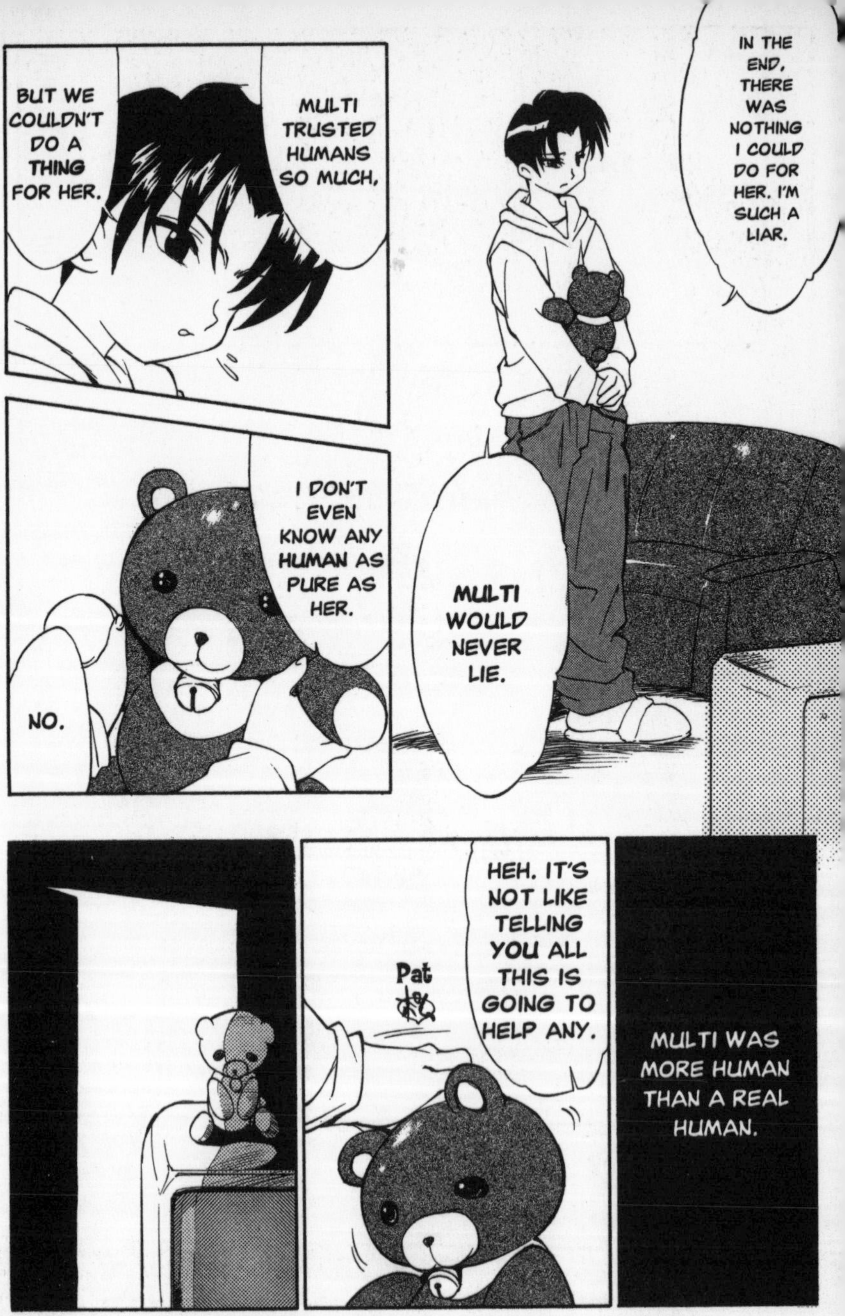

MULTI TRUSTED HUMANS SO MUCH,
BUT WE COULDN'T DO A THING FOR HER.
I DON'T EVEN KNOW ANY HUMAN AS PURE AS HER.
NO.
MULTI WOULD NEVER LIE.
IN THE END, THERE WAS NOTHING I COULD DO FOR HER. I'M SUCH A LIAR.
Pat
HEH. IT'S NOT LIKE TELLING YOU ALL THIS IS GOING TO HELP ANY.
MULTI WAS MORE HUMAN THAN A REAL HUMAN.

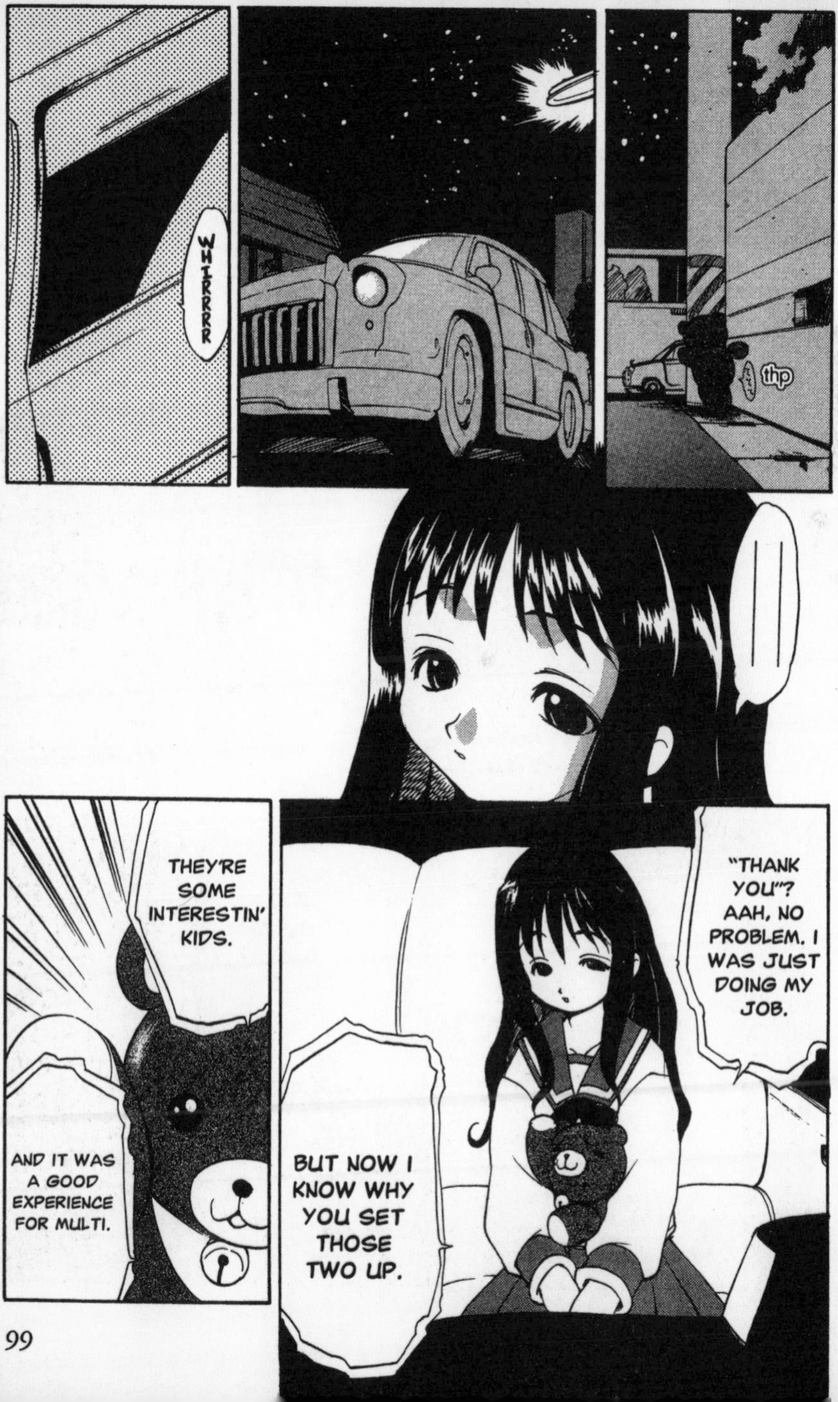
WHIRRRR
thp
"THANK YOU"? AAH, NO PROBLEM. I WAS JUST DOING MY JOB.
BUT NOW I KNOW WHY YOU SET THOSE TWO UP.
THEY'RE SOME INTERESTIN' KIDS.
AND IT WAS A GOOD EXPERIENCE FOR MULTI.

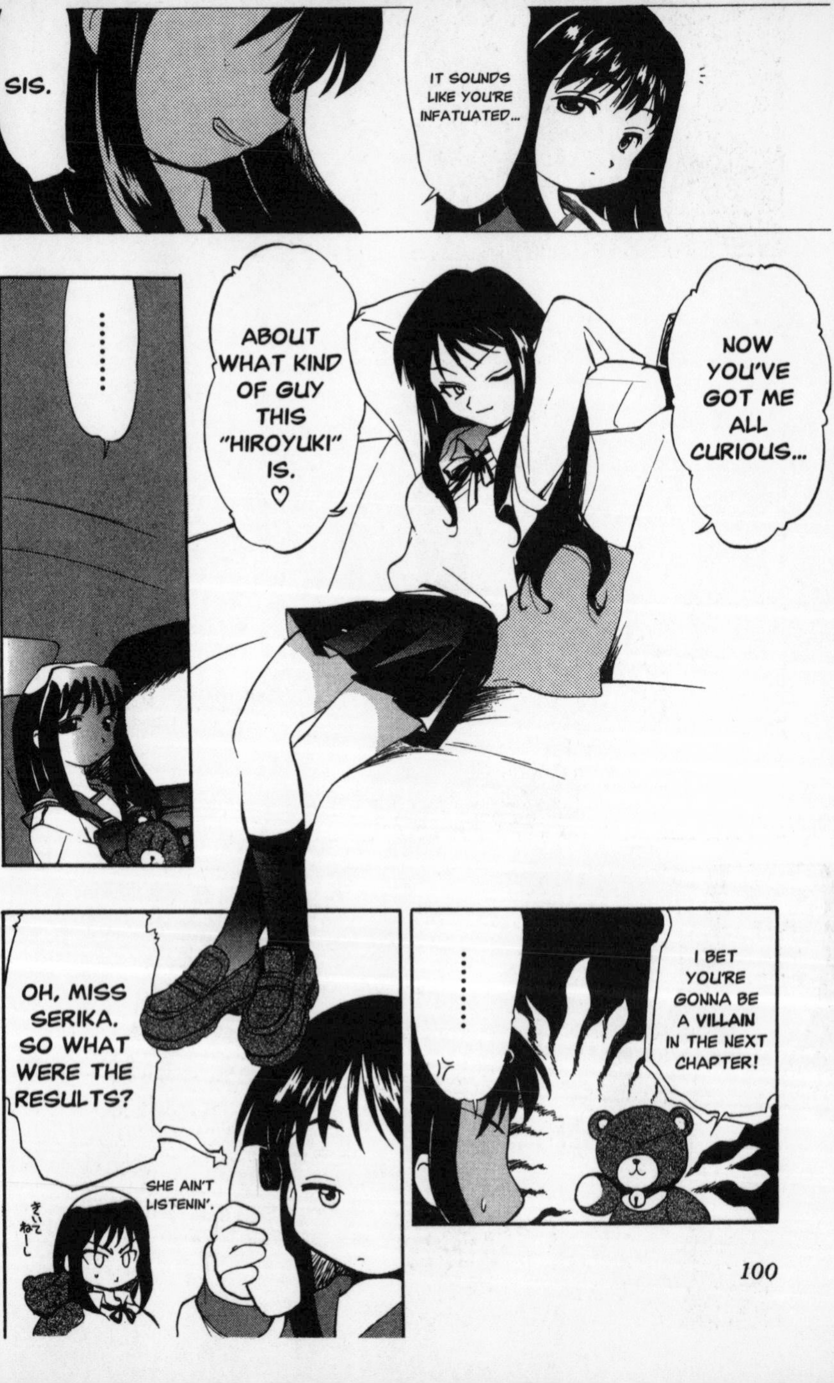
IT SOUNDS LIKE YOU'RE INFATUATED...
SIS.
NOW YOU'VE GOT ME ALL CURIOUS...
ABOUT WHAT KIND OF GUY THIS "HIROYUKI" IS. ♡
....
I BET YOU'RE GONNA BE A VILLAIN IN THE NEXT CHAPTER!
....
OH, MISS SERIKA. SO WHAT WERE THE RESULTS?
SHE AIN'T LISTENIN'.
きいてねーし

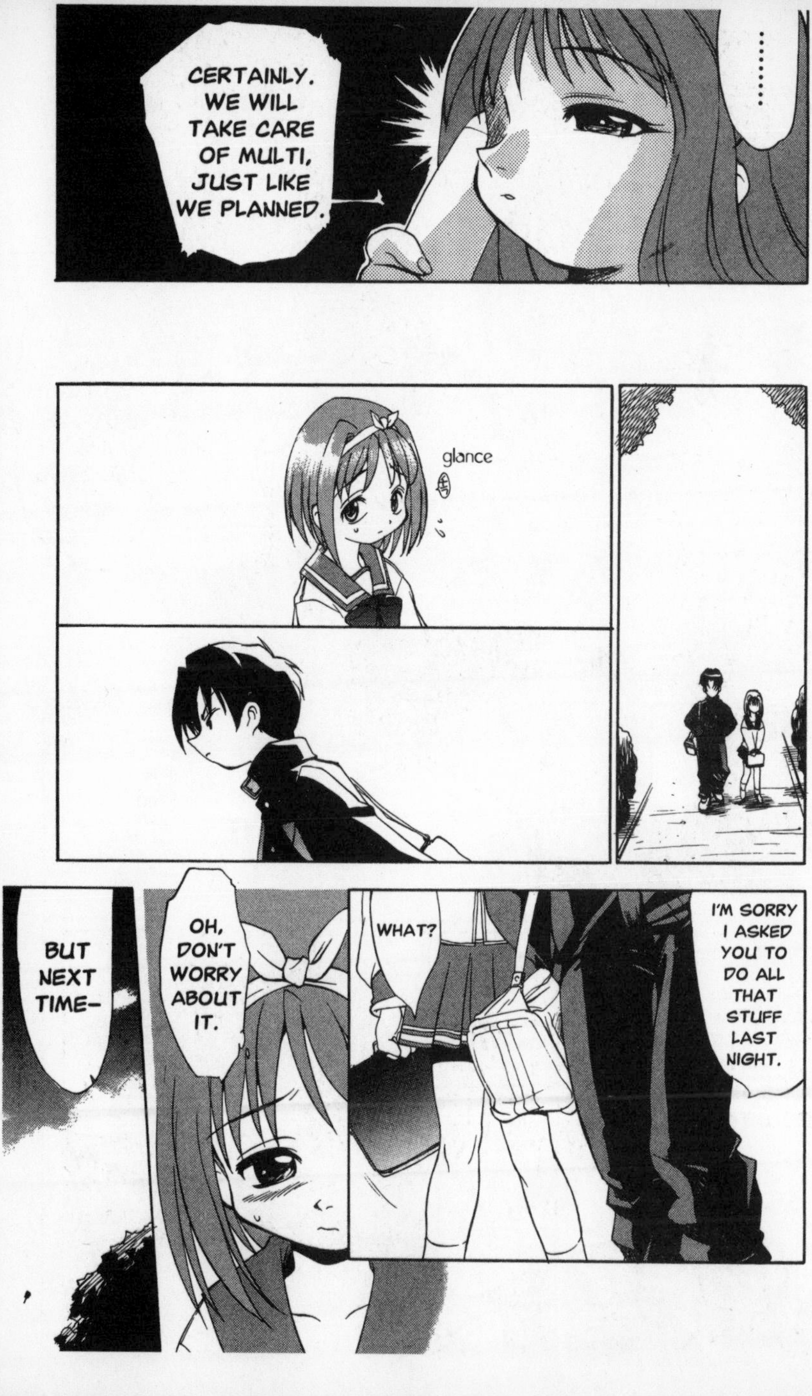
......
CERTAINLY. WE WILL TAKE CARE OF MULTI, JUST LIKE WE PLANNED.
glance
I'M SORRY I ASKED YOU TO DO ALL THAT STUFF LAST NIGHT.
WHAT?
OH, DON'T WORRY ABOUT IT.
BUT NEXT TIME-

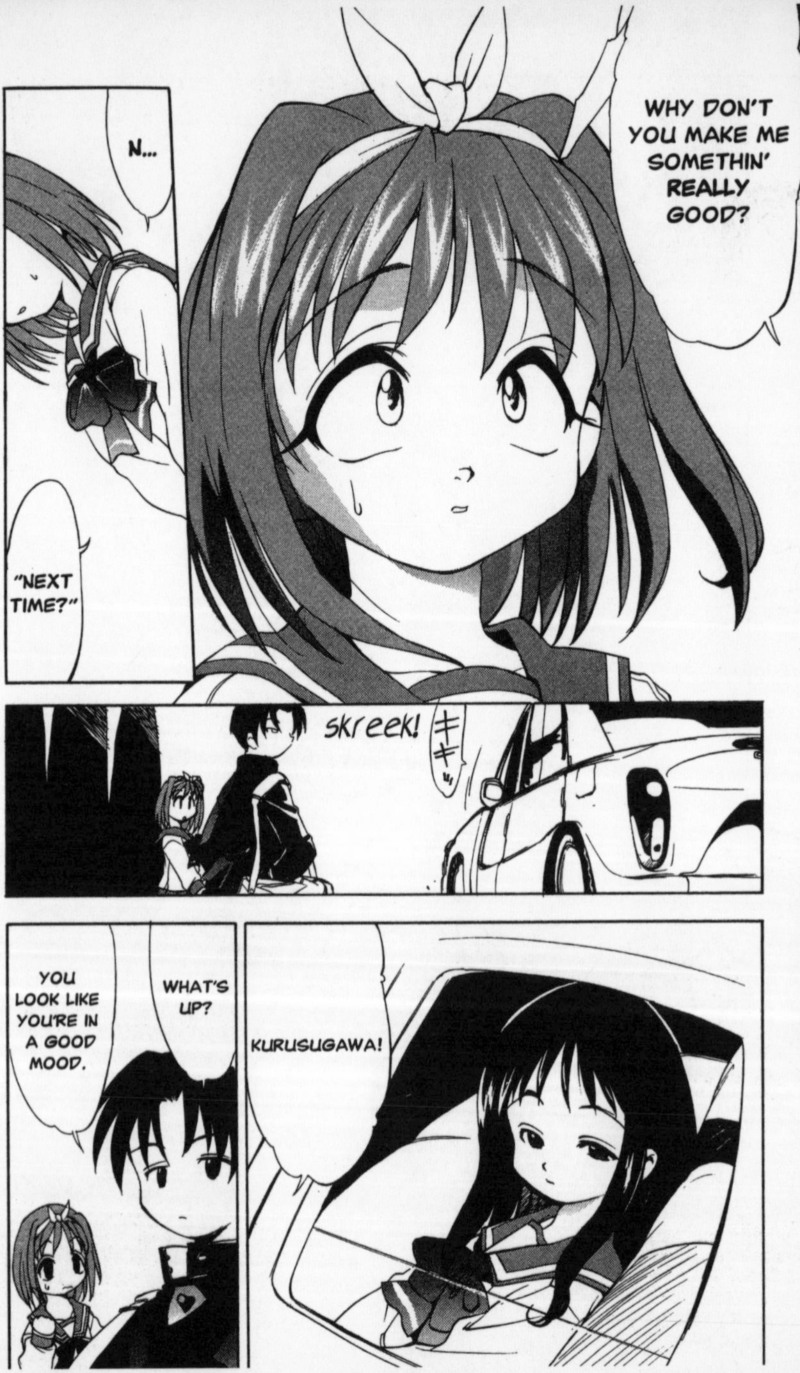
WHY DON'T YOU MAKE ME SOMETHIN' REALLY GOOD?
N...
"NEXT TIME?"
キキッ
SKREEK!
KURUSUGAWA!
WHAT'S UP?
YOU LOOK LIKE YOU'RE IN A GOOD MOOD.

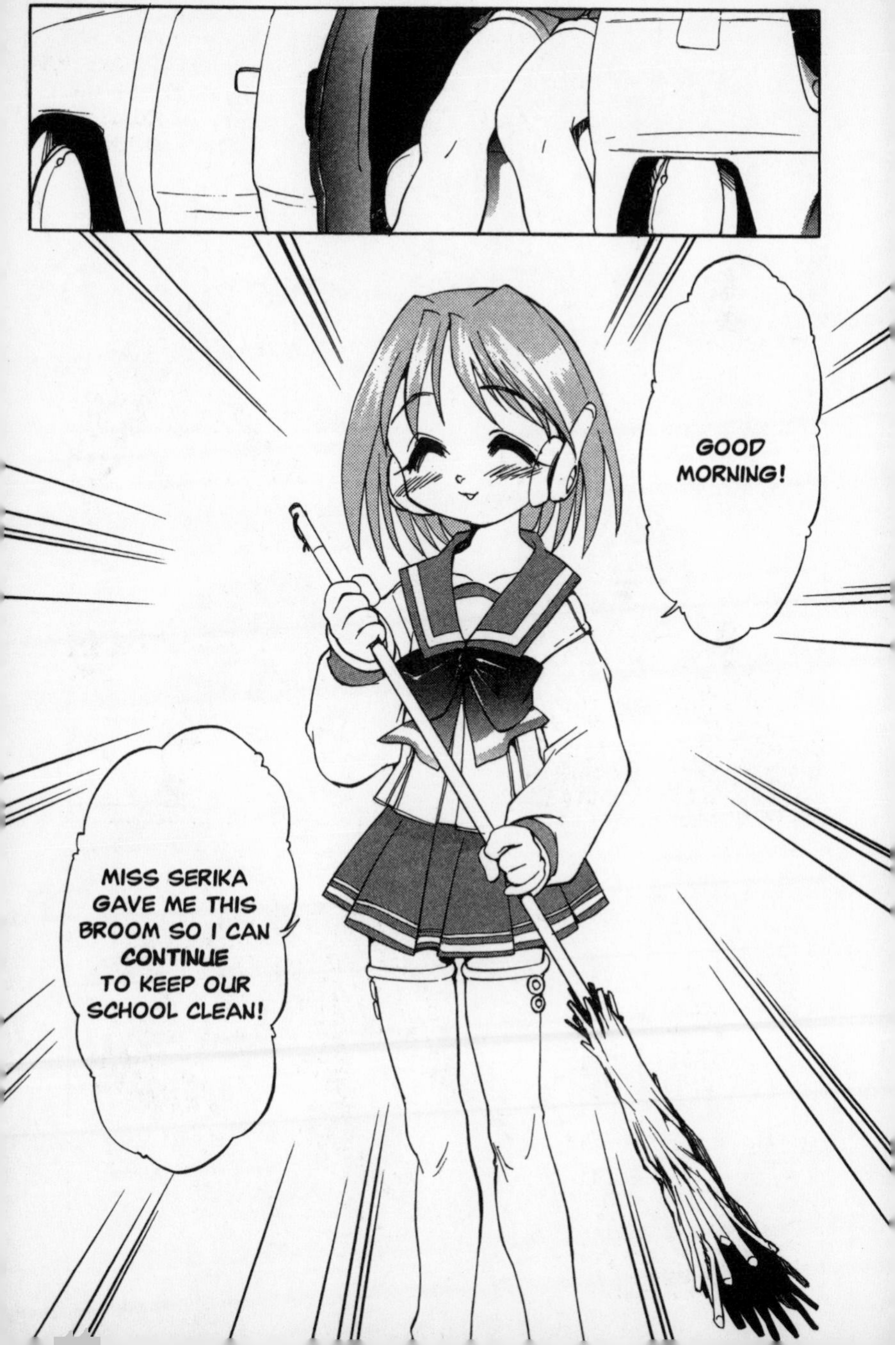
GOOD MORNING!
MISS SERIKA GAVE ME THIS BROOM SO I CAN CONTINUE TO KEEP OUR SCHOOL CLEAN!

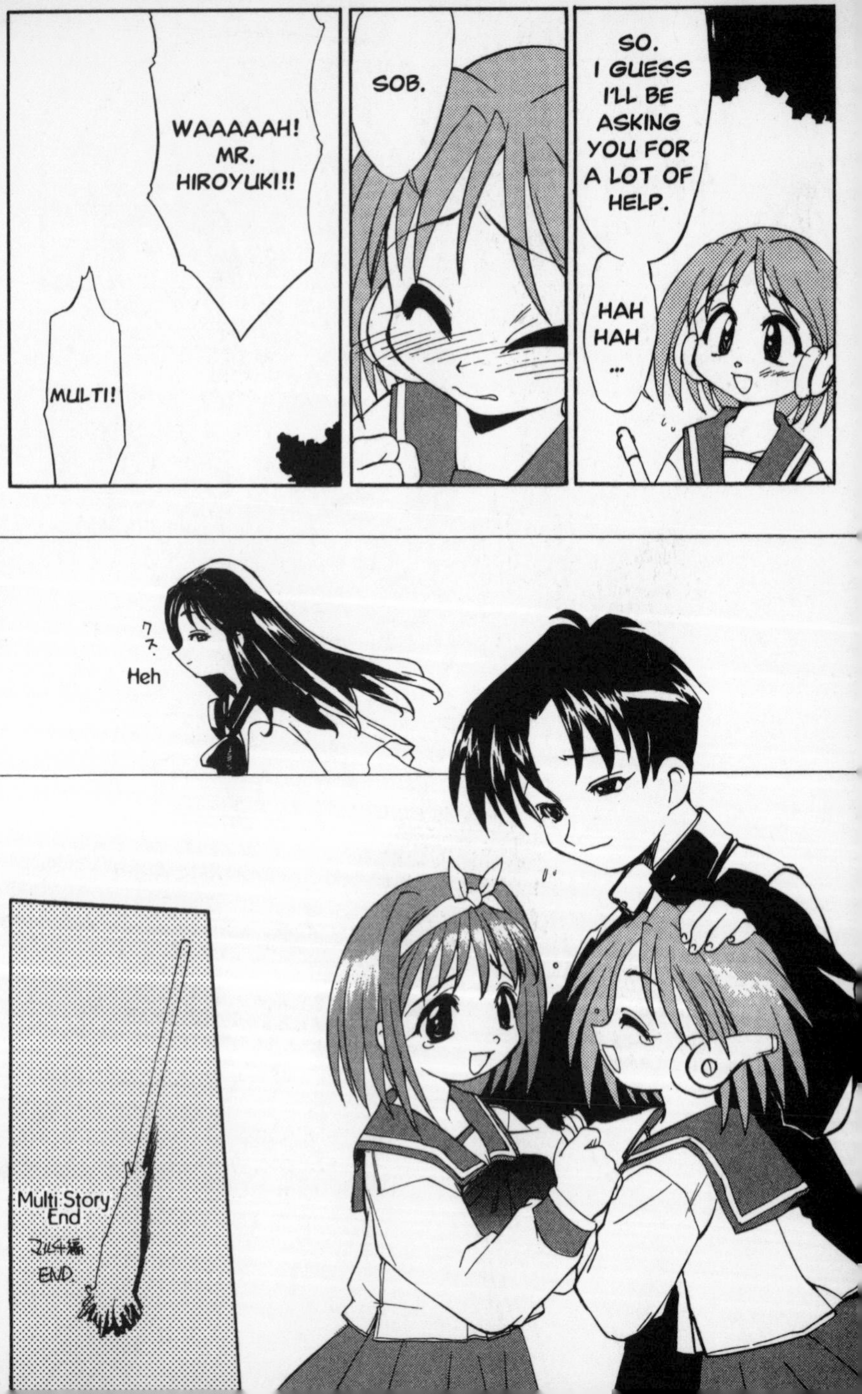
SO. I GUESS I'LL BE ASKING YOU FOR A LOT OF HELP.
HAH HAH ...
SOB.
WAAAAAH! MR. HIROYUKI!!
MULTI!
クス.
Heh
Multi Story End
マルチ編
END.

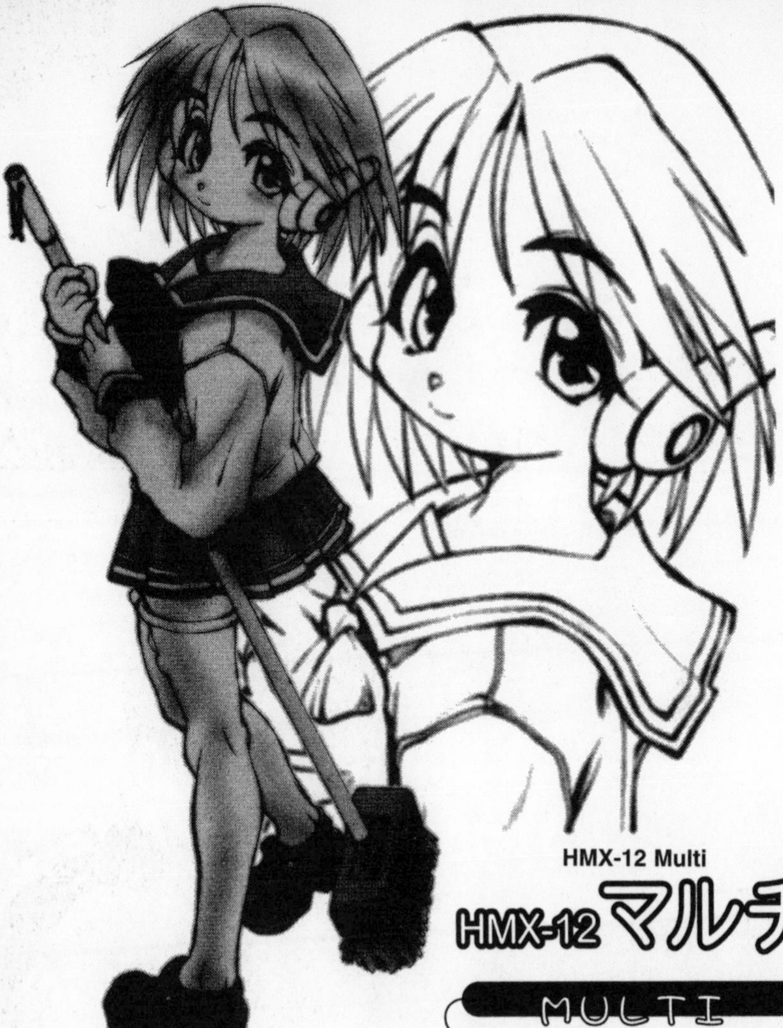

HMX-12 Multi

HMX-12 マルチ

MULTI

MULTI IS THE PUREST GIRL IN THE WORLD. IT DOESN'T MATTER THAT SHE'S A ROBOT – WE HAVE TO MAKE A PEACEFUL WORLD, WHERE A GIRL LIKE HER CAN BE HAPPY!

Episode 3
『"Magical Girl"』
~Serika Kurusugawa~

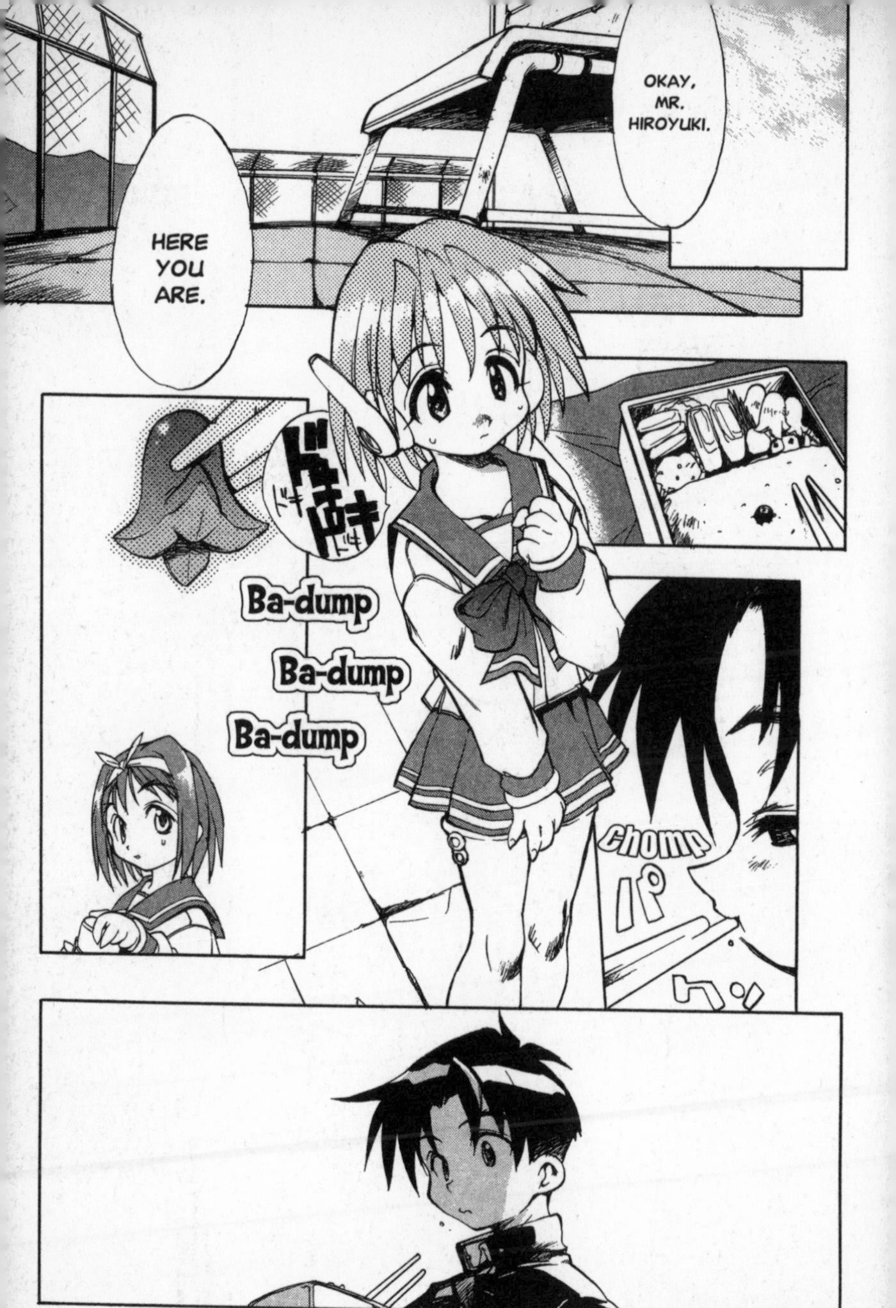
OKAY, MR. HIROYUKI.
HERE YOU ARE.
Ba-dump
Ba-dump
Ba-dump
chomp

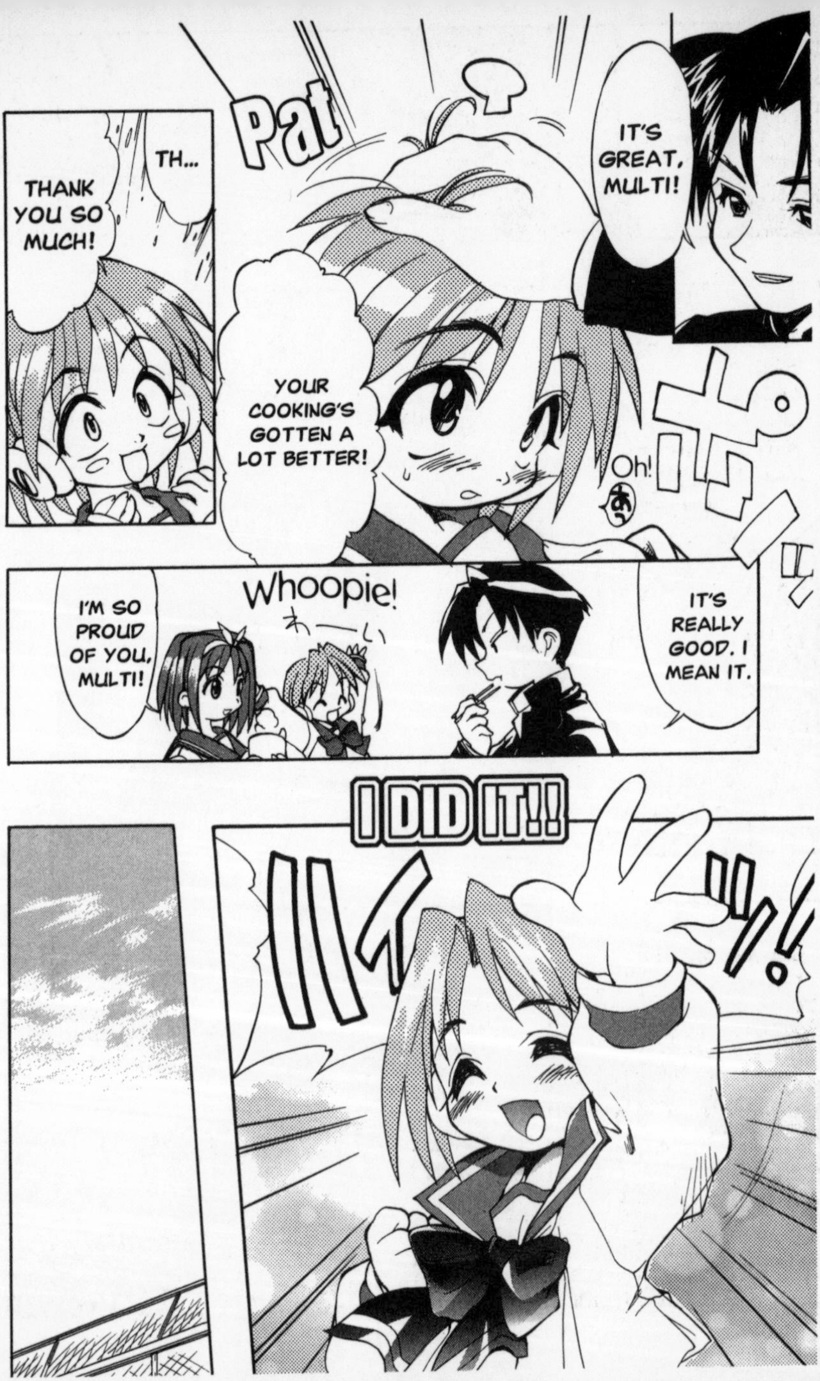
IT'S GREAT, MULTI!
Pat
YOUR COOKING'S GOTTEN A LOT BETTER!
Oh!
TH...
THANK YOU SO MUCH!
IT'S REALLY GOOD. I MEAN IT.
Whoopie!
わーい
I'M SO PROUD OF YOU, MULTI!
I DID IT!!

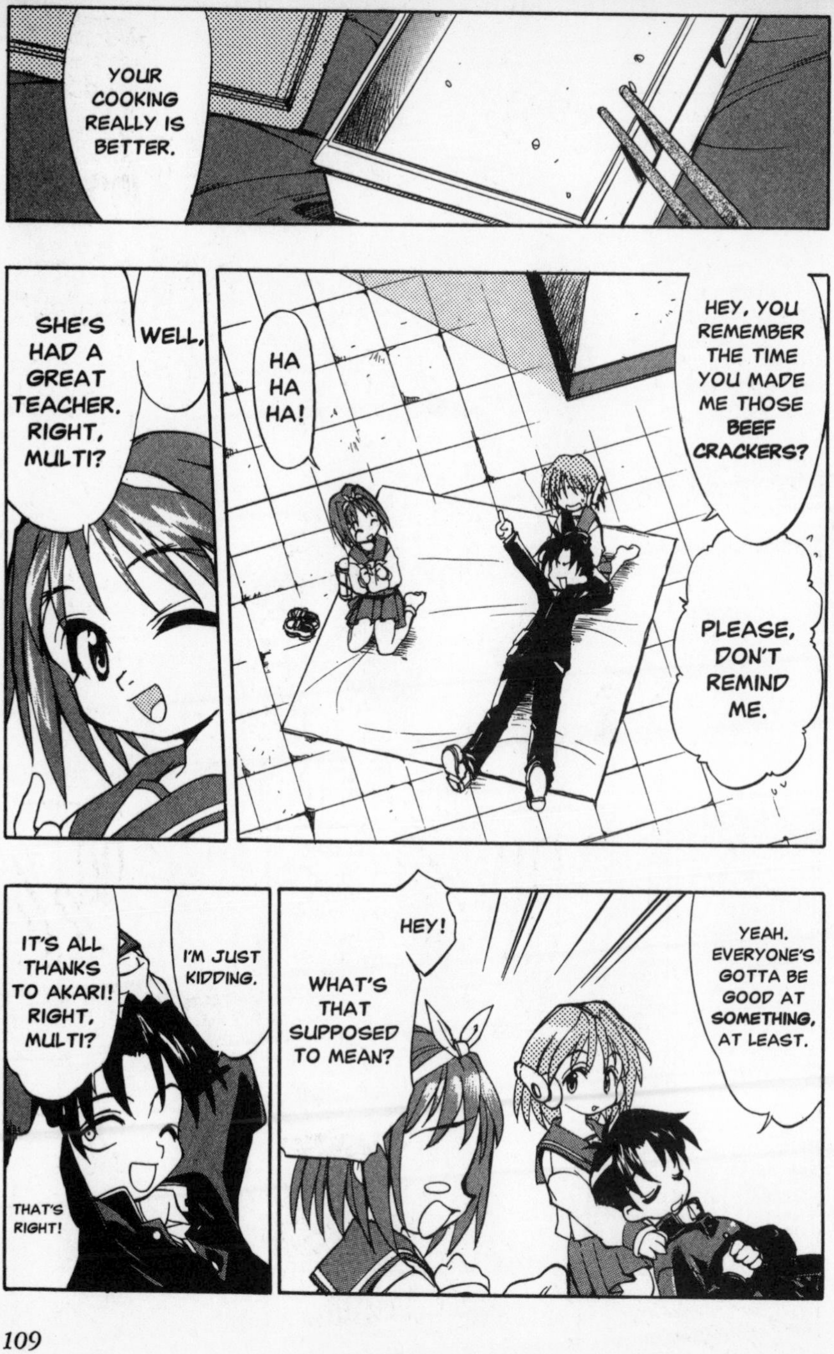
YOUR COOKING REALLY IS BETTER.
HEY, YOU REMEMBER THE TIME YOU MADE ME THOSE BEEF CRACKERS?
PLEASE, DON'T REMIND ME.
HA HA HA!
WELL,
SHE'S HAD A GREAT TEACHER. RIGHT, MULTI?
YEAH. EVERYONE'S GOTTA BE GOOD AT SOMETHING, AT LEAST.
HEY!
WHAT'S THAT SUPPOSED TO MEAN?
I'M JUST KIDDING.
IT'S ALL THANKS TO AKARI! RIGHT, MULTI?
THAT'S RIGHT!

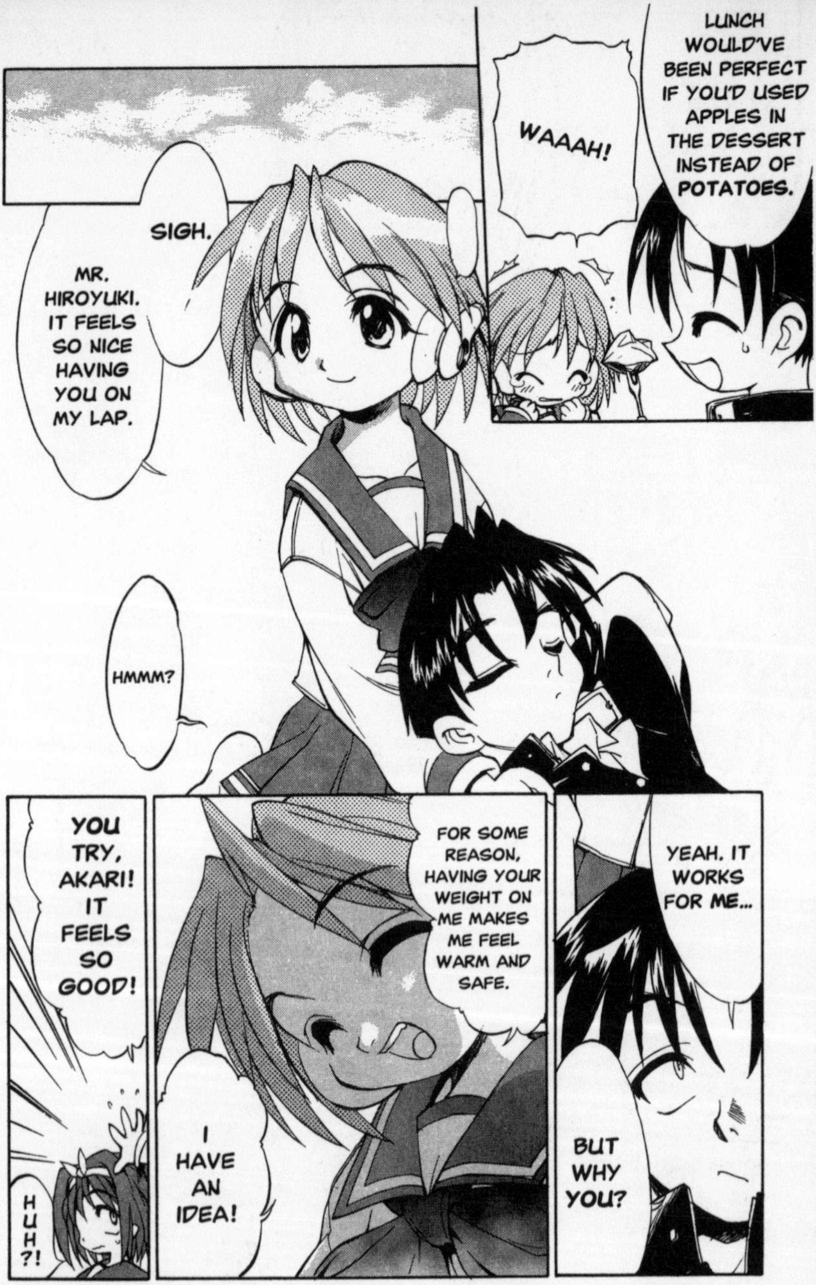

LUNCH WOULD'VE BEEN PERFECT IF YOU'D USED APPLES IN THE DESSERT INSTEAD OF POTATOES.
WAAAH!
SIGH.
MR. HIROYUKI. IT FEELS SO NICE HAVING YOU ON MY LAP.
HMMM?
YEAH. IT WORKS FOR ME...
BUT WHY YOU?
FOR SOME REASON, HAVING YOUR WEIGHT ON ME MAKES ME FEEL WARM AND SAFE.
I HAVE AN IDEA!
YOU TRY, AKARI! IT FEELS SO GOOD!
HUH?!

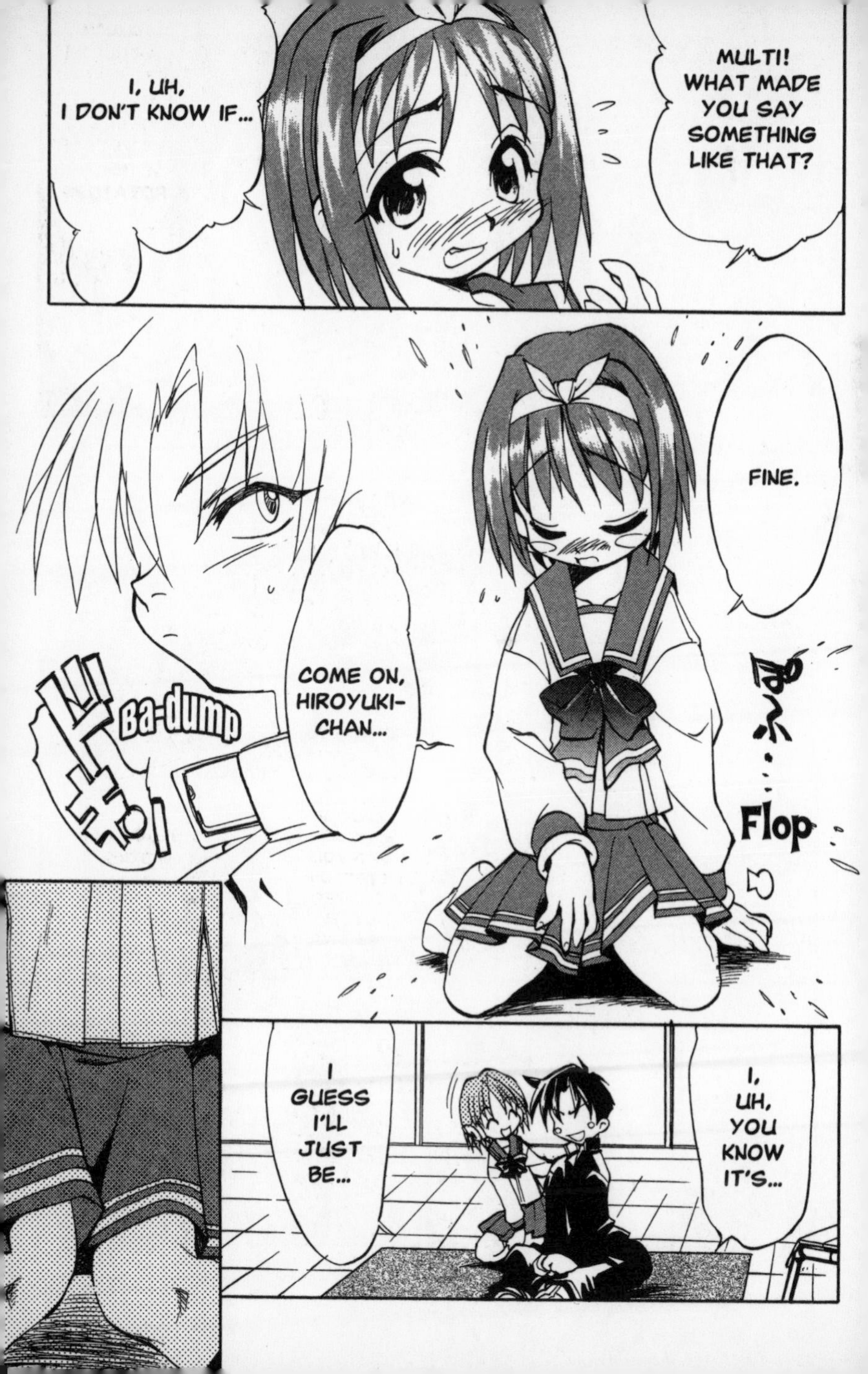
MULTI! WHAT MADE YOU SAY SOMETHING LIKE THAT?
I, UH, I DON'T KNOW IF...
FINE.
Flop
COME ON, HIROYUKI-CHAN...
Ba-dump
I, UH, YOU KNOW IT'S...
I GUESS I'LL JUST BE...

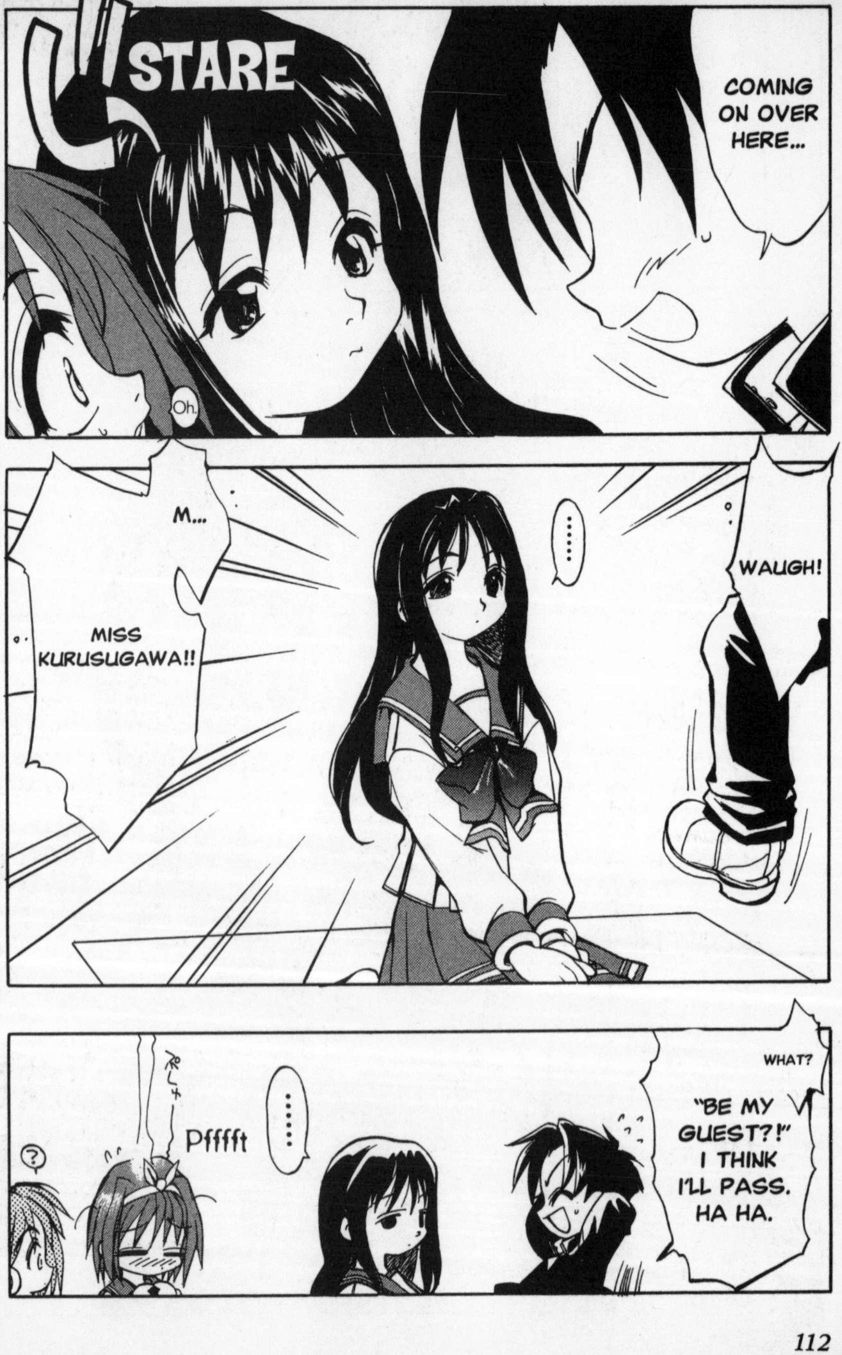
COMING ON OVER HERE...
STARE
Oh.
WAUGH!
......
M...
MISS KURUSUGAWA!!
WHAT?
"BE MY GUEST?!" I THINK I'LL PASS. HA HA.
......
Pfffft
?

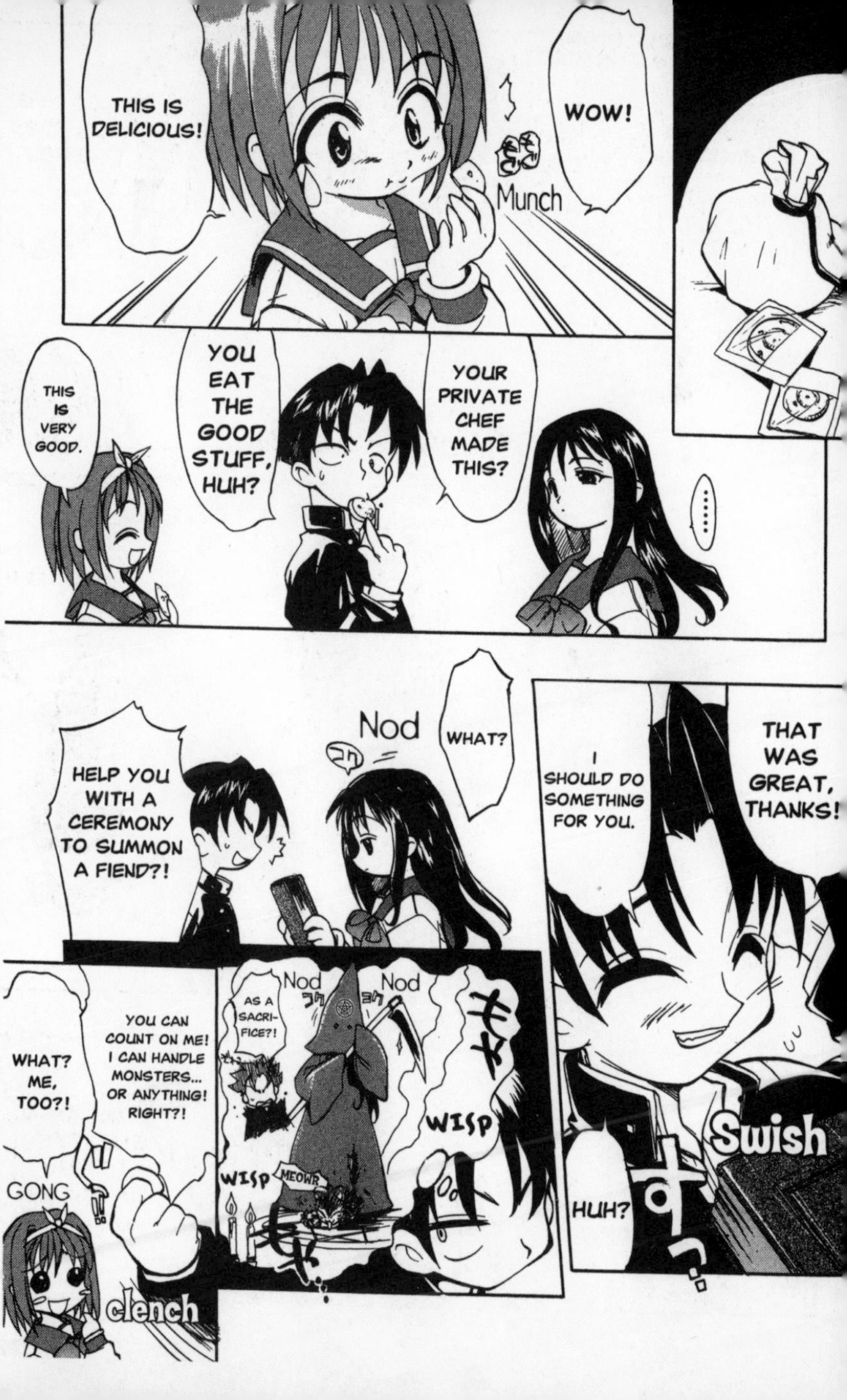
WOW!
Munch
THIS IS DELICIOUS!
YOUR PRIVATE CHEF MADE THIS?
YOU EAT THE GOOD STUFF, HUH?
THIS IS VERY GOOD.
......
THAT WAS GREAT, THANKS!
I SHOULD DO SOMETHING FOR YOU.
HUH?
Swish
WHAT?
Nod
HELP YOU WITH A CEREMONY TO SUMMON A FIEND?!
Nod
Nod
AS A SACRIFICE?!
WISP
WISP
MEOWR
YOU CAN COUNT ON ME! I CAN HANDLE MONSTERS... OR ANYTHING! RIGHT?!
WHAT? ME, TOO?!
GONG
clench

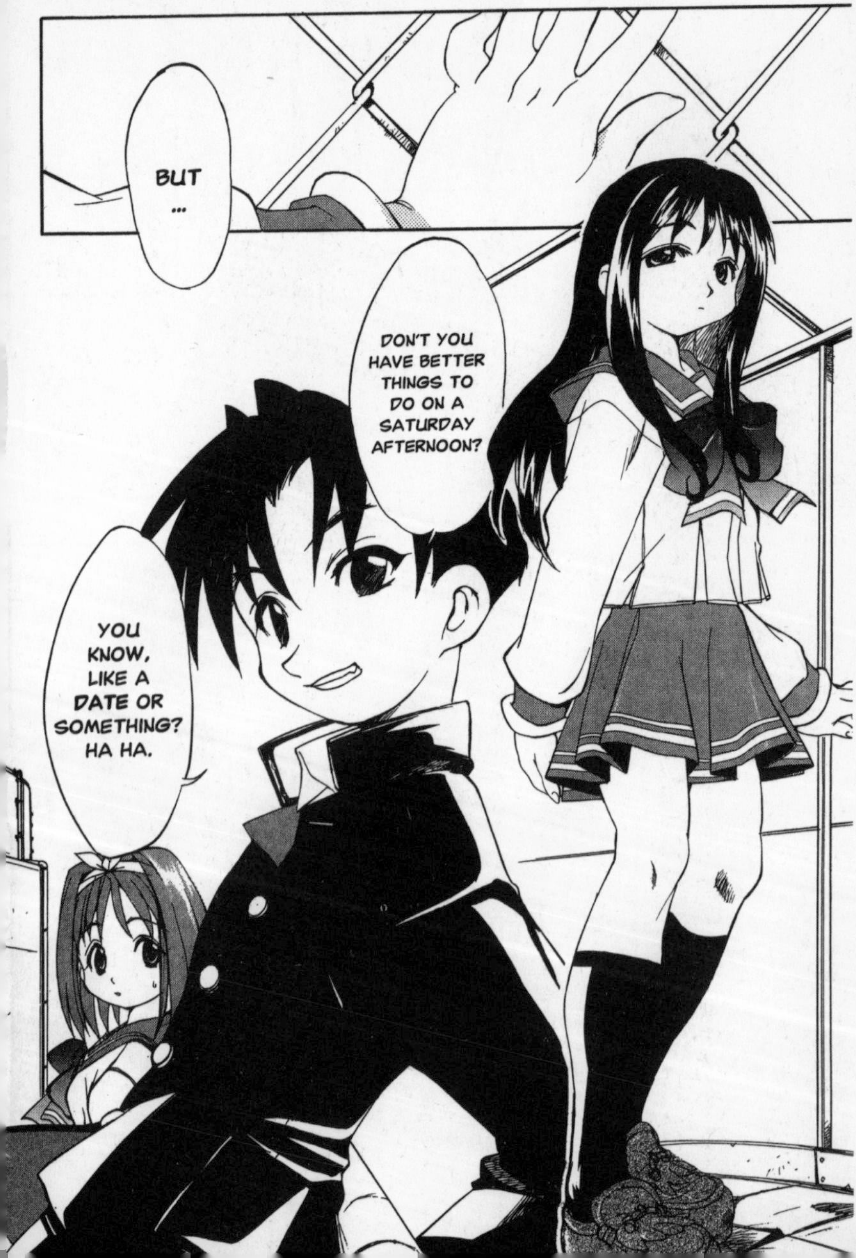
BUT ...
DON'T YOU HAVE BETTER THINGS TO DO ON A SATURDAY AFTERNOON?
YOU KNOW, LIKE A DATE OR SOMETHING? HA HA.

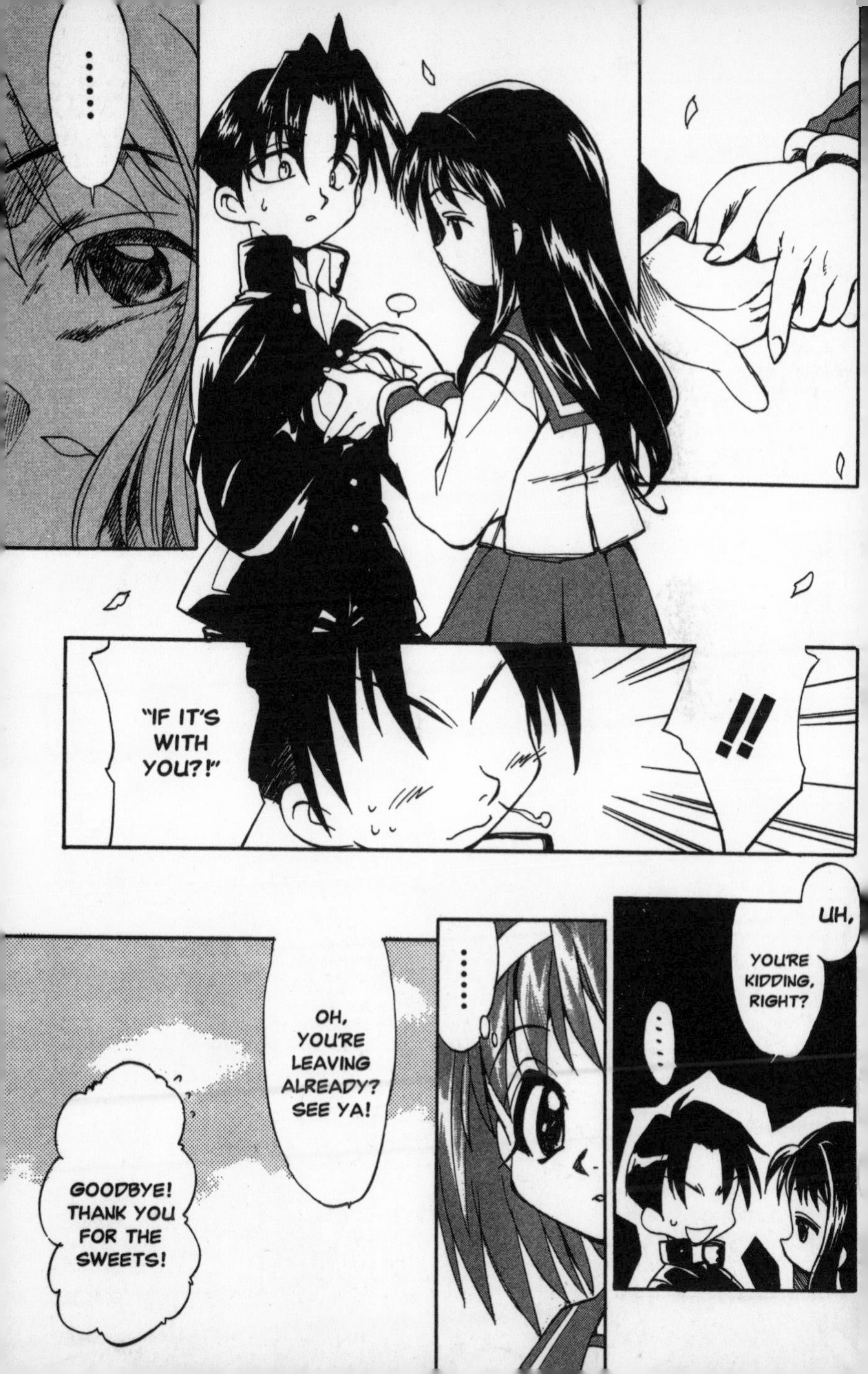

......
"IF IT'S WITH YOU?!"
!!
UH, YOU'RE KIDDING, RIGHT?
......
......
OH, YOU'RE LEAVING ALREADY? SEE YA!
GOODBYE! THANK YOU FOR THE SWEETS!

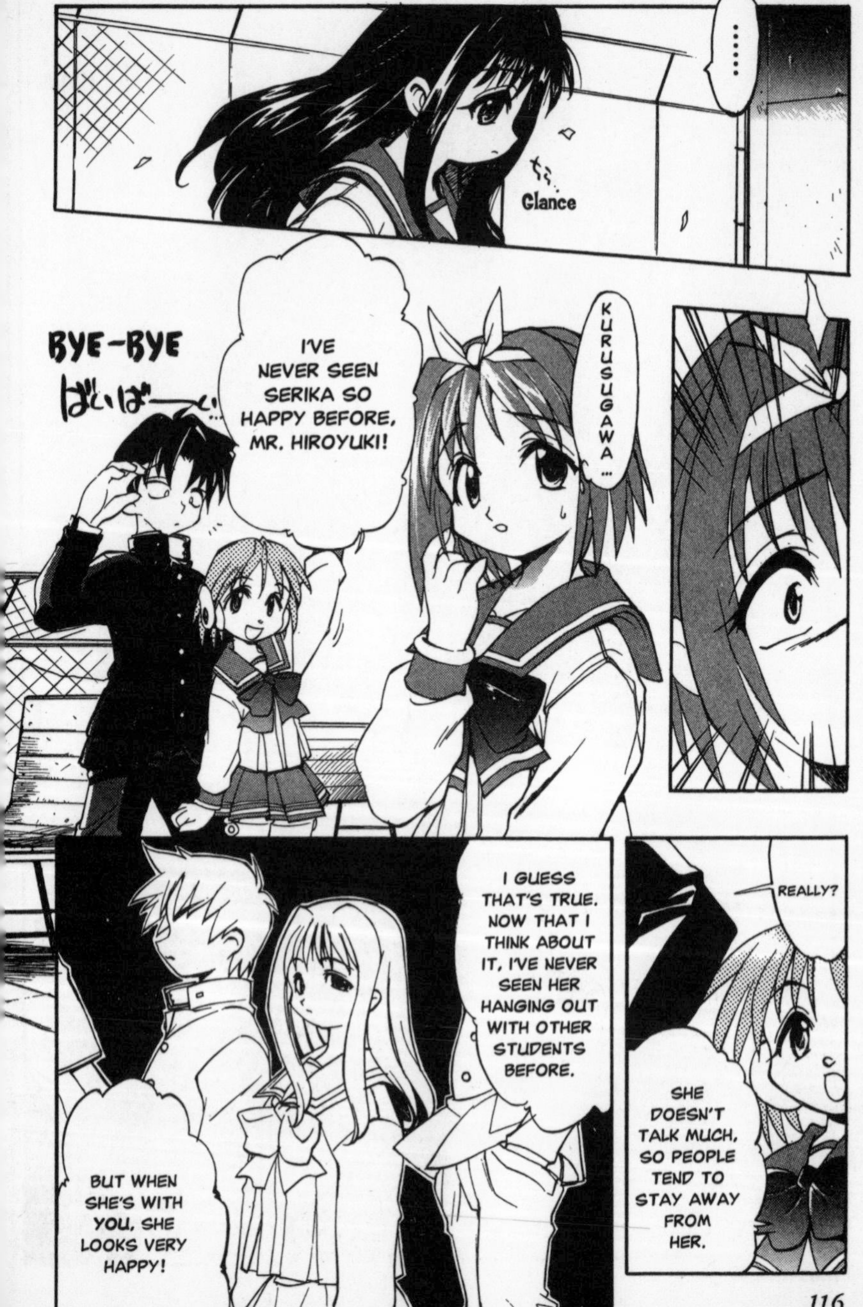

......
Glance
Kurusugawa...
I'VE NEVER SEEN SERIKA SO HAPPY BEFORE, MR. HIROYUKI!
BYE-BYE
ばいばーい
REALLY?
I GUESS THAT'S TRUE. NOW THAT I THINK ABOUT IT, I'VE NEVER SEEN HER HANGING OUT WITH OTHER STUDENTS BEFORE.
SHE DOESN'T TALK MUCH, SO PEOPLE TEND TO STAY AWAY FROM HER.
BUT WHEN SHE'S WITH YOU, SHE LOOKS VERY HAPPY!

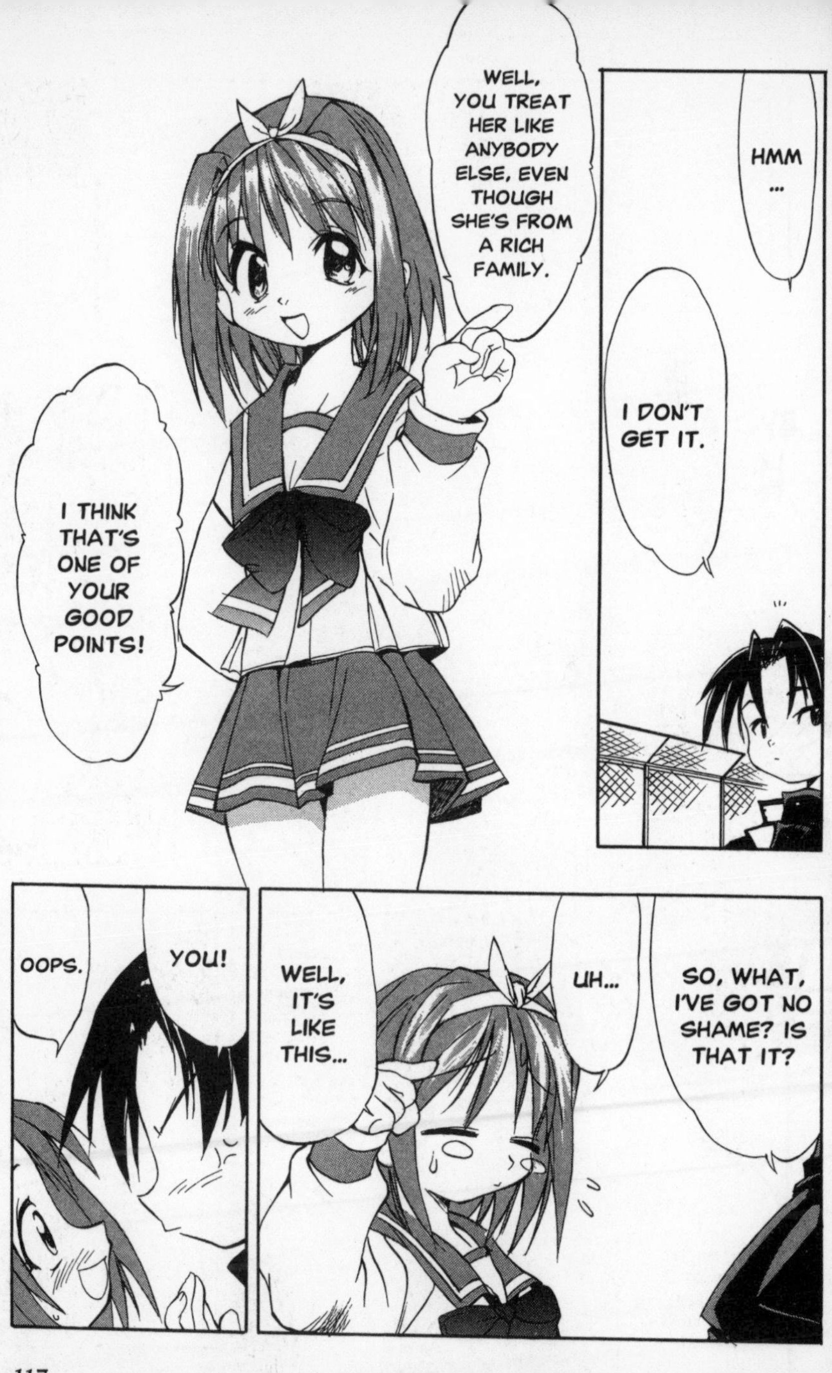
HMM ...
I DON'T GET IT.
WELL, YOU TREAT HER LIKE ANYBODY ELSE, EVEN THOUGH SHE'S FROM A RICH FAMILY.
I THINK THAT'S ONE OF YOUR GOOD POINTS!
SO, WHAT, I'VE GOT NO SHAME? IS THAT IT?
UH...
WELL, IT'S LIKE THIS...
YOU!
OOPS.

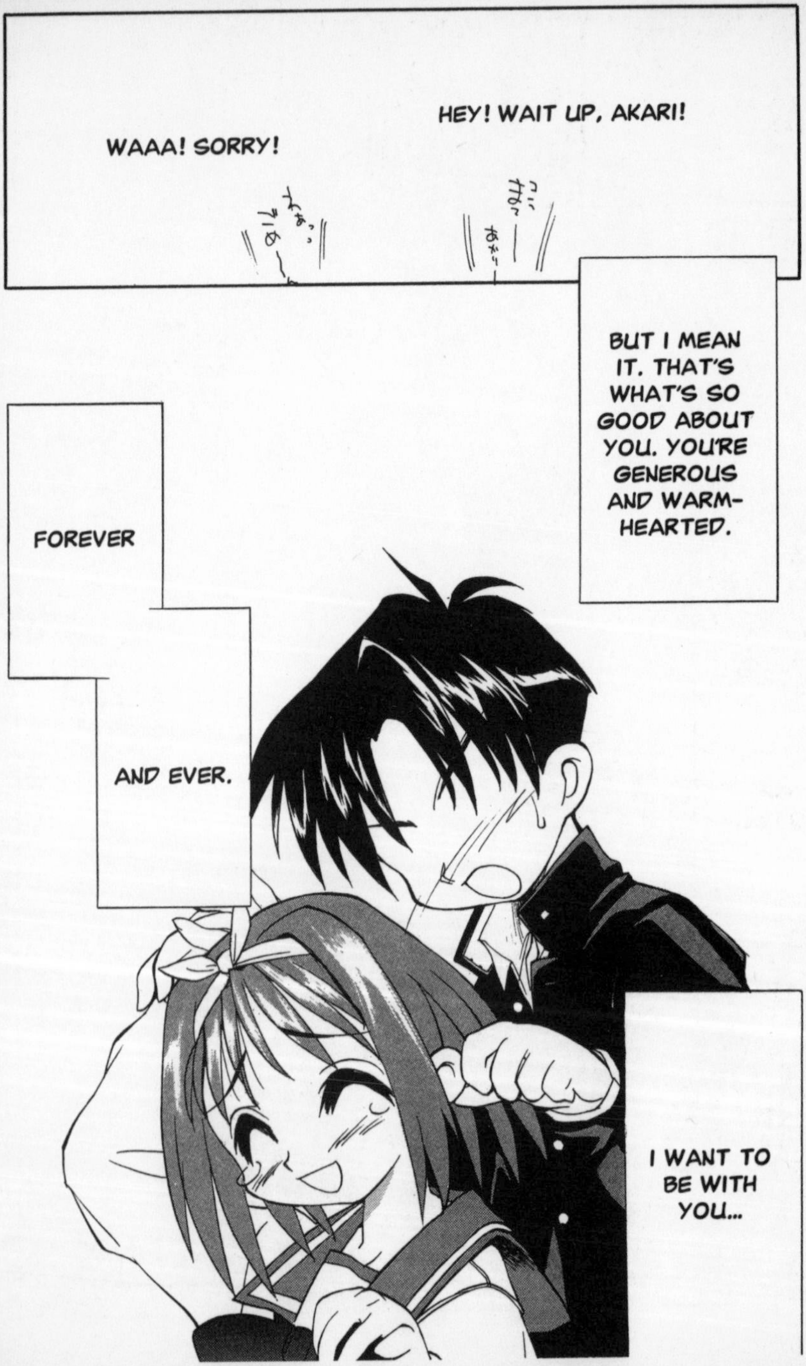
HEY! WAIT UP, AKARI!
WAAA! SORRY!
BUT I MEAN IT. THAT'S WHAT'S SO GOOD ABOUT YOU. YOU'RE GENEROUS AND WARM-HEARTED.
FOREVER
AND EVER.
I WANT TO BE WITH YOU...

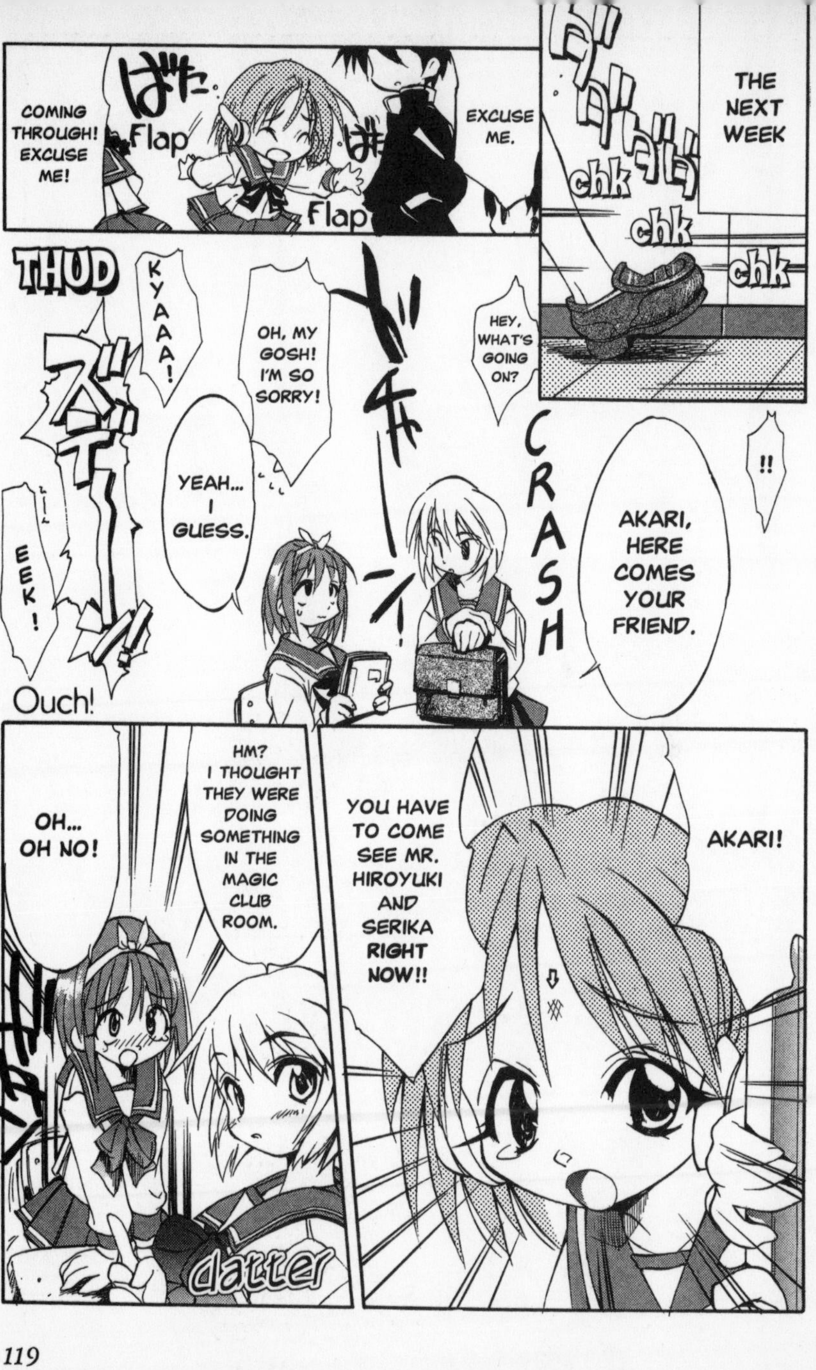
THE NEXT WEEK
chk
chk
chk
EXCUSE ME.
COMING THROUGH! EXCUSE ME!
Flap
Flap
HEY, WHAT'S GOING ON?
!!
AKARI, HERE COMES YOUR FRIEND.
CRASH
OH, MY GOSH! I'M SO SORRY!
YEAH... I GUESS.
KYAAA!
THUD
EEK!
Ouch!
AKARI!
YOU HAVE TO COME SEE MR. HIROYUKI AND SERIKA RIGHT NOW!!
HM? I THOUGHT THEY WERE DOING SOMETHING IN THE MAGIC CLUB ROOM.
OH... OH NO!
clatter

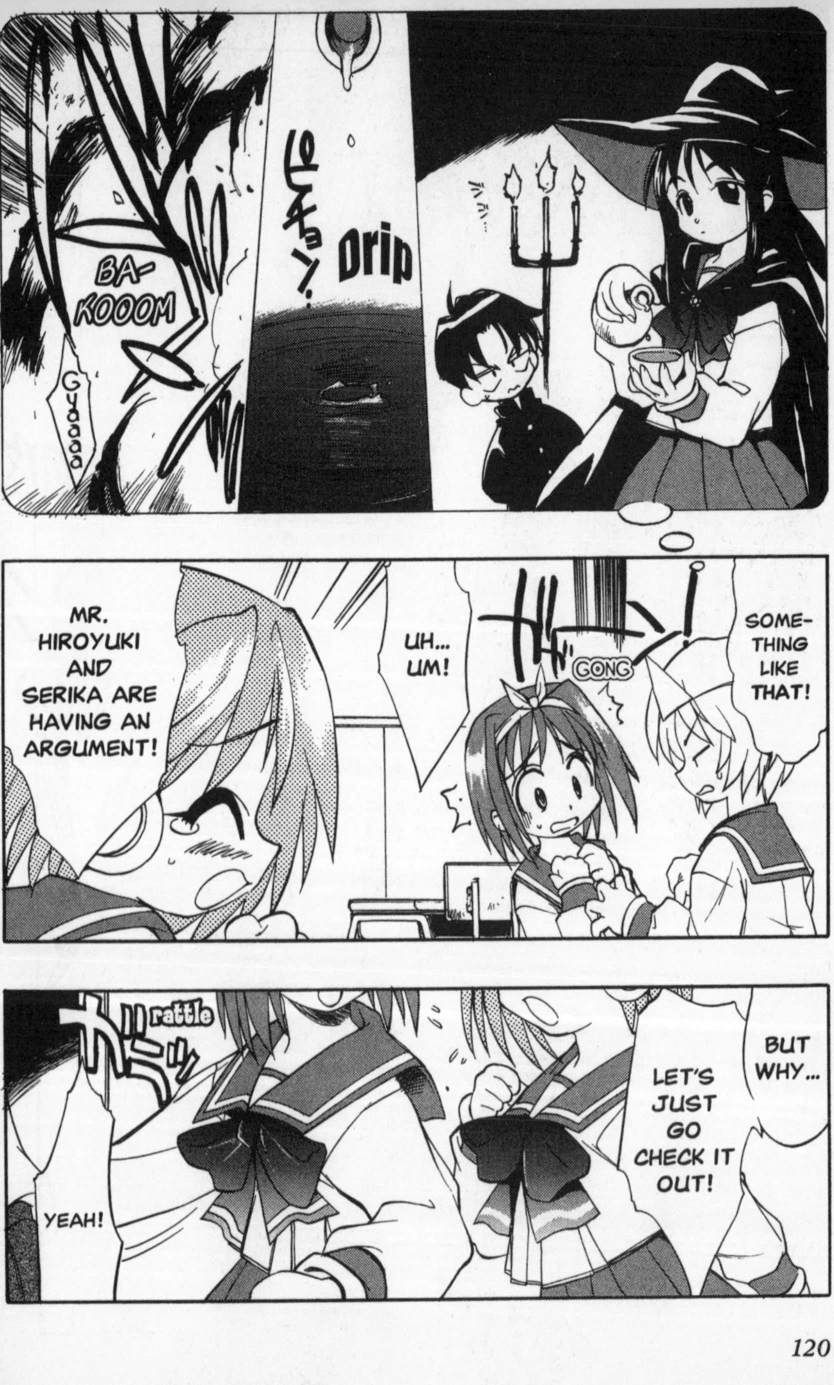

ピチョン!
Drip
BA-KOOOM
Gyaaaa
SOME-THING LIKE THAT!
GONG
UH... UM!
MR. HIROYUKI AND SERIKA ARE HAVING AN ARGUMENT!
BUT WHY...
LET'S JUST GO CHECK IT OUT!
rattle
YEAH!

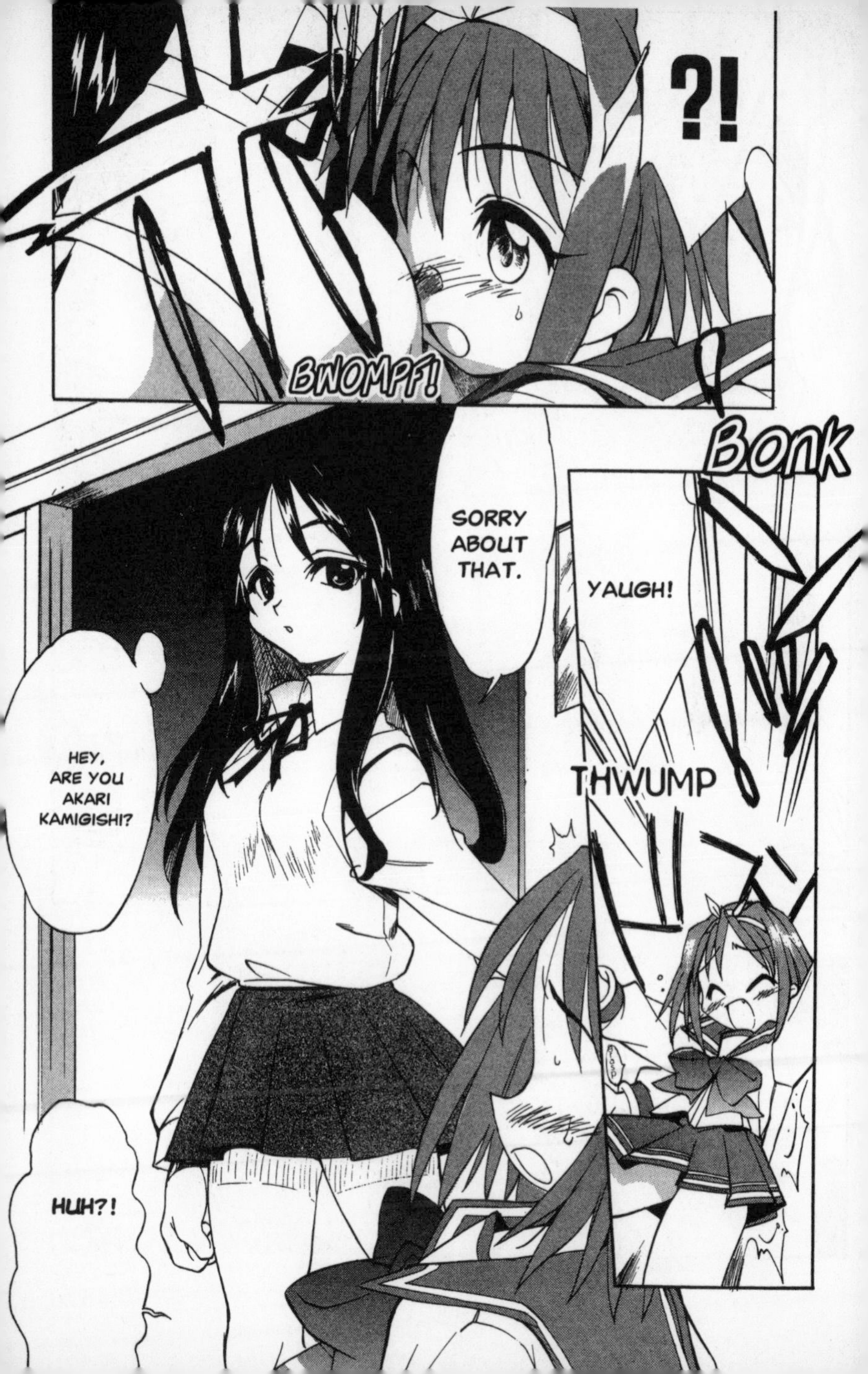
?!
BWOMPF!
Bonk
YAUGH!
THWUMP
SORRY ABOUT THAT.
HEY, ARE YOU AKARI KAMIGISHI?
HUH?!

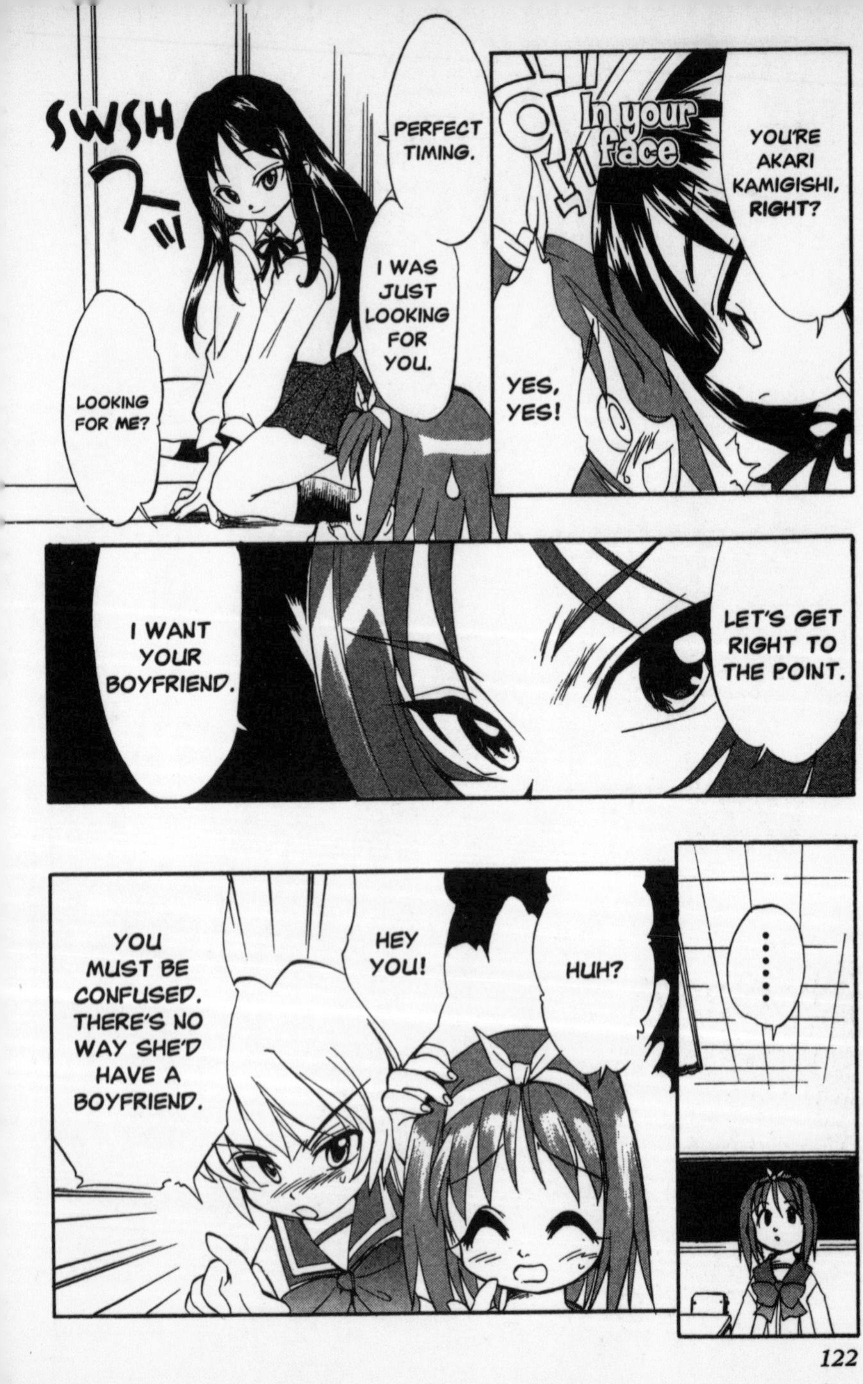
In your face
YOU'RE AKARI KAMIGISHI, RIGHT?
YES, YES!
SWSH
PERFECT TIMING.
I WAS JUST LOOKING FOR YOU.
LOOKING FOR ME?
LET'S GET RIGHT TO THE POINT.
I WANT YOUR BOYFRIEND.
......
HUH?
HEY YOU!
YOU MUST BE CONFUSED. THERE'S NO WAY SHE'D HAVE A BOYFRIEND.

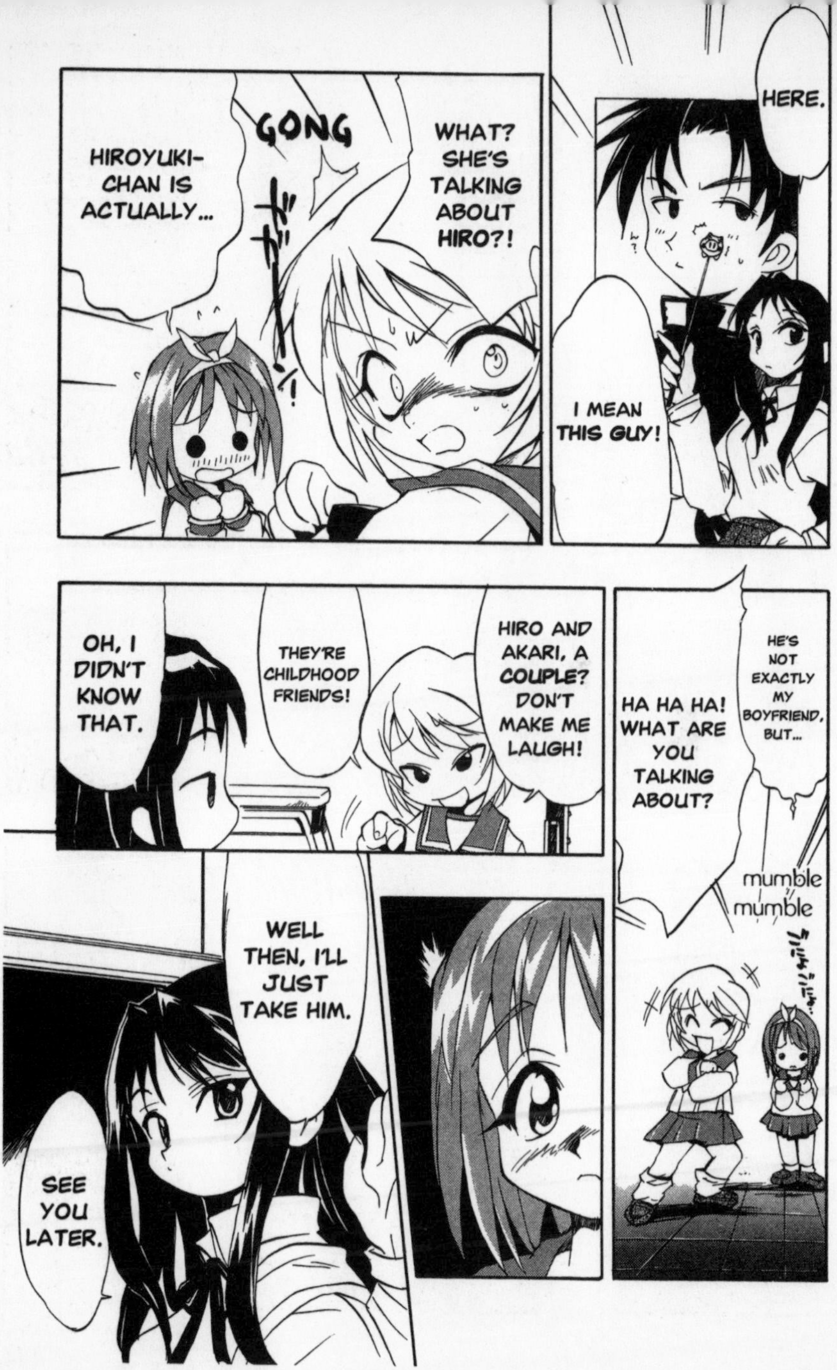
HERE.
I MEAN THIS GUY!
WHAT? SHE'S TALKING ABOUT HIRO?!
GONG
HIROYUKI-CHAN IS ACTUALLY...
HE'S NOT EXACTLY MY BOYFRIEND, BUT...
HA HA HA! WHAT ARE YOU TALKING ABOUT?
mumble mumble
HIRO AND AKARI, A COUPLE? DON'T MAKE ME LAUGH!
THEY'RE CHILDHOOD FRIENDS!
OH, I DIDN'T KNOW THAT.
WELL THEN, I'LL JUST TAKE HIM.
SEE YOU LATER.

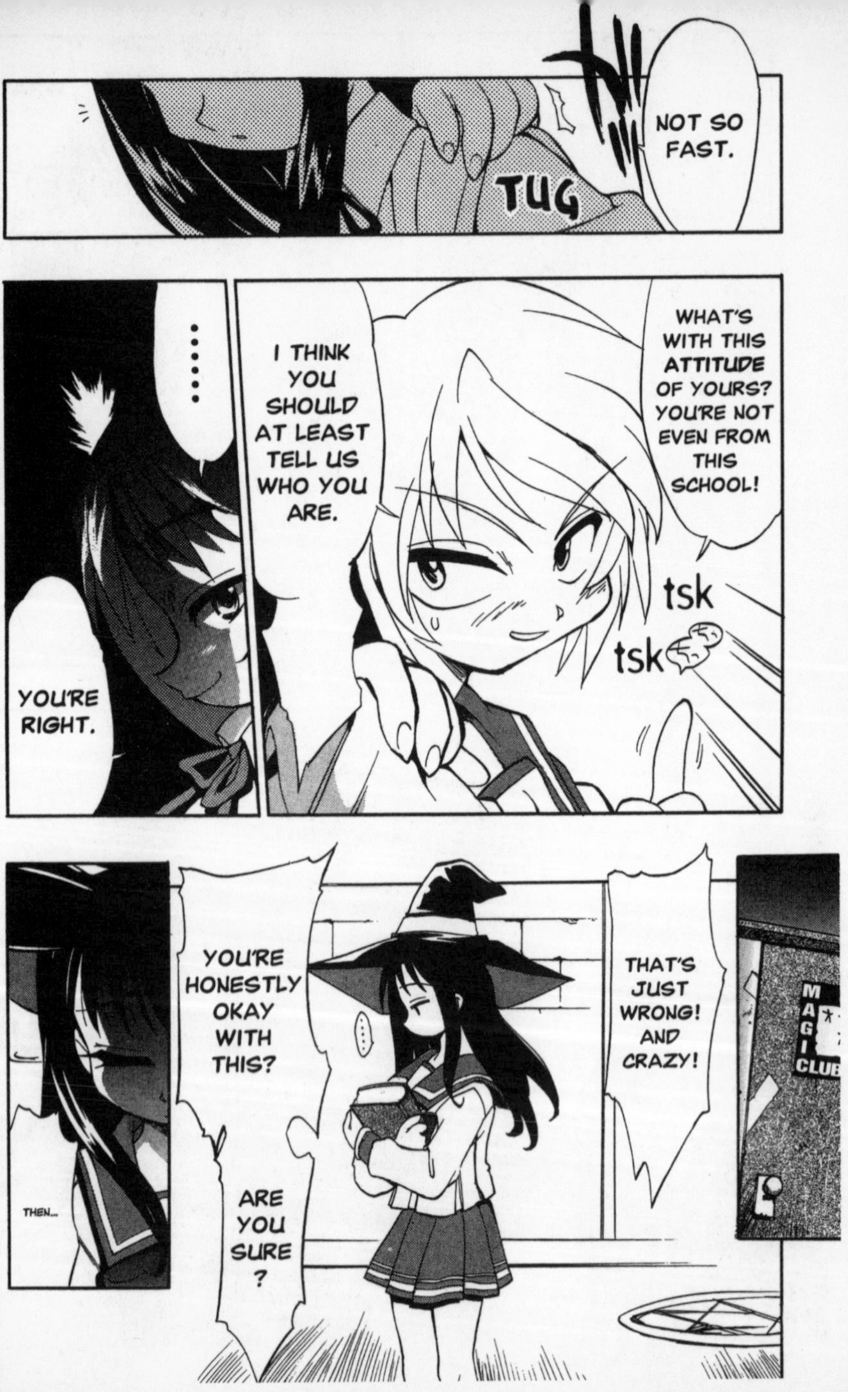
NOT SO FAST.
TUG
WHAT'S WITH THIS ATTITUDE OF YOURS? YOU'RE NOT EVEN FROM THIS SCHOOL!
tsk
tsk
I THINK YOU SHOULD AT LEAST TELL US WHO YOU ARE.
......
YOU'RE RIGHT.
MAGI CLUB
THAT'S JUST WRONG! AND CRAZY!
YOU'RE HONESTLY OKAY WITH THIS?
...
ARE YOU SURE?
THEN...

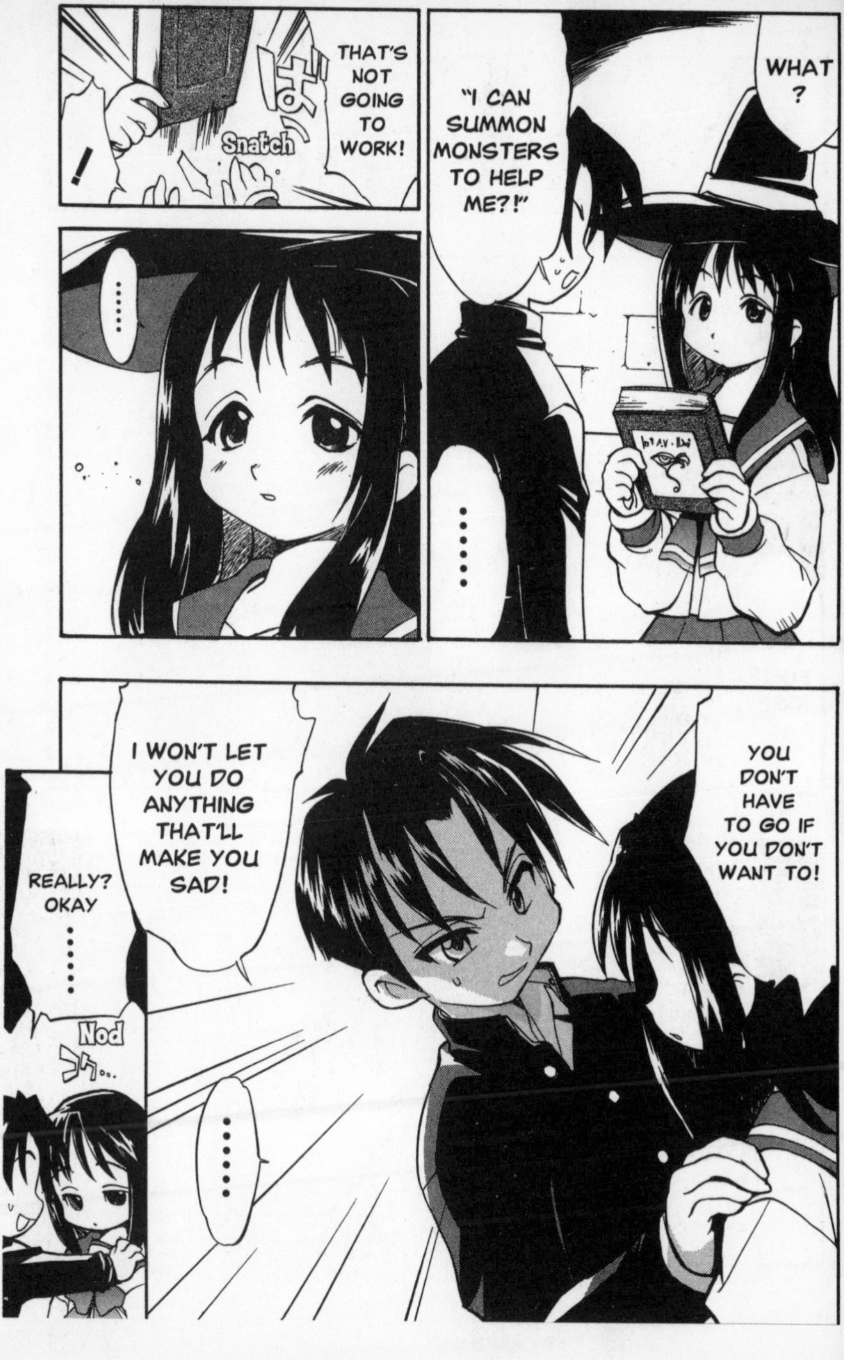
WHAT?
"I CAN SUMMON MONSTERS TO HELP ME?!"
THAT'S NOT GOING TO WORK!
Snatch
!
......
......
YOU DON'T HAVE TO GO IF YOU DON'T WANT TO!
I WON'T LET YOU DO ANYTHING THAT'LL MAKE YOU SAD!
......
REALLY? OKAY ......
Nod

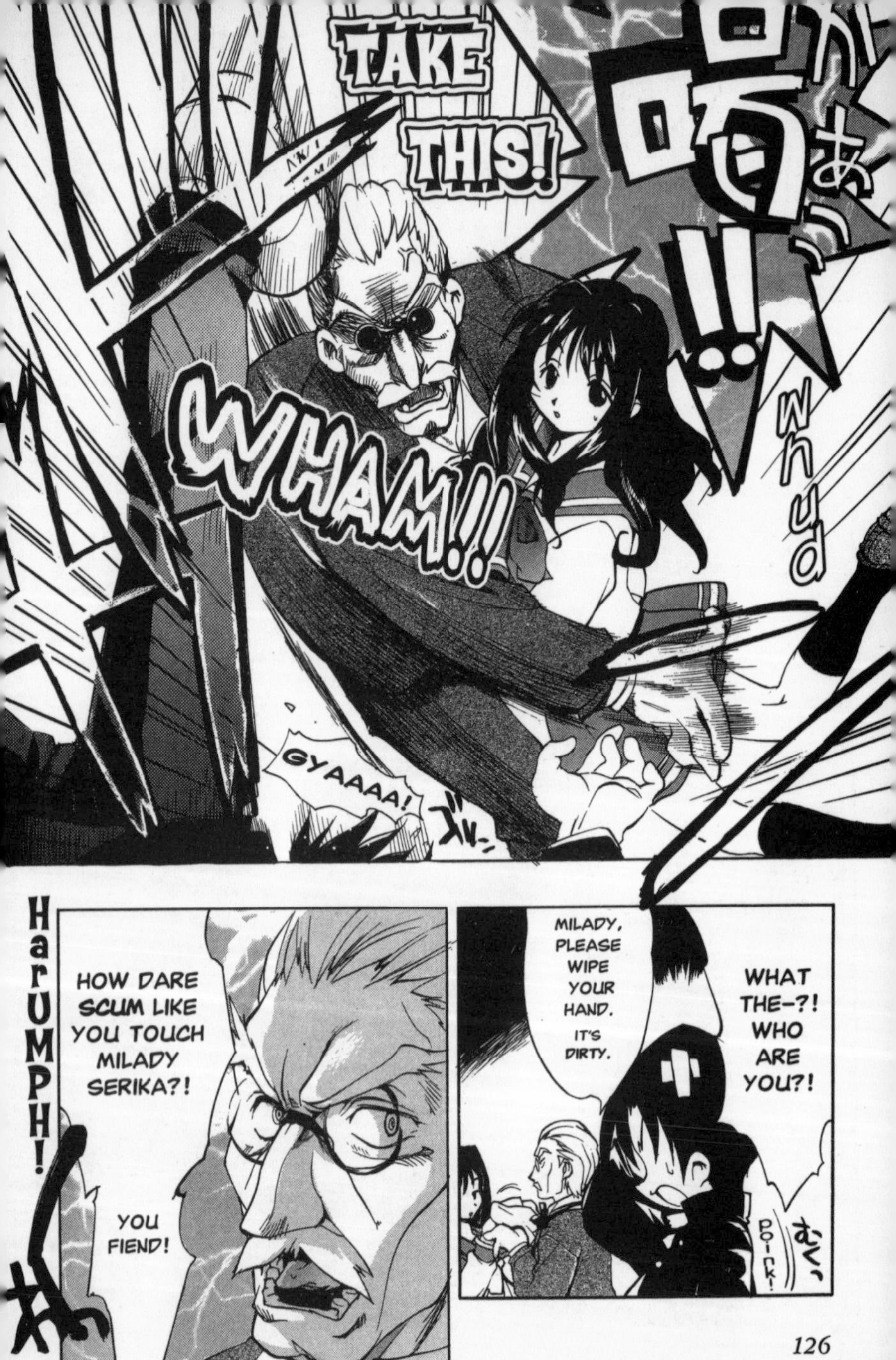
TAKE THIS!
Whud
WHAM!!!
GYAAAA!
WHAT THE-?! WHO ARE YOU?!
MILADY, PLEASE WIPE YOUR HAND.
IT'S DIRTY.
poink!
HarUMPH!
HOW DARE SCUM LIKE YOU TOUCH MILADY SERIKA?!
YOU FIEND!

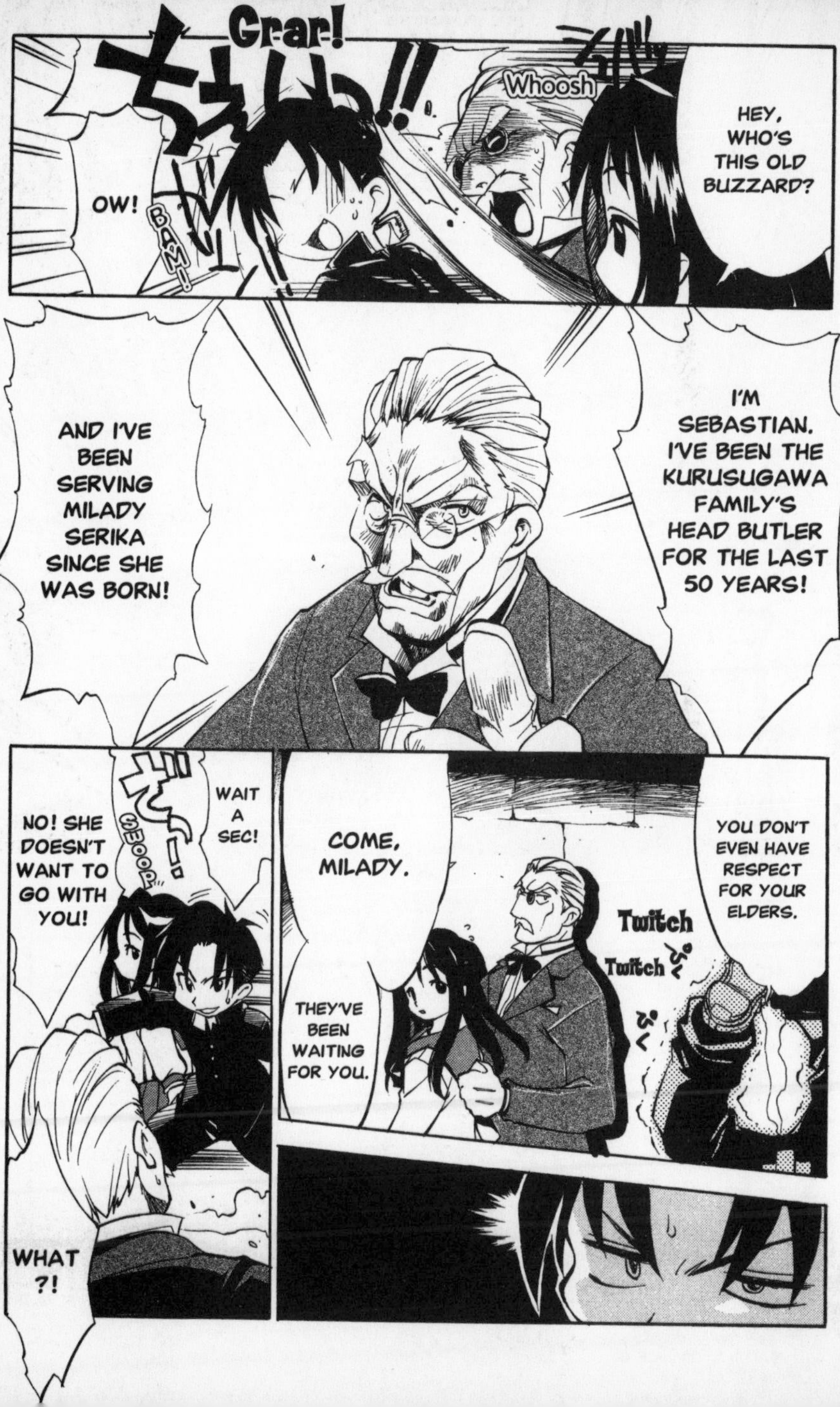
HEY, WHO'S THIS OLD BUZZARD?
Whoosh
Grar!
OW!
BAM!
I'M SEBASTIAN. I'VE BEEN THE KURUSUGAWA FAMILY'S HEAD BUTLER FOR THE LAST 50 YEARS!
AND I'VE BEEN SERVING MILADY SERIKA SINCE SHE WAS BORN!
YOU DON'T EVEN HAVE RESPECT FOR YOUR ELDERS.
Twitch
Twitch
COME, MILADY.
THEY'VE BEEN WAITING FOR YOU.
WAIT A SEC!
SWOOP
NO! SHE DOESN'T WANT TO GO WITH YOU!
WHAT?!

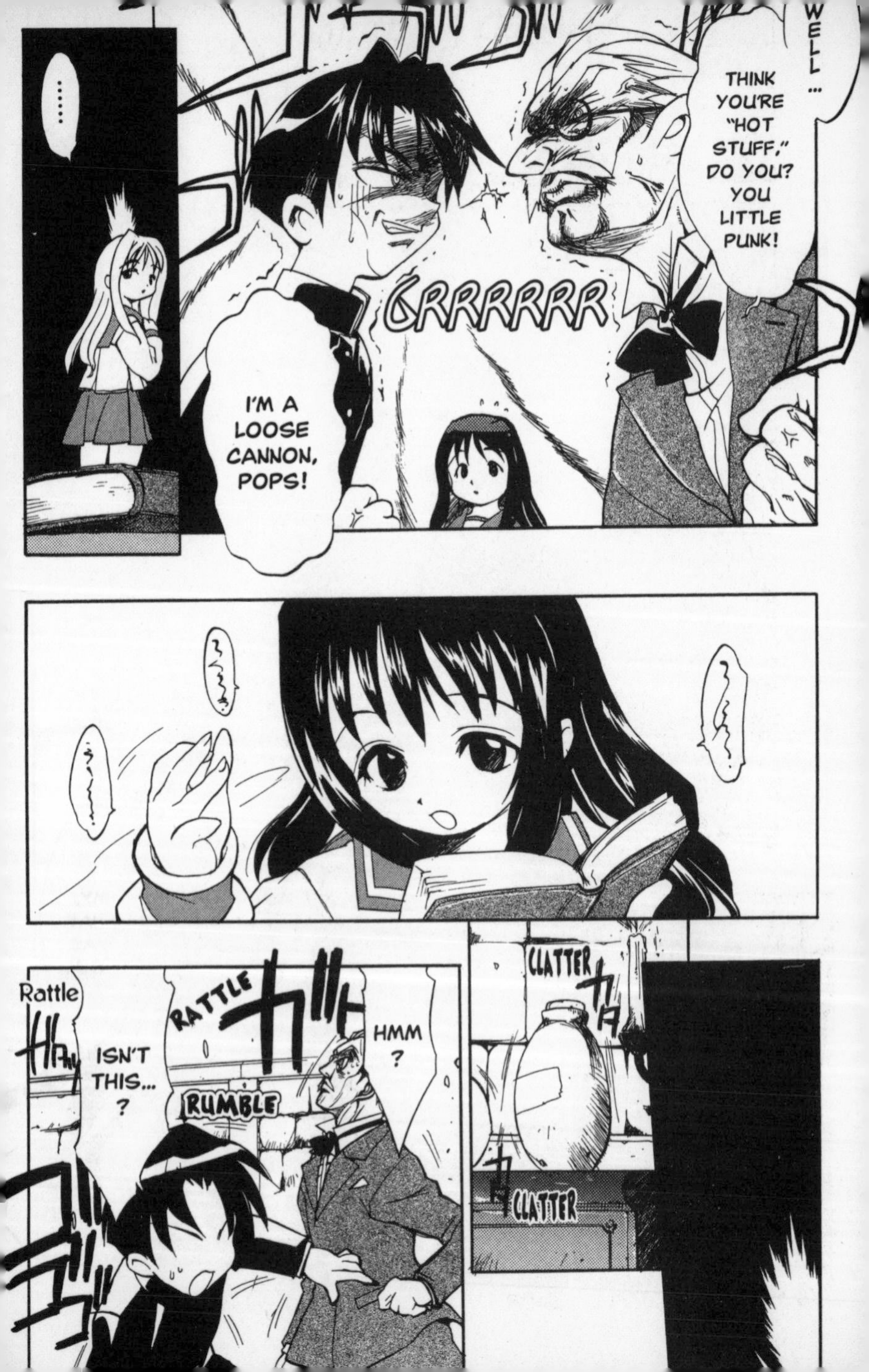
WELL ...
THINK YOU'RE "HOT STUFF," DO YOU? YOU LITTLE PUNK!
GRRRRRRR
I'M A LOOSE CANNON, POPS!
......
CLATTER
CLATTER
HMM ?
RATTLE
RUMBLE
Rattle
ISN'T THIS... ?

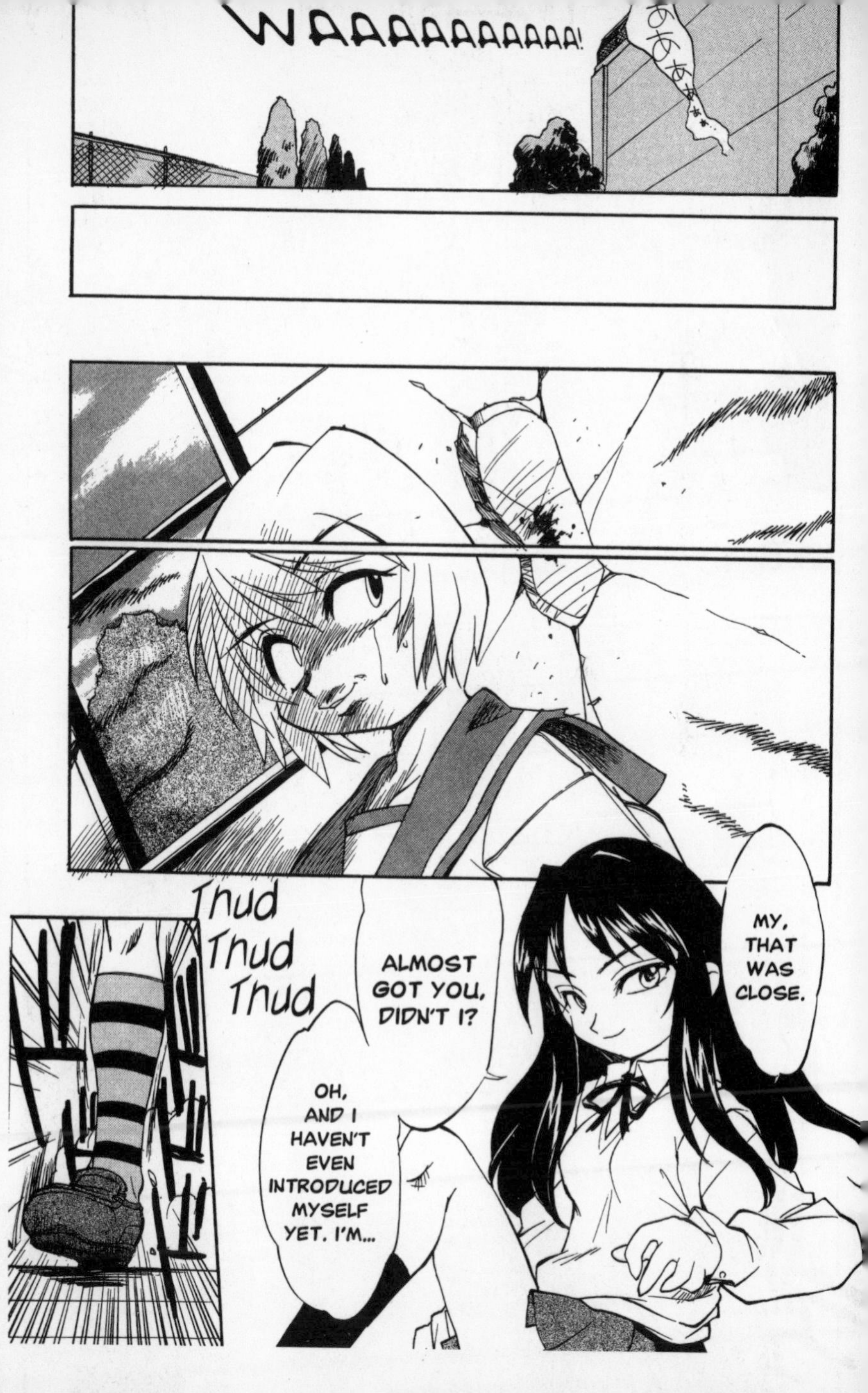
WAAAAAAAAAA!
ああああ
MY, THAT WAS CLOSE.
ALMOST GOT YOU, DIDN'T I?
Thud Thud Thud
OH, AND I HAVEN'T EVEN INTRODUCED MYSELF YET. I'M...

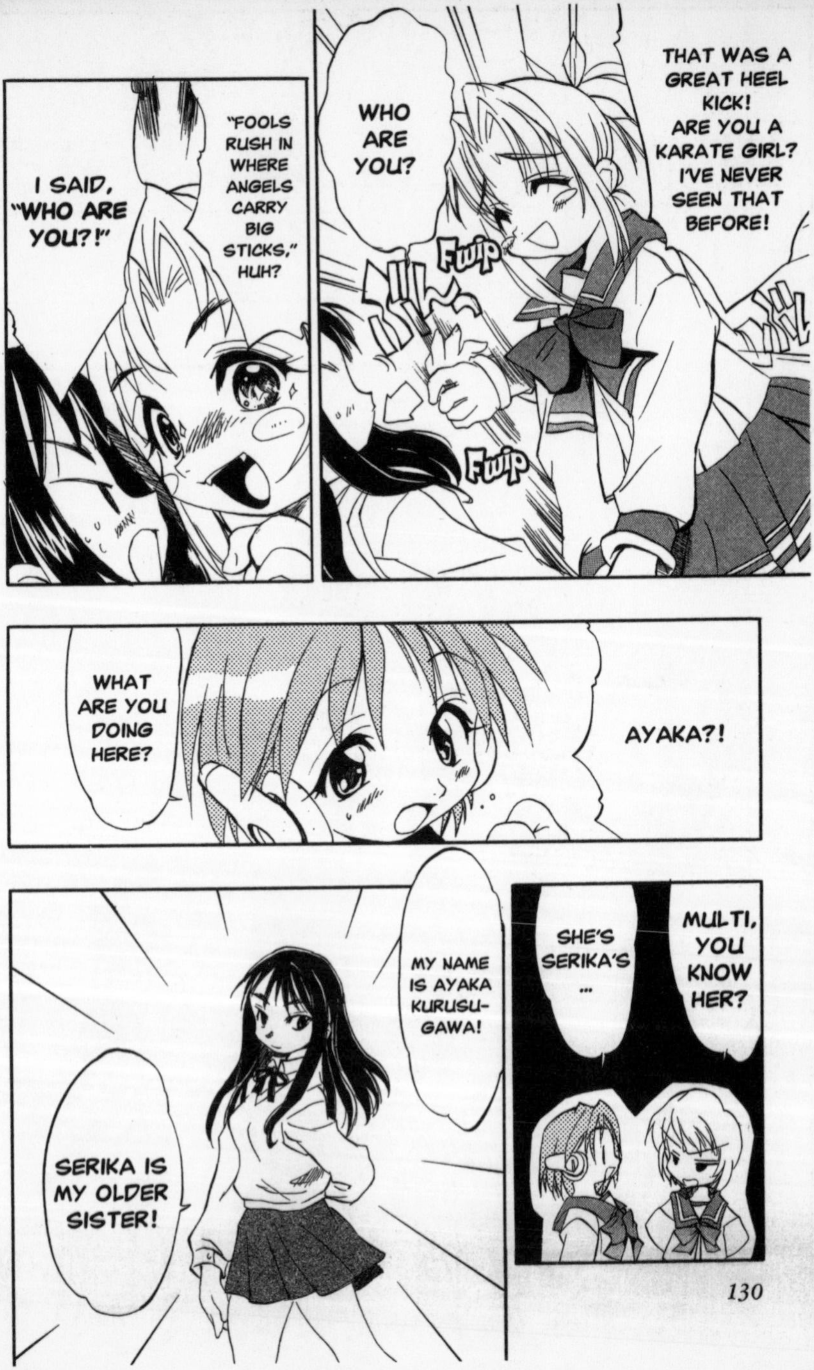
THAT WAS A GREAT HEEL KICK! ARE YOU A KARATE GIRL? I'VE NEVER SEEN THAT BEFORE!
WHO ARE YOU?
Fwip
Fwip
"FOOLS RUSH IN WHERE ANGELS CARRY BIG STICKS," HUH?
I SAID, "WHO ARE YOU?!"
...
AYAKA?!
WHAT ARE YOU DOING HERE?
MULTI, YOU KNOW HER?
SHE'S SERIKA'S ...
MY NAME IS AYAKA KURUSUGAWA!
SERIKA IS MY OLDER SISTER!

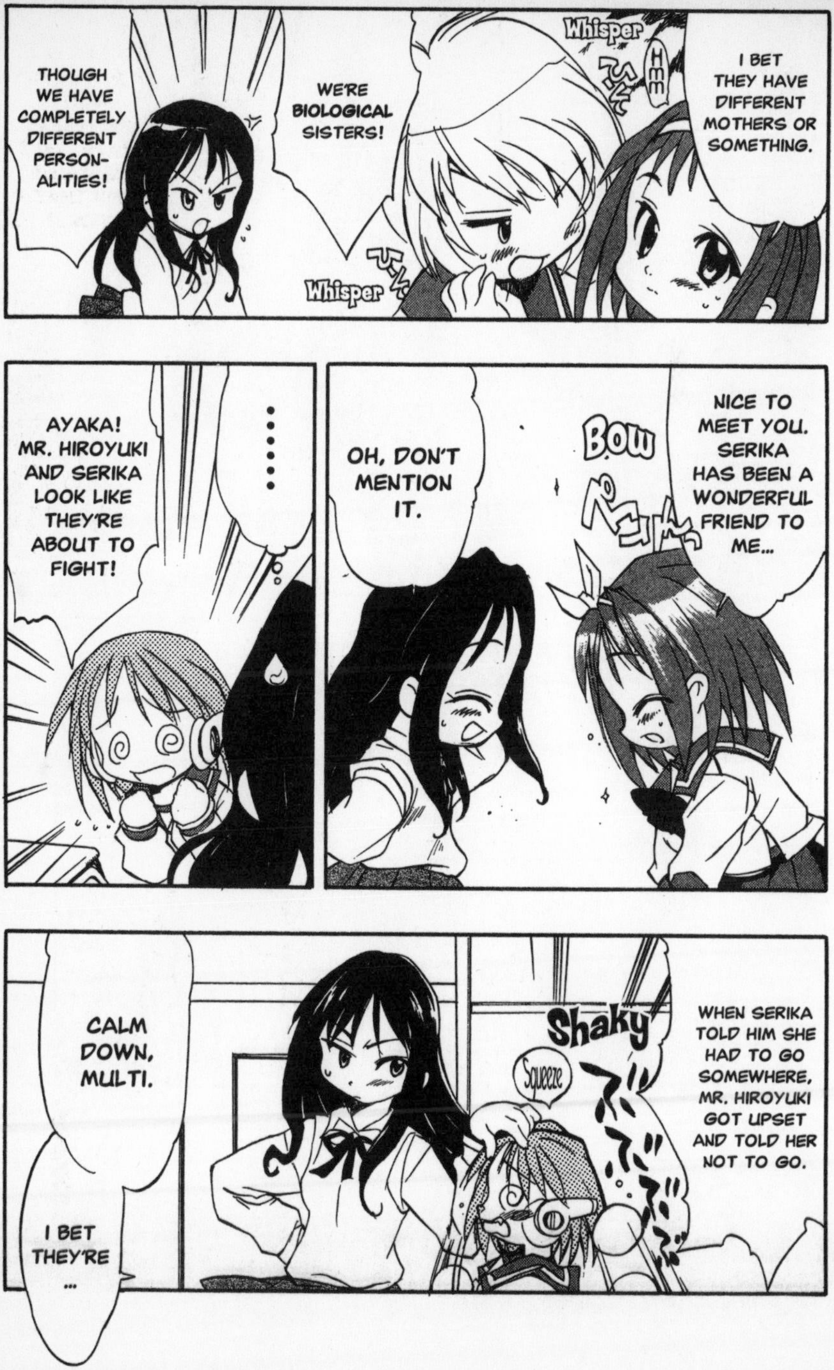
I BET THEY HAVE DIFFERENT MOTHERS OR SOMETHING.
Whisper
HMM
WE'RE BIOLOGICAL SISTERS!
THOUGH WE HAVE COMPLETELY DIFFERENT PERSON-ALITIES!
Whisper
NICE TO MEET YOU. SERIKA HAS BEEN A WONDERFUL FRIEND TO ME...
Bow
OH, DON'T MENTION IT.
......
AYAKA! MR. HIROYUKI AND SERIKA LOOK LIKE THEY'RE ABOUT TO FIGHT!
WHEN SERIKA TOLD HIM SHE HAD TO GO SOMEWHERE, MR. HIROYUKI GOT UPSET AND TOLD HER NOT TO GO.
Shaky
Squeeze
CALM DOWN, MULTI.
I BET THEY'RE ...

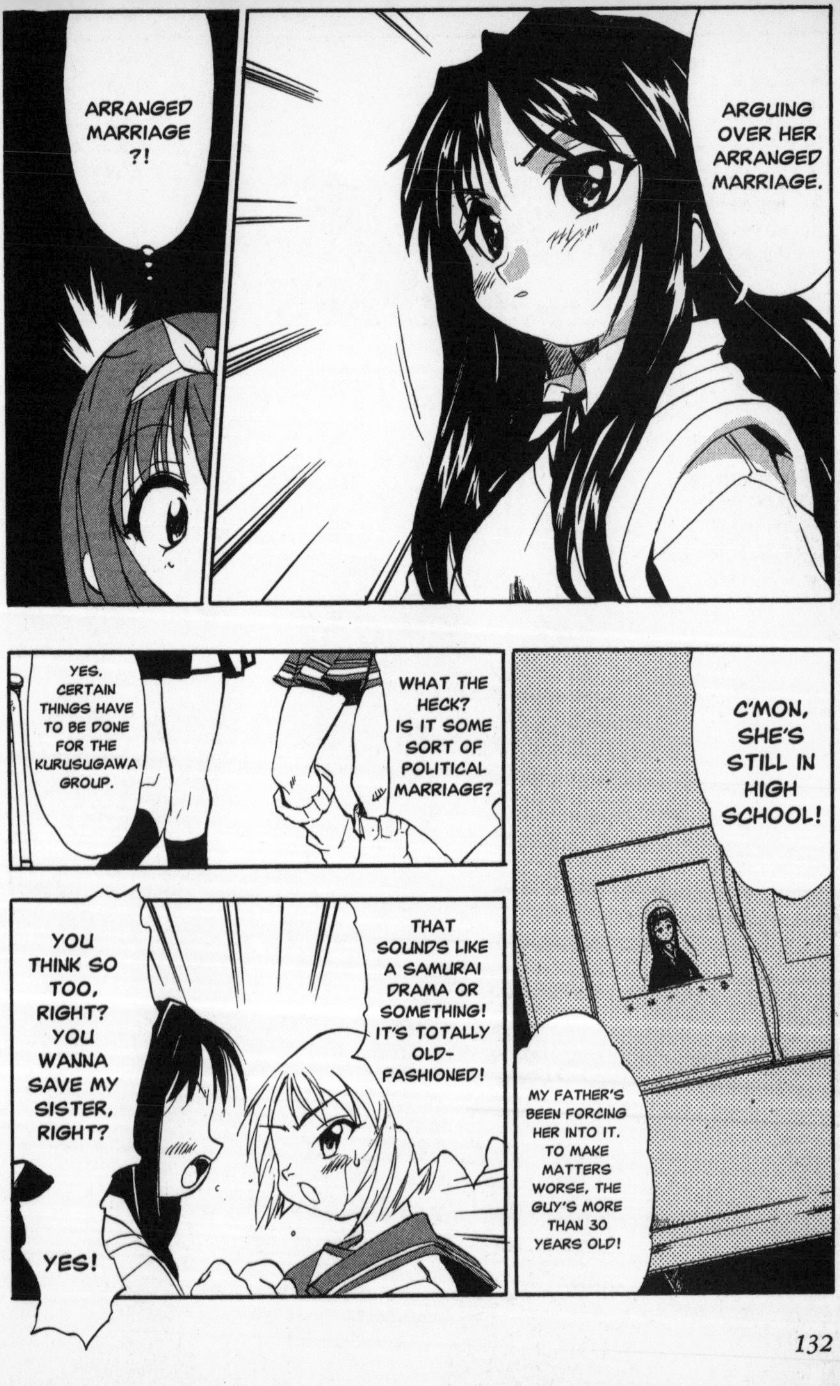
ARGUING OVER HER ARRANGED MARRIAGE.
ARRANGED MARRIAGE ?!
C'MON, SHE'S STILL IN HIGH SCHOOL!
MY FATHER'S BEEN FORCING HER INTO IT. TO MAKE MATTERS WORSE, THE GUY'S MORE THAN 30 YEARS OLD!
WHAT THE HECK? IS IT SOME SORT OF POLITICAL MARRIAGE?
YES. CERTAIN THINGS HAVE TO BE DONE FOR THE KURUSUGAWA GROUP.
THAT SOUNDS LIKE A SAMURAI DRAMA OR SOMETHING! IT'S TOTALLY OLD-FASHIONED!
YOU THINK SO TOO, RIGHT? YOU WANNA SAVE MY SISTER, RIGHT?
YES!

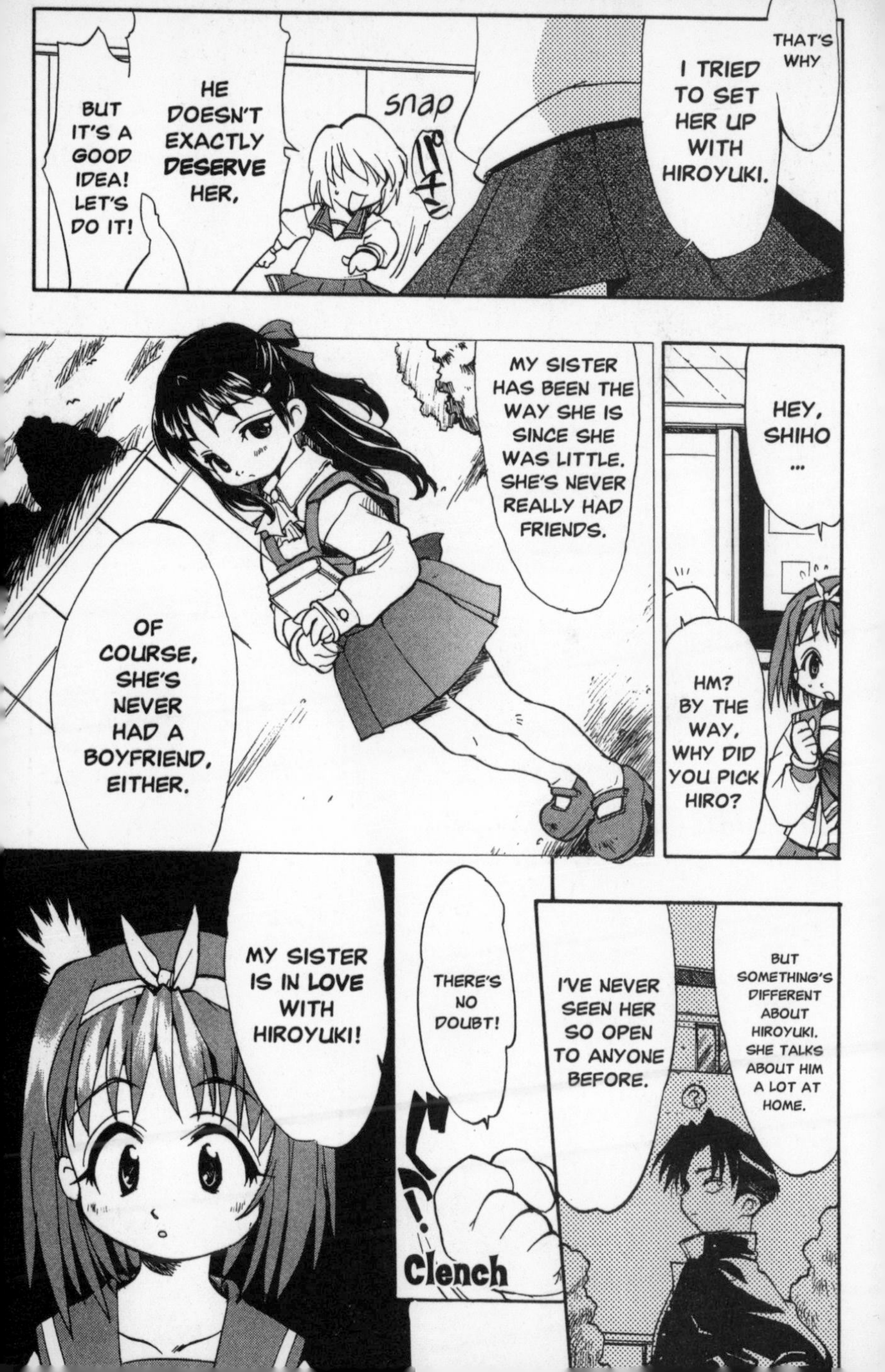
THAT'S WHY
I TRIED TO SET HER UP WITH HIROYUKI.
Snap
HE DOESN'T EXACTLY DESERVE HER,
BUT IT'S A GOOD IDEA! LET'S DO IT!
HEY, SHIHO ...
HM? BY THE WAY, WHY DID YOU PICK HIRO?
MY SISTER HAS BEEN THE WAY SHE IS SINCE SHE WAS LITTLE. SHE'S NEVER REALLY HAD FRIENDS.
OF COURSE, SHE'S NEVER HAD A BOYFRIEND, EITHER.
BUT SOMETHING'S DIFFERENT ABOUT HIROYUKI. SHE TALKS ABOUT HIM A LOT AT HOME.
I'VE NEVER SEEN HER SO OPEN TO ANYONE BEFORE.
THERE'S NO DOUBT!
Clench
MY SISTER IS IN LOVE WITH HIROYUKI!

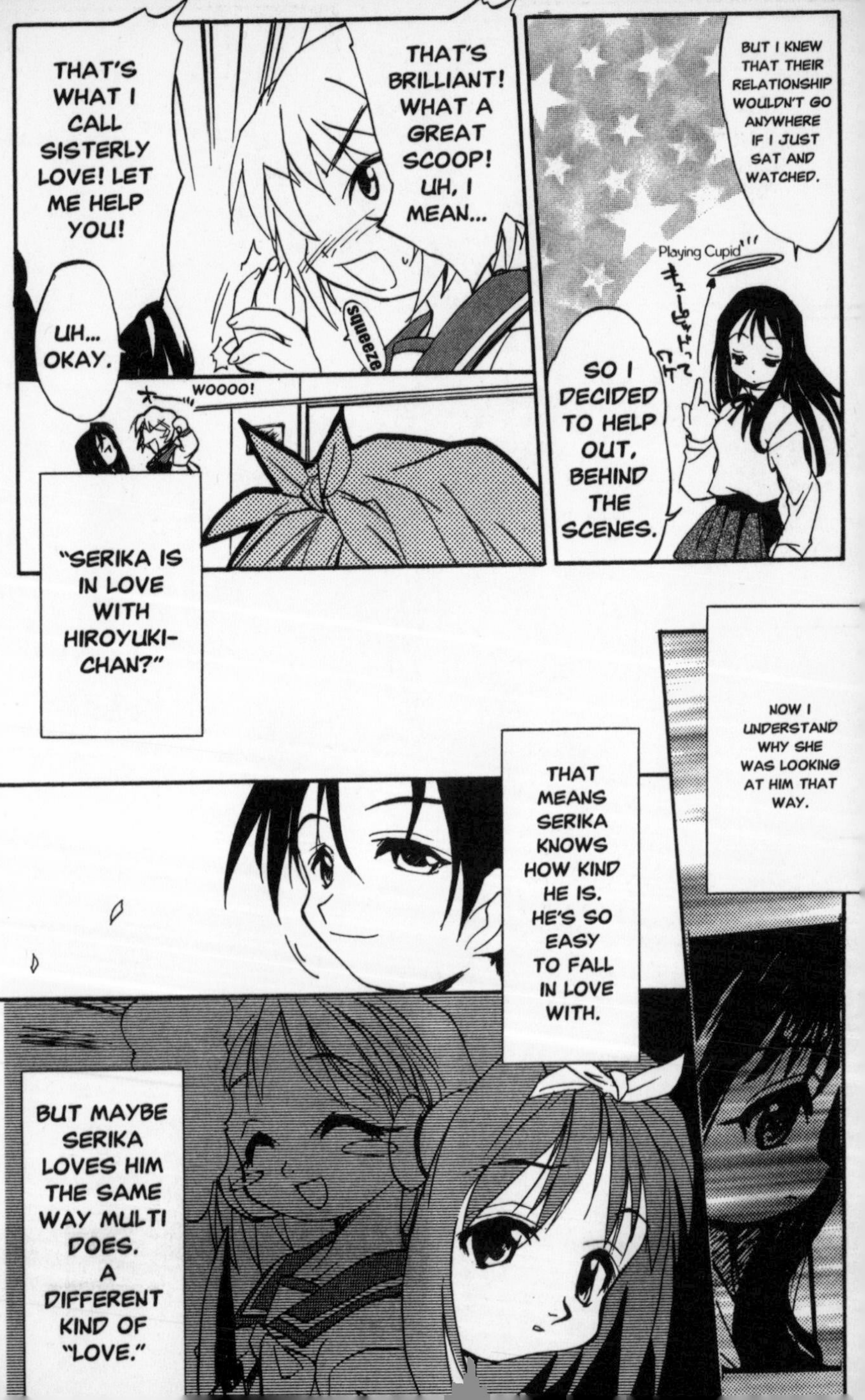
BUT I KNEW THAT THEIR RELATIONSHIP WOULDN'T GO ANYWHERE IF I JUST SAT AND WATCHED.
Playing Cupid
SO I DECIDED TO HELP OUT, BEHIND THE SCENES.
THAT'S BRILLIANT! WHAT A GREAT SCOOP! UH, I MEAN...
THAT'S WHAT I CALL SISTERLY LOVE! LET ME HELP YOU!
squeeze
UH... OKAY.
WOOOO!
"SERIKA IS IN LOVE WITH HIROYUKI-CHAN?"
NOW I UNDERSTAND WHY SHE WAS LOOKING AT HIM THAT WAY.
THAT MEANS SERIKA KNOWS HOW KIND HE IS. HE'S SO EASY TO FALL IN LOVE WITH.
BUT MAYBE SERIKA LOVES HIM THE SAME WAY MULTI DOES. A DIFFERENT KIND OF "LOVE."

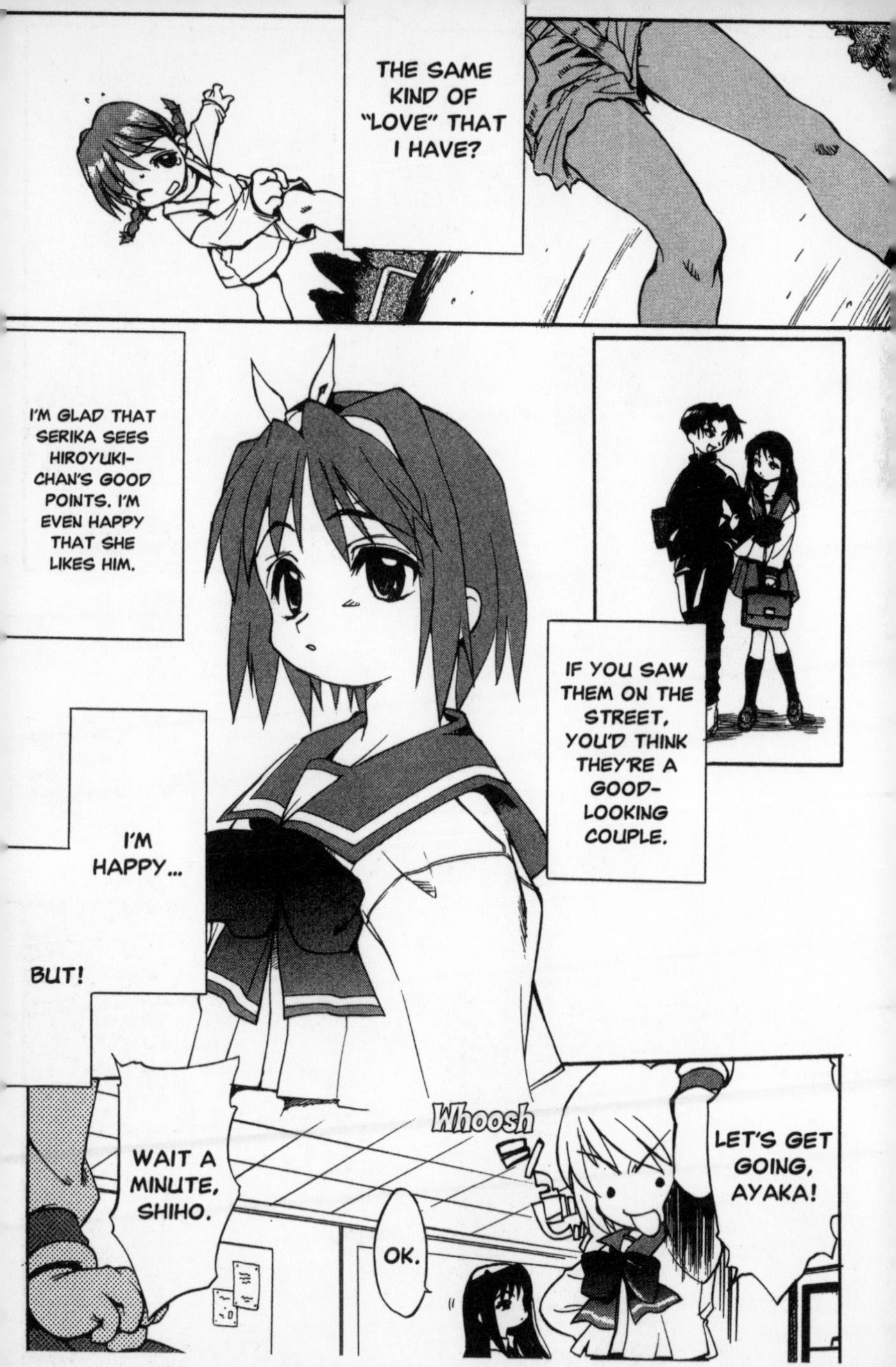
THE SAME KIND OF "LOVE" THAT I HAVE?
I'M GLAD THAT SERIKA SEES HIROYUKI-CHAN'S GOOD POINTS. I'M EVEN HAPPY THAT SHE LIKES HIM.
IF YOU SAW THEM ON THE STREET, YOU'D THINK THEY'RE A GOOD-LOOKING COUPLE.
I'M HAPPY...
BUT!
LET'S GET GOING, AYAKA!
Whoosh
OK.
WAIT A MINUTE, SHIHO.

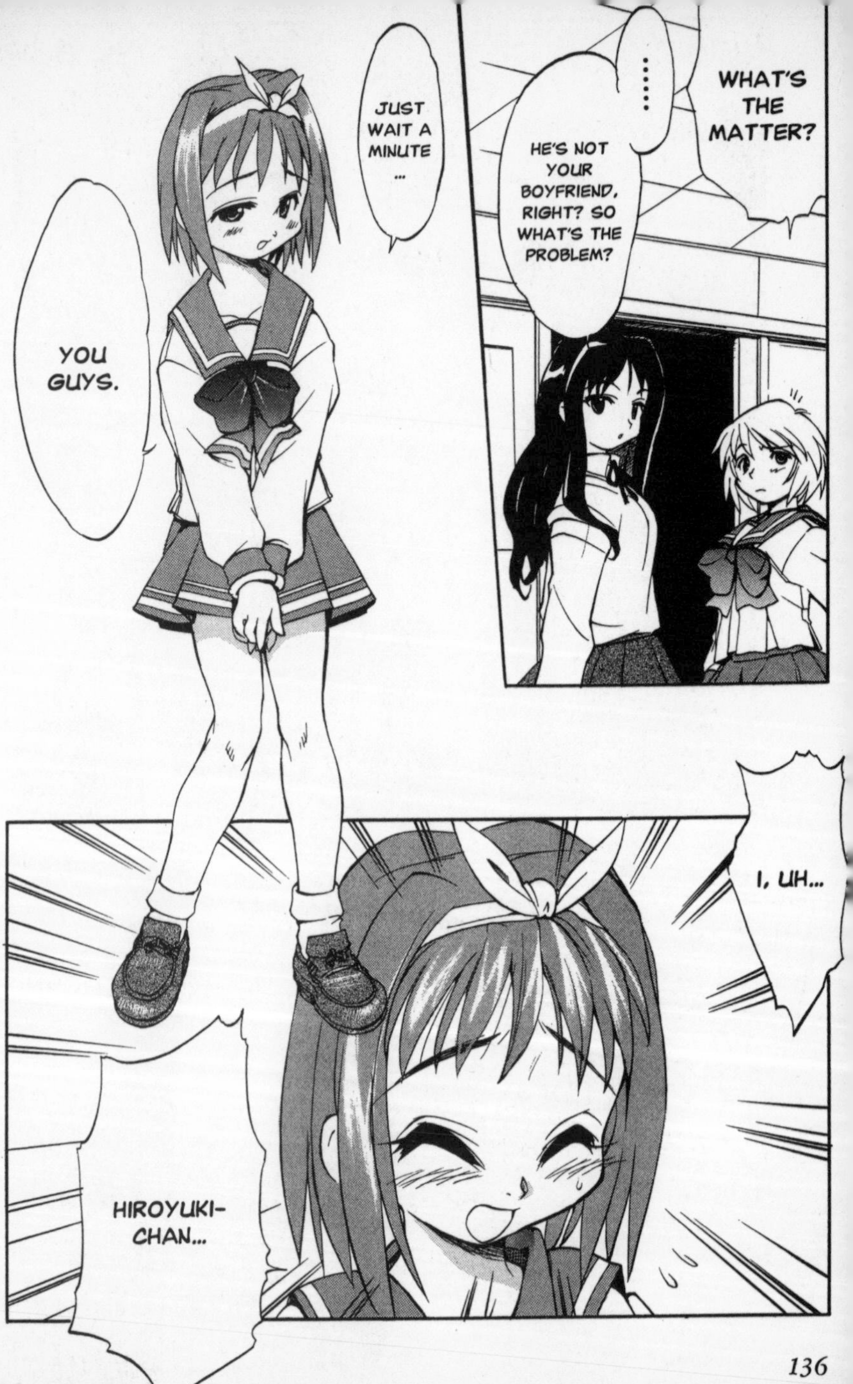
WHAT'S THE MATTER?
......
HE'S NOT YOUR BOYFRIEND, RIGHT? SO WHAT'S THE PROBLEM?
JUST WAIT A MINUTE ...
YOU GUYS.
I, UH...
HIROYUKI-CHAN...

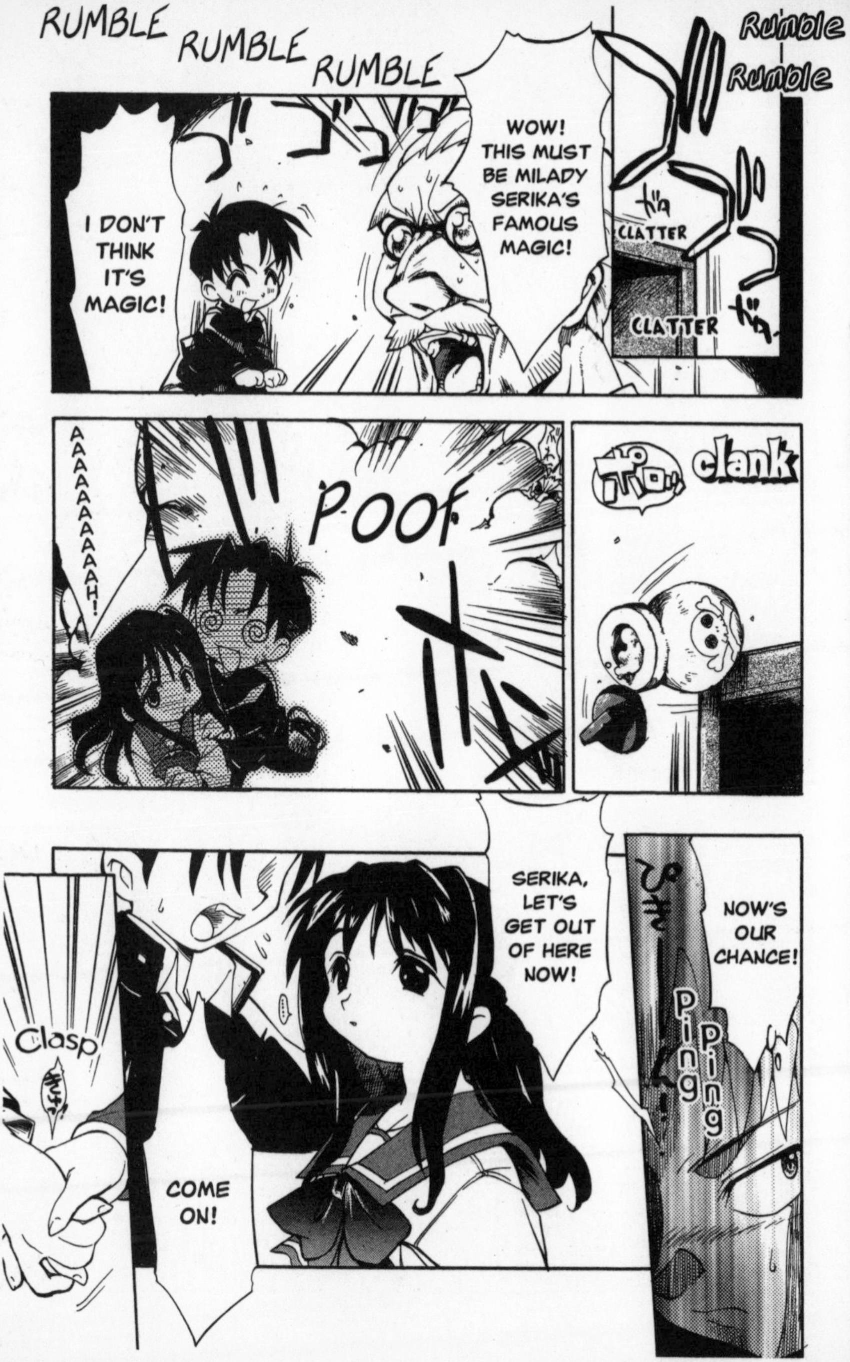

RUMBLE RUMBLE RUMBLE
Rumble Rumble
CLATTER
CLATTER
WOW! THIS MUST BE MILADY SERIKA'S FAMOUS MAGIC!
I DON'T THINK IT'S MAGIC!
clank
POOF
AAAAAAAAAAAH!
NOW'S OUR CHANCE!
Ping Ping
SERIKA, LET'S GET OUT OF HERE NOW!
Clasp
COME ON!

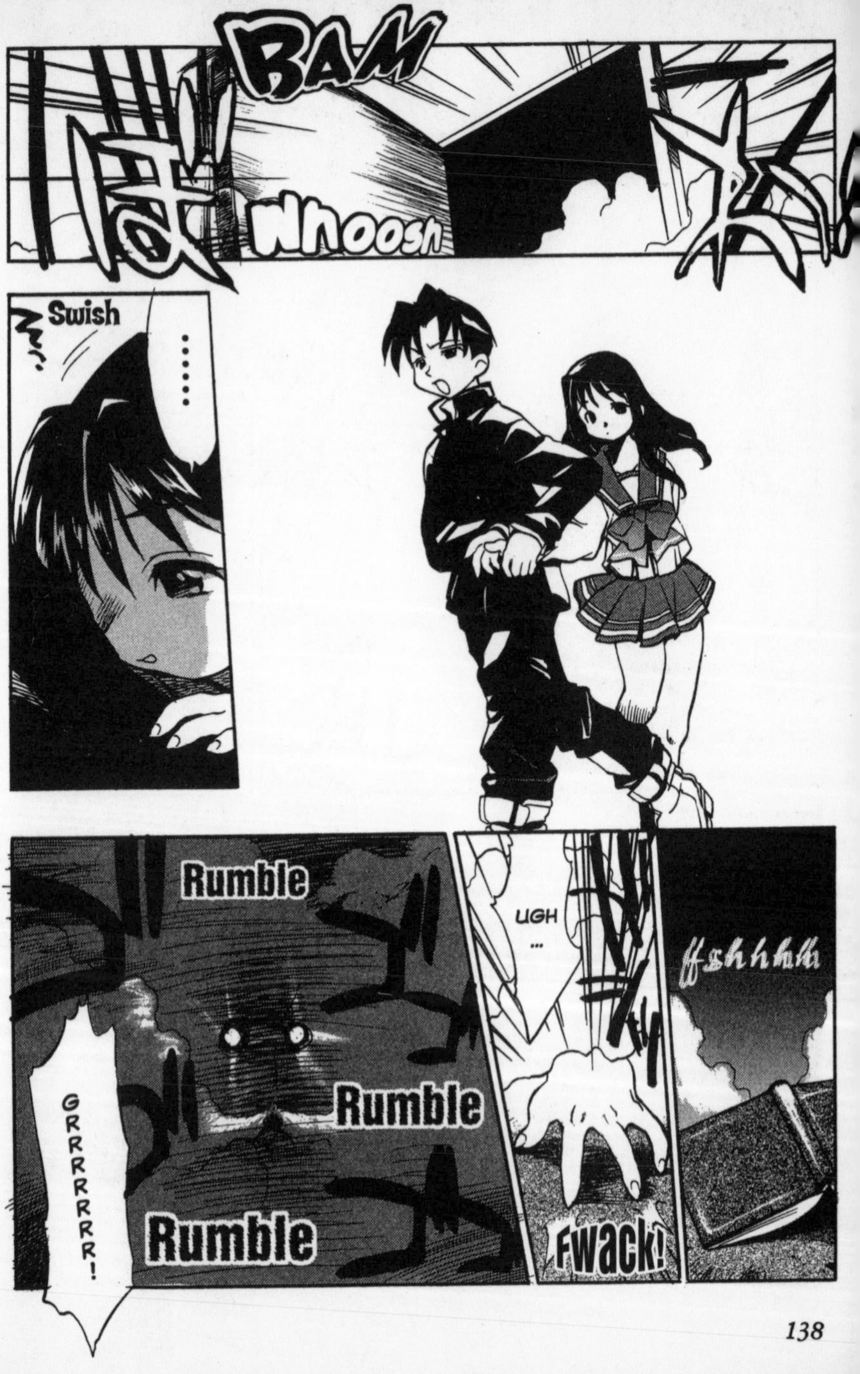
BAM
Whoosh
Swish
......
Rumble
Rumble
Rumble
GRRRRRR!
UGH
...
Fwack!
ffshhhh

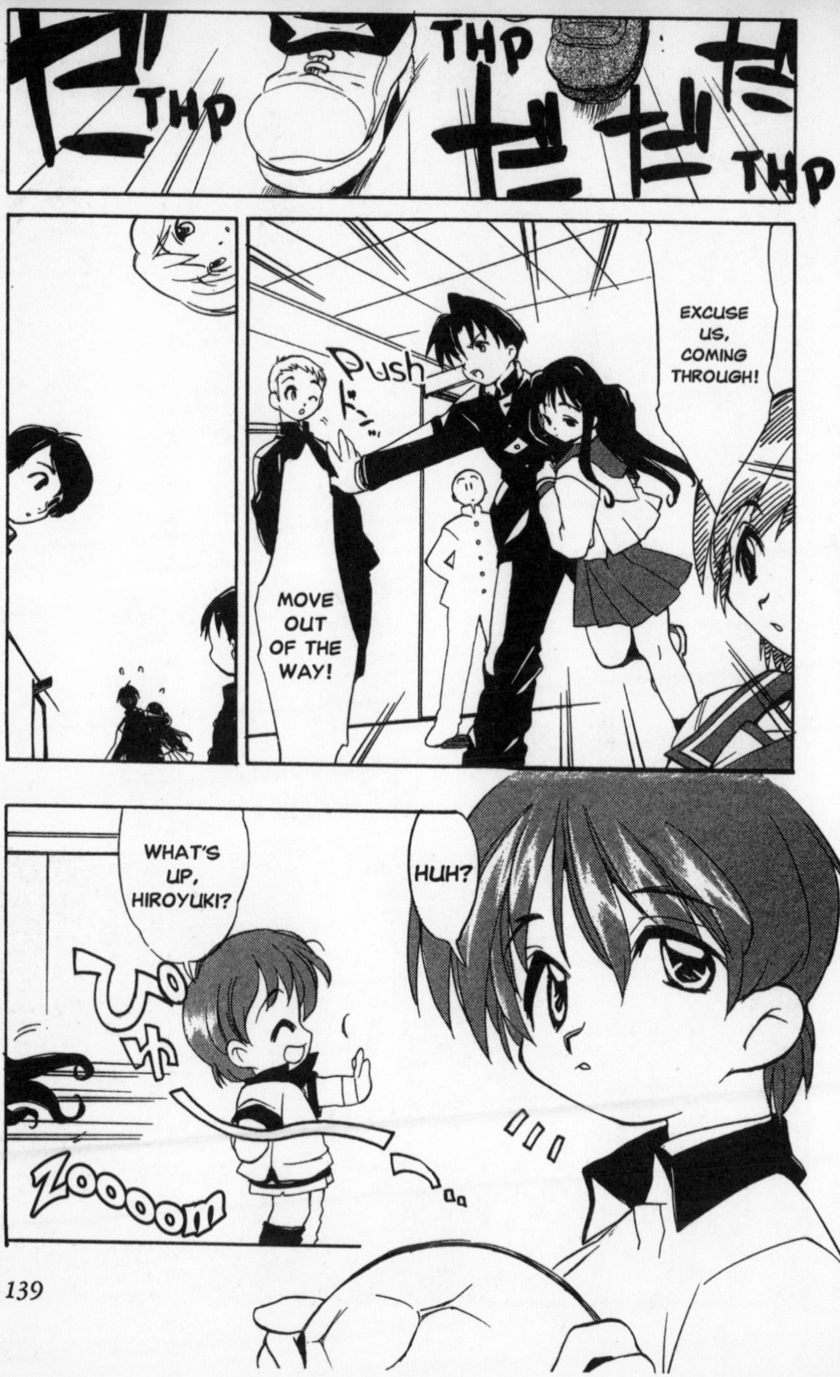
THP
THP
THP
EXCUSE US, COMING THROUGH!
Push
MOVE OUT OF THE WAY!
HUH?
WHAT'S UP, HIROYUKI?
Zoooom

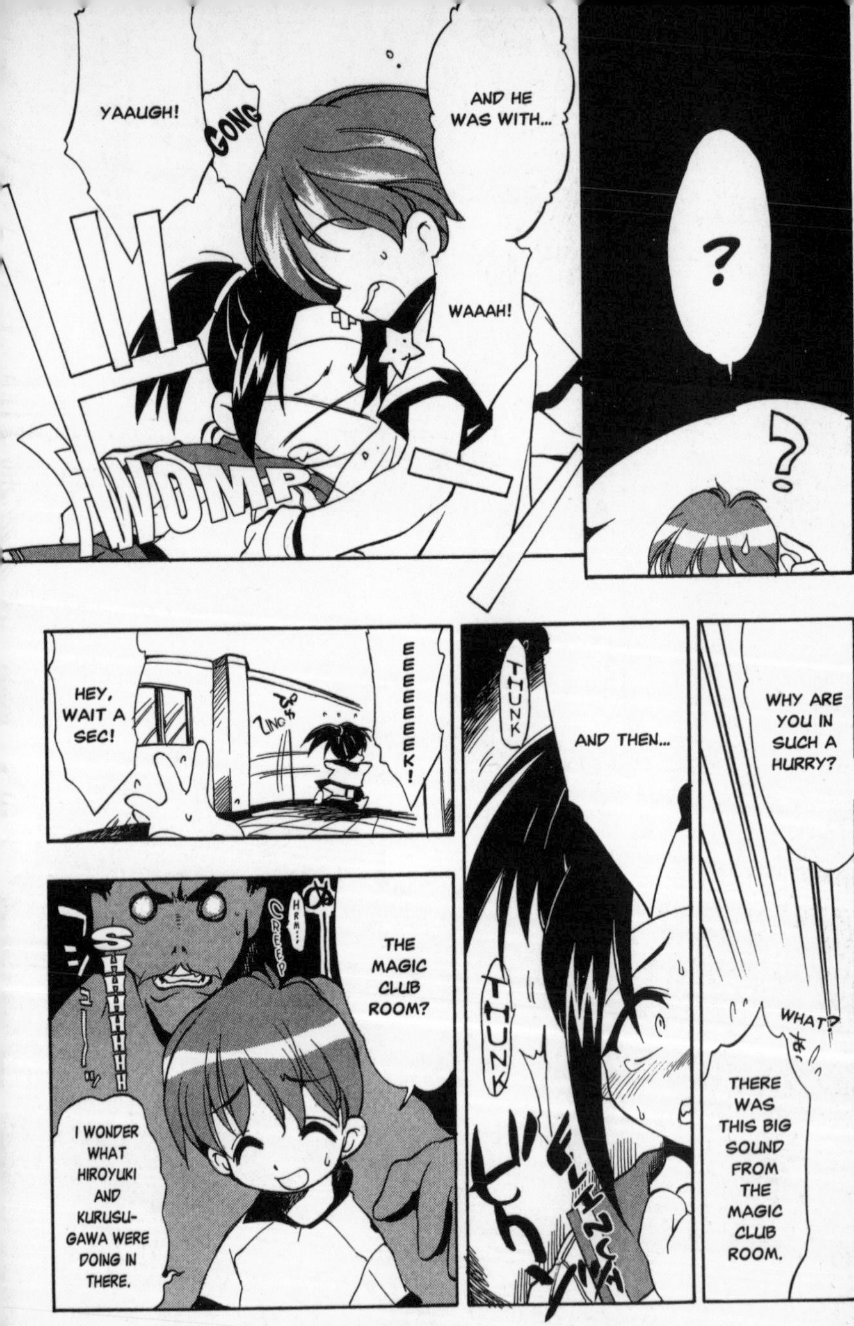
?
?
AND HE WAS WITH...
WAAAH!
GONG
YAAUGH!
WOMP
WHY ARE YOU IN SUCH A HURRY?
WHAT?
THERE WAS THIS BIG SOUND FROM THE MAGIC CLUB ROOM.
AND THEN...
THUNK
THUNK
EEEEEEEEK!
HEY, WAIT A SEC!
THE MAGIC CLUB ROOM?
HRM...
CREEP
SHHHHHH
I WONDER WHAT HIROYUKI AND KURUSU-GAWA WERE DOING IN THERE.

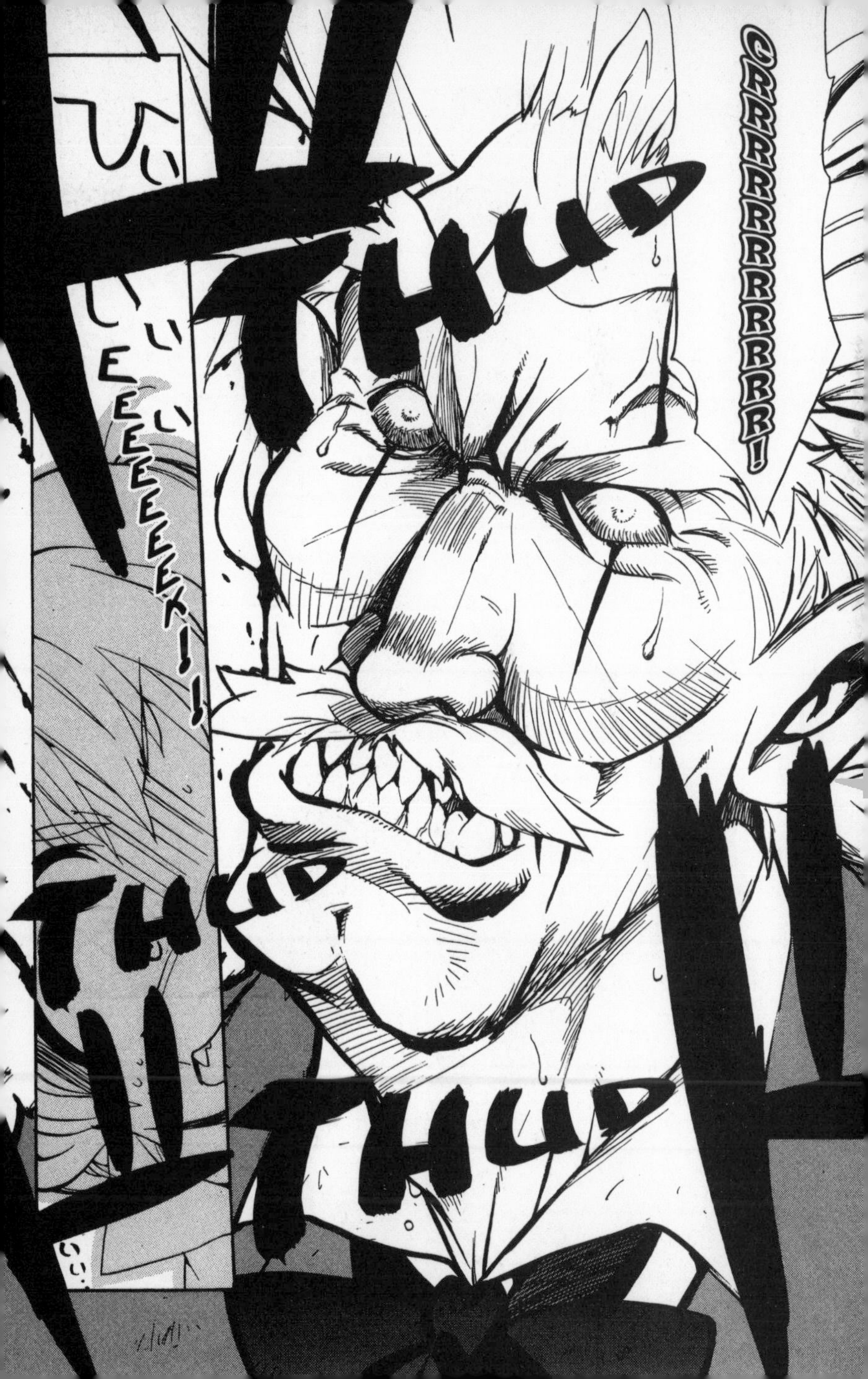

GRRRRRRRRRRR!
THUD
EEEEEEEK!!
THUD
THUD

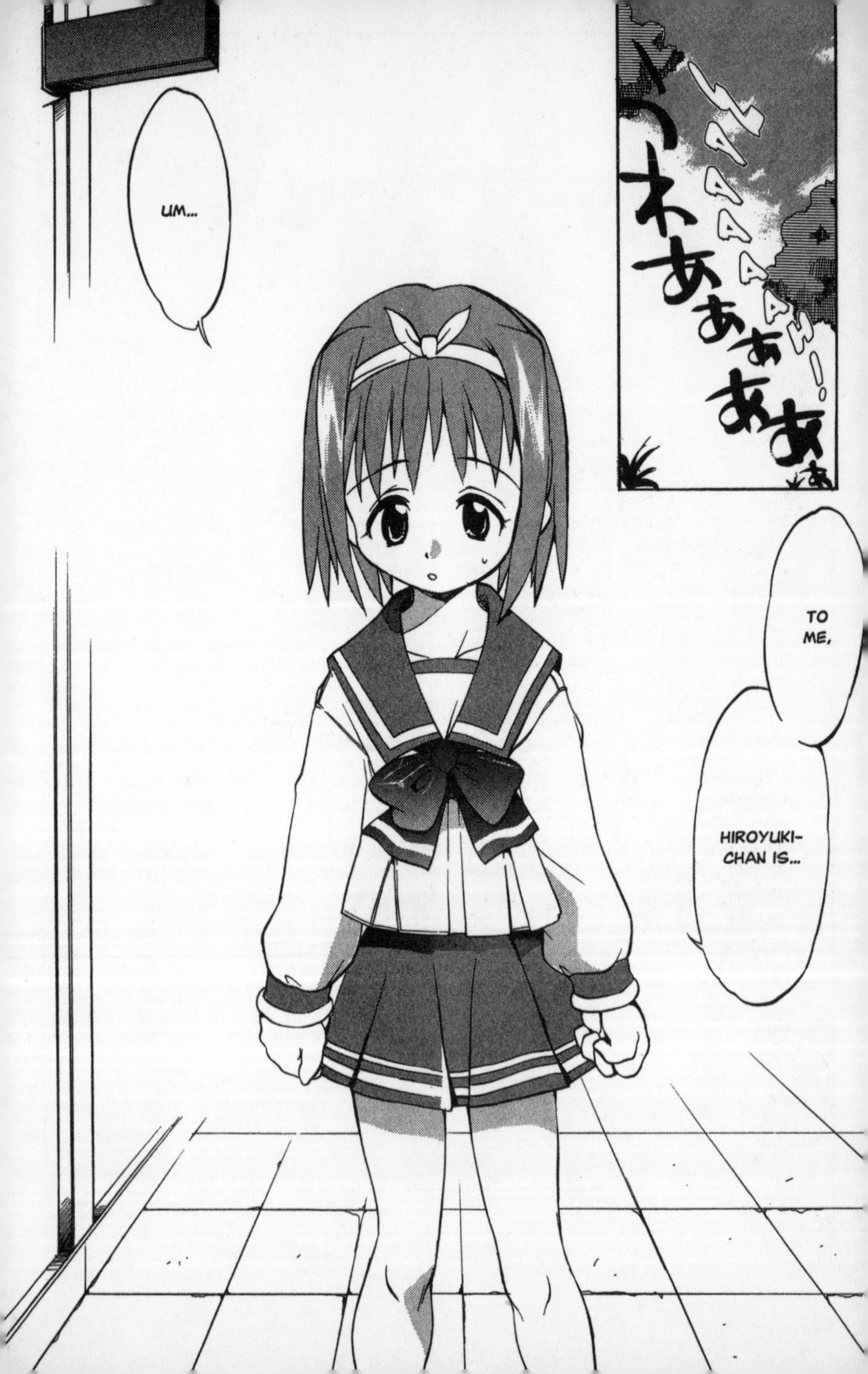
WAAAAAH!
TO ME,
HIROYUKI-CHAN IS...
UM...

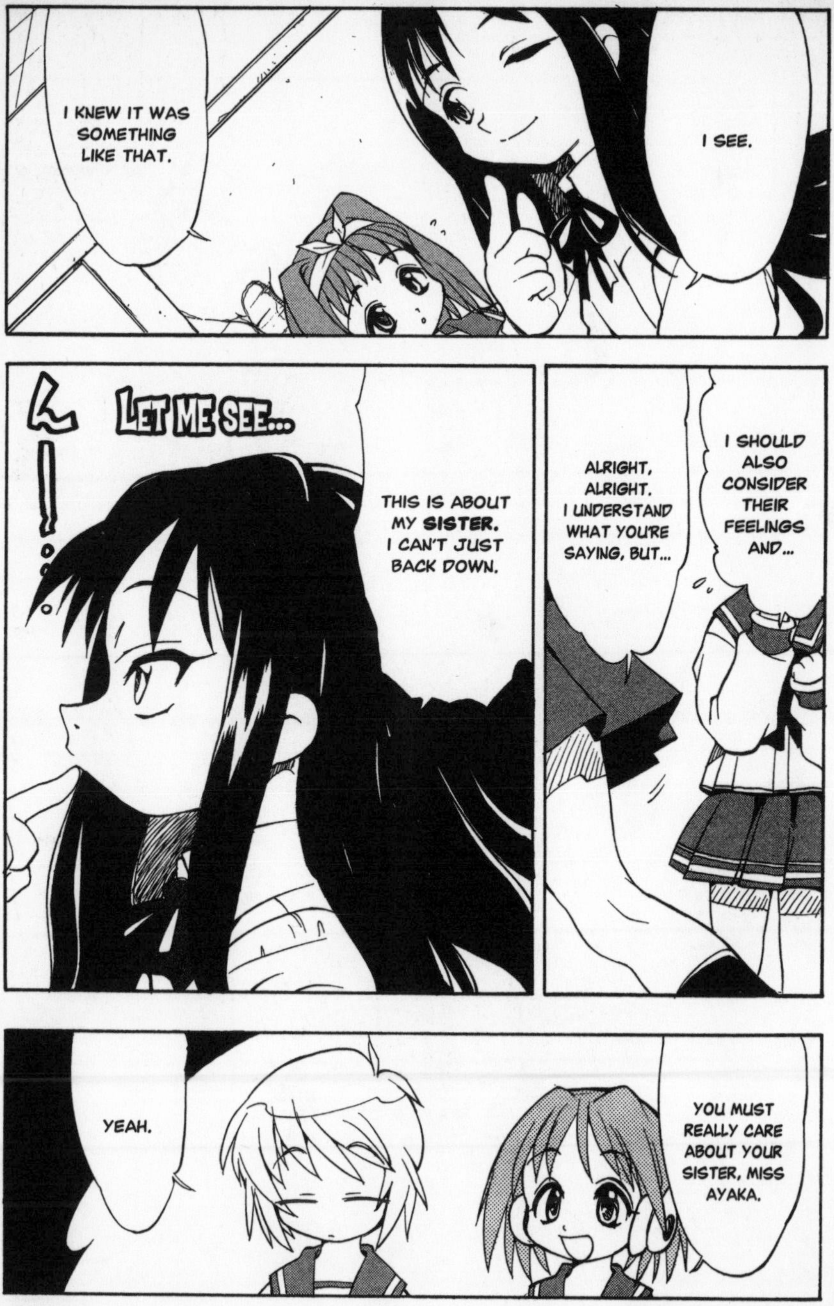
I SEE.
I KNEW IT WAS SOMETHING LIKE THAT.
I SHOULD ALSO CONSIDER THEIR FEELINGS AND...
ALRIGHT, ALRIGHT. I UNDERSTAND WHAT YOU'RE SAYING, BUT...
THIS IS ABOUT MY **SISTER.** I CAN'T JUST BACK DOWN.
LET ME SEE...
YOU MUST REALLY CARE ABOUT YOUR SISTER, MISS AYAKA.
YEAH.

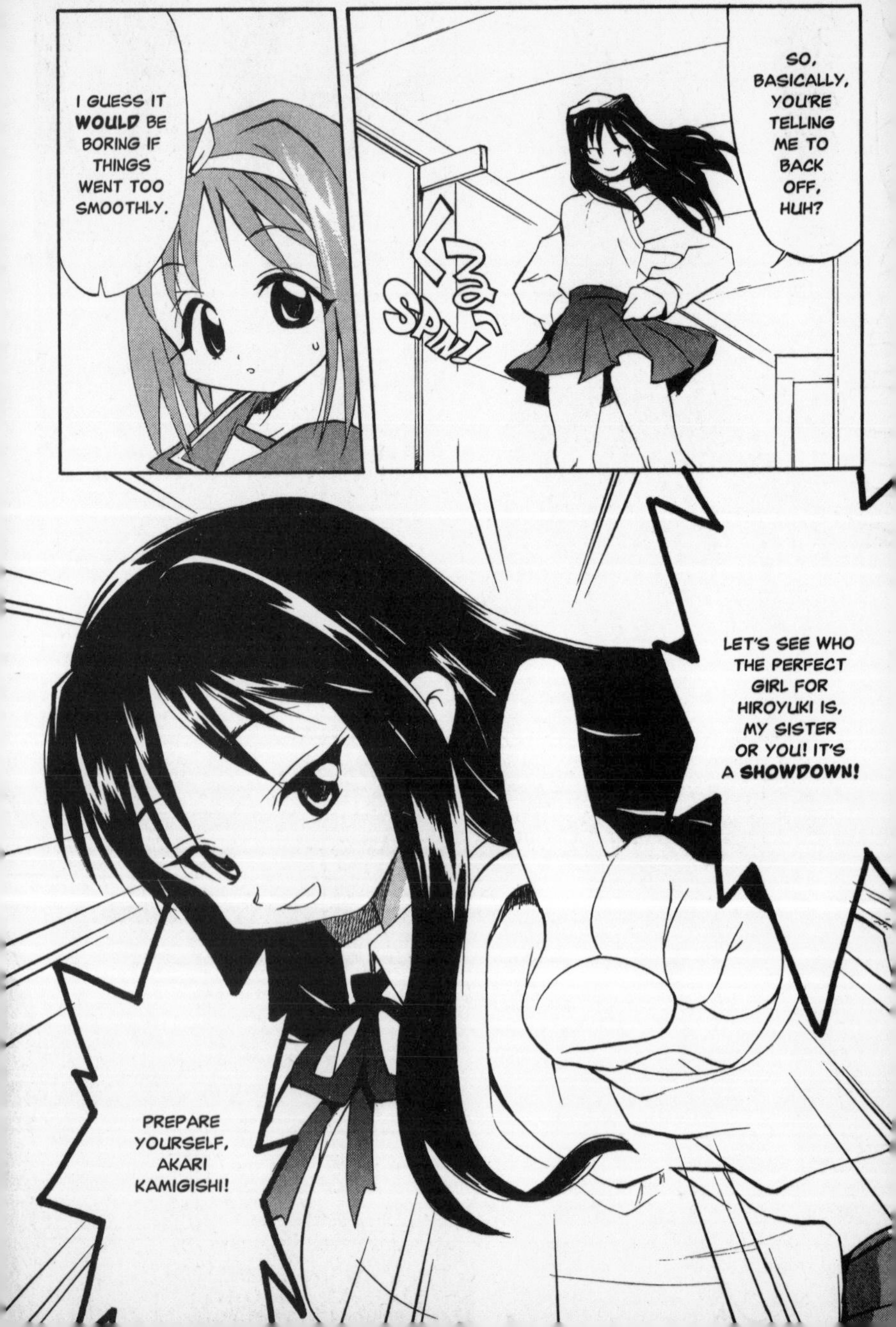
SO, BASICALLY, YOU'RE TELLING ME TO BACK OFF, HUH?
SPIN!
I GUESS IT **WOULD** BE BORING IF THINGS WENT TOO SMOOTHLY.
LET'S SEE WHO THE PERFECT GIRL FOR HIROYUKI IS, MY SISTER OR YOU! IT'S A **SHOWDOWN!**
PREPARE YOURSELF, AKARI KAMIGISHI!

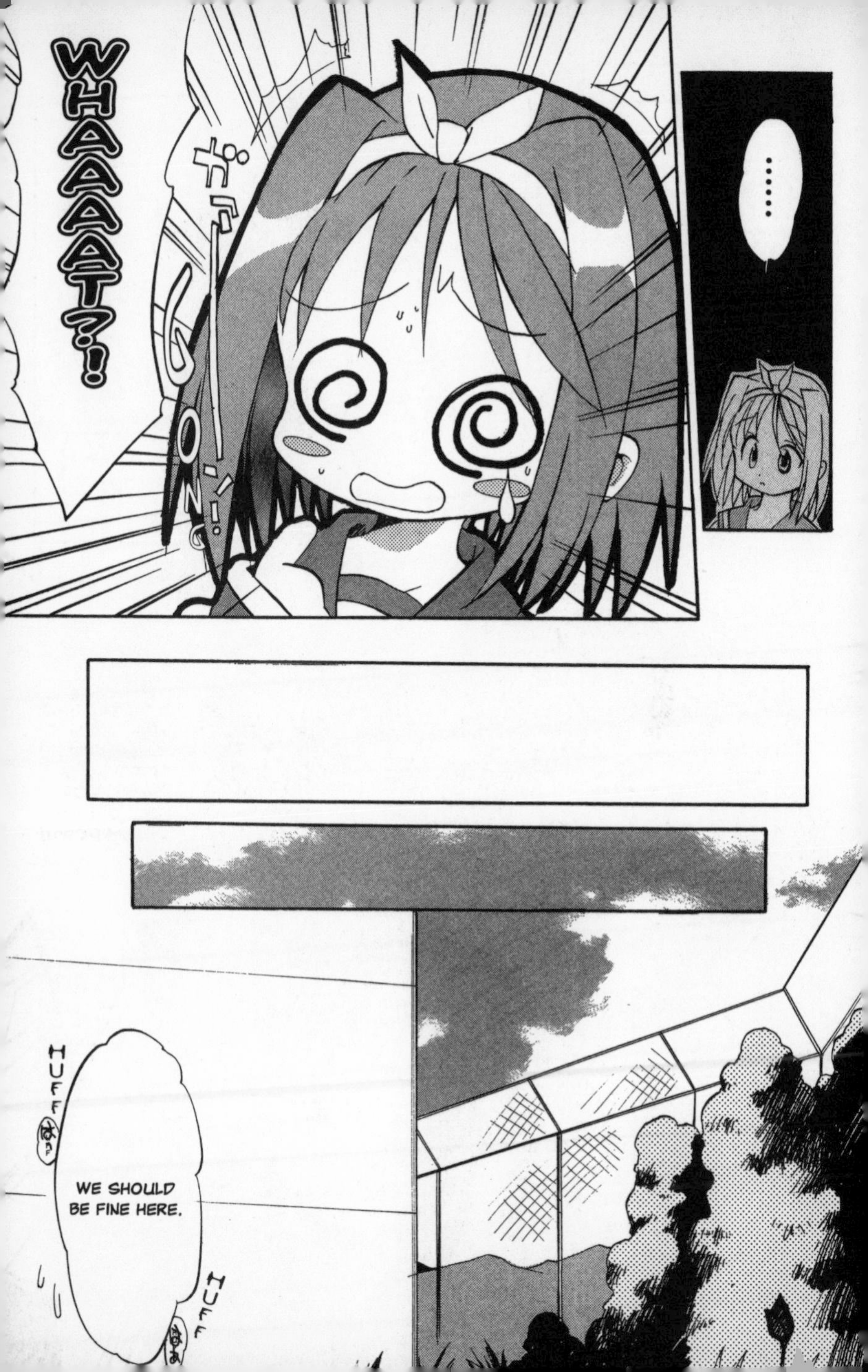

......
WHAAAAAT?!
HUFF
WE SHOULD BE FINE HERE.
HUFF

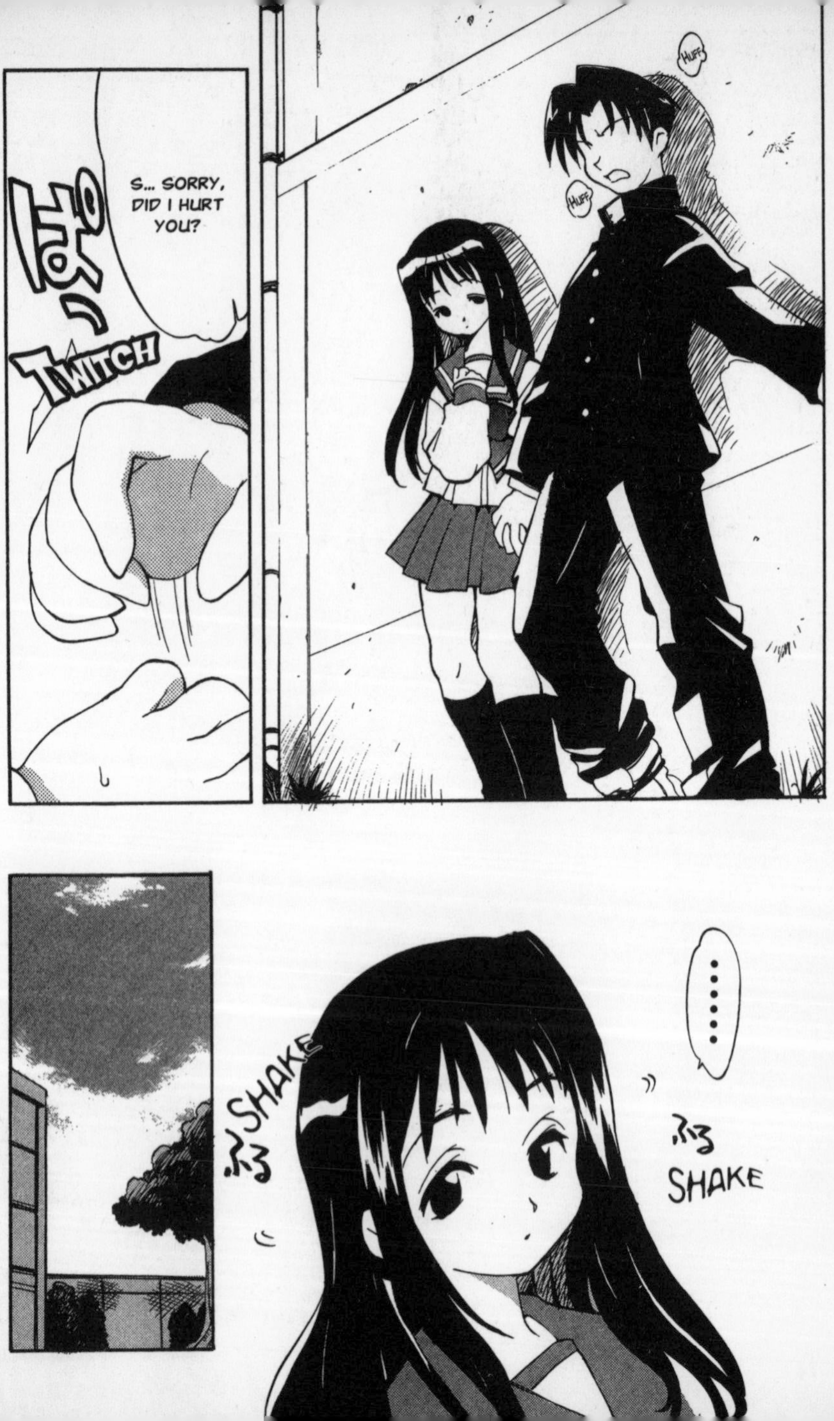
HUFF
HUFF
S... SORRY, DID I HURT YOU?
TWITCH
......
ふる SHAKE
ふる SHAKE

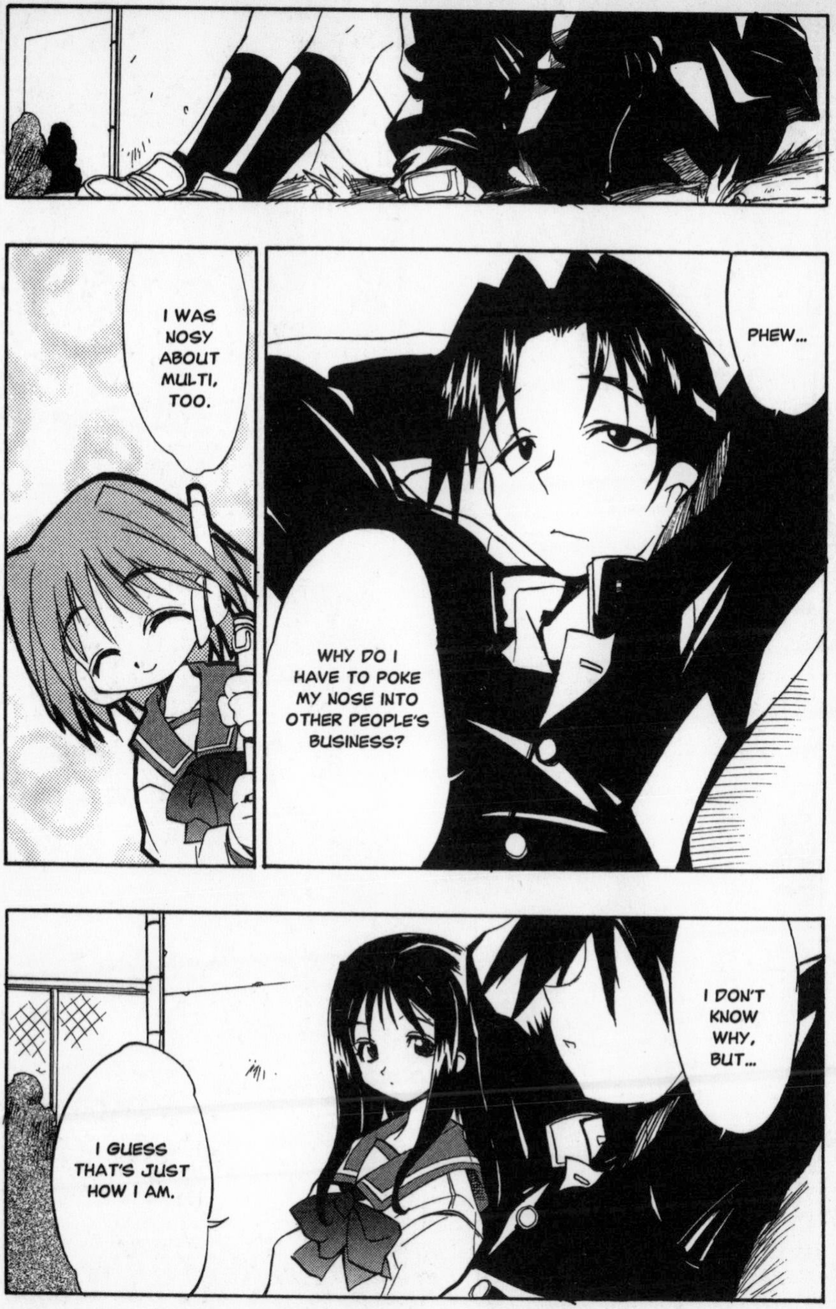
PHEW...
WHY DO I HAVE TO POKE MY NOSE INTO OTHER PEOPLE'S BUSINESS?
I WAS NOSY ABOUT MULTI, TOO.
I DON'T KNOW WHY, BUT...
I GUESS THAT'S JUST HOW I AM.

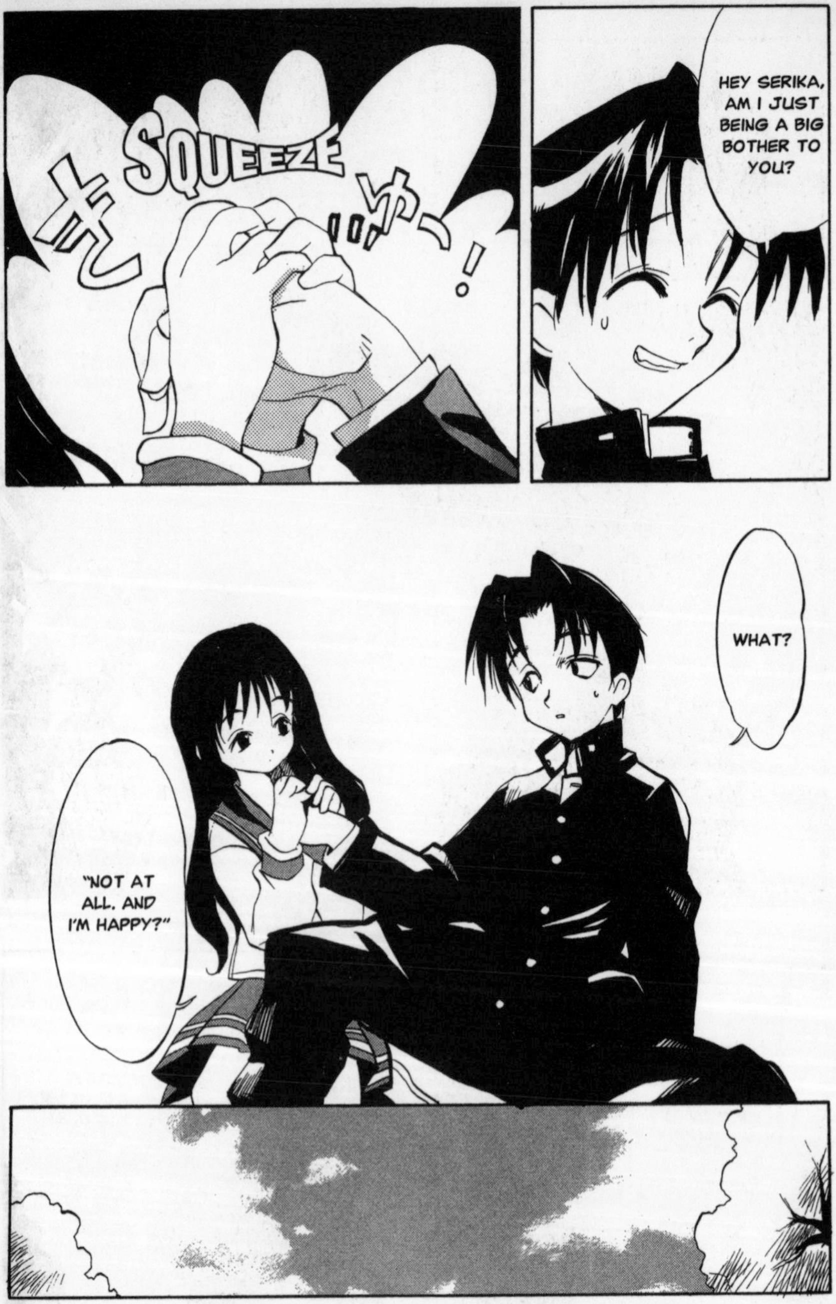
HEY SERIKA, AM I JUST BEING A BIG BOTHER TO YOU?
SQUEEZE
WHAT?
"NOT AT ALL. AND I'M HAPPY?"

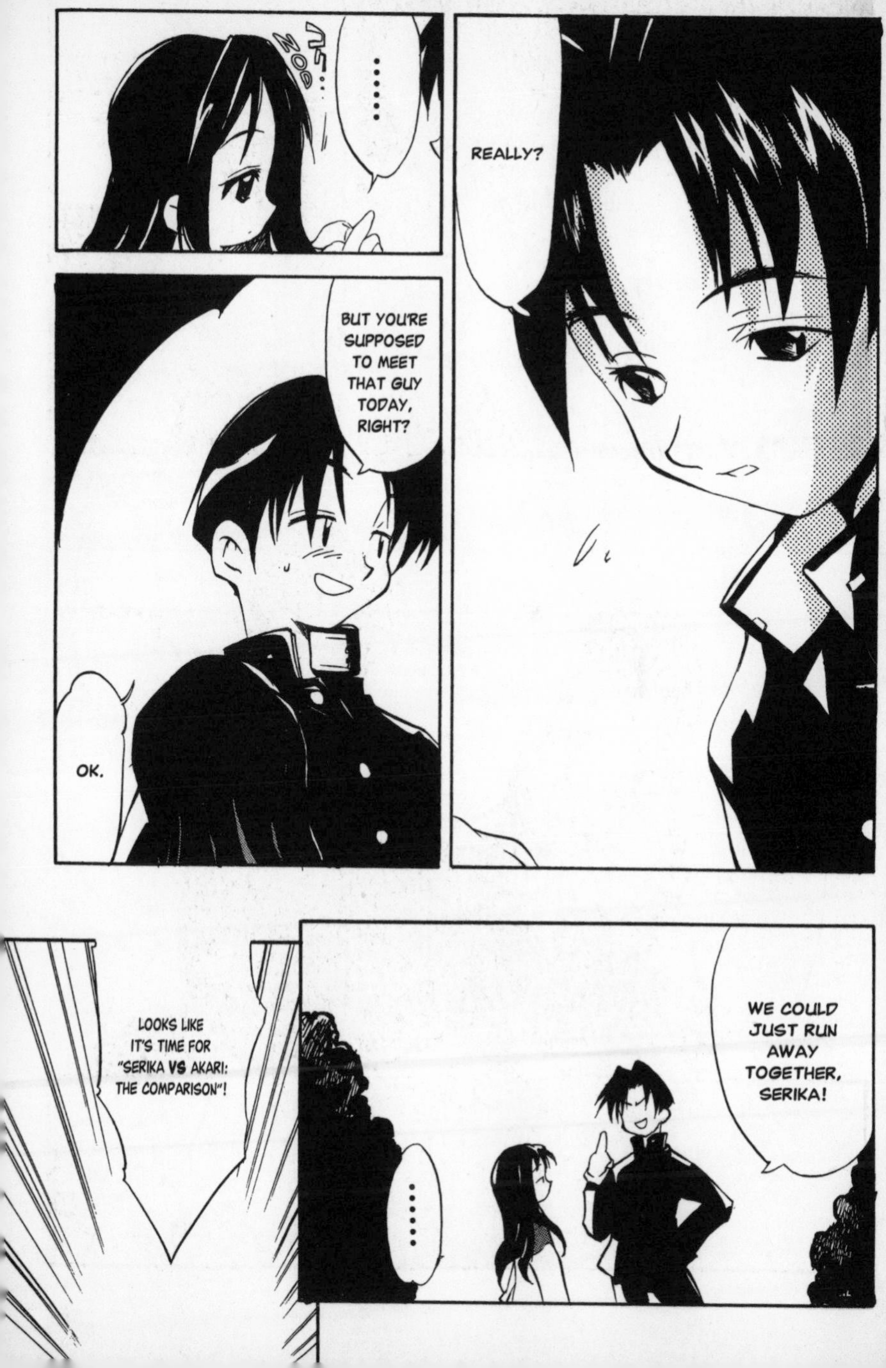

REALLY?
ZOOP
......
BUT YOU'RE SUPPOSED TO MEET THAT GUY TODAY, RIGHT?
OK.
WE COULD JUST RUN AWAY TOGETHER, SERIKA!
......
LOOKS LIKE IT'S TIME FOR "SERIKA VS AKARI: THE COMPARISON"!

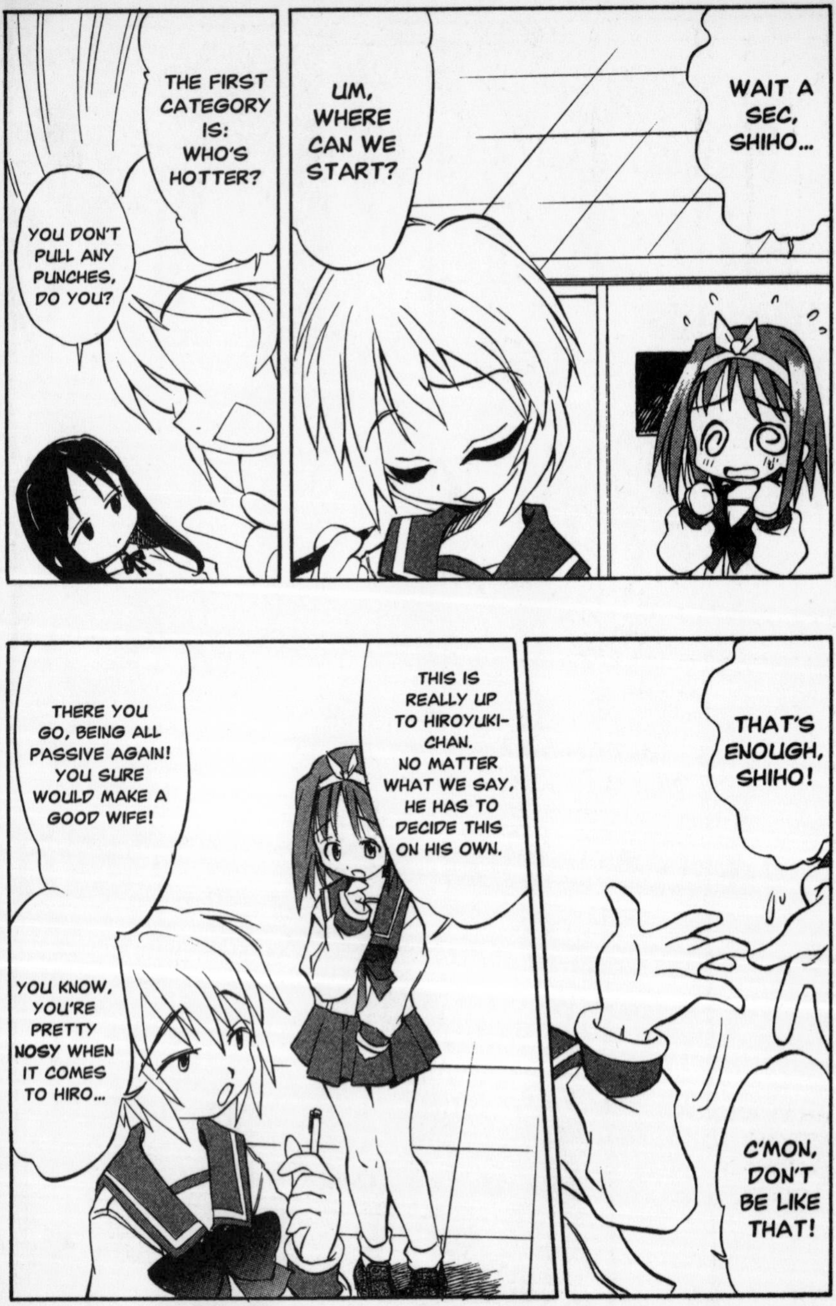
WAIT A SEC, SHIHO...
UM, WHERE CAN WE START?
THE FIRST CATEGORY IS: WHO'S HOTTER?
YOU DON'T PULL ANY PUNCHES, DO YOU?
THAT'S ENOUGH, SHIHO!
C'MON, DON'T BE LIKE THAT!
THIS IS REALLY UP TO HIROYUKI-CHAN. NO MATTER WHAT WE SAY, HE HAS TO DECIDE THIS ON HIS OWN.
THERE YOU GO, BEING ALL PASSIVE AGAIN! YOU SURE WOULD MAKE A GOOD WIFE!
YOU KNOW, YOU'RE PRETTY NOSY WHEN IT COMES TO HIRO...

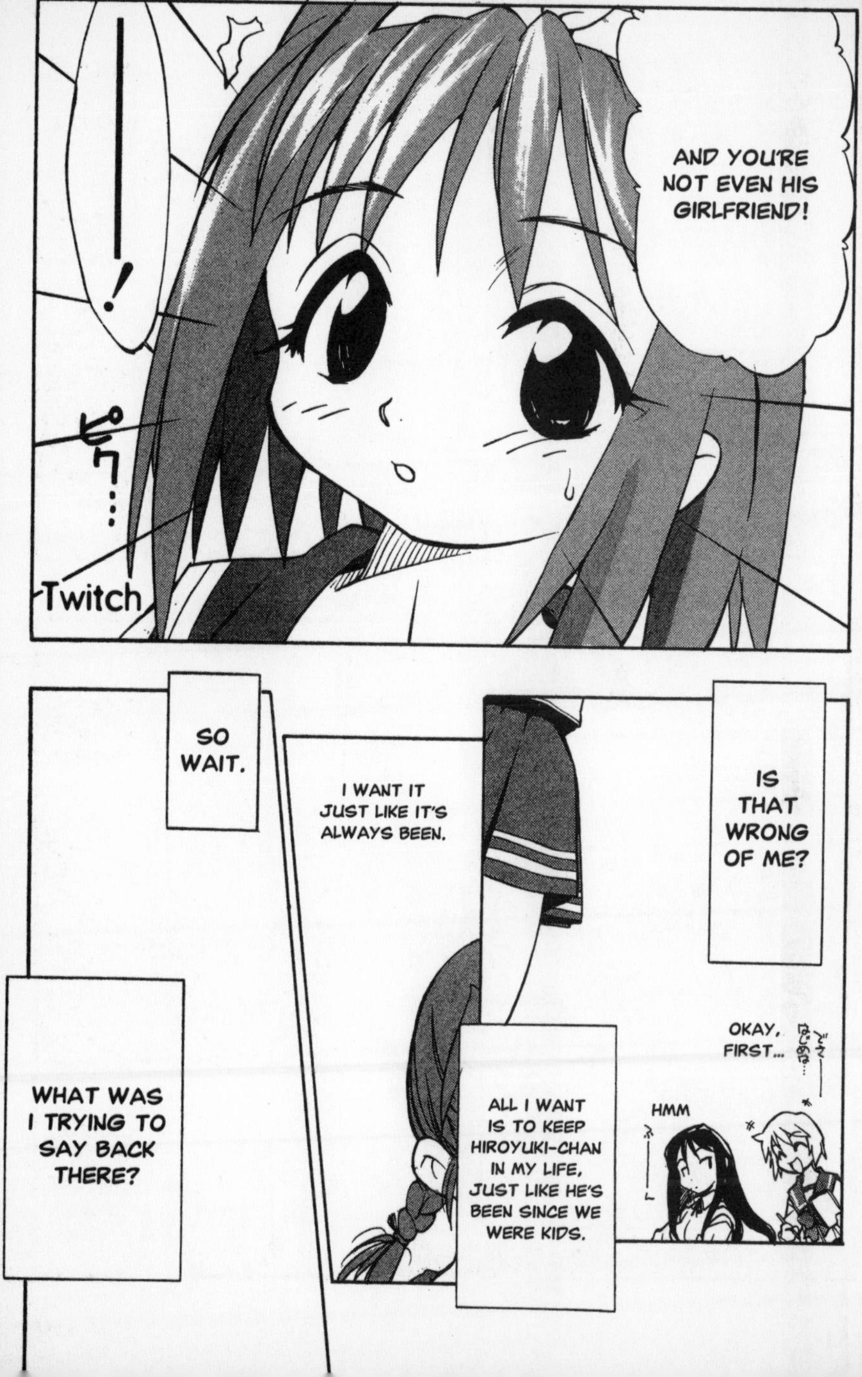
AND YOU'RE NOT EVEN HIS GIRLFRIEND!
—!
ピク…
Twitch
IS THAT WRONG OF ME?
I WANT IT JUST LIKE IT'S ALWAYS BEEN.
SO WAIT.
OKAY, FIRST...
HMM
ALL I WANT IS TO KEEP HIROYUKI-CHAN IN MY LIFE, JUST LIKE HE'S BEEN SINCE WE WERE KIDS.
WHAT WAS I TRYING TO SAY BACK THERE?

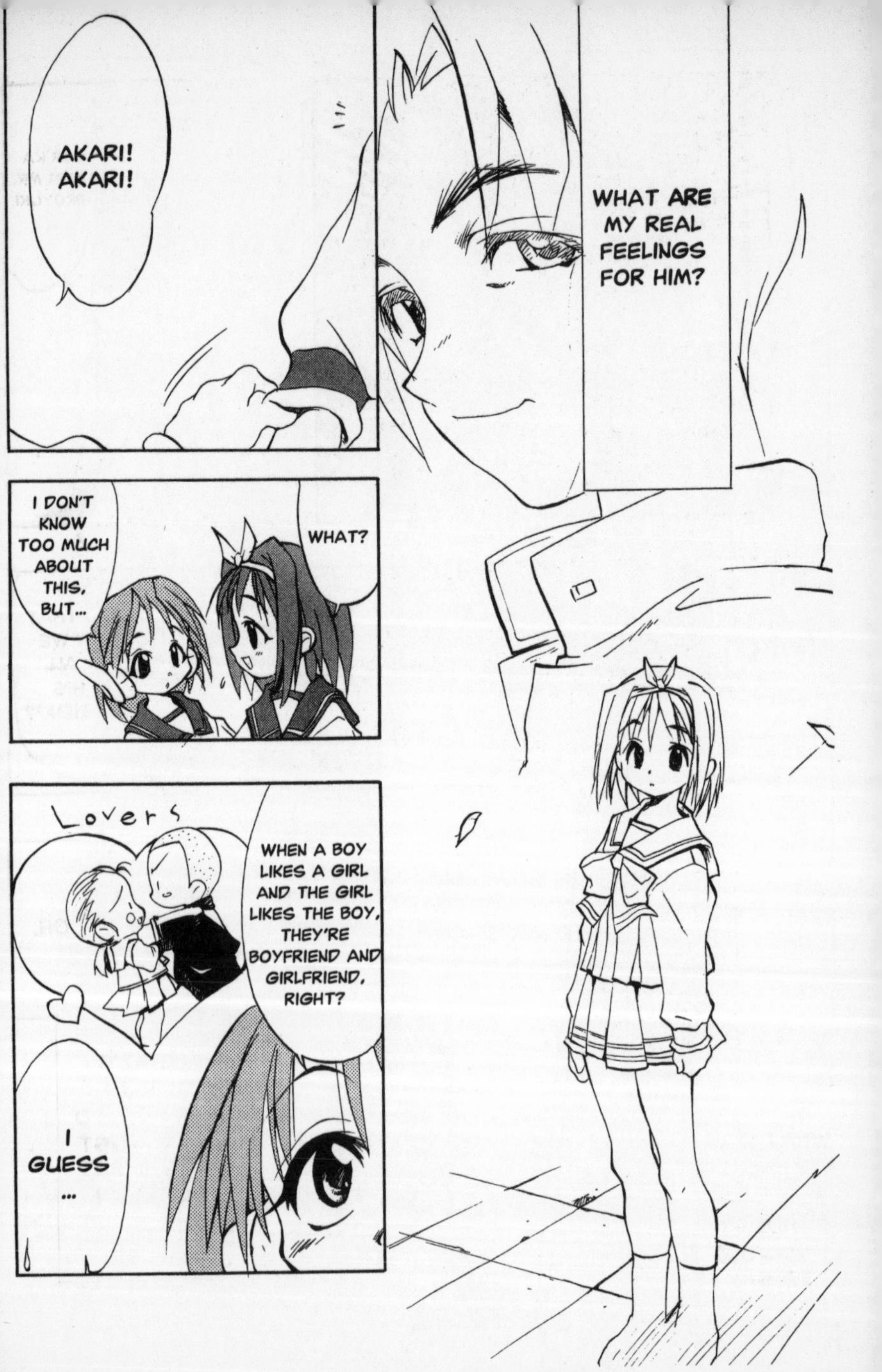
WHAT ARE MY REAL FEELINGS FOR HIM?
AKARI! AKARI!
WHAT?
I DON'T KNOW TOO MUCH ABOUT THIS, BUT...
WHEN A BOY LIKES A GIRL AND THE GIRL LIKES THE BOY, THEY'RE BOYFRIEND AND GIRLFRIEND, RIGHT?
Lovers
I GUESS ...

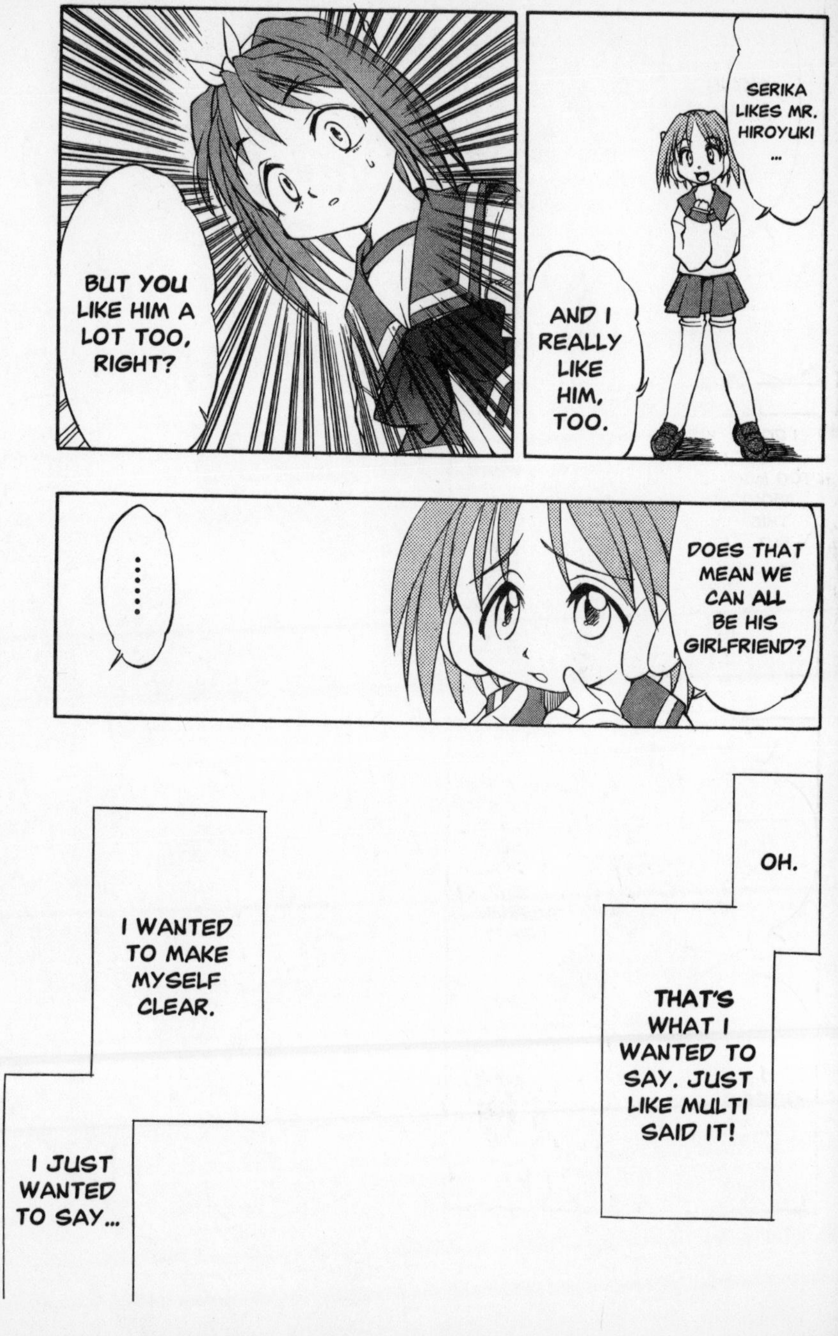
SERIKA LIKES MR. HIROYUKI ...
AND I REALLY LIKE HIM, TOO.
BUT YOU LIKE HIM A LOT TOO, RIGHT?
DOES THAT MEAN WE CAN ALL BE HIS GIRLFRIEND?
......
OH.
THAT'S WHAT I WANTED TO SAY. JUST LIKE MULTI SAID IT!
I WANTED TO MAKE MYSELF CLEAR.
I JUST WANTED TO SAY...

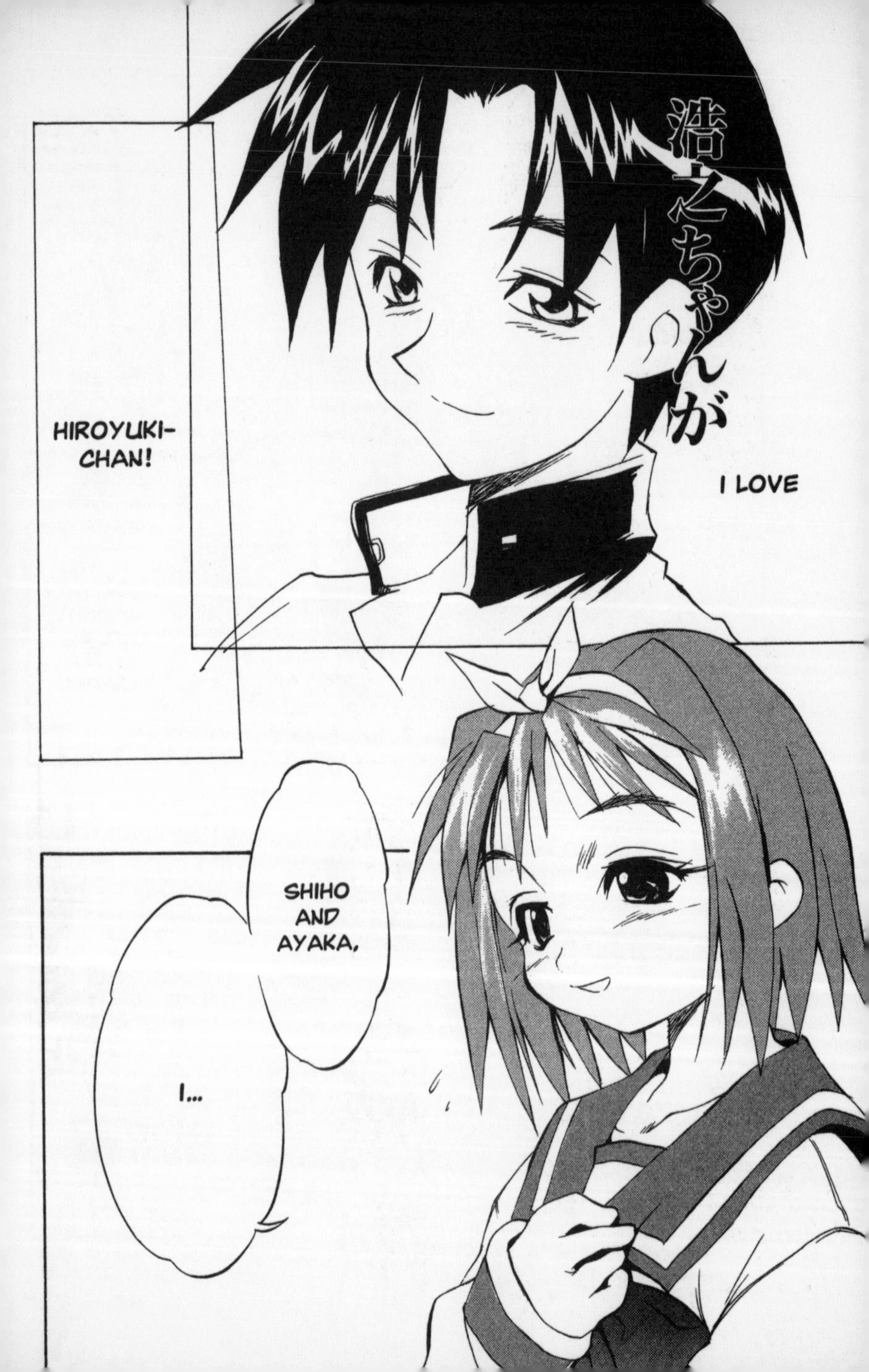
浩之ちゃんが
I LOVE
HIROYUKI-CHAN!
SHIHO AND AYAKA,
I...

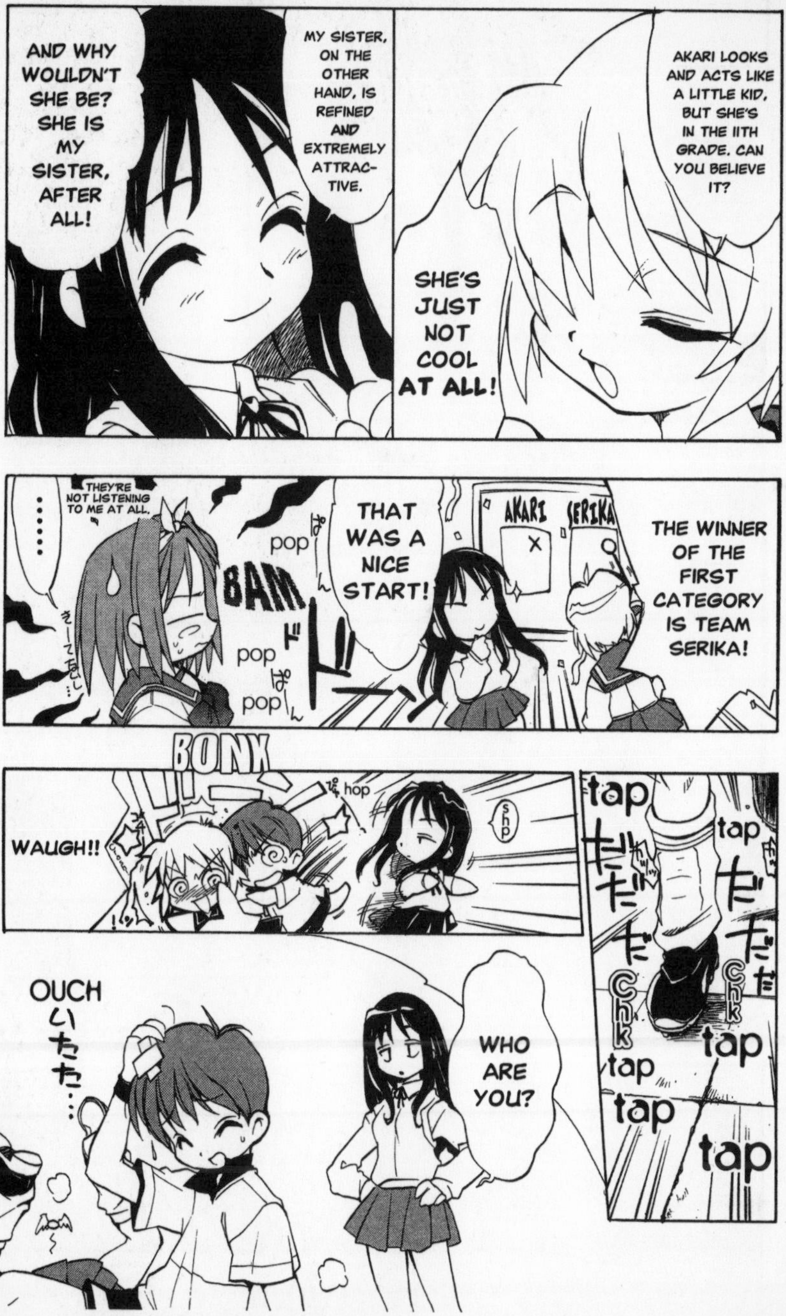
AKARI LOOKS AND ACTS LIKE A LITTLE KID, BUT SHE'S IN THE 11TH GRADE. CAN YOU BELIEVE IT?
SHE'S JUST NOT COOL AT ALL!
MY SISTER, ON THE OTHER HAND, IS REFINED AND EXTREMELY ATTRACTIVE.
AND WHY WOULDN'T SHE BE? SHE IS MY SISTER, AFTER ALL!
THE WINNER OF THE FIRST CATEGORY IS TEAM SERIKA!
AKARI
SERIKA
THAT WAS A NICE START!
BAM
pop
pop
pop
THEY'RE NOT LISTENING TO ME AT ALL.
......
tap
tap
chk
chk
tap
tap
tap
tap
BONK
hop
shp
WAUGH!!
WHO ARE YOU?
OUCH
いたた…

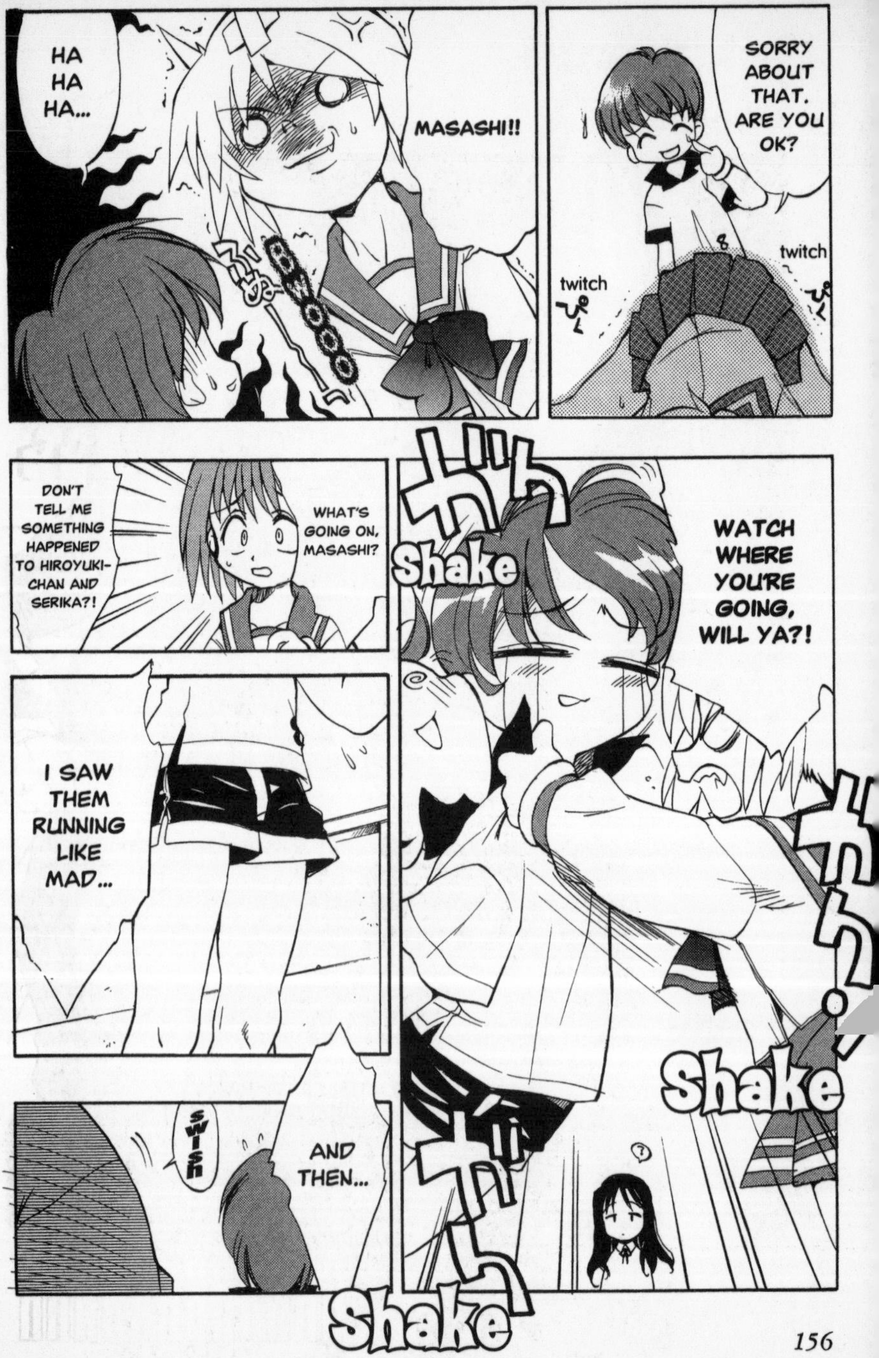
SORRY ABOUT THAT. ARE YOU OK?
twitch
twitch
MASASHI!!
HA HA HA...
WATCH WHERE YOU'RE GOING, WILL YA?!
Shake
Shake
Shake
WHAT'S GOING ON, MASASHI?
DON'T TELL ME SOMETHING HAPPENED TO HIROYUKI-CHAN AND SERIKA?!
I SAW THEM RUNNING LIKE MAD...
AND THEN...
swish

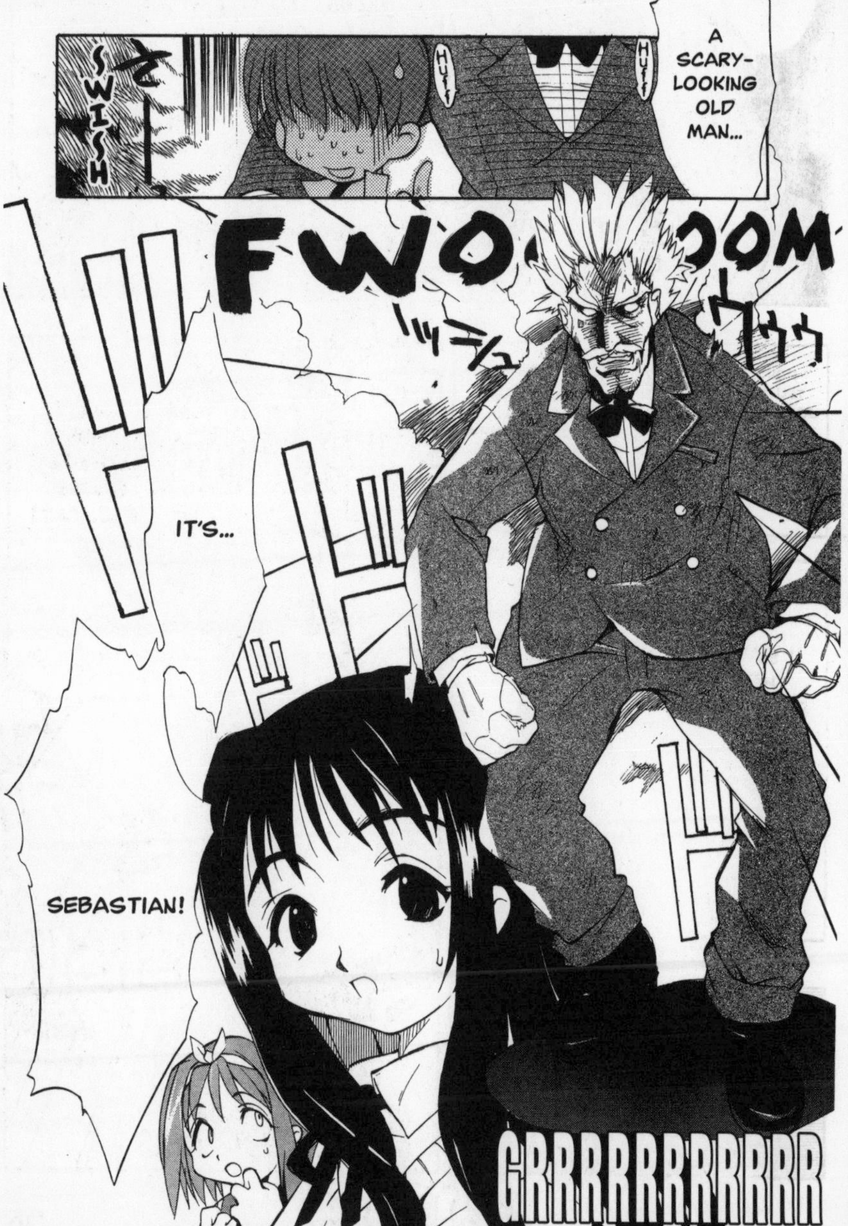
A SCARY-LOOKING OLD MAN...
HUFF
HUFF
SWISH
FWO-OOM
IT'S...
SEBASTIAN!
GRRRRRRRRRRR

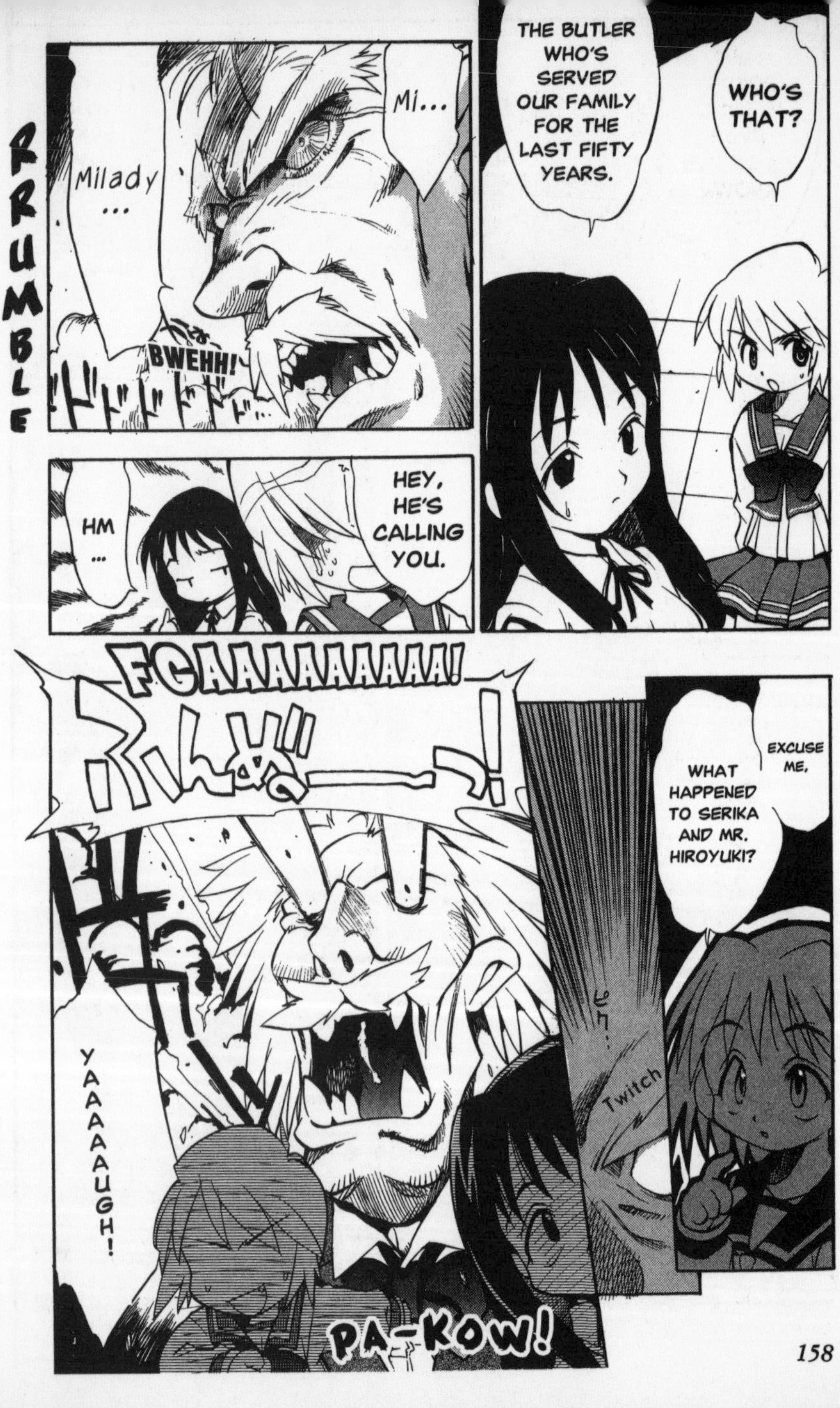
WHO'S THAT?
THE BUTLER WHO'S SERVED OUR FAMILY FOR THE LAST FIFTY YEARS.
Mi...
Milady ...
RRUMBLE
BWEHH!
HEY, HE'S CALLING YOU.
HM ...
EXCUSE ME,
WHAT HAPPENED TO SERIKA AND MR. HIROYUKI?
Twitch
FGAAAAAAAAAA!
ふんぬ――っ!
YAAAAAUGH!
PA-KOW!

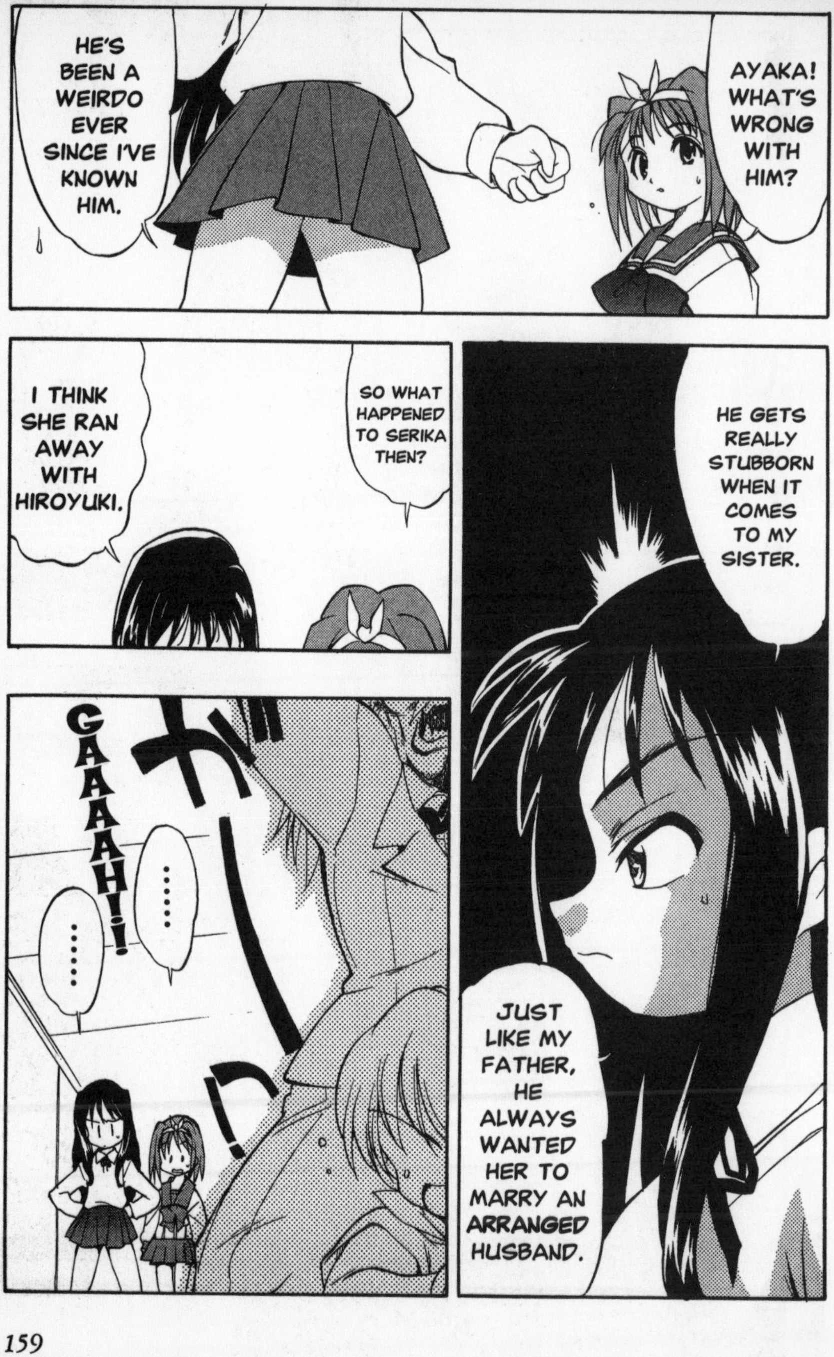
AYAKA! WHAT'S WRONG WITH HIM?
HE'S BEEN A WEIRDO EVER SINCE I'VE KNOWN HIM.
HE GETS REALLY STUBBORN WHEN IT COMES TO MY SISTER.
JUST LIKE MY FATHER, HE ALWAYS WANTED HER TO MARRY AN ARRANGED HUSBAND.
SO WHAT HAPPENED TO SERIKA THEN?
I THINK SHE RAN AWAY WITH HIROYUKI.
GAAAAAH!!
......
......

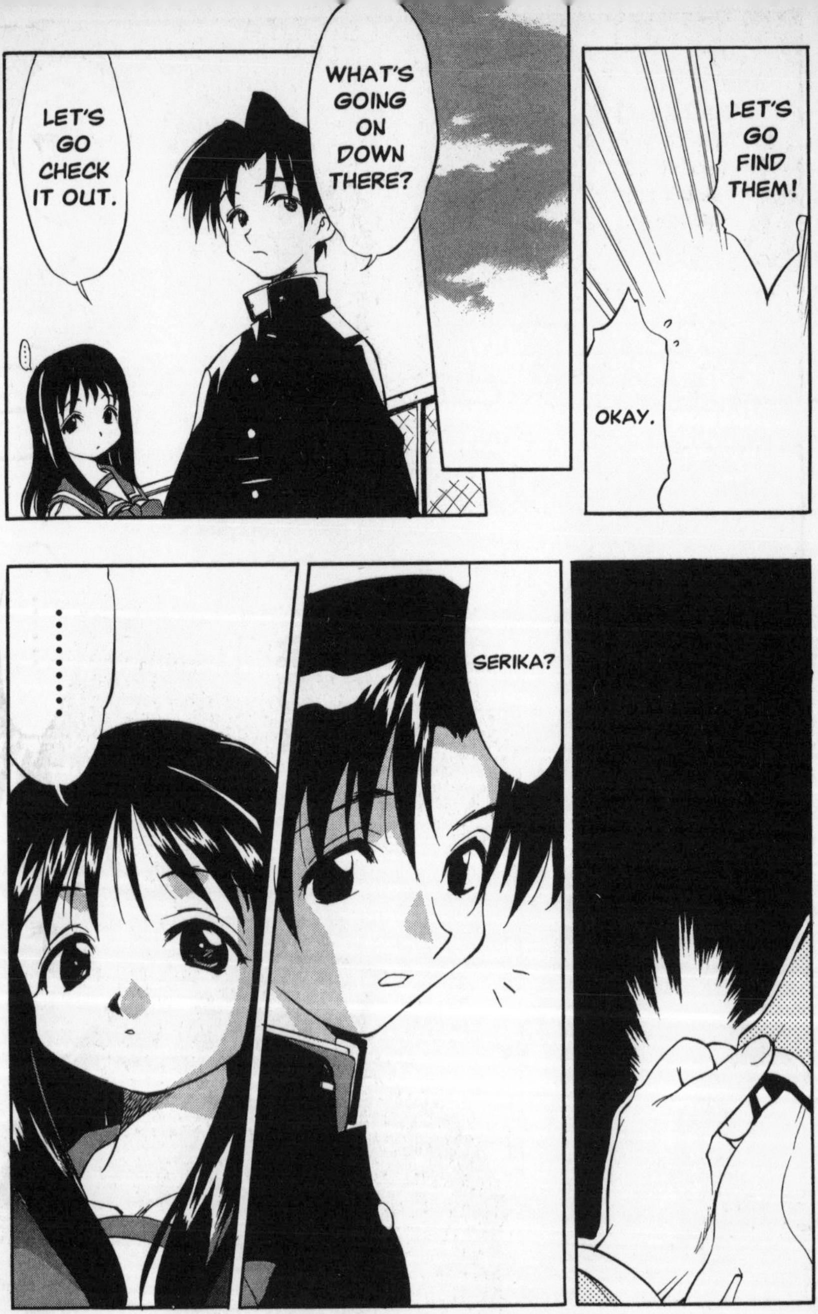
LET'S GO FIND THEM!
OKAY.
WHAT'S GOING ON DOWN THERE?
LET'S GO CHECK IT OUT.
...
SERIKA?
....

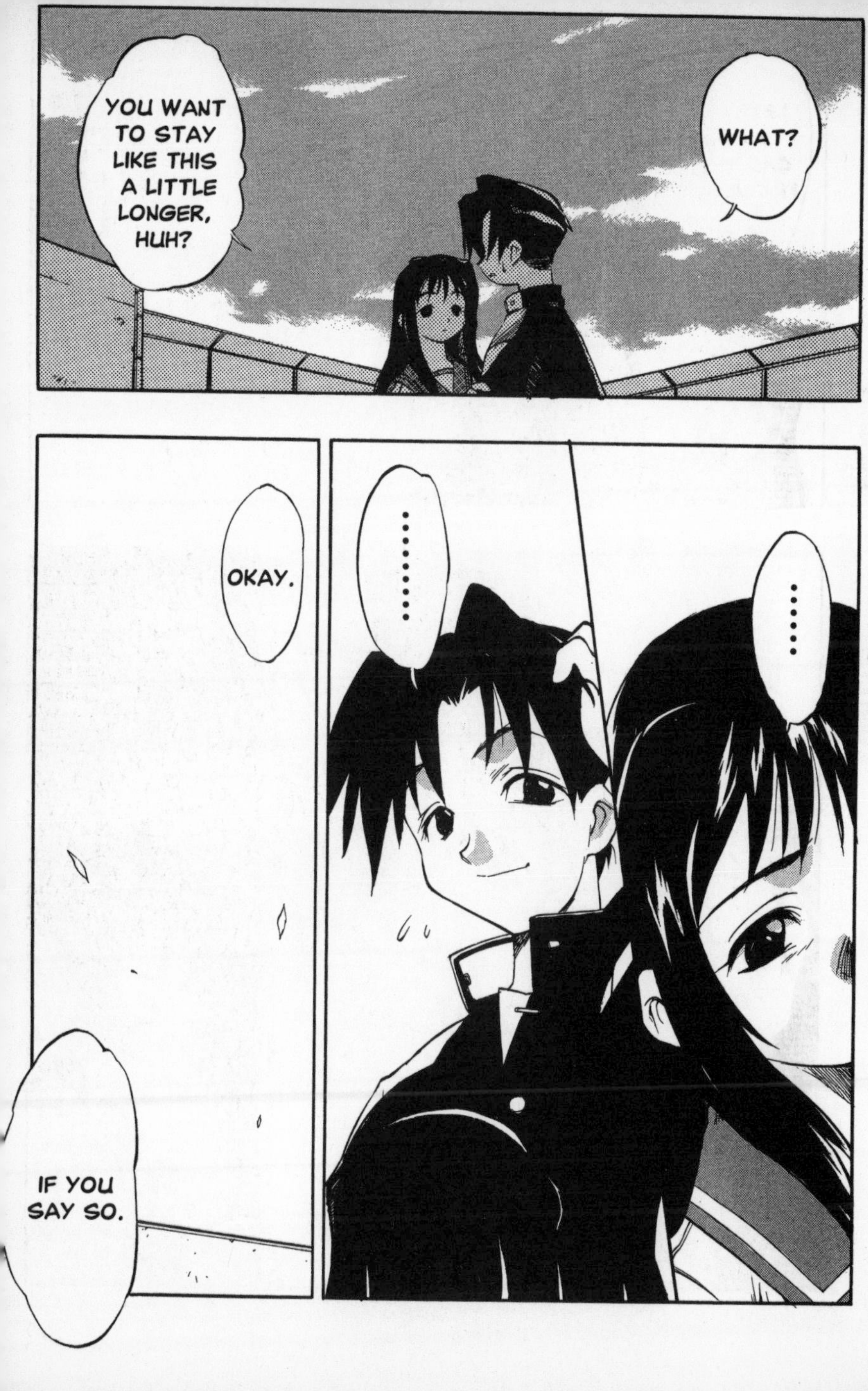
WHAT?
YOU WANT TO STAY LIKE THIS A LITTLE LONGER, HUH?
......
....
OKAY.
IF YOU SAY SO.

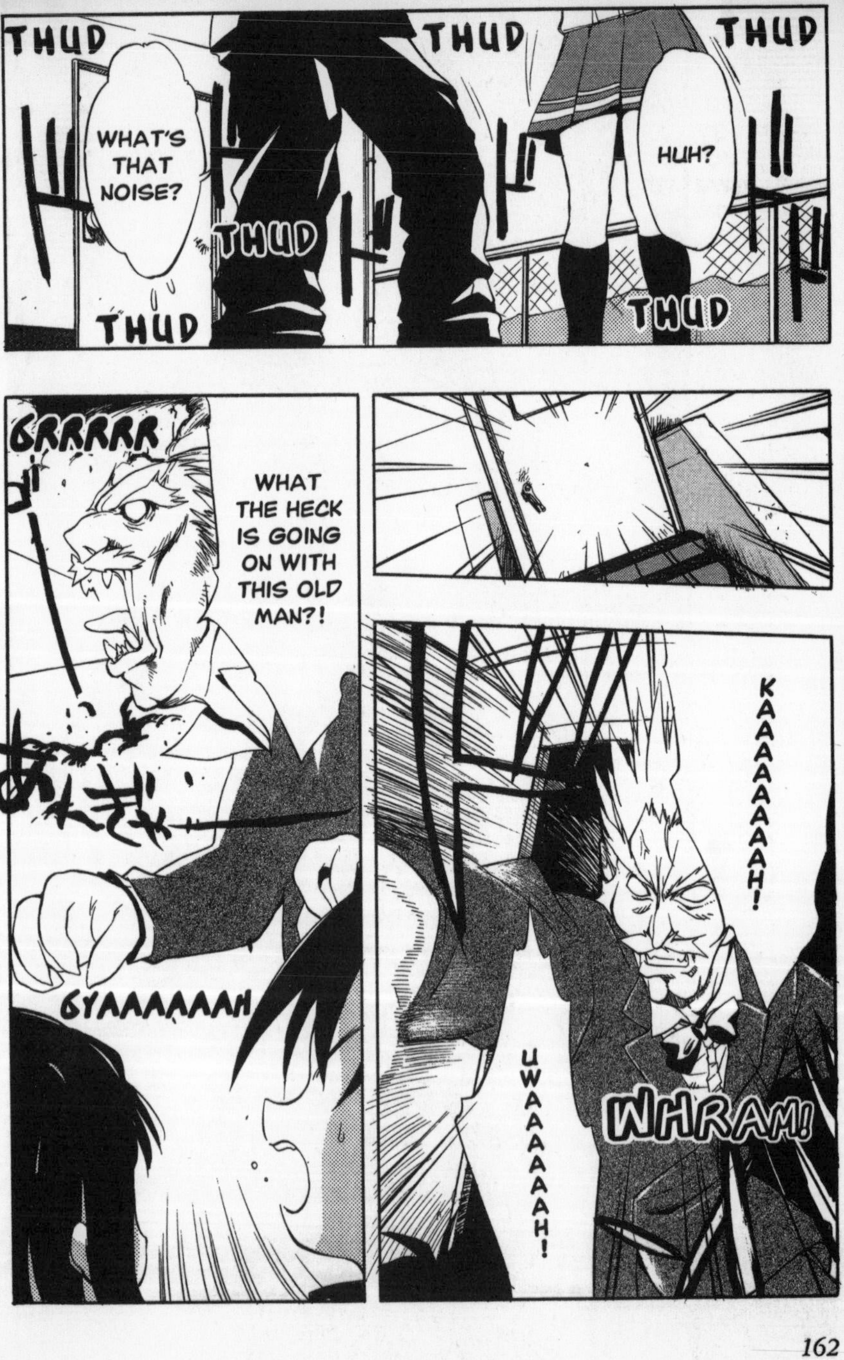
THUD
THUD
THUD
WHAT'S THAT NOISE?
HUH?
THUD
THUD
THUD
GRRRRR
WHAT THE HECK IS GOING ON WITH THIS OLD MAN?!
GYAAAAAAH
KAAAAAAAAAH!
UWAAAAAAAH!
WHRAM!

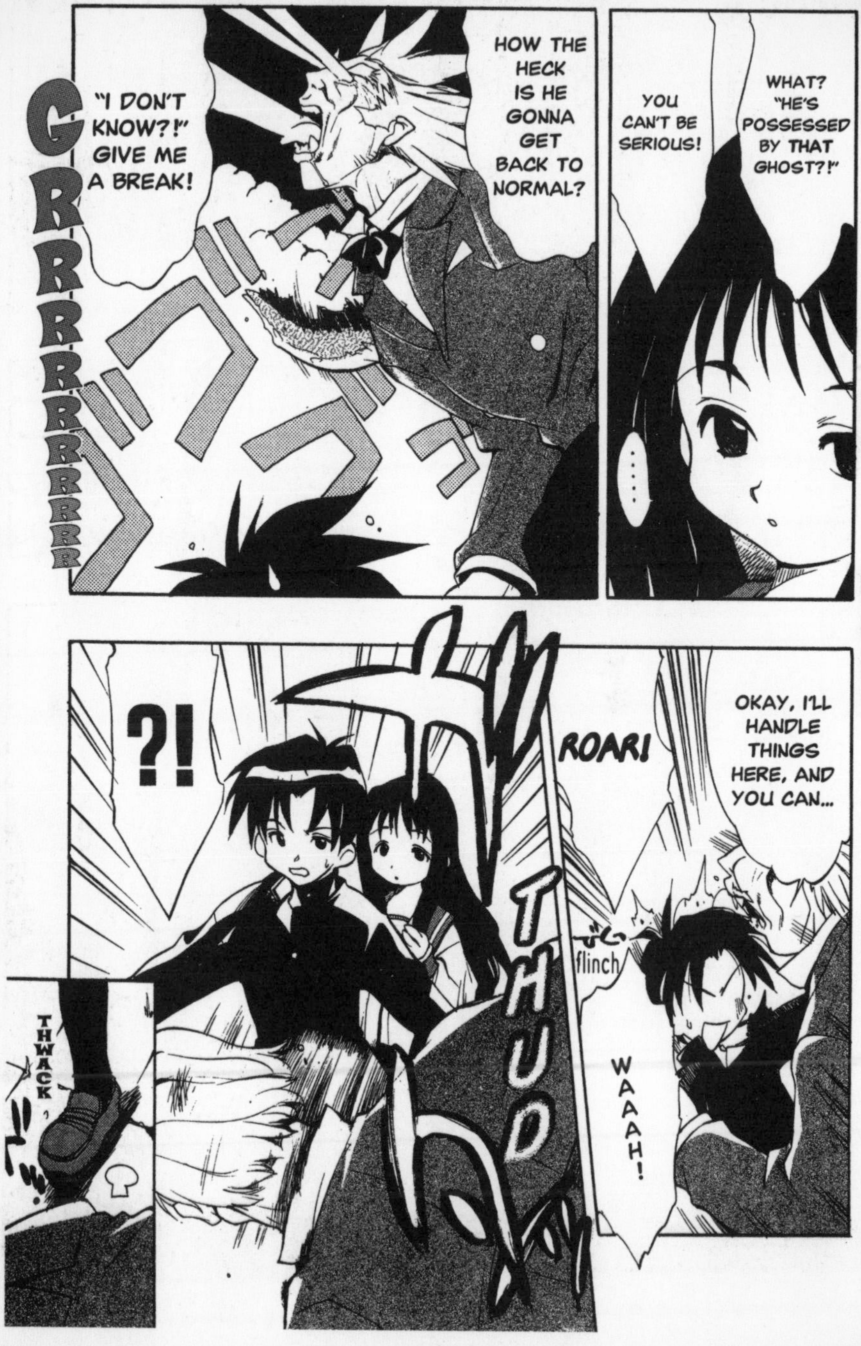
WHAT? "HE'S POSSESSED BY THAT GHOST?!"
YOU CAN'T BE SERIOUS!
.....
HOW THE HECK IS HE GONNA GET BACK TO NORMAL?
"I DON'T KNOW?!" GIVE ME A BREAK!
GRRRRRRRRRR
OKAY, I'LL HANDLE THINGS HERE, AND YOU CAN...
flinch
WAAAH!
ROAR!
THUD
?!
THWACK

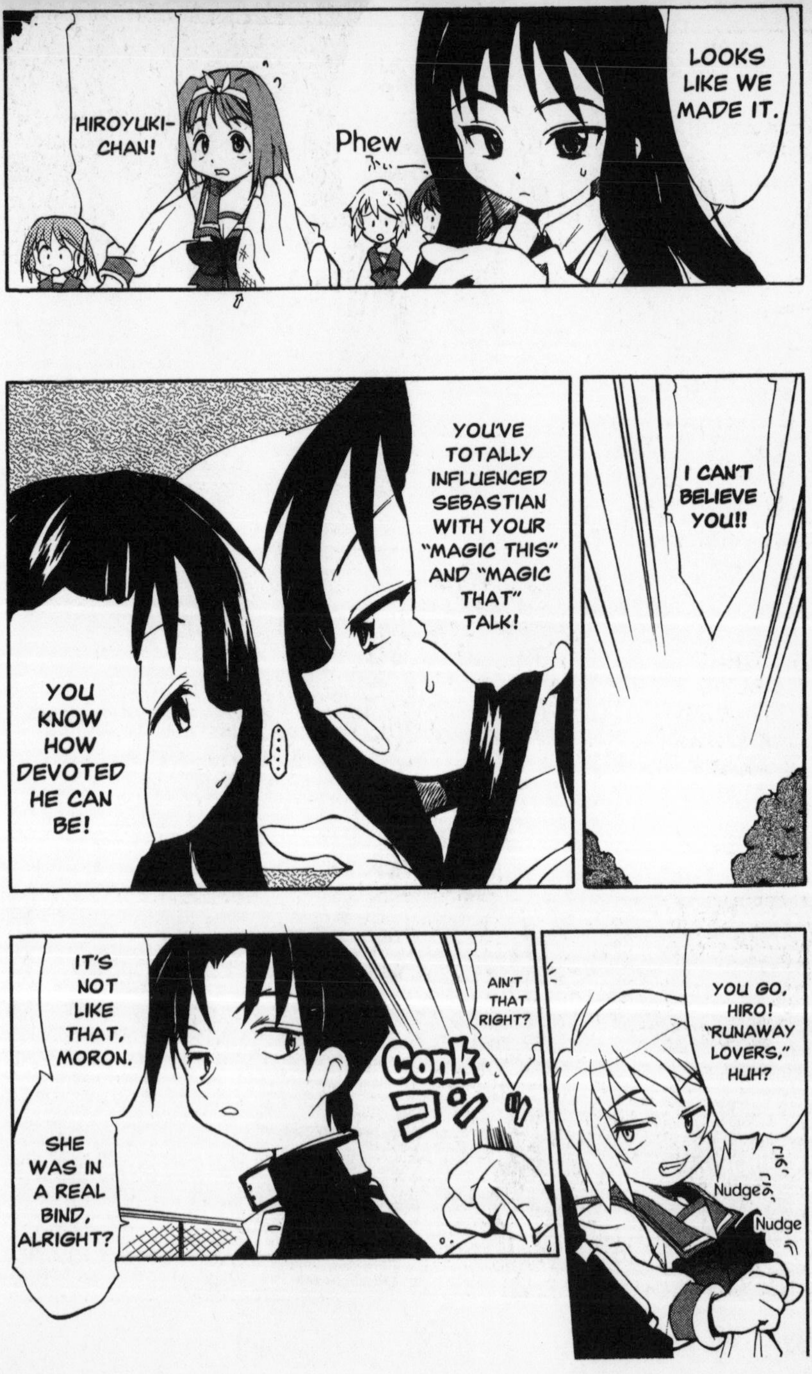
LOOKS LIKE WE MADE IT.
Phew
HIROYUKI-CHAN!
I CAN'T BELIEVE YOU!!
YOU'VE TOTALLY INFLUENCED SEBASTIAN WITH YOUR "MAGIC THIS" AND "MAGIC THAT" TALK!
YOU KNOW HOW DEVOTED HE CAN BE!
YOU GO, HIRO! "RUNAWAY LOVERS," HUH?
Nudge
Nudge
AIN'T THAT RIGHT?
Conk
IT'S NOT LIKE THAT, MORON.
SHE WAS IN A REAL BIND, ALRIGHT?

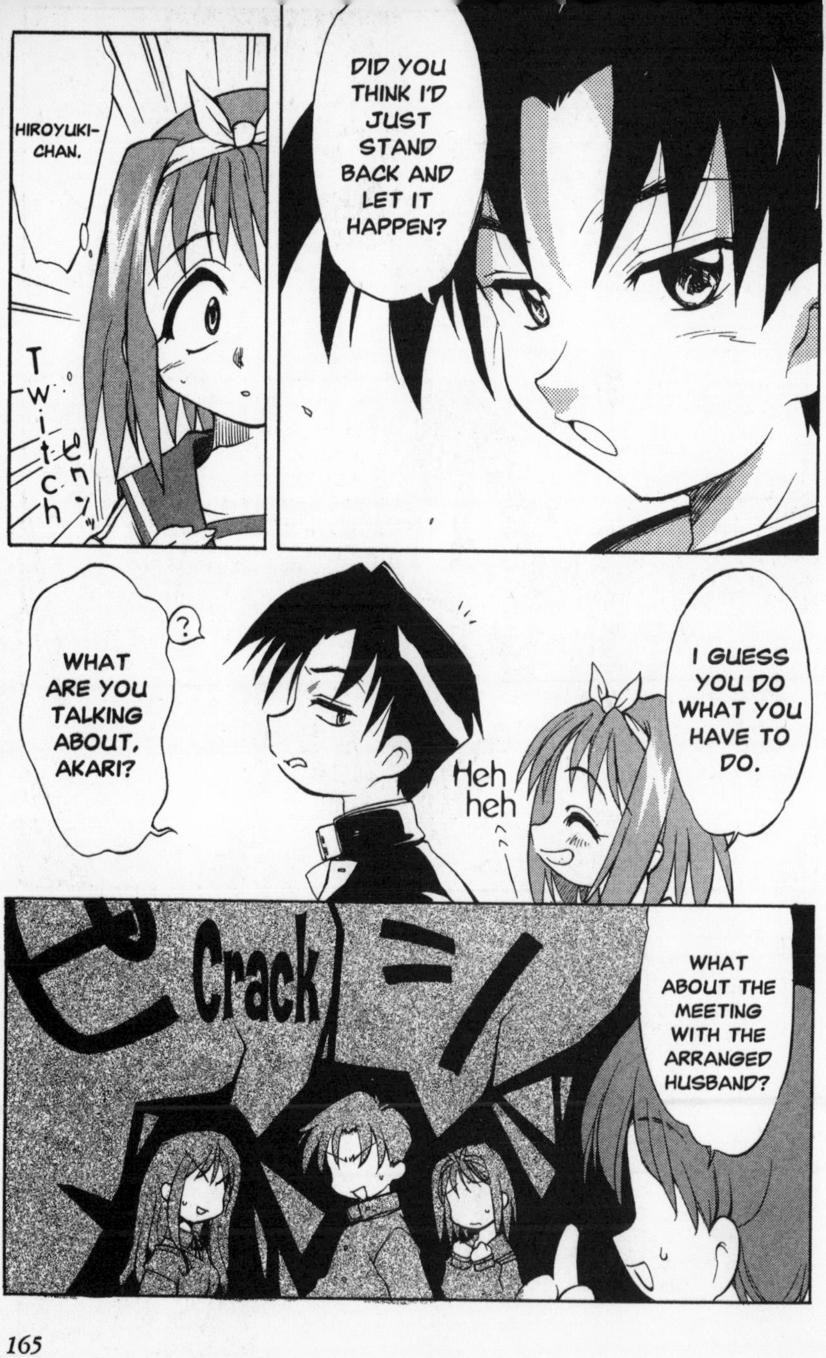
DID YOU THINK I'D JUST STAND BACK AND LET IT HAPPEN?
HIROYUKI-CHAN.
Twitch
I GUESS YOU DO WHAT YOU HAVE TO DO.
Heh heh
WHAT ARE YOU TALKING ABOUT, AKARI?
WHAT ABOUT THE MEETING WITH THE ARRANGED HUSBAND?
Crack

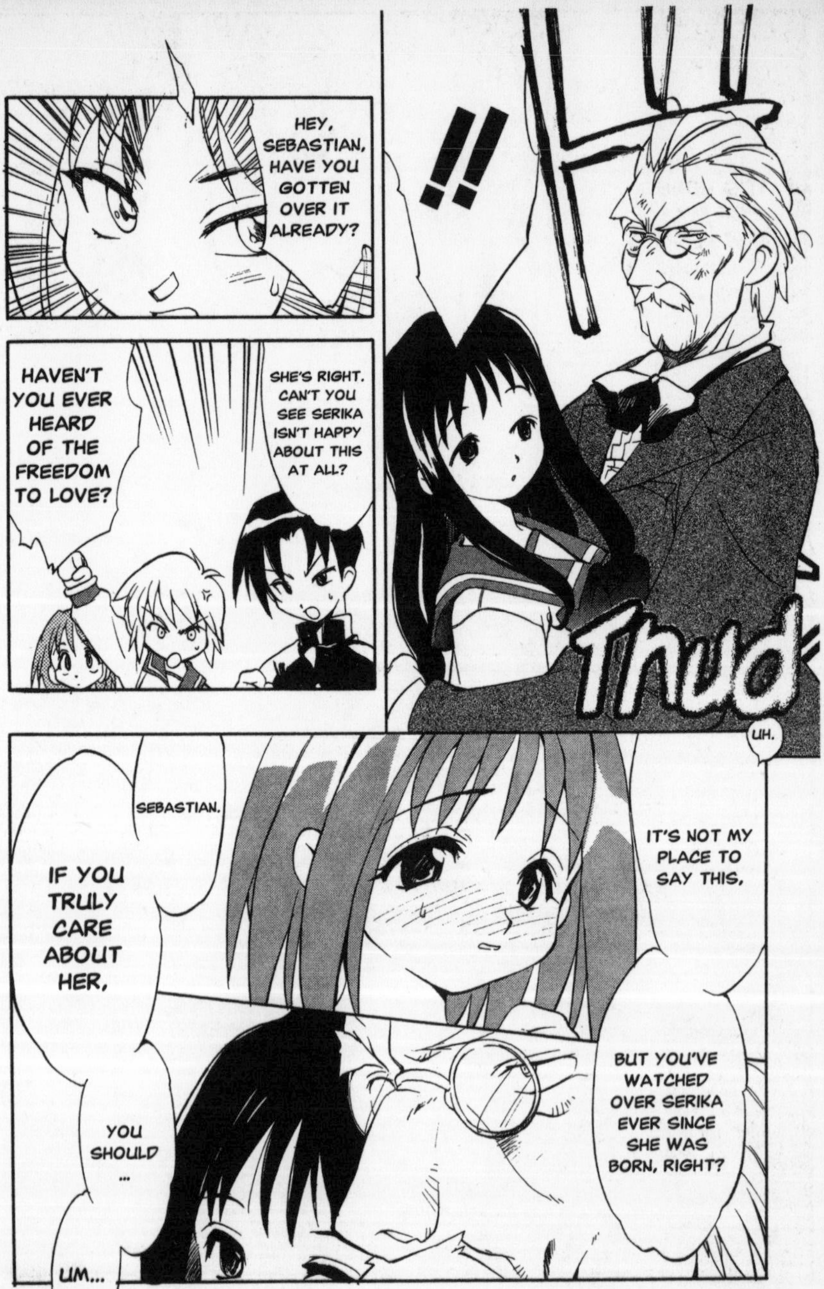
!!
THUD
HEY, SEBASTIAN, HAVE YOU GOTTEN OVER IT ALREADY?
SHE'S RIGHT. CAN'T YOU SEE SERIKA ISN'T HAPPY ABOUT THIS AT ALL?
HAVEN'T YOU EVER HEARD OF THE FREEDOM TO LOVE?
UH.
IT'S NOT MY PLACE TO SAY THIS,
BUT YOU'VE WATCHED OVER SERIKA EVER SINCE SHE WAS BORN, RIGHT?
SEBASTIAN.
IF YOU TRULY CARE ABOUT HER,
YOU SHOULD ...
UM...

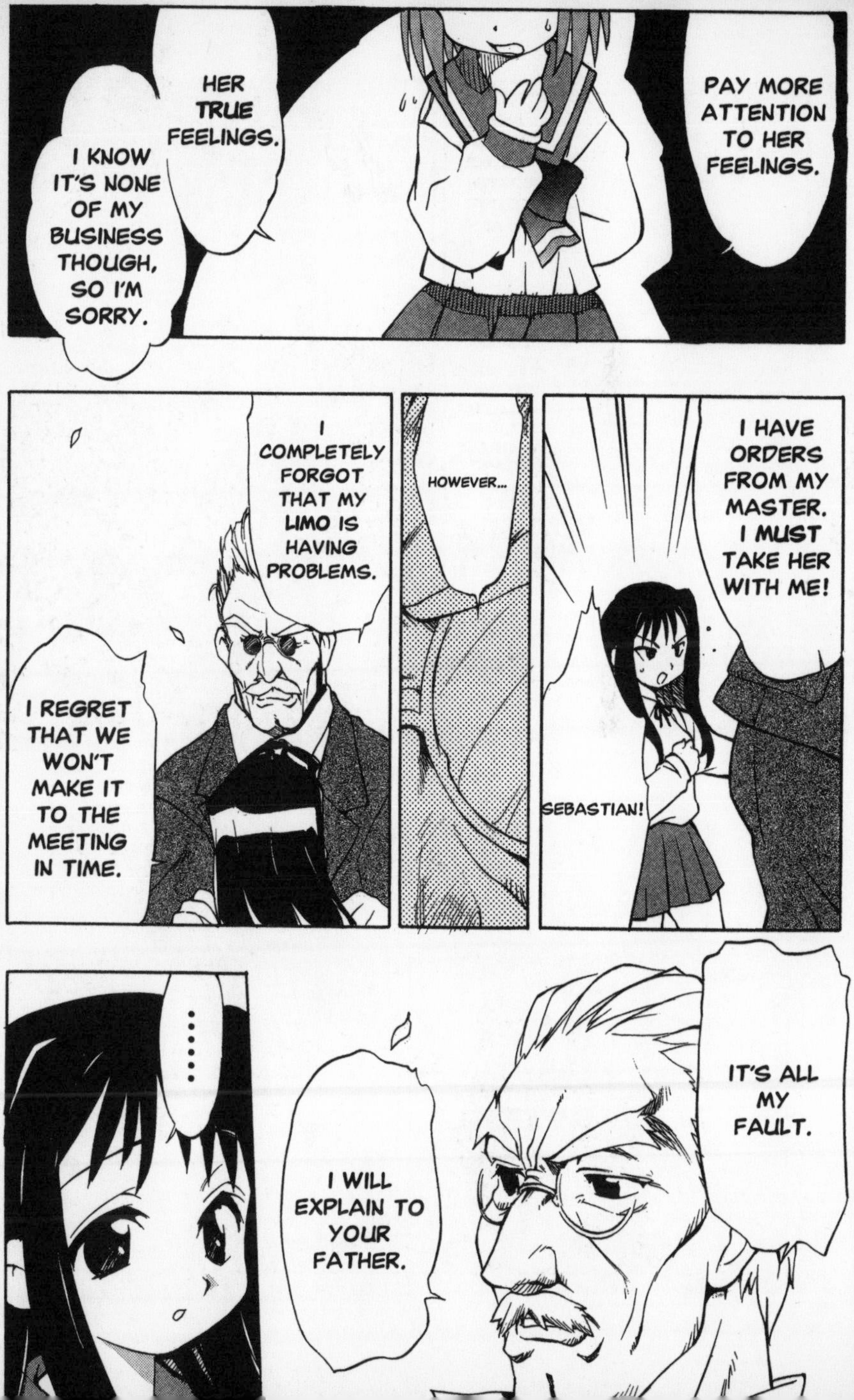
PAY MORE ATTENTION TO HER FEELINGS.
HER TRUE FEELINGS.
I KNOW IT'S NONE OF MY BUSINESS THOUGH, SO I'M SORRY.
I HAVE ORDERS FROM MY MASTER. I MUST TAKE HER WITH ME!
SEBASTIAN!
HOWEVER...
I COMPLETELY FORGOT THAT MY LIMO IS HAVING PROBLEMS.
I REGRET THAT WE WON'T MAKE IT TO THE MEETING IN TIME.
IT'S ALL MY FAULT.
I WILL EXPLAIN TO YOUR FATHER.
......

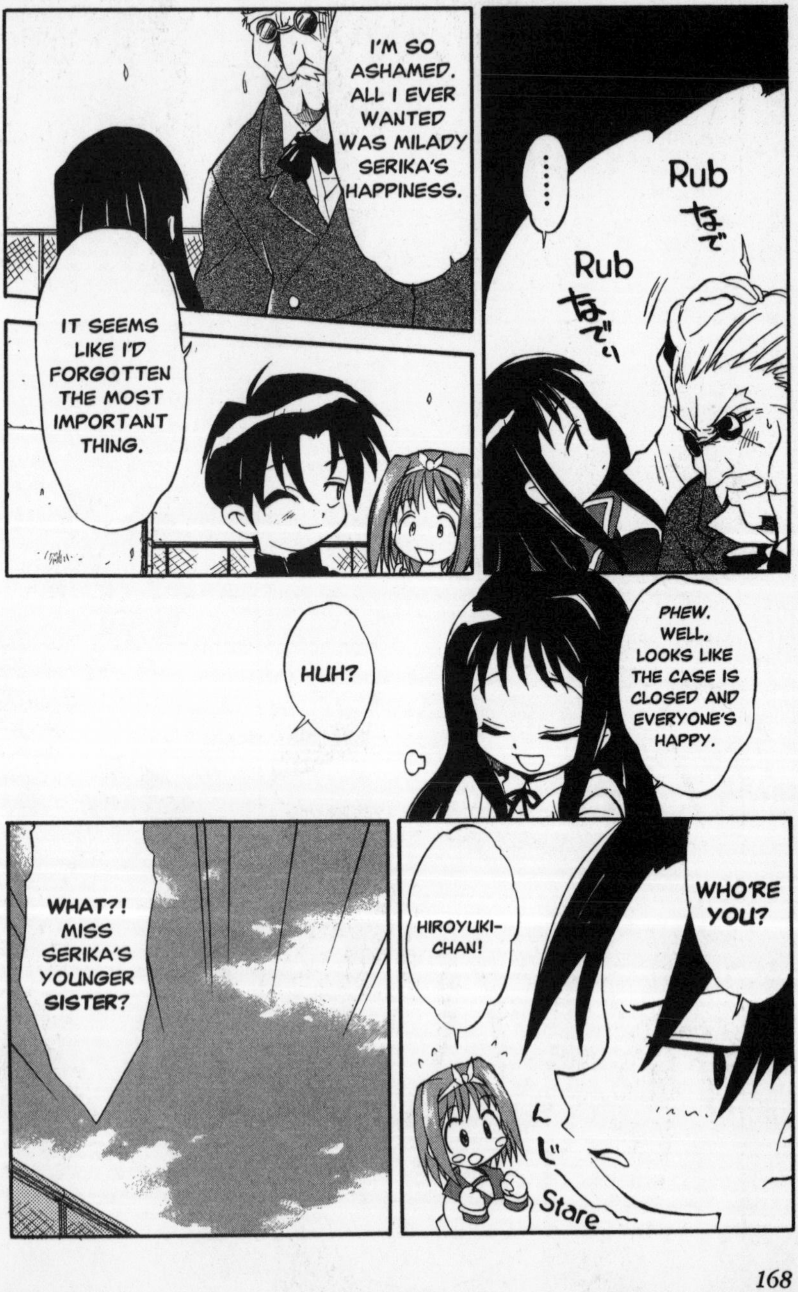
......
Rub
なで
Rub
なでり
I'M SO ASHAMED. ALL I EVER WANTED WAS MILADY SERIKA'S HAPPINESS.
IT SEEMS LIKE I'D FORGOTTEN THE MOST IMPORTANT THING.
PHEW. WELL, LOOKS LIKE THE CASE IS CLOSED AND EVERYONE'S HAPPY.
HUH?
WHO'RE YOU?
HIROYUKI-CHAN!
んじ
Stare
WHAT?! MISS SERIKA'S YOUNGER SISTER?

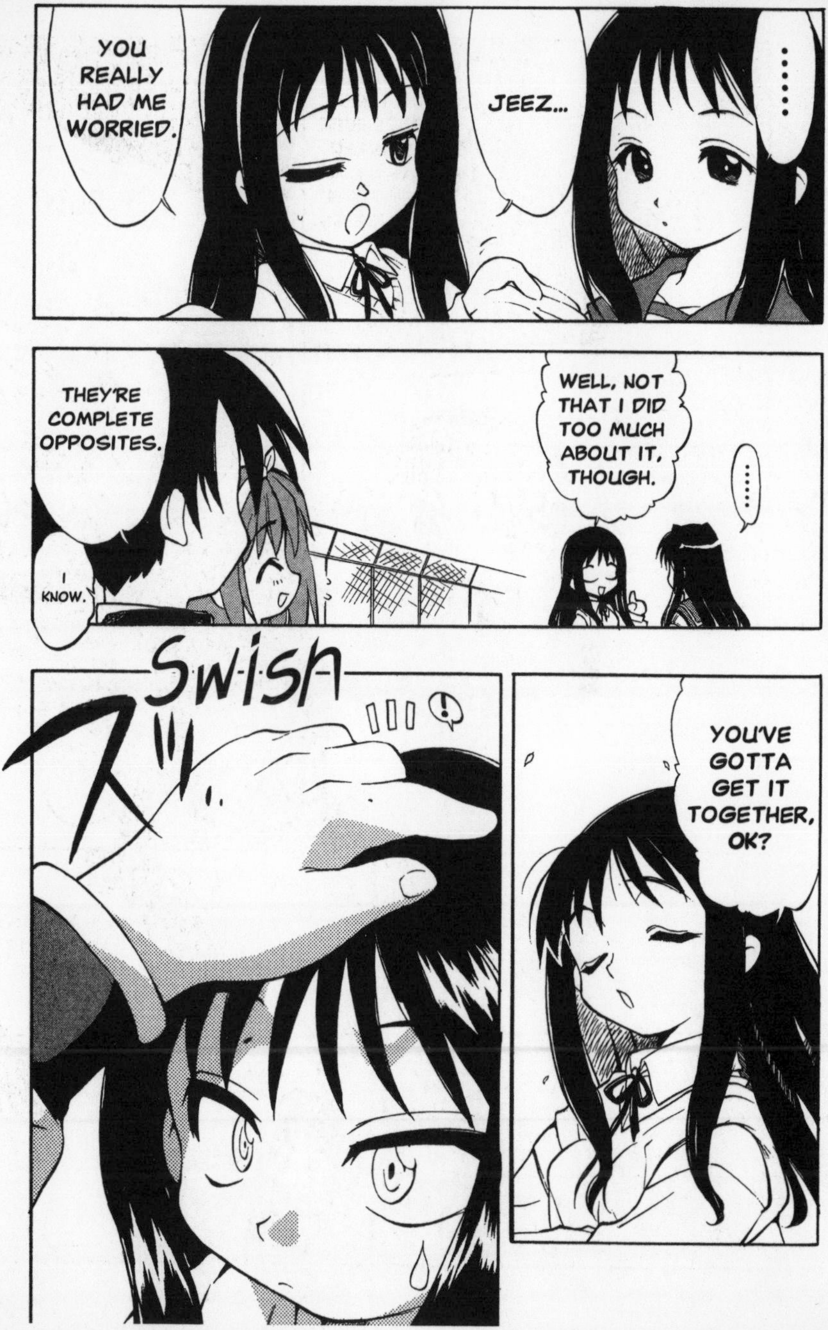
......
JEEZ...
YOU REALLY HAD ME WORRIED.
......
WELL, NOT THAT I DID TOO MUCH ABOUT IT, THOUGH.
THEY'RE COMPLETE OPPOSITES.
I KNOW.
YOU'VE GOTTA GET IT TOGETHER, OK?
SWISH

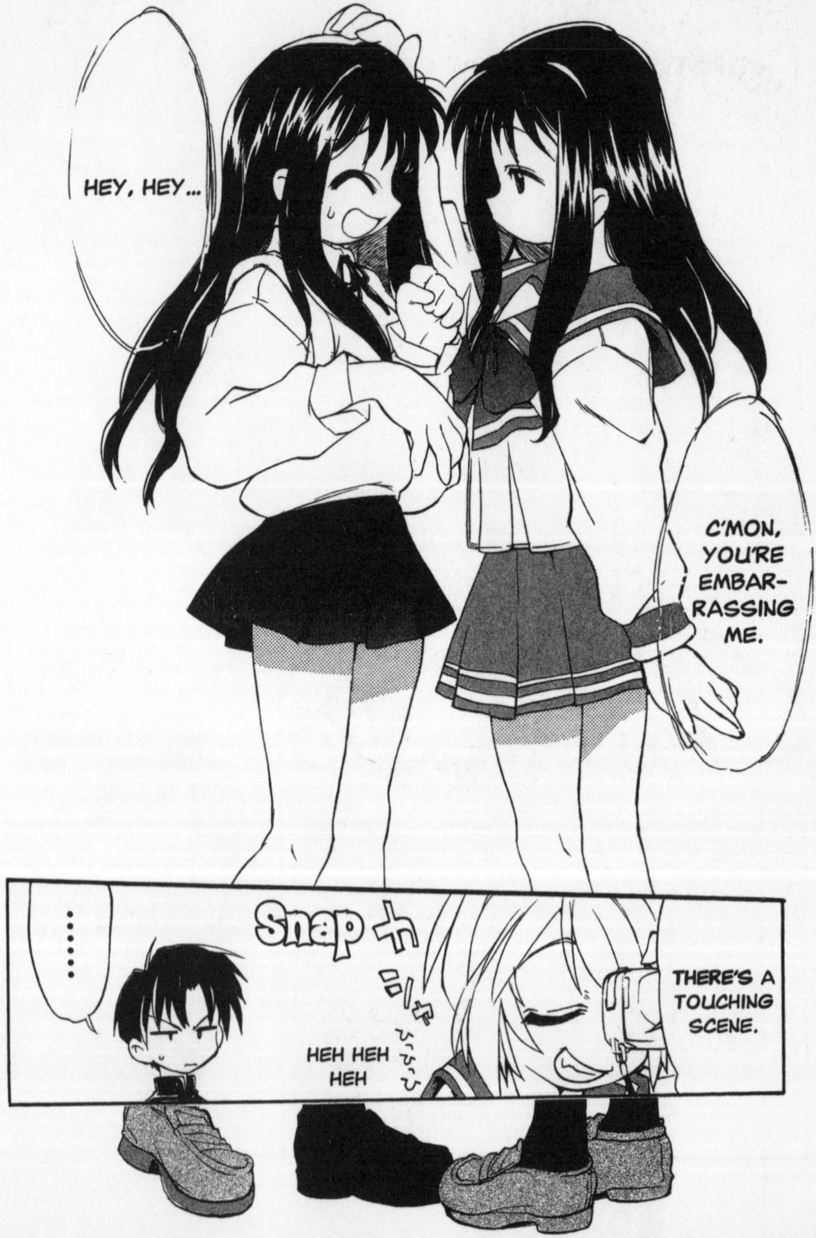
C'MON, YOU'RE EMBARRASSING ME.
HEY, HEY...
THERE'S A TOUCHING SCENE.
HEH HEH HEH
Snap
......

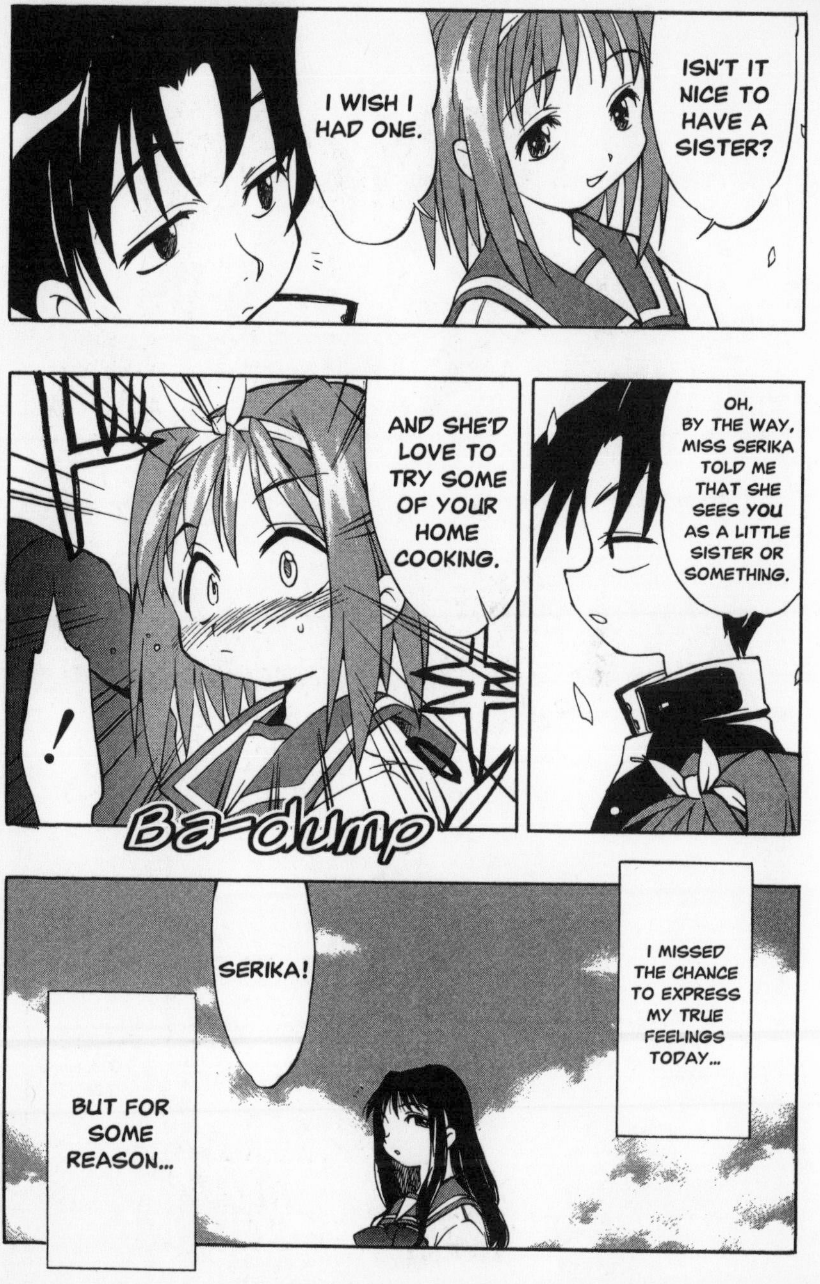

ISN'T IT NICE TO HAVE A SISTER?
I WISH I HAD ONE.
OH, BY THE WAY, MISS SERIKA TOLD ME THAT SHE SEES YOU AS A LITTLE SISTER OR SOMETHING.
AND SHE'D LOVE TO TRY SOME OF YOUR HOME COOKING.
!
Ba-dump
I MISSED THE CHANCE TO EXPRESS MY TRUE FEELINGS TODAY...
SERIKA!
BUT FOR SOME REASON...

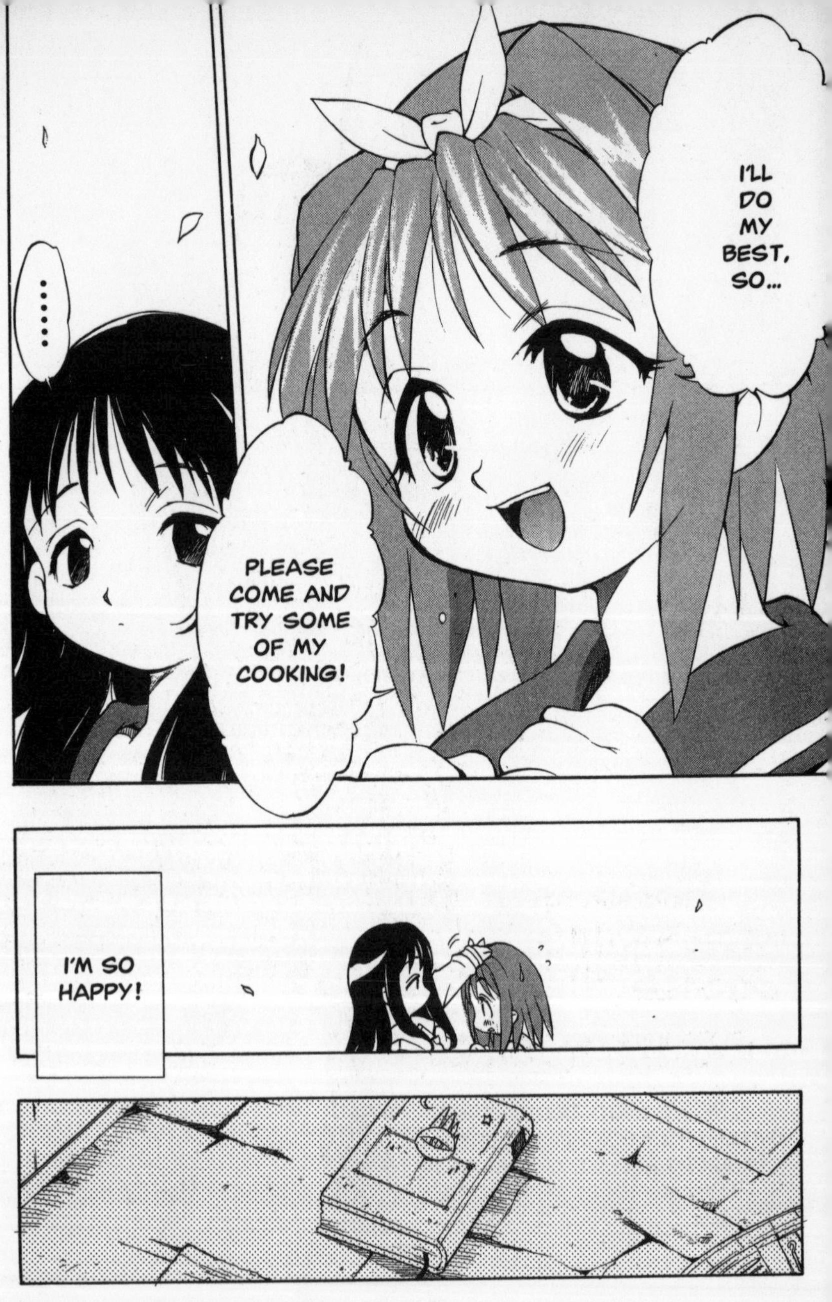
I'LL DO MY BEST, SO...
PLEASE COME AND TRY SOME OF MY COOKING!
......
I'M SO HAPPY!

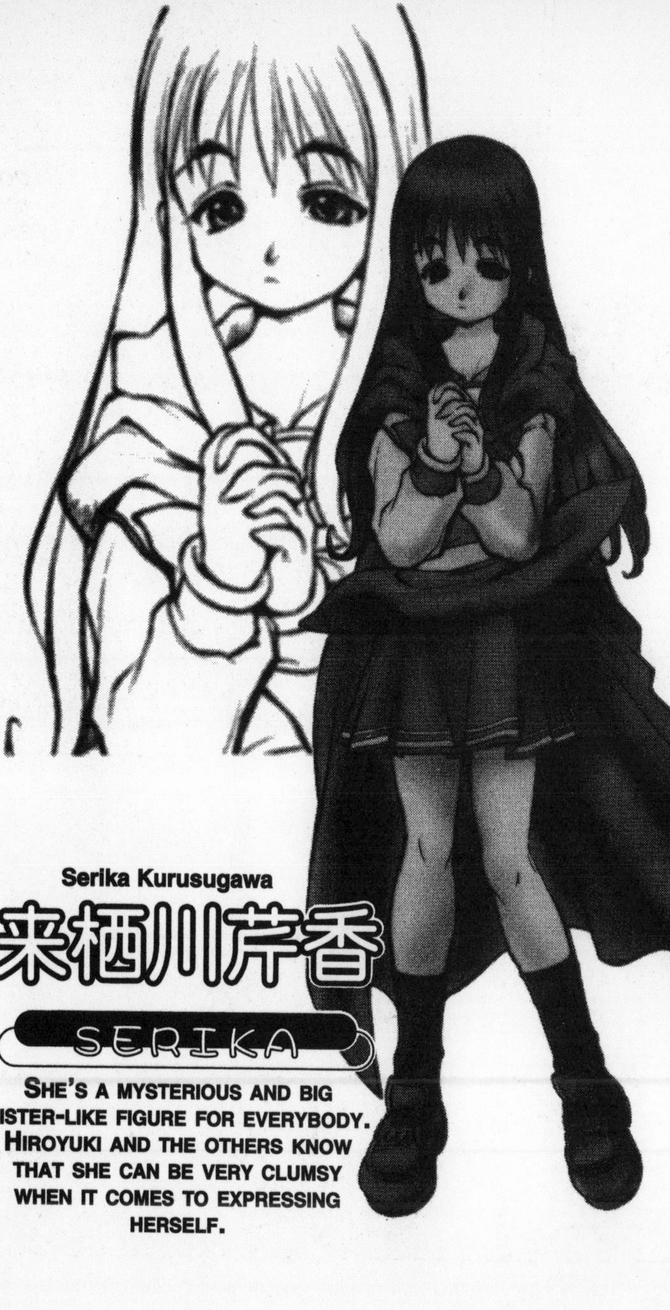

Serika Kurusugawa

来栖川芹香

SERIKA

SHE'S A MYSTERIOUS AND BIG SISTER-LIKE FIGURE FOR EVERYBODY. HIROYUKI AND THE OTHERS KNOW THAT SHE CAN BE VERY CLUMSY WHEN IT COMES TO EXPRESSING HERSELF.

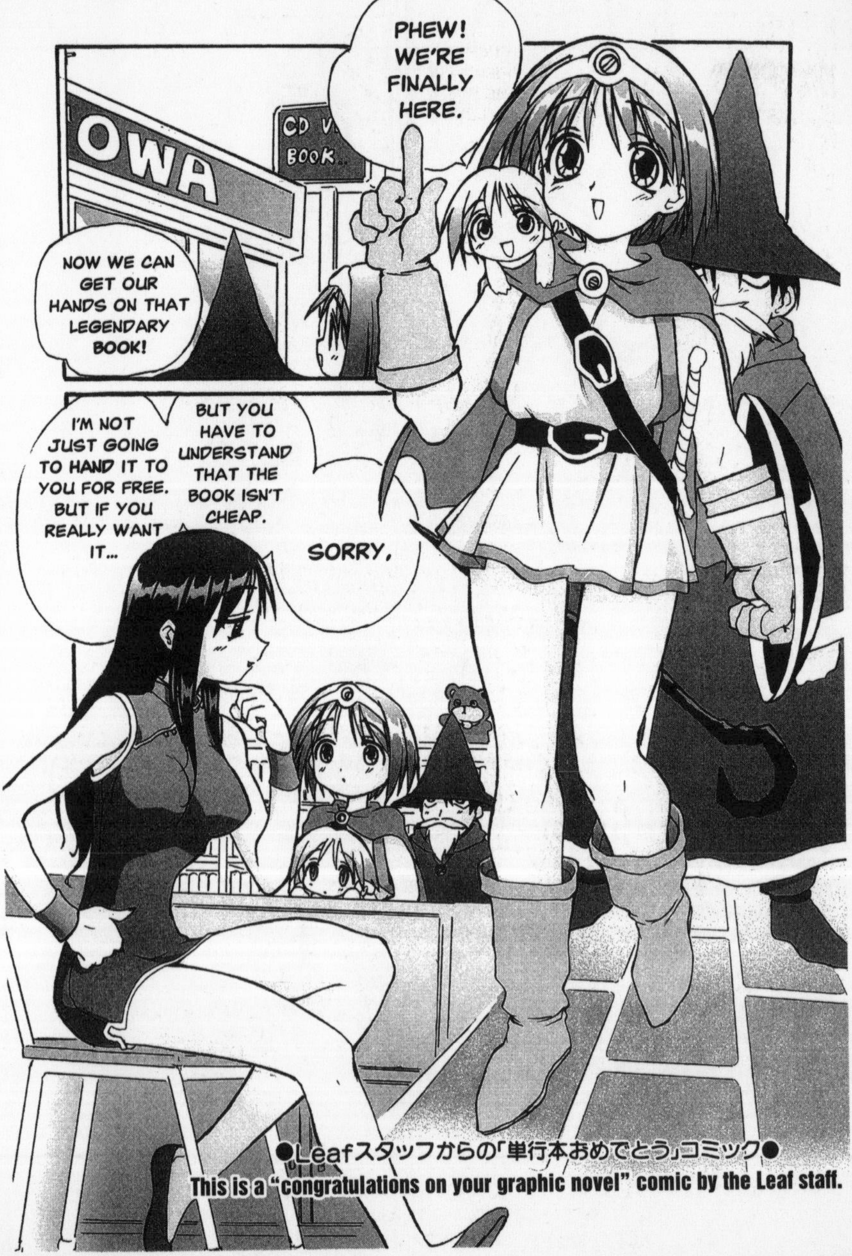
PHEW! WE'RE FINALLY HERE.
NOW WE CAN GET OUR HANDS ON THAT LEGENDARY BOOK!
SORRY,
BUT YOU HAVE TO UNDERSTAND THAT THE BOOK ISN'T CHEAP.
I'M NOT JUST GOING TO HAND IT TO YOU FOR FREE. BUT IF YOU REALLY WANT IT...

●Leafスタッフからの「単行本おめでとう」コミック●
This is a "congratulations on your graphic novel" comic by the Leaf staff.

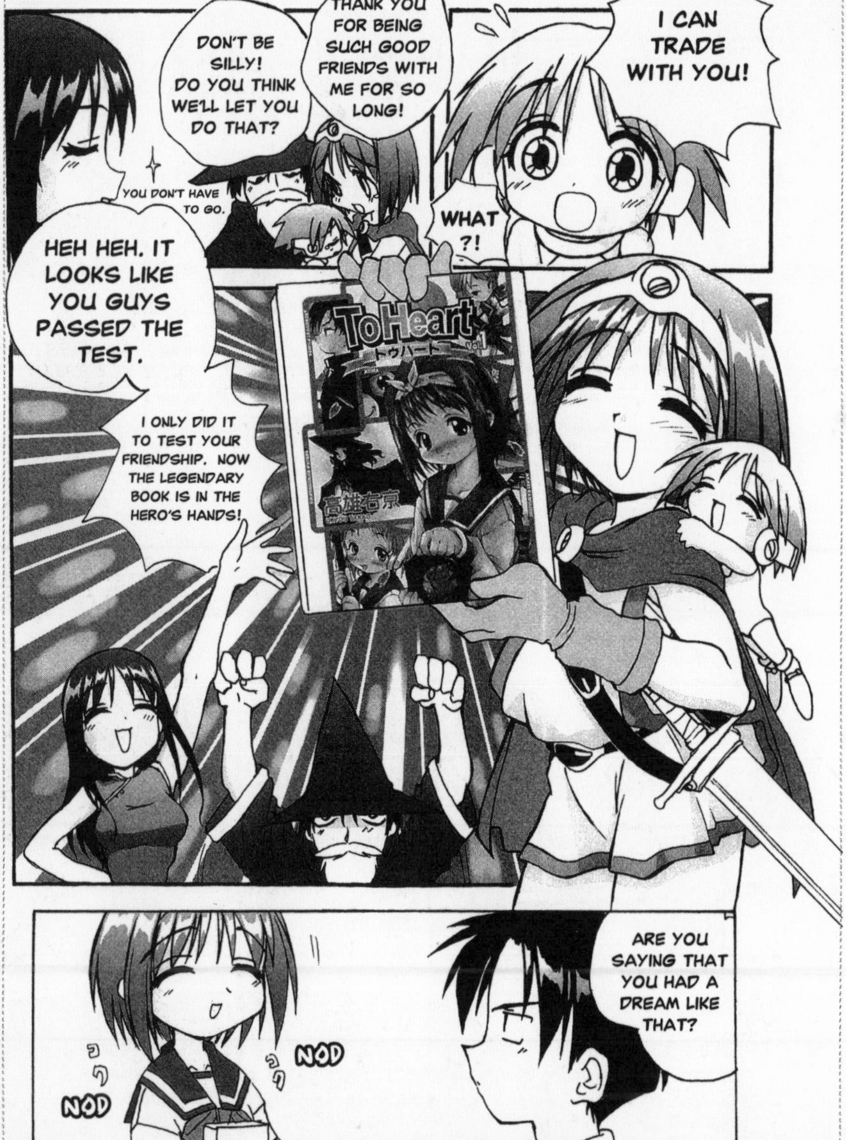
I CAN TRADE WITH YOU!
WHAT ?!
THANK YOU FOR BEING SUCH GOOD FRIENDS WITH ME FOR SO LONG!
DON'T BE SILLY! DO YOU THINK WE'LL LET YOU DO THAT?
YOU DON'T HAVE TO GO.
HEH HEH. IT LOOKS LIKE YOU GUYS PASSED THE TEST.
I ONLY DID IT TO TEST YOUR FRIENDSHIP. NOW THE LEGENDARY BOOK IS IN THE HERO'S HANDS!
ToHeart vol.1
トゥハート
高雄右京
ARE YOU SAYING THAT YOU HAD A DREAM LIKE THAT?
NOD
NOD

CONGRATULATIONS ON YOUR GRAPHIC NOVEL RELEASE, MR. TAKAO!
MINAZUKI & TAKAHASHI
ASSISTANTS, NANOTSUKI & ROMYU

TO HEART
VOLUME ONE
©AQUAPLUS
©UKYOU TAKAO 1998

First published in 1998 by Media Works Inc., Tokyo, Japan.
English translation rights arranged with Media Works Inc.

Translator **KAY BERTRAND**
Lead Translator/Translation Supervisor **JAVIER LOPEZ**
ADV Manga Translation Staff **AMY FORSYTH, BRENDAN FRAYNE,** and **EIKO McGREGOR**

Print Production/ Art Studio Manager **LISA PUCKETT**
Art Production Manager **RYAN MASON**
Sr. Designer/Creative Manager **JORGE ALVARADO**
Graphic Designer/Group Leader **SHANNON RASBERRY**
Graphic Designer **LANCE SWARTOUT**
Graphic Artists **CHRIS LAPP, KRISTINA MILESKI, NATALIA MORALES,** and **NANAKO TSUKIHASHI**

International Coordinator **TORU IWAKAMI**
International Coordinator **ATSUSHI KANBAYASHI**

Publishing Editor **SUSAN ITIN**
Assistant Editor **MARGARET SCHAROLD**
Editorial Assistant **VARSHA BHUCHAR**
Proofreader **SHERIDAN JACOBS**

Research/ Traffic Coordinator **MARSHA ARNOLD**

President, C.E.O & Publisher **JOHN LEDFORD**

Email: editor@adv-manga.com
www.adv-manga.com
www.advfilms.com

For sales and distribution inquiries please call 1.800.282.7202

ADV MANGA is a division of A.D. Vision, Inc.
10114 W. Sam Houston Parkway, Suite 200, Houston, Texas 77099

English text © 2004 published by A.D. Vision, Inc. under exclusive license.
ADV MANGA is a trademark of A.D. Vision, Inc.

ISBN: 1-4139-0022-4
First printing, April 2004
10 9 8 7 6 5 4 3 2
Printed in Canada